Practical Business Intelligence

with SQL Server 2005

Microsoft Windows Server System Series

Books in the **Microsoft Windows Server System Series** are written and reviewed by the world's leading technical authorities on Microsoft Windows technologies, including principal members of Microsoft's Windows and Server Development Teams. The goal of the series is to provide reliable information that enables administrators, developers, and IT professionals to architect, build, deploy, and manage solutions using the Microsoft Windows Server System. The contents and code of each book are tested against, and comply with, commercially available code. This series should be an invaluable resource for any IT professional or student working in today's Windows environment.

TITLES IN THE SERIES

Paul Bertucci, *Microsoft SQL Server High Availability,* 0-672-32625-6 (Sams)

Peter Blackburn and William R. Vaughn, *Hitchhiker's Guide to SQL Server 2000 Reporting Services,* 0-321-26828-8 (Addison-Wesley)

William Boswell, *Learning Exchange Server 2003,* 0-321-22874-X (Addison-Wesley)

Roberta Bragg, *Windows Server 2003 Security,* 0-321-30501-9 (Addison-Wesley)

Eric L. Brown, *SQL Server 2005 Distilled,* 0-321-34979-2 (Addison-Wesley)

Bill English, Olga Londer, Shawn Shell, Todd Bleeker, and Stephen Cawood, *Microsoft Content Management Server 2002: A Complete Guide,* 0-321-19444-6 (Addison-Wesley)

John C. Hancock and Roger Toren, *Practical Business Intelligence with SQL Server 2005,* 0-321-35698-5 (Addison-Wesley)

Don Jones, *Managing Windows® with VBScript and WMI,* 0-321-21334-3 (Addison-Wesley)

Sakari Kouti and Mika Seitsonen, *Inside Active Directory, Second Edition: A System Administrator's Guide,* 0-321-22848-0 (Addison-Wesley)

Jason Nadrowski and Stacy Draper, *SharePoint 2003 Advanced Concepts,* 0-321-33661-5 (Addison-Wesley)

Shyam Pather, *Microsoft SQL Server 2000 Notification Services,* 0-672-32664-7 (Sams)

Jeffrey R. Shapiro and Marcin Policht, *Building High Availability Windows Server™ 2003 Solutions,* 0-321-22878-2 (Addison-Wesley)

Buck Woody, *Administrator's Guide to SQL Server 2005,* 0-321-39797-5 (Addison-Wesley)

For more information please go to www.awprofessional.com/msserverseries

Practical Business Intelligence

with SQL Server 2005

John C. Hancock
Roger Toren

♦Addison-Wesley

Upper Saddle River, NJ • Boston • Indianapolis
San Francisco • New York • Toronto • Montreal
London • Munich • Paris • Madrid • Cape Town
Sydney • Tokyo • Singapore • Mexico City

Many of the designations used by manufacturers and sellers to distinguish their products are claimed as trademarks. Where those designations appear in this book, and the publisher was aware of a trademark claim, the designations have been printed with initial capital letters or in all capitals.

The authors and publisher have taken care in the preparation of this book, but make no expressed or implied warranty of any kind and assume no responsibility for errors or omissions. No liability is assumed for incidental or consequential damages in connection with or arising out of the use of the information or programs contained herein.

The publisher offers excellent discounts on this book when ordered in quantity for bulk purchases or special sales, which may include electronic versions and/or custom covers and content particular to your business, training goals, marketing focus, and branding interests. For more information, please contact:

> U.S. Corporate and Government Sales
> (800) 382-3419
> corpsales@pearsontechgroup.com

For sales outside the U.S., please contact:
> International Sales
> international@pearsoned.com

 This Book Is Safari Enabled

The Safari Enabled icon on the cover of your favorite technology book means the book is available through Safari Bookshelf. When you buy this book, you get free access to the online edition for 45 days. Safari Bookshelf is an electronic reference library that lets you easily search thousands of technical books, find code samples, download chapters, and access technical information whenever and wherever you need it.

To gain 45-day Safari Enabled access to this book:

- Go to http://www.awprofessional.com/safarienabled.

- Complete the brief registration form.

- Enter the coupon code SZFV-KJ4G-5ZQY-SKG7-NVH6.

If you have difficulty registering on Safari Bookshelf or accessing the online edition, please e-mail customer-service@safaribooksonline.com.

Visit us on the Web: www.awprofessional.com

Copyright © 2007 Pearson Education, Inc.

ISBN 0-321-35698-5

Text printed in the United States on recycled paper at R.R. Donnelley & Sons in Crawfordsville, Indiana.
First printing, September 2006

Library of Congress Cataloging-in-Publication Data

Hancock, John C. (John Christian), 1973-
  Practical business intelligence with SQL Server 2005 / John C. Hancock, Roger Toren.
    p. cm.
  Includes bibliographical references and index.
  ISBN 0-321-35698-5 (pbk. : alk. paper) 1. Business intelligence. 2. SQL server. 3. Client/server computing. I. Toren, Roger. II. Title.

  HD38.7.H36 2006
  005.75'85—dc22

                       2006017671

Contents

Acknowledgments

We would like to thank Jan Shanahan of Microsoft for her early support of the project and practical advice, without which this book may never have got off the ground.

We would like to thank our colleagues at Microsoft Consulting Services in Canada for their help: Simona Marin, Shaun Tinline-Jones, and Tamer Farag for working through the text and providing feedback; Jonathan Stynder, for SharePoint assistance; Vince Bryden, for professional services metrics advice; and Rob Wood, for a wealth of practical e-commerce advice. We want to thank Darren Massel for early encouragement and extensive feedback on the book as it progressed. We are also grateful to our manager, Steven Major, whose support and enthusiasm from the beginning was invaluable in keeping us going.

We also need to thank many members of the SQL Server product teams for taking the time to work with us on their areas of expertise in the text—any remaining errors that we may have managed to sneak past them are purely a reflection of our own stubbornness. In particular, we want to thank Zhaohui Tang and Jamie MacLennan for data mining advice, Dave Wickert for real-world advice, and especially Thierry D'Hers for his extensive and valuable feedback.

We also want to thank the great team at Addison-Wesley for their professionalism and patience, and all of the reviewers for their input.

Roger would like to thank his family, Nadine, Erik, and Julia, for their patience on this journey. He would also like to thank many of the customers he has worked with from Toronto to Tokyo for their great questions and the opportunity to work with them on their business problems, which helped to frame much of the content of our book.

John would like to thank his wife, Nicolette, for her enthusiasm and encouragement throughout the long book project. He would also like to thank his family for all their support, and in particular Dr. J. D. Hancock for his precedent-setting early practical work. John would like to dedicate his work on this book to Rita Smith for her encouragement of him and so many others, and to Irene Mosley for her kindness and support.

About the Authors

John C. Hancock is a Senior Consultant with Microsoft Consulting Services in Toronto, Canada, specializing in Business Intelligence technologies. He has worked with some of Microsoft's largest and most strategic clients, and his consulting experience has included architectural consulting, project team lead positions, performance optimization, and development of customized training courses and materials. Recently he has worked extensively in the field of intelligence systems for law enforcement. Prior to Microsoft, he worked as an independent consultant in the United Kingdom and South Africa. He holds a Bachelor of Science (Honors) degree in mathematics and computer science.

Roger Toren is a Principal Consultant with MCS, based in Vancouver, Canada, focusing on guiding customers in the design and implementation of Business Intelligence solutions with SQL Server 2005. He was the lead author on the *SQL Server 2000 High Availability* guide. He has more than 35 years of experience in IT, covering a wide variety of industries, including banking, insurance, retail, education, health care, geo-spatial analysis, and nuclear research. He holds a Bachelor of Science degree in physics and a Masters of Science degree in computing science. Prior to joining Microsoft, he taught undergraduate courses in computing science, worked as an independent consultant, and served as Associate Director in the technology practice of a major global consulting firm.

About the Technical Editor

Bob Reinsch is a senior technical trainer for Foss Training Center in Leawood, Kansas. He has been a Microsoft Certified Trainer and Systems Engineer for 10 years, and he resides in Lawrence, Kansas, with his wife and three kids. When he is not in the classroom, consulting on messaging or security matters, or spending time with his family, he can be found either strumming a guitar or building a new one. He can be contacted at bob@piercingblue.com.

Preface

Each of the areas in the Microsoft Business Intelligence (BI) platform could take a whole book to describe in detail. Why then are we attempting to cover all aspects of BI solutions in one book? The answer is that people who design, build, and manage a BI solution need to have a good understanding of how all the BI components in SQL Server 2005 can work together, from relational databases to store the data, Integration Services to move and transform the data, Analysis Services to provide a platform to analyze and query the data, and Reporting Services to present the information to users.

We really wanted to avoid just giving a superficial or "marketing" view of all the different aspects of the BI platform, so we have designed this book in a practical way. If you were starting out to build a BI solution for a business problem and had a clearly defined budget and deliverables, you would not necessarily learn every technical aspect of all the SQL Server components, just those areas you need to deliver business value.

Books are available that cover specific technologies in depth, such as On Line Analytical Processing (OLAP) or data mining, and other books describe areas such as how to properly design data warehouses—this book combines the essentials of both areas to teach you how to design good solutions and describes the concrete steps and best practices to build a working solution in SQL Server 2005, without trying to cover every technology in depth.

Structure of This Book

Instead of structuring this book around the technology and trying hard to list and explain every feature in the platform, we pick a specific business issue for each chapter and show you how a complete solution could be built, touching on all the key technologies and design challenges along the way. We selected the business areas from various vertical industries that we have worked with, such as health care or financial services. Although all these vertical industries might not be applicable to your job, you can apply the lessons you learn to your own environment. In some cases, we have taken the liberty of simplifying the business problem to convey more clearly a specify point in a BI solution to a broader audience. It is not our intent to turn readers into industry experts.

The authors have both worked as BI consultants for many years and have a fundamental belief that you cannot learn to build effective solutions from a technology reference book or a step-by-step guide to using technical features. Instead, we share our thoughts on design decisions at every point along the way to building a working solution and explain the tradeoffs and consequences in the real world. Each chapter focuses on some specific technology areas and builds on your knowledge from previous chapters, so we recommend that you read through them in sequence.

The first chapter, "Introduction to Business Intelligence," introduces the terms and concepts behind BI, including data warehousing and dimensional modeling, and is recommended both for readers who are new to BI as well as experienced practitioners who can see how and where we apply standard BI techniques to our recommended solutions. The second chapter, "Introduction to SQL Server 2005," gives a high-level overview of all the components of the Microsoft BI platform and is intended to serve as an orientation for the technology so that later chapters are free to focus on solutions.

The Business Focus

In all the remaining chapters, we followed the same pattern. Every chapter starts in the same place that your projects will be starting: with a business problem. We give you an overview of the solution we are proposing at roughly the same level of detail that you might have in mind at the beginning of a BI project and explain some of the business benefits that the customer might expect to get from the solution.

The next section of the chapter walks you through the data model for the solution. We believe that more BI projects get into trouble in the data modeling stage than anywhere else (except possibly data quality—more on this later in the book), so we typically cover the data model in detail for each solution. Data modeling is fundamentally a practical discipline; if you are new to it, you will only get any good through practice, so we have tried to take you through our thought processes as we design the data models. Experienced data modelers can have fun reading the section and second-guessing our designs.

The technical solution section of the chapter describes how you can use the technology to build the solution we outlined in the early part of the chapter. We describe the relevant SQL Server features and give some advice on things to be aware of, by referring to the particular business solution we are building in the chapter. We cover the major technology areas that you can expect to encounter in most BI projects and provide some pointers to other interesting technical features that you might want to investigate further.

It would be nice if we could stop work at the point when the solution has been developed, but in the real world, you are going to need to deploy the solution from development into a production environment, maintain it by making changes and enhancements, and know how to operate it on an ongoing basis. The section on managing the solution covers all these topics with specific reference to the particular technology areas from the chapter.

We focus our attention on specific areas of the business problem and technologies to describe a working solution, so we end each chapter with some ideas for next steps to enhance the solution by adding new business areas or using other SQL Server features.

Quick Start Sections

Each chapter contains some Quick Start sections, which are detailed exercises that you can follow along to get practice using SQL Server tools to implement key sections of the solution. The Quick Starts are not intended as a step-by-step guide to all the features in SQL Server 2005, but rather cover in detail the steps you need to take to get a particular aspect of a working solution to the point where you can use what you have just built to further explore all the ideas presented in the chapter. Practical experience with the technology is crucial for you to understand the platform fully, even if your role is in architecture or operations.

When we tested this book with readers, they all had slightly different ways of using the Quick Start sections. Some people prefer to read through a whole chapter, and then when they have chance to sit in front of a computer, they work through all the Quick Starts in the chapter and start trying out their own ideas. Others read the book and try out both the detailed Quick Starts and other technical areas we mention in the chapter as they come across them. Regardless of the approach you take, remember that the Quick Starts are there to get you started: Trying out your own ideas is the best way to master what is, after all, a large and comprehensive BI platform.

You can find sample files and setup instructions for the Quick Starts on the Addison-Wesley Web site. Go to the book's Web page (http://www.awprofessional.com/title/0321356985), and in the More Information section, click the Quick Starts link.

Audience

The audience for this book includes all members of teams involved in BI projects. Technical decision makers will benefit from the business-focused sections and information on vertical market solutions to be able to envision the kinds of solutions that are possible. Architects and IT professionals will use this book to learn about the SQL Server BI platform and how to use the various components in their environment (and prepare for the kinds of problems that BI projects face). Developers and database administrators who will be building and managing the solutions will benefit from the industry-specific solution descriptions and will gain hands-on experience with the technology through the technology walkthroughs.

CHAPTER 1

Introduction to Business Intelligence

Before looking at building Business Intelligence (BI) solutions with SQL Server 2005, it's important to get an understanding of the underlying concepts. This chapter covers the basics of what makes BI systems different from transaction systems and looks at some modeling techniques and technologies for providing the performance and flexibility that users need. We end the chapter by providing some practical project advice and point out some of the pitfalls of BI projects.

What Is Business Intelligence?

Business Intelligence is a set of concepts, methods, and technologies designed to pursue the elusive goal of turning all the widely separated data in an organization into useful information and eventually into knowledge.

This information has historically been delivered to an organization's analysts and management through reporting and analysis capabilities, but increasingly BI is being delivered to all parts of an organization by integrating smarter capabilities into the applications and tools that people use to perform their everyday jobs. The most successful BI solutions can create exceptionally valuable capabilities for an organization, such as the ability to proactively spot opportunities to increase revenue or improve operational processes and practices.

In the past, BI projects have often suffered from over-hyped attempts to highlight the potential value without consideration of the work that is required within an organization. Simply building a BI capability doesn't mean that it will easily be able to move off the whiteboards and out of the server rooms and into the hands of a user community that is ready and prepared to do something with the information. The best BI solutions pay as much attention to the "business" as the "intelligence," and in this book we look at both sides with a focus on the practical aspects required for success.

Transaction Systems and the Search for Information

Every company of a reasonable size has some major systems that run the business. These systems are known as OLTP (**online transaction processing**) systems and are often responsible for the vital processes such as handling orders and invoices. Because of their key role, they usually end up storing the most critical information that the business relies on, such as the list of how much money customers owe or how much the company owes in tax.

Most OLTP systems handle many thousands of individual transactions in a day. The goals of transaction systems are primarily to provide consistency of the information and the ability to support additions and modifications to typically small pieces of data at a time. These requirements are fairly standard across many OLTP systems and have led to the broad adoption of a specific approach to organizing the data in these databases.

The data model for these systems is usually produced through a process of entity-relationship (ER) modeling, which leads to a normalized structure in which each entity has its own separate table that is related to the others, as shown in Figure 1-1. The normalized data model is a great fit for OLTP's requirements because it ensures that every piece of information exists only in one place and can be updated easily and efficiently.

These data models typically contain dozens or even hundreds of separate tables, most of which are connected to the others through large numbers of relationships. The normalized relational database has become such a common feature of systems that many database administrators (DBAs) and application designers can glance at a new report and automatically form a picture in their heads of a normalized data model that would fit.

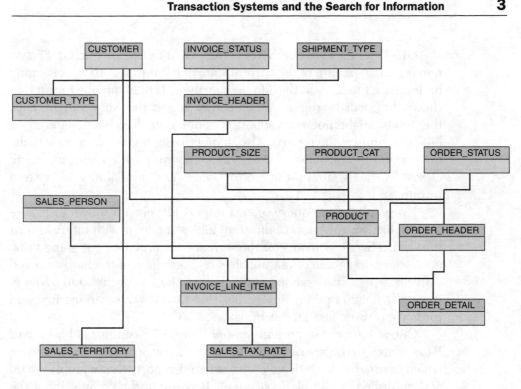

Figure 1-1 OLTP database schema

Many people use reports directly from their company's enterprise resource planning (ERP) system or other major systems all the time, but the kind of information that can easily be retrieved is restricted by the design and purpose of a transaction system. Using operational systems for standard reporting works well for operational-level data such as reports on specific customer records or order transactions, but trying to understand your entire business by analyzing detailed transactions is unlikely to prove successful.

Why OLTP Reporting and Analysis Fails to Deliver

The really interesting questions that business users would like to answer almost always touch much more data than single transactions or records, such as "Which product category sold best in the northwest last year?" followed by "So, what kinds of customers were buying that product category in the region?."

OLTP systems are the systems that run a business. The OLTP system is a "live" picture of the current state of the business that is changing underneath the users as they do their analysis. If they run one report that shows the totals by region, then another report that shows the details, the totals might not correspond if more data has been entered in between running the reports. Also, trying to use these systems to actually understand the business as it runs is a risky proposition because it will almost certainly affect the performance and availability of system resources.

Every interesting query against the OLTP schema shown in Figure 1-1 will likely involve lots of different tables and joins with filters against the data. The performance of those queries is probably not going to be good for any database of reasonable size, regardless of the hardware and software you are using. Even optimizing the tables for this kind of query is usually not an option: Remember that OLTP systems must first and foremost provide fast, atomic updates.

One of the most important reasons that OLTP systems fail to deliver BI is related to the restricted ways that users can access the information, which is usually via static or parameterized reports that were designed and published by the IT department. Because of the complexity of the database and the performance implications of a user possibly launching a huge, poorly designed query that takes eight hours to complete on the live OLTP system, the users are restricted to accessing specific sets of information in a prescribed way.

The promise of "end-user reporting" tools that people could use to create their own reports on their desktops never really materialized. Even when reporting tools started to get user-friendly Windows interfaces, the complexity of the schema in the transaction systems defeated most attempts to provide access directly to users. Ultimately, they are still restricted by the database design and the operational requirements for the transaction system.

Despite all the drawbacks we have just described, there is an even more compelling problem with trying to use an OLTP system directly as the vehicle for intelligent analysis. Every organization we have ever worked with has valuable information that is spread out in different areas, from the HR department's system to the spreadsheet that contains next year's budget. The solution to the problem of providing access to information must lie outside a single transaction system. The solution lies in a separate system: a data warehouse.

Data Warehouses

The data warehouse is the place where a consistent view of an organization's data can be published for users to be able to access it. The first characteristic of the data warehouse is that it is separate. If we are really serious about providing easy access to all the information, we have to create a separate relational database with a design and an operational approach that is optimized for queries rather than atomic transactions—this is the data warehouse.

Data from all the source systems is loaded into the warehouse (see Figure 1-2) through a process of extraction, transformation, and loading that produces a clean, validated repository of information. This information is organized and presented to the users in a way that enables them to easily formulate their business questions, and the answers are returned orders of magnitudes faster than similar queries against the transaction systems so that the users can immediately reformulate their question and get more details.

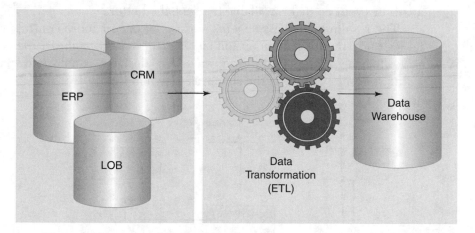

Figure 1-2   Data warehouse loaded from source systems

The Data Warehouse Design

The data warehouse is still a relational database, but that doesn't mean we are constrained to stick to the fully normalized, entity-relationship (ER) schema that is so appropriate for OLTP systems. Over time, the various approaches to designing a database schema that is optimized for understanding and querying information have been consolidated into an approach called a **dimensional model**.

At the center of the dimensional model are the numeric **measures** that we are interested in understanding, such as sales revenue or profit margins. Related measures are collected into **fact tables** that contain columns for each of the numeric measures. Every time something measurable happens, such as a sales transaction, an inventory balance or when an event occurs, a new record is added to the fact table with these numeric values.

There are usually many different ways that people can look at these measures. For example, they could look at totals for a product category or show the totals for a particular set of stores. These different ways of looking at the information are called **dimensions**, where a dimension is a particular area of interest such as Product, Customer, or Time. Every dimension table has a number of columns with descriptive text, such as product category, color, and size for a Product dimension. These descriptive columns are known as **attributes**; the more interesting attributes you can make available to users, the better.

The resulting database schema consists of one or more central fact tables, and a number of dimension tables that can be joined to these fact tables to analyze them in different ways. This design is usually known as a **star schema** because of the shape, as shown in Figure 1-3.

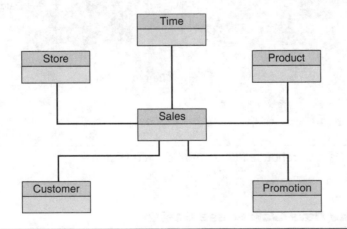

Figure 1-3   Star schema

If you have a strong background in OLTP databases, the idea of not necessarily normalizing data is probably at this moment causing you to reconsider the money you just spent on this book. Rest assured: We are not advocating ditching normalization altogether, but this is just one tool in our kit. Dimensional databases have different purposes, and different constraints. We can make appropriate decisions about the correct design of a particular database by looking at the ways it will be used, rather than necessarily trying to apply standard OLTP designs to every database.

Time and the Data Warehouse

Probably the most important dimension in any data warehouse is the **Time** dimension. This is the dimension that allows users to summarize the information in the fact tables in a way that matches up to the real world. They can use this dimension to look at totals for the current calendar year or to compare the percentage improvement over the previous fiscal period, for example. Although modern query languages have many flexible functions for working with date values, the best way to accommodate all the real-world complexities of analyzing information by time is to add a Time dimension table to the data warehouse, loaded with records starting from the earliest fact record that is available.

An important characteristic of the data warehouse is that it **stores history**. This idea is often misinterpreted because OLTP systems also store transactions going back in time (some for many years), so why is this feature of the data warehouse so important? Actually, there is a lot more to storing history accurately than just keeping a set of transactions around. For example, if every sales manager in the OLTP system is related to a set of customers in a sales territory, what happens when the sales territories' boundaries have been updated and you try to run an analysis for previous calendar years? The data warehouse must be capable of accurately reproducing the state of the business in the past as well as the present.

Most measures in a fact table are **additive**. That is, all the numbers can be added up across any time period that a user selects, whether that is a single day or several months. The benefit of additive measures is that they can easily be used to create summaries by simply summing the numbers. Some measures may not be additive across time periods or some other dimension and are known as **semi-additive**. Examples of these include monthly balances such as inventory on hand or account balances.

Getting Data into the Data Warehouse

Because the data warehouse is separate from all the other systems, an important part of the data warehouse process is copying data from the various source systems, restructuring it as necessary, and loading it into the warehouse. This process is often known as **ETL**, or extraction, transformation, and loading, sometimes with an additional M on the end (ETLM) to remind us of the need to actively manage this process.

The exact approach that you take for a given data warehouse depends on a lot of factors such as the nature of the source systems and business requirements for timely data, but a typical ETL process is a batch process that is run on a daily or weekly basis. The first part of the process involves extracting data from the source systems, either through direct queries against the systems using a data access interface such as ODBC or OLE DB or through the export of data files from within the systems.

This source data is then transformed into the correct format, which involves the obvious tasks such as matching data types and formats but also more complex responsibilities such as checking that valid business keys are supplied. When the data is in the right format, it is added to the data warehouse tables. Fact table loading usually involves appending a new set of records to the existing set of records for a particular date range. Updates to fact records are relatively uncommon in practice, but you can accommodate them with some special handling.

Dimension table loading often involves appending new records, but sometimes takes the form of updates to the attributes on existing records. These updates can have the unfortunate side effect of destroying our ability to look at historical data in the context that existed at that time. If it is important for a particular dimension to preserve the ability to look at data using the attribute values that existed in the past, the dimension is known as a **slowly changing dimension** (SCD), and Chapter 8, "Managing Changing Data," describes some well-established techniques for dealing with this.

Some ETL processes include a temporary database called a **staging database**, which is used to store a copy of the data that is currently being processed on the way to the data warehouse. The data in the staging area can then be manipulated by very efficient SQL operations such as joins. The disadvantage of having a staging area is that the data needs to be written more than once on the way from the source system into the data warehouse, which can add a lot of overhead to the process. SQL

Server's ETL facilities use a "pipeline" approach that can often address all the ETL requirements without requiring a data staging step.

The best way to think of ETL is not as a process of copying and transforming data from one system to another, but rather as a process of publishing data. The publishing process includes a great deal of focus on data quality and provides a management process to catch any errors or omissions and correct them before the users can access the information.

What Is the Difference Between a Data Warehouse and a Data Mart?

The difference between the terms *data warehouse* and *data mart* is largely a matter of perspective. A data mart was classically an initiative within a single department with a specific subject area, such as a "Marketing Data Mart" or a "Finance Data Mart." These projects were usually undertaken in isolation without a consistent vision across the company, so this approach led to problems because there was no driver to agree on consistent dimensions across these data marts.

In contrast, a centralized data repository that served multiple communities in the organization was termed a data warehouse, or enterprise data warehouse. Data marts would sometimes use this central data warehouse as a source of information.

In this book, we stick with the term *data warehouse* whenever we are referring to the dimensional relational database, which is the source for all of our BI capabilities.

In summary, our proposed approach is to build a consistent relational data warehouse with a dimensional schema optimized for queries. Even so, real-world applications often involve millions or billions of transactions with complex ad-hoc queries, and even the best relational query engine is going to take some time to return information. Because our goals are to provide fast and intuitive access to information, is relational database technology the best we can do?

OLAP to the Rescue

Relational databases have become so popular and ubiquitous that many IT professionals think that every data storage and querying problem can (and should) be solved by a relational database. Similarly, when XML was first popularized, many people thought exactly the same thing about XML. The reality of course is that although structures such as relational databases and XML files have a wide range of uses, we should follow a practical rather than dogmatic approach and apply the right tool for the job.

Any BI solution that we put in place should ideally be available across the whole company, follow a multidimensional approach that matches up with the real-world concepts, be easy to use by nontechnical users, and have really great performance. This is quite a tall order, but the technology to achieve all of this is available.

On-Line Analytical Processing (**OLAP**) is a different kind of database technology designed specifically for BI. Instead of organizing information into tables with rows and columns like a relational database, an OLAP database stores data in a multidimensional format. Rather than trying to get a relational database to meet all the performance and usability needs we described previously, we can build an OLAP database that the users can query instead and periodically load it with data from the relational data warehouse, as shown in Figure 1-4. SQL Server includes an OLAP database engine called Analysis Services.

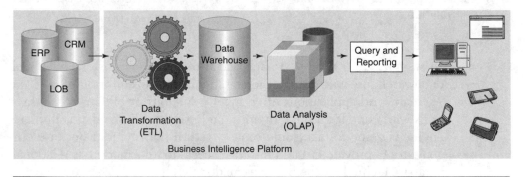

Figure 1-4   Source to DW to OLAP to users flow

The central concept in an OLAP database is the **cube**. An OLAP cube consists of data from one or more fact tables and presents information to the users in the form of measures and dimensions. OLAP database technology also generally includes a calculation engine for adding complex analytical logic to the cube, as well as a query language. Because the standard relational query language, SQL, is not well suited to working with cubes and dimensions, an OLAP-specific query language has been developed called **MDX** (Multidimensional Expressions), which is supported by several OLAP database engines.

The term *cube* comes from the general idea that the data structure can contain many dimensions rather than just a two-dimensional table with rows and columns. Because a real-life geometric cube is a three-dimensional object, it is tempting to try and explain OLAP technology using that metaphor, but it quickly becomes confusing to many people (including the authors!) because most OLAP cubes contain more than three dimensions. Suffice to say, a cube is a data structure that allows numeric measures to be analyzed across many different dimensions.

Loading Information into OLAP Databases

As you have seen in the section on ETL, data from source systems is transformed and loaded into the relational data warehouse. To make this data available to users of the OLAP database, we need to periodically **process** the cube. When a cube is processed, the OLAP engine issues a set of SQL queries against the relational data warehouse and loads the resulting records into an OLAP cube structure.

In principle, an OLAP cube could be loaded directly from the source systems and instantly provide a dimensional model for accessing the information and great performance. In that case, why do we need a relational data warehouse as well? The most important reason is data quality. The data warehouse contains consolidated, validated, and stable information from many source systems and is always the best source of data for an OLAP cube.

Getting Information out of OLAP Databases

Users usually interact with a relational database (including a data warehouse) by running predefined reports that are either created for them by IT departments or built by the users themselves using a report writing application. Reports can often take several minutes to run even in a well-designed star schema data warehouse, which doesn't lend itself to the kinds of interactive queries that can really allow the user to understand new information.

The key to the success of using OLAP databases in an interactive, user-friendly way is their performance. Queries against an OLAP cube, even ones that summarize years of history and huge amounts of transactions, typically return results in a couple of seconds at most, which is orders of magnitude faster than similar relational queries. This makes it feasible to build client applications that allow users to build queries by dragging and dropping measures and dimension attributes and see results almost instantly.

Many users, especially analysts and other power users, have conventionally used rich BI client applications specifically designed for querying OLAP databases. These tools typically include features such as charting and visualization and can really improve the effectiveness of analytical tasks. As the need for access to information becomes more widespread across the organization, BI capabilities are being included in tools that most people have access to, such as Web portals and Excel spreadsheets.

Information is often presented at a summarized level with the ability to **drill down** to see more details (that is, to pick a particular area of interest and then expand it). For example, someone may begin with looking a list of sales revenue against quota for all the geographic regions in a country and see that a particular region has not reached their target for the period. They can highlight the row and drill down to see all the individual cities within that region, to try and understand where the problem may be.

Why Is OLAP So Fast?

So how does an OLAP database engine achieve such great performance? The short answer is pretty simple: It cheats. When somebody runs an ad-hoc query that asks for a total of all sales activity in a certain region over the past three years, it is very unlikely that a database engine could sum billions of records in less than a second. OLAP solves this problem by working out some of the answers in advance, at the time when the cube is processed.

In addition to the detailed fact data, OLAP cubes also store some precalculated summaries called **aggregates**. An example of an aggregate is a set of totals by product group and month, which would contain far fewer records than the original set. When a query is executed, the

OLAP database engine decides whether there is an appropriate aggregate available or whether it needs to sum up the detailed records themselves. A properly tuned OLAP database can respond to most queries using aggregates, and this is the source of the performance improvement.

If you try to work out the total possible number of different aggregates in a cube with a reasonable number of dimensions, you will quickly realize that the number of combinations is staggering. It is clear that OLAP database engines cannot efficiently store all possible aggregations; they must pick and choose which ones are most effective. To do this, they can take advantage of the situation shown in Figure 1-5. Because products roll up to product categories, and months roll up to quarters and years, if an aggregate on product by month is available, several different queries can quickly be answered. If a query is executed that calls for totals by year and product category, the OLAP database engine can sum up the records in the product by month aggregate far more quickly than using the detailed records.

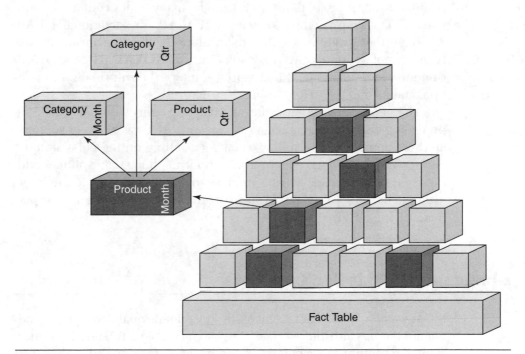

Figure 1-5   OLAP aggregations

Another key to OLAP database engine performance is where and how they store the detailed and aggregated data. There are a few different approaches to this question, but the most common answer is for the OLAP database engine to create optimized structures on disk. This approach is known as **MOLAP**, or Multidimensional OLAP. Modern platforms such as Analysis Services can support billions of records in highly optimized, compressed MOLAP structures.

Regardless of whether a query is answered from a precalculated aggregate or the detail-level records themselves, every query is answered completely from the MOLAP structure. In fact, after the daily cube processing has loaded data into the cube, you could even stop the relational database server without affecting cube users, because the relational database is never used for end-user queries when using MOLAP structures.

In some older technologies, MOLAP did not scale well enough to meet everybody's needs, so some analytical solutions stored the detailed information and the aggregates in relational database tables instead. In addition to a fact table, there would also be many tables containing summaries. This approach is known as **ROLAP**, or Relational OLAP. Although these solutions scaled relatively well, their performance was typically not as good as MOLAP solutions, so **HOLAP** (Hybrid OLAP) solutions were introduced that stored some of the information in relational tables and the rest in MOLAP structures.

The good news is that as far as Analysis Services is concerned, the preceding discussion is no longer a real issue. Analysis Services supports all three approaches by simply changing a setting on the cube, and the current version will have no trouble supporting huge data volumes with excellent performance, leaving you free to concentrate on a more interesting question: How should you structure the information in your particular BI solution?

Dimensional Modeling Concepts

So far we have looked at several of the key dimensional concepts, including dimensions, attributes, measures, and fact tables. You need to understand a few other areas before we can move on to actually building a BI solution.

Hierarchies

As you have seen, dimensions consist of a list of descriptive attributes that are used to group and analyze information. Some of these attributes are strongly related, and can be grouped into a **hierarchy**. For example, product category, product subcategory and product stock-keeping unit (SKU) could be grouped into a hierarchy called Product Categorization. When the hierarchy is used in a query, the results would show the totals for each product category, and then allow the user to drill down into the subcategories, and then into the product SKUs that make up the subcategory, as shown in Figure 1-6.

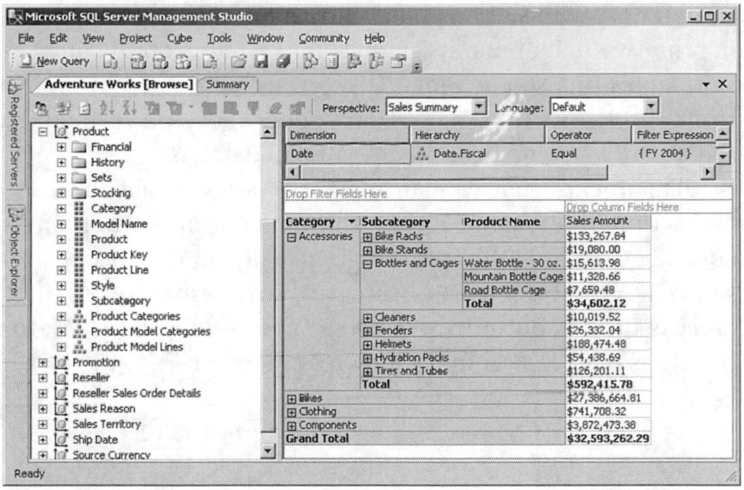

Figure 1-6   Product hierarchy drilldown

Hierarchies are useful for comprehending large amounts of information by presenting summary information and allowing people to drill down for more details in the areas of interest. OLAP technology has typically been built around hierarchy definitions; in fact, many OLAP tools in the past only allowed users to create queries using the predefined hierarchies. The reason for this was that the aggregates, which are the source of OLAP's performance, were all designed around the hierarchy levels.

Stars and Snowflakes

The simplest dimensional model has the "star" design shown in Figure 1-3, with a single table for each dimension such as Product or Customer. This means that the tables are not fully normalized, because attributes such as product category description are repeated on every product record for that category. In the past, the star schema was an attractive design because you could allow users to access the relational database directly without them having to worry about joining multiple separate dimension tables together and because relational databases did not used to do a very good job of optimizing queries against more complex schemas.

Modern BI solutions have an entirely different approach to providing the two main benefits that used to come from having single dimension tables in a star schema: If users are accessing all their information from an OLAP cube, the usability and query performance come from the OLAP layer, not from the relational database.

This means that we can move beyond dogmatically denormalizing every dimension table into a star schema and where necessary take advantage of a different design usually known as a **snowflake**. A snowflake dimension has been partly renormalized so that the single table is broken out into several separate tables with one-to-many relationships between them, as shown in Figure 1-7.

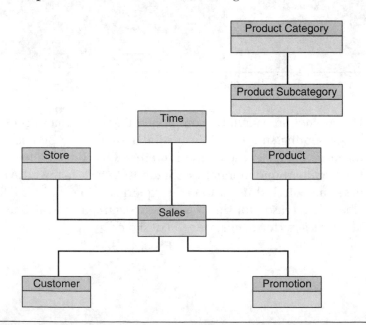

Figure 1-7　Snowflake design

So now that we have two different possible designs, a single-dimension table in a star design or multiple tables in a snowflake design, how do you know which one to use and when? Because the OLAP cube is providing the performance and user-friendly model, the main criterion for choosing between star and snowflake is how it will affect your ETL process.

Choosing Between Star and Snowflake for a Dimension

A single dimension table is often the easiest design to handle for the ETL process, especially when all the information in the dimension comes from a single source system. We can simply set up a query on the source system that joins all the various component tables together and presents a nice simple set of source columns to the ETL process. It's then easy to use SQL Server's ETL features to detect which rows have been added or changed and make the appropriate updates to the dimension table.

A snowflake design starts to get much more attractive when some of the dimension's attributes come from a different source. For example, a Geography dimension might consist of some attributes that describe a customer's physical address and other attributes that describe which sales territory the address is located within. If the customer addresses are coming from the main OLTP system but the master list of sales territories is just a spreadsheet, it might make the ETL process easier if you snowflake the Geography dimension into Sales Territory and Location tables that can then be updated separately (and yes, it is permissible to use "snowflake" as a verb in BI circles—just be prepared to defend yourself if you do it within earshot of an English major).

The other reason that designers sometimes choose a snowflake design is when the dimension has a strong natural hierarchy, such as a Product dimension that is broken out into Category, Subcategory, and Product SKU levels. If those three levels map to normalized dimension tables in the source system, it might be easier to manage the ETL process if the dimension consists of three tables rather than one. Also, because of the way Analysis Services queries the data warehouse to load the data for a dimension's attributes, a snowflake design can improve the performance of loading large Analysis Services dimensions.

You might also think that by renormalizing the dimension tables into a snowflake structure, you will save lots of disk space because the descriptions won't be repeated on every dimension record. Actually, although it is technically correct that the total storage used by dimensions is smaller in a snowflake schema, the relatively huge size of the fact tables compared with the dimension tables means that almost any attempt to optimize the dimensions to save on data warehouse space is going to be a drop in the ocean.

Using Surrogate Keys

Most dimensions that you create from data in source systems will have an obvious candidate for a primary key. In the case of a Product dimension, the primary key in the source system might be a product code, or a customer number in the case of a Customer dimension. These keys are examples of **business keys**, and in an OLTP environment they are often used as the primary key for tables when you are following a standard E/R modeling approach.

You may think that the best approach would be to use these business keys as the primary key on all of your dimension tables in the data warehouse, too. In fact, we recommend that in the data warehouse, you never use business keys as primary identifiers. Instead, you can create a new column containing an integer key with automatically generated values, known as a **surrogate key**, for every dimension table.

These surrogate keys are used as primary identifiers for all dimension tables in the data warehouse, and every fact table record that refers to a dimension always uses the surrogate key rather than the business key. All relationships in the data warehouse use the surrogate key, including the relationships between different dimension tables in a snowflake structure. Because the data warehouse uses surrogate keys and the source systems use business keys, this means that one important step in the ETL process is to translate the business keys in the incoming transaction records into data warehouse surrogate keys before inserting the new fact records.

You also need to keep the original business key on the dimension record in addition to the new surrogate key. In some cases, users have become used to working with some business keys such as product codes and might want to use these keys as an attribute in their queries. Also, even though the business key may not always uniquely identify the dimension record anymore for reasons explained in Chapter 8, they are required for the ETL process to be able to translate the business keys on the incoming fact records.

Using surrogate rather than business keys is another of those areas that appears to contradict best practices for OLTP databases, so why would we do this? One reason is to have independence from a single source system, so that they can change their internal coding structures and also so that we can acquire new companies and systems without having to modify the data warehouse structure.

Another advantage of using surrogate keys is data storage size. Unlike trying to optimize dimension table sizes, which is more or less irrelevant in the general scheme of things, any tiny difference that you can make to the size of the fact table often translates into huge space savings. Using 4-byte (or even smaller) integer keys for all dimension keys on the fact table rather than long product codes or customer identifiers means you save gigabytes of storage on a typical fact table.

A Practical Approach to Dimensional Modeling

This section provides an introduction to dimensional modeling rather than a misguided attempt to teach modeling in a few pages. Modeling is a practical discipline, and the reality is that you will only get good at it through practice—that is why each chapter in this book walks you through some of the data modeling decisions for a given business solution.

The primary difference between E/R modeling and dimensional modeling is that for E/R modeling, you mostly look at the data and apply normalization rules, whereas for dimensional modeling, you listen to the users and apply your common sense. The OLAP cubes and subsequent analyses that are built on top of a relational database schema are not the right places to transform a complicated schema into a simple, user-friendly model—you will be building the simplicity right into your schema.

A well-designed dimensional model uses the names and concepts that the business users are familiar with rather than the often-cryptic jargon-ridden terms from the source systems. The model will consist of fact tables and their associated dimension tables and can generally be understood by even nontechnical people.

Designing a Dimensional Data Model

The first question you will probably have when starting your first BI project will be "Where on earth should I start?." Unlike most modeling exercises, there will probably be fairly limited high-level business requirements, and the only information you will probably have to work with is the schemas of the source systems and any existing reports. You should start by interviewing (and listening to) some of the users of the proposed information and collect any requirements along with any available sample reports before beginning the modeling phase.

After you have this information in hand, you can move on to identifying which business processes you will be focusing on to deliver the requirements. This is usually a single major process such as sales or shipments, often building on an existing data warehouse that supports solutions from previous iterations of the BI process.

The remaining steps in the modeling process are essentially to identify the dimensions, measures, and the level of detail (or **grain**) of every fact table that we will be creating. The grain of a fact table is the level of detail that is stored in the table and is determined by the levels of the dimensions we include. For example, a fact table containing daily sales totals for a retail store has a grain of Day by Store by Product.

This process is often described in sequence, but the reality of doing dimensional modeling is that you will cycle through these steps a number of times during your design process, refining the model as you go. It's all very well when books present a dimensional data model as if it sprang to life by itself; but when you are swamped by the information you have collected, it helps to have some concrete goals to focus on.

Making a List of Candidate Attributes and Dimensions

When you are reviewing the information you have collected, look for terms that represent different ways of looking at data. A useful rule of thumb is to look for words such as *by* (as in, "I need to see profitability *by* product category"). If you keep a list of all these candidate attributes when you find them, you can start to group them into probable dimensions such as Product or Customer.

One thing to be careful of is synonyms: People often have many different ways of naming the same thing, and it is rare that everyone will agree on the definition of every term. Similarly, people in different parts of the business could be using the same term to mean different things. An important job during the modeling process is to identify these synonyms and imprecise names and to drive the business users toward consensus on what terms will mean in the data warehouse. A useful by-product of this process can be a data dictionary that documents these decisions as they are made.

Making a List of Candidate Measures

At the same time that you are recording the attributes that you have found, you will be looking for numeric measures. Many of the candidate measures that you find will turn out to be derived from a smaller set of basic measures, but you can keep track of all them because they might turn out to be useful calculations that you can add into the OLAP cube later. The best candidates for measures are additive and atomic. That is, they can be added up across all the dimensions, including time, and they are not composed from other measures.

Grouping the Measures with the Same Grain into Fact Tables

Figuring out how to group measures into fact tables is a much more structured process than grouping related attributes into dimension tables. The key concept that determines what measures end up on a fact table is that every fact table has only one grain. After you have your list of candidate measures, you can set up a spreadsheet as shown in Table 1-1 with the candidate dimensions on the columns and the candidate measures on the rows.

For each measure, you need to figure out the grain or level of detail you have available. For example, for a specific sales amount from a sales transaction, you can figure out the customer that it was sold to, the product SKU that they bought, and the day that they made the purchase, so the granularity of the sales amount measure is Product SKU by Customer by Day. For budget amount, the business is only producing monthly budgets for each product category, so the granularity is Product Category by Month.

From the example in Table 1-1, we end up with two different fact tables. Because the Sales Amount and Quantity measures both have the same granularity, they will be on the Sales fact table, which will also include Product, Customer, and Date dimension keys. A separate Budget fact table will have Product Category and Date dimension keys and a Budget Amount measure.

Table 1-1   Measures and Their Granularity Levels

	Product	Customer	Date
Sales Amount	SKU	Customer	Day
Quantity	SKU	Customer	Day
Budget Amount	Category	N/A	Month

Identifying the granularity of every measure sounds simple in principle but often turns out to be difficult in practice. So, how do you know when you have made a mistake? One common sign is when you end up with some records in the fact table with values for one set of measures and nulls for the remainder. Depending on how you load the data, you could also see that a given numeric quantity ends up being repeated on multiple records on a fact table. This usually occurs when you have a measure with a higher granularity (such as Product Category rather than Product SKU) than the fact table.

Fitting the Source Data to the Model

The output of the modeling process previously outlined is a set of dimension and fact table designs. It is important to recognize that you need actual data to validate the design, so we recommend creating the dimension and fact tables and loading some test data into them during the design process. SQL Server Integration Services (SSIS) is a great help here because you can easily use it to populate tables, as we show in Chapter 4, "Integrating Data."

Note that the reason for including real data in your modeling process is certainly not to bend your model to fit some data model issue in a source system—the right place to correct those kinds of issues is in the ETL process that loads the data, not by messing up your design. Loading test data during the design phase is really a recognition that even skilled dimensional modelers don't expect to get it right the first time. You need to build in prototyping and early demonstrations to prospective users to gather feedback during the modeling process.

Business Intelligence Projects

Large data warehousing projects have over time developed a bad reputation for being money pits with no quantifiable benefits. This somewhat gloomy picture can probably be explained by looking at many different systemic factors, but the fundamental issue was probably that the only thing many of these projects produced was gigantic wall-sized schema diagrams and the general unavailability of conference room B for 18 months or so.

A Business Value-Based Approach to BI Projects

Our recommended approach to BI projects is to focus on the business value of a proposed solution. That is, every BI project should have a clearly defined business case that details how much money will be spent and exactly what the expected business benefits are. As described in the final section of this chapter, these benefits may or may not be financially quantifiable, but they must be clearly defined and include some criteria to assess the results.

We recommend an **iterative approach** of short (three months or so) projects that focus on one specific business case. This approach has a lot of benefits in that it provides opportunity for improvement and learning through the different phases and can more easily adapt to changing business conditions as well as delivering business value along with way.

Instead of thinking about BI as a single large project that can deliver a defined set of features and then stop, you need to think about BI as an iterative process of building complete solutions. Each phase or version that you ship needs to have a clearly defined business case and include all the standard elements that lead to successful solutions, such as a deployment plan and training for end users.

In general, if a team realizes that it is not going to meet the deadline for this phase, they should be cutting scope. This usually means focusing attention on the key areas that formed the business case and moving the less-valuable features to a subsequent release. This kind of discipline is essential to delivering business value, because if your timelines slip and your costs increase, the expected return on investment will not materialize and you will have a much harder time getting commitment for a follow-up project. Of course, you can't cut many of the features that are essential to the "value" part of the equation either.

The challenge with this iterative approach is that without a careful approach to the data architecture, you might end up with disconnected islands of information again. The solution to this problem is that the architectural team needs to focus on **conformed dimensions**.

This means that whenever a particular dimension shows up in different areas, possibly from different source systems, the design approach must force all areas to use a single version of the schema and data for that dimension. Using conformed dimensions everywhere is a difficult process that costs more in the short term but is absolutely essential to the success of BI in an organization in order to provide "one version of the truth."

Kimball and Inmon

No overview of an approach to BI projects would really be complete without mentioning two of the giants in the field, who have somewhat different approaches. There are many comparisons of the two approaches (some biased, and some less so), but in general Ralph Kimball's approach is to build a dimensional data warehouse using a series of interconnected projects with heavy emphasis on conformed dimensions. Bill Inmon's approach is to introduce a fully normalized data warehouse into which all the data for a corporation is loaded, before flowing out into dependant data marts or data marts for specific purposes. This approach was previously known as Enterprise Data Warehouse, but more recently has become known by the somewhat awkward term Corporate Information Factory or CIF.

Our approach is more aligned with Kimball's because in our experience, it's difficult to justify the effort and expense of creating and maintaining an additional normalized data warehouse, especially because of the difficulty of tying concrete returns on the investment back to this central data warehouse.

Business Intelligence Project Pitfalls

Many technology books present BI as if the actual process of delivering a solution was so elementary and so obviously added value that readers are often surprised to find out that a significant number of BI projects are failures. That is, they don't provide any value to the business and are scrapped either during development or after they are delivered, often at great cost.

Throughout this book, we try to reinforce the practices that in our experience have led to successful BI solutions, but it is also important to highlight some of the major common factors that lead to failed BI projects.

Lack of Business Involvement

The team that is designing the solution must have strong representation from the business communities that will be using the final product, because a BI project team that only consists of technical people will almost always fail. The reason is that BI projects attempt to address one of the trickiest areas in IT, and one that usually requires practical business experience—providing the users with access to information that they didn't already know that can actually be used to change their actions and decisions.

BI projects have another interesting challenge that can only be solved by including business people on the team: Users usually can't tell you what they want from a BI solution until they see something that is wrong. The way to deal with this is to include lots of early prototyping and let the business representatives on the team help the technical people get it right before you show it to all the users.

If you get this wrong and produce a solution without appropriate business input, the major symptom only appears afterward when it becomes clear that no one is using the solution. This is sometimes tricky to establish, unless you take the easy approach and switch off the solution to see how many people complain (not recommended; when you start to lose user trust in a system that is always available and always correct, you will have a nearly impossible time trying to recover it).

Data Quality, Data Quality, Data Quality

A lack of attention to the area of data quality has sunk more BI projects than any other issue in our experience. Every single BI project is always going to have issues with data quality. (Notice that we are not hedging our bets here and saying "most BI projects.") If you have started a BI project and think you don't have a data quality problem, set up a cube and let a few business people have access to it and tell them the revenue numbers in the cube will be used to calculate their next bonus.

Dealing with Data Quality Problems

Data quality problems come in many shapes and sizes, some of which have technology fixes and many of which have business process fixes. Chapter 7, "Data Quality," discusses these in more detail, but the basic lesson in data quality is to start early in the project and build a plan to identify and address the issues. If you mess this up, the first users of your new BI solution will quickly figure it out and stop trusting the information.

Data quality challenges can often be partly addressed with a surprising technique: communication. The data is not going to be perfect, but people have probably been relying on reports from the source transaction systems for years, which, after all, use the same data. Although one approach is to never show any information to users unless it's perfect, in the real world you might have to resort to letting people know exactly what the data quality challenges are (and your plan to address them) before they access the information.

Auditing

The technical people who will be building the BI solution are typically terrible at spotting data quality issues. Despite being able to spot a missing curly bracket or END clause in hundreds of lines of code, they usually don't have the business experience to distinguish good data from bad data. A critical task on every BI project is to identify a business user who will take ownership of data quality auditing from day one of the project and will work closely with the project team to reconcile the data back to the source systems. When the solution is deployed, this quality assurance mindset must continue (by appointing a data quality manager).

One of the most obviously important tasks is checking that the numbers (or measures from the fact table) match up with the source systems. Something that might not be so obvious is the impact that errors in dimension data can have. For example, if the parenting information in product category and subcategory data is not correct, the numbers for the product SKU-level measures will roll up incorrectly, and the totals will be wrong. Validating dimension structures is a critical part of the process.

The Really Big Project

A fairly common approach to BI projects is to spend a year or two building a huge data warehouse with some cubes and deploying a fancy BI client tool. As discussed earlier, we favor a business value-based approach using smaller, targeted projects instead. Assuming that you manage to deliver a solution that the business can use as part of their decision-making process, you must accept that the BI solution starts to get out of sync with the business on the day that you ship it. If the company has committed to a strategy that requires real insight, the BI project will never actually be completed.

Problems Measuring Success

If you commit to the idea of focusing on business value for your BI solutions, one major challenge that you will face is figuring out whether you succeeded. Unlike transaction systems for which you can more easily do things such as measure the return on investment (ROI) by comparing the cost of doing business before and after the system is deployed, the success of BI projects is usually much harder to measure.

Working out the "cost" part of the equation is hard enough, factoring in indirect costs such as maintenance and support of the solution after it has been deployed in addition to hard costs such as software, hardware, and labor. Of course, you cannot stop at working out the costs of the BI solution—you must also estimate the costs of *not* having the BI solution. For example, most organizations have people who spend many hours every month or quarter exercising their Excel skills to glue together data from different systems, which will typically take less time and be more accurate when they can access a proper data warehouse instead.

The "benefit" side is even more difficult. How do you quantify the benefits of having access to better information? The intangible benefits such as increased agility and competitiveness are notoriously difficult to quantify, and the best approach in putting together a business case is usually to describe those areas without trying to assign financial numbers. Some of the most successful BI projects are aligned with business initiatives so that the cost of the BI system can be factored into the overall cost of the business initiative and compared with its tangible benefits.

Summary

This chapter looked at some of the key Business Intelligence concepts and techniques. We showed that OLTP systems typically have a normalized database structure optimized for updates rather than queries. Trying to provide access to this data is difficult because the complex schemas of OLTP databases makes them difficult for end users to work with, even when simplifying views are provided; furthermore, there are usually multiple data sources in an organization that need to be accessed together.

We propose building a data warehouse relational database with a design and an operational approach optimized for queries. Data from all the source systems is loaded into the warehouse through a process of extraction, transformation, and loading (ETL). The data warehouse uses a dimensional model, where related numeric measures are grouped into fact tables, and descriptive attributes are grouped into dimension tables that can be used to analyze the facts.

A separate OLAP database that stores and presents information in a multidimensional format is built on top of the data warehouse. An OLAP cube includes precalculated summaries called aggregates that are created when the data is loaded from the data warehouse and that can radically improve the response times for many queries.

We also looked at some of the key concepts in dimensional modeling. A hierarchy is a set of attributes grouped together to provide a drill-down path for users. In a snowflake dimension design, the dimension is stored as several separate related tables, and we often recommend taking this approach when it will improve the performance or maintainability of the data-loading process. We recommend using surrogate keys for every dimension table, which are generated integer values that have no meaning outside the data warehouse.

We also covered some of the potential pitfalls of BI projects. Some of the key areas to focus on are making sure the business is involved and using an iterative approach that actually delivers value along the way. We recommend that BI project teams pay careful attention to issues of data quality.

CHAPTER 2

Introduction to SQL Server 2005

SQL Server 2005 is a complete, end-to-end platform for Business Intelligence (BI) solutions, including data warehousing, analytical databases (OLAP), extraction, transformation, and loading (ETL), data mining, and reporting. The tools to design and develop solutions and to manage and operate them are also included.

It can be a daunting task to begin to learn about how to apply the various components to build a particular BI solution, so this chapter provides you with a high-level introduction to the components of the SQL Server 2005 BI platform. Subsequent chapters make use of all these components to show you how to build real-world solutions, and we go into much more detail about each of the technologies along the way.

SQL Server Components

SQL Server 2005 consists of a number of integrated components, as shown in Figure 2-1. When you run the SQL Server installation program on a server, you can choose which of these services to install. We focus on those components relevant to a BI solution, but SQL Server also includes all the services required for building all kinds of secure, reliable, and robust data-centric applications.

Development and Management Tools

SQL Server includes two complementary environments for developing and managing BI solutions. **SQL Server Management Studio** replaces both Enterprise Manager and Query Analyzer used in SQL Server 2000. SQL Server Management Studio enables you to administer all the aspects of solutions within a single management environment. Administrators can manage many different servers in the same place, including the database engine, Analysis Services, Integration Services, and Reporting Services components. A powerful feature of the Management Studio is that every command that an administrator performs using the tool can also be saved as a script for future use.

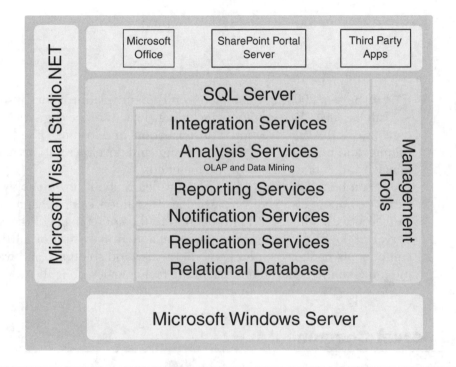

Figure 2-1   SQL Server components

For developing solutions, BI developers can use the new **Business Intelligence Development Studio**. This is a single, rich environment for building Analysis Services cubes and data mining structures, Integration Services packages, and for designing reports. BI Development Studio is built on top of the Visual Studio technology, so it integrates well with existing tools such as source control repositories.

Deploying Components

You can decide where you would like to install the SQL Server components based on the particular environment into which they are deployed. The installation program makes it easy to pick which services you want to install on a server, and you can configure them at the same time.

In a large solution supporting thousands of users with a significantly sized data warehouse, you could decide to have one server running the database engine to store the data warehouse, another server running Analysis Services and Integration Services, and several servers all running Reporting Services. Each of these servers would, of course, need to be licensed for SQL Server, because a single server license does not allow you to run the various components on separate machines.

Figure 2-2 shows how these components fit together to create an environment to support your BI solution.

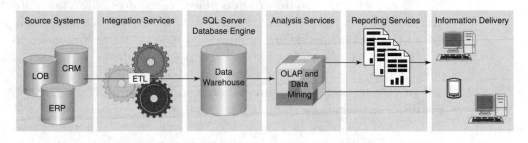

Figure 2-2   SQL Server BI architecture

SQL Server Database Engine

The SQL Server 2005 database engine is the service that provides support for relational databases. It is a highly reliable, available, and scalable database server. As shown in Figure 2-2, its primary role in BI solutions is to be the long-term authoritative data store for enterprise data from which Analysis Services will build OLAP databases and cubes.

Usually a single server machine runs a single **instance** of the database engine, but each server can be configured to run more than one instance of the database engine at the same time if necessary. Each instance has its own completely separate set of databases and tables. It is usually better to have a single instance on a machine because the overall performance of the server will be improved and the administration simplified, but sometimes it is useful to be able to run multiple isolated environments on the same large server, such as when you need to run different versions or service pack levels to support existing applications. SQL Server 2005 supports up to 50 instances on a single server.

Management

SQL Server 2005 greatly simplifies the job of managing a database because it is largely self-tuning. Whether you need to manage a few or hundreds of SQL Servers, tools are included that will reduce the cost of implementing and maintaining SQL Server instances. Most management operations can be performed with the database online.

For backup and index maintenance operations, a wizard will create and deploy scheduled **maintenance plans**. It requires only a few minutes to implement a maintenance plan for a SQL Server instance. Backups of the data or the log are performed online, so there is no need to take the database down to create a backup. Most index reorganizations or rebuilds are also performed with the database online.

To help track down resource-intensive queries or operations, **SQL Profiler** can monitor all statements or a subset of the statements sent to SQL Server, as shown in Figure 2-3. You can see the statement, who issued it, how long it ran, and many other metrics and attributes. You can view the list directly or record it to a table or file. You can capture the text of a query and have the **Database Engine Tuning Advisor** provide suggestions for creating new indexes to help the query perform better.

SQL Server is extensively instrumented to provide information about how it is using resources. To monitor the resource consumption or internal metrics of SQL Server's operation, you can run the System Monitor (previously known as Perfmon). You can use this information to determine or predict requirements for additional resources.

If you are managing more than a few SQL Servers, a separate product called Microsoft Operations Manager (**MOM**) can collect events and errors raised by each instance and filter out the important information for forwarding to the system operators. With the MOM interface, you can see at a glance the state of any of the servers. Predictive logic in MOM can alert you to potential issues before they become critical issues.

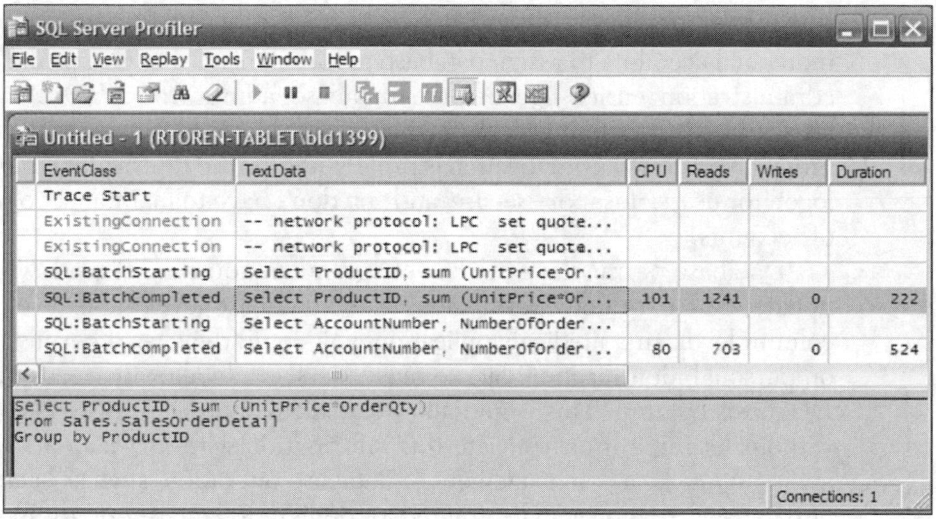

Figure 2-3   Analyzing query performance with SQL Server Profiler

Scheduled Execution of Processes

SQL Server Agent is a Windows service that can schedule and execute jobs. A job is a sequence of one or more steps. A step can invoke an operating system command, SQL script, Analysis Services query or command, Integration Services package, an ActiveX script, or a replication management command. The job can be executed on demand or scheduled to recur on a regular basis. The sequence of job steps can be conditional on the results of a prior job step. Notifications can be sent via e-mail, pager, or net send command on the success or failure of the job.

Security

SQL Server supports authentication of connections using either Windows authentication alone or Windows and SQL Server authentication. Windows authentication uses your Windows credentials to identify you; SQL authentication uses a login name and password that a SQL Server administrator creates for you. This login is valid only for connecting to a single SQL Server instance.

SQL Server 2005 authentication has been enhanced over that of SQL Server 2000 to provide security rules such as password expiration and strong password requirements. Access to a database is not possible without an authenticated connection. You can use Windows groups or individual accounts to assign database permissions. Using groups makes administration easier because the database administrator (DBA) no longer needs to administer individual users, just a smaller number of groups. Windows authentication is preferred because it provides a single logon for users, it is more secure, and you don't have to maintain two sets of accounts.

Database permissions can be very granular. You can set read, write, update, delete, or deny permissions at the database level, table level, or column level. In a medical application, you could deny read permission on personal identification data to most users, while allowing reads on a Diagnosis column. This would allow statistical analysis of disease data, without letting a user associate this information with any patient. The ability to invoke any management or database operation, such as backup or database creation, can be granted, or denied, to any user or group. As with all rights and permissions in SQL Server, deny overrides any granting of rights or permissions.

Transmissions "over the wire" can be encrypted to protect data being sent between the client and server. You can also encrypt stored data down to the column level, using certificates, symmetric keys, or asymmetric keys.

Availability

SQL Server provides a wide range of options to ensure availability under almost any circumstances. Whether you need server redundancy simply to be able to perform server maintenance, or geographically remote synchronized databases for disaster recovery, you will find the features and tools to support these requirements. **Clustering** provides automatic failover to one or more alternative servers connected to the same storage area network (SAN). Database **mirroring** is a cost-effective solution that provides complete synchronization over the network between databases and fast automatic failover to a completely separate set of servers and storage. **Replication** offers the ability to synchronize a subset of the database with another active server. All the options maintain transactional integrity.

Scalability

You can run SQL Server on either 32-bit or 64-bit Windows platforms, but the file structures are exactly the same, so you can freely move databases from 32-bit to 64-bit and back again. 64-bit architecture gives you the advantages of a much larger and more efficient memory space, and more processors per server. The reason memory space is important is to support larger data and query caches. You can use up to 32TB of RAM on a 64-bit platform.

You can also add more processors to improve performance or handle a larger workload. Eight-way servers are commonplace now and are appropriate for many situations. For larger data warehouses, you can scale up SQL Server to 128 processors on a single server.

Multi-terabyte data warehouses are supported with good design and infrastructure in most contexts. The maximum single database size is 1,048,516 terabytes. We will avoid becoming famous for stating that this "should be enough for anyone." However, it is likely enough for the next few years, for most uses.

Support for Very Large Databases

Partitioned tables and **distributed partitioned views** are two features of the database engine that enhance support for very large databases. A partitioned table appears as a single table to a query, but the rows in the table are physically divided across a number of filegroups in the same database. A distributed partitioned view is similar in concept, but the tables are distributed across several SQL Servers and presented to the user through a view. If the SQL Servers are multiple instances on a single server, this is called simply a partitioned view. These features offer improvements in performance through parallel queries and through manageability and maintenance (because you can treat each partition independently in many respects).

Integration Services

SQL Server Integration Services (SSIS) provides the data ETL services that you use to deliver clean, validated data to your data warehouse. Integration Services also enables you to invoke administrative tasks, monitor external events, and maintain audit logs of Integration Services runtime events. The design and runtime environments are totally new in SQL Server 2005, replacing Data Transformation Services (DTS) of SQL Server 2000. DTS packages may continue to be executed, but not modified, because Integration Services has a completely different architecture.

Integration Services is an independent service that you can choose to install and run on any server, as shown in Figure 2-4, regardless of whether the SQL Server engine is installed on that server. You create **packages** to access, cleanse, and conform source data; load data into the relational data warehouse and Analysis Services databases; and audit the overall ETL process. Packages are usually executed by a job scheduled by the SQL Agent, or an active package can wait on an external event such as the arrival of a file.

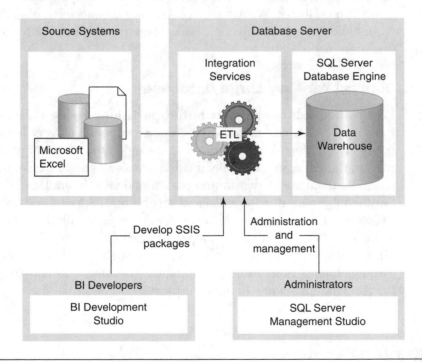

Figure 2-4   Integration Services architecture

Designing Packages

BI Development Studio is the development environment for Integration Services packages. You create an Integration Services **project**, which may contain one or more packages. A graphical designer is used to build the packages, and you can configure most complex tasks or transforms via a wizard. The designer retains metadata about all the data flowing through the package. You can break data flows, insert new transforms, and reconnect the data flow without fear of losing column mappings going into or out of a transform.

A package primarily contains one or more **control flows**, and usually a **data flow** invoked by the control flow. You can think of a control flow as a high-level description of the steps needed to accomplish a major task. For example, the steps to update the data warehouse might be "initiate an FTP download from regional offices," "load the sales data," and "load the inventory data."

The details of how to load the sales and inventory data are not part of the control flow, but are each a separate data flow. The data flow tasks would define the source for the data, which columns you needed, probably some key lookups, validation, and eventually would write the transformed data to the data warehouse.

Defining the Control Flow

Even though our goal is frequently just to move data from our sources to the data warehouse, quite a bit of administration and overhead is required to implement a full production-ready ETL solution. You might need to empty tables, update audit logs, or wait for an event to occur indicating the availability of new data. Some tasks must be performed before others. This is what a control flow is for. Integration Services provides a number of different types of tasks that you can link together to perform all the steps necessary for your ETL solution.

You graphically design the control flow by dragging tasks from the toolbox onto the work surface, as shown in Figure 2-5. Simple tasks do things such as execute an SQL statement, invoke a data flow task, or invoke another package. Variables can be defined and used to pass information between tasks or to other packages. You can define a sequence for their execution by linking one task to another, or you can define a group of tasks that can execute in parallel by putting them in a sequence container and simply linking other tasks to or from the container. You can put a set of tasks in a loop to be executed until some condition is satisfied, or have them repeated while enumerating the values on a list, such as a list of file names to be loaded.

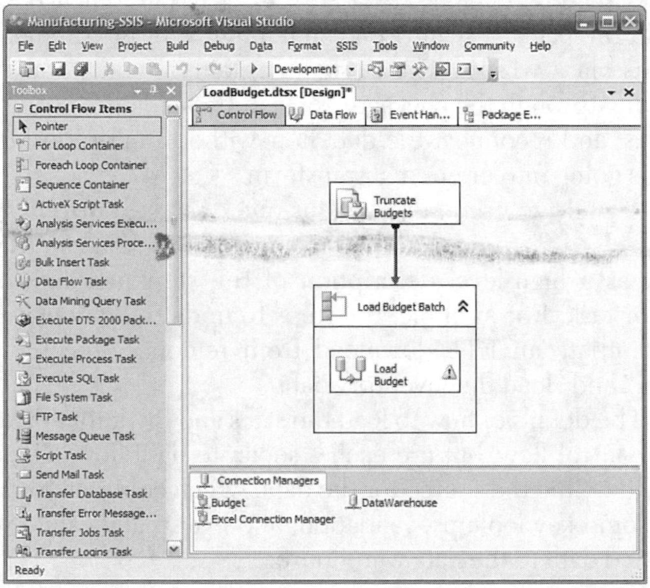

Figure 2-5   Control flow in a package

Other tasks are related to interacting with external events and processes rather than data. You can work with a message queue to send or wait for a message. You can listen for any Windows Management Instrumentation (WMI) event, such as a new file added to a directory, and begin the control flow task when this occurs. You can use a web service to receive data or a command to initiate processing. You can initiate FTP sessions to send or receive data files between systems with no other common interface.

Defining Data Flows

A data flow defines where the data comes from (the data source), the transformations required to make it ready for the data warehouse, and where the data goes to (the data destination), as shown in Figure 2-6. This is generally the core of a package. Many data flows can be invoked by a control flow, and they may be invoked in parallel. A data flow is initiated when a data flow task is executed in a control flow.

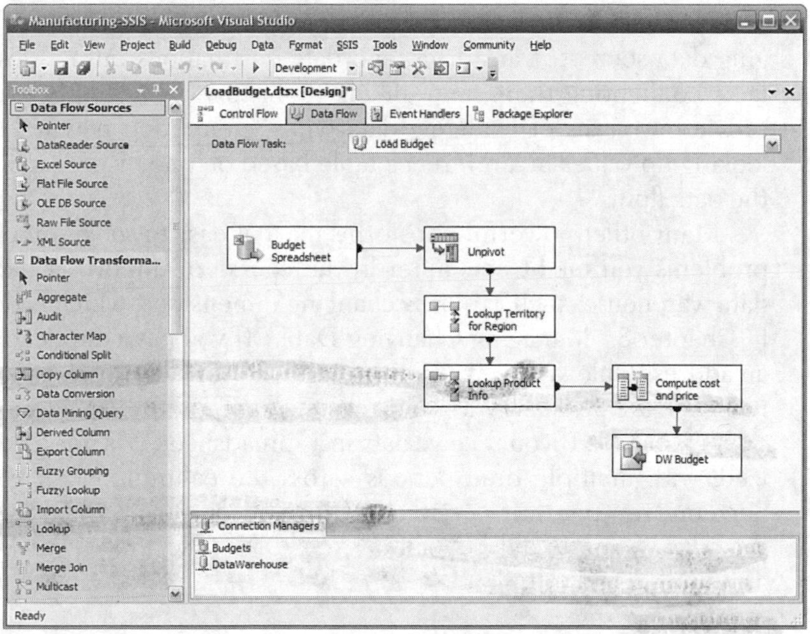

Figure 2-6   Data flow

Data Sources and Destinations

Integration Services supports a wide variety of **data sources** and **data destinations**. Common relational databases such as SQL Server, Oracle, and DB2 are supported directly "out of the box." In addition, Excel, Access, XML documents, and flat files connectors are provided. Connections can also be made to Analysis Services cubes, Directory Services, and Outlook, among many other services with OLE DB providers. You can use Integration Services for essentially all your ETL requirements between any data sources and destinations. There is no requirement at all that a SQL Server database be either the source or the destination of a data flow.

Data Transformations

Data **transformations** are used to define the specific actions to be performed on the data in a data flow task as it flows from a data source to a data destination. You graphically design the sequence of actions by dragging data sources, transforms, and data destinations onto a design surface, configuring them, and linking them together. Simple transforms provide a means of changing data types, computing new columns, or looking up values in a reference table based on one or more columns in the data flow.

Many other powerful transforms make it easy to solve some difficult problems you might encounter in the course of importing data into a data warehouse, such as slowly changing dimensions, which is described in Chapter 8, "Managing Changing Data." If you have duplicate rows in an address table, a **Fuzzy Grouping** transform will provide a ranking of rows that are probably the same, even with minor differences in spelling or punctuation. If you receive data in a spreadsheet, it is often denormalized, with multiple time periods across the columns when you really need one row per time period. An **Unpivot** transform will normalize the data stream, putting each column on its own row, retaining the row key and adding an additional key to indicate which column the row corresponds to.

You can also add transforms to split or merge a data flow. If you need to process some rows differently than others based on some value in the row, you can use a **Conditional Split** transform to create multiple independent data flows. You can perform unique transforms on each data flow, and then send each one to unique destinations in the data warehouse or other data target, or you can merge some of the data flows back into the main stream.

Data flows quickly through most transforms thanks to the new **pipeline architecture** in Integration Services. You will see that a typical data flow consists of reading data from a source, passing it through several transforms, and the finally writing it to a destination. The data is not written to disk between each transform. Instead, it is retained in memory and passed between the transforms. For large volumes of data, a block of records is read from the source and then passed on to the first transform. When the transform completes its work on the block, it passes the data on to the next transform and then receives another block to continue working. Both transforms can now work in parallel. This design means there is little overhead spent writing intermediate results to disk only to be read back in again immediately.

Debugging

Debugging packages is easy, too. When the package is executed in the BI Development Studio, each task is color coded by its state. Running tasks are yellow, successfully completed tasks turn green, and failing tasks turn red. Row counts display along each data flow path so that you can observe the progress and traffic along each path. If you need to view the data flowing along a path, you can add a data viewer to the path. A data viewer can show you the value of each column in each row in a grid, or you can choose to view column values as a histogram, scatter plot, or column chart. If a transform or task fails, a descriptive error is written to a progress file. You can set **breakpoints** at any task, or at any point in a script task or transform, step through each task or script, and view the values of variables as they change.

Data Quality

The ETL process is critical to ensuring high quality of the data reaching the data warehouse. Integration Services transforms are designed so that data containing errors can be redirected to a different path for remediation. Common errors such as missing business keys or string truncation errors automatically raise an error condition by default, but you can specify alternative actions. You can also use a Conditional Split transform to redirect rows with values that are out of a predefined range. Nearly every transform provides multiple data flow outputs that you can simply drag to some other transform to create a new data flow that you use to handle the data that has failed some test.

Deploying and Configuring Packages

You can deploy packages to other environments such as test or production one at a time from the development studio, or in a batch using a command line. Using package configuration sources, you can reconfigure properties such as connection strings, server names, or parameters at runtime. The source for these properties can be environment variables, the registry, a database table, or an XML file.

Executing Packages

Integration Services packages can be run from the BI Development Studio designer, by starting them in SQL Server Management Studio, from a command line, or through the SQL Agent to schedule the execution. You can also invoke a package from another package. You can pass parameters to the packages using any of these methods. The parameters can set package variables that can be used to set task and transform properties, such as a server name, or to control other aspects of the package execution. You can use Management Studio to view or stop currently executing packages, regardless of how they were started.

Analysis Services

SQL Server Analysis Services is an engine designed to support storing and querying large amounts of data based on dimensional models. Analysis Services implicitly understands concepts such as dimensions, hierarchies, slicing, and filtering. Using Analysis Services, you no longer need to worry about how to construct complex SQL statements to do the kind of analysis of your data commonly performed in BI applications.

In addition to simply presenting a set of values as output, Analysis Services can assist in interpreting these values. Data mining capabilities in Analysis Services can provide insight into the relationships between different aspects of your data (for example, how level of education correlates with credit risk). Another common application in BI is key performance indicators (KPI), where you are measuring success against some pre-established goals.

Analysis Services Architecture

Analysis Services reads data from one or more sources to populate the dimensions and cubes you have designed. It is a distinct service from the SQL Server database engine. Most common data sources can be used by Analysis Services as data sources. You can just as easily create Analysis Services databases with Oracle or Access databases as you can with SQL Server databases.

Like the SQL Server database engine, Analysis Services is a server application, as shown in Figure 2-7, not an end-user application. Queries in the form of Multidimensional Expressions (**MDX**) statements are submitted to the server, and results are typically returned to the user through Excel, Reporting Services, Business Scorecard Manager, or third-party tools such as ProClarity, Cognos, and Panorama. Communication with end-user applications is done using XML for Analysis (**XMLA**), an open standard for interfacing with data sources. The XMLA council has more than 20 vendors (and many more subscribers to the standard).

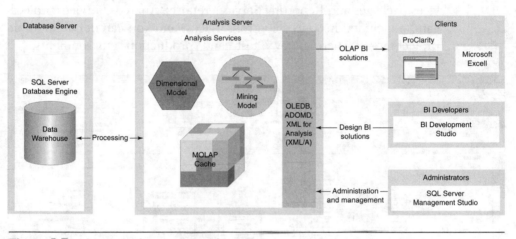

Figure 2-7   Analysis Services architecture

Usually a single server machine runs a single instance of Analysis Services, just like the SQL Server database engine, but you can configure a server to run more than one instance of the Analysis Services engine at the same time if necessary.

With Analysis Services 2005, you can have on-demand, real-enough-time, or real-time updating of the analysis database. The notification of new data being available can be automatic if you are using SQL Server or via polling for other databases. You choose how long to wait before processing new data, and how old the data is allowed to be, and Analysis Services will ensure that if the data is not available in its database within that timeframe, it will revert to the relational data store until it is available. This feature is called **proactive caching** and is an important feature not just for real-time scenarios but for high availability, too. Updating performed using proactive caching does not mean taking the database offline.

Development Environment

In a BI development environment, you need to specify what the data sources are, what your dimensions and measures are, the goals of your KPIs, and other design criteria. This is not an end-user task, but a task for a BI developer.

BI Development Studio is the graphical development environment where you create your Analysis Services database design, as shown in Figure 2-8. This is the same environment used to develop Integration Services packages and Reporting Services reports. Analysis Services projects can be included in source control services, and you can define multiple project targets, such as "dev," "test," and "production" environments.

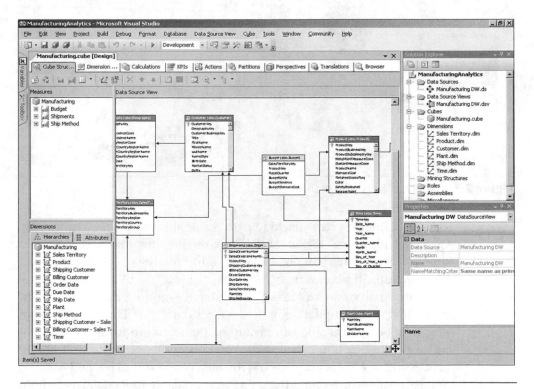

Figure 2-8 Cube designer in BI Development Studio

Building a basic cube is extremely simply, thanks to a wizard. All you need to do is to tell the wizard which tables to include, and it will determine which tables represent dimensions and which represent facts. If you have enough data in the tables, the wizard can determine some of the natural hierarchies of each dimension. You can be well on your way to having the framework for a cube within minutes. Many other wizards are available to help you build special objects such as time dimensions.

In the designer, you also specify any KPI, actions, data partitioning, and other options you require. The result of building an Analysis Services project is an XML file that completely describes your design. You can have this file deployed to any server running Analysis Services, which creates the Analysis Services database and performs the initial population of the dimensions and cubes. You can use the Analysis Services Deployment Wizard to deploy your database to other servers and environments, and as part of the deployment, specify properties to change so that the solution will work in the new environment, such as the data source server, the log files, and so on.

You can also reverse engineer an existing Analysis Services database into a BI Development Studio project. This is important because you can make changes to a live database through the SQL Management Studio, or through programmatic means; neither method modifies the underlying project.

Managing and Securing Analysis Services

You use SQL Server Management Studio as shown in Figure 2-9 to perform routine maintenance, manage security, and to browse the dimensions and cubes.

If you need to understand the kinds of queries being presented to a cube, you can use SQL Profiler (the same one used to trace relational queries). You can filter on the duration of a query, who issued the query, and many other attributes. You can capture the query string, put it into an Analysis Services query window in Management Studio, and execute it to review its results and test modifications to the query.

Analysis Services by default requires authentication of connections using Windows authentication. When you log in to Windows, you are authenticated, and the credentials you receive are used by Analysis Services to determine your permissions. In this default mode, access to a database is not possible without an authenticated connection and explicit permission granted for that database. In Analysis Services, you create **roles** to which you give permissions to all or portions of a cube. You can place Windows groups or individual user accounts in these roles. Using groups makes administration easier because you no longer need to administer individual users, just a smaller number of groups, and the specific groups rarely change.

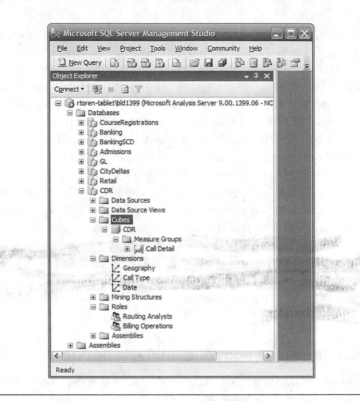

Figure 2-9   Management Studio with Analysis Services

You can configure Analysis Services to use Basic or Digest authentication or to simply grant unauthorized users access (although, of course, the latter is not generally recommended).

The Unified Dimensional Model

OLAP technology can usually support all the different design elements covered in Chapter 1, "Introduction to Business Intelligence," including the ability to easily handle stars or snowflakes and to define hierarchies from the attributes in a dimension. However, in the past there has always been one major reason that people continued to use relational reporting as well as OLAP. Most OLAP technologies restrict users to drilling down through summary data along predefined hierarchies; so when users get to a point in their analysis where they want to see detailed transactional information, they need to switch to a relational report.

SQL Server 2005 includes some OLAP innovations that can unify these previously separate relational and dimensional reporting models, called the **Unified Dimension Model** (UDM). The term UDM refers to the extended set of capabilities offered by Analysis Services 2005, which essentially means that cubes are not restricted to providing classic drilldown access through a star or snowflake schema, but can support detail-level reporting from complex real-world source databases.

The major difference is that users of Analysis Services 2005 cubes are not restricted to a predefined set of hierarchies for querying the cube. Instead, they can use any descriptive attribute on a dimension to analyze information. This means that in addition to the classic OLAP-style reports with summary information, users can include attributes such as order numbers to generate reports with the most detailed level of information available, such as a list of order-line items.

Support for Large and Mission-Critical BI Solutions

As BI solutions become a key part of the strategy of a company, BI will quickly move from being simply an important initiative to a mission-critical system. In large and more complex BI solutions, Analysis Services' support for availability, scalability, and very large volumes of data become essential.

Availability

Analysis Services is cluster-aware. It can be placed in a failover cluster to provide fault tolerance or in a load-balanced cluster to provide more resources to support additional users or more complex queries. Database synchronization provides a means to propagate changes from an Analysis Services database to other databases in a load-balanced cluster. The cubes remain online during synchronization and present a consistent view to the users. When synchronization is complete, the new version of the database is presented to the users.

Scalability

Analysis Services can be run on either 32-bit or 64-bit Windows platforms and can use as many processors as the operating system will support. Typically, you would use 2-way to 16-way servers, but you can go up to 128 processors. This extreme is usually unnecessary because Analysis

Services databases can also be deployed to as many servers as required to support the volume of queries you have. Databases can be transparently synchronized from a master database to the other servers to support this scenario.

Support for Very Large Databases

When cubes become large, they could require a long time to process after the addition of new data. Analysis Services supports partitioning of cubes, and you only have to process partitions where the underlying data has changed. You usually partition over time, so by designing your partitions so that only the most recent ones are updated, you can reduce the overall processing time significantly (often to just a few minutes).

Reporting Services

SQL Server Reporting Services is a server-based platform for designing, managing, and delivering both interactive reports and traditional printed reports. Although Reporting Services is a component of SQL Server 2005 and uses a SQL Server database as the catalogue, you can include data in your reports from any database with an OLE DB or ODBC driver. This version of Reporting Services also has great integration with Analysis Services, making it easy to build reports that take advantage of the rich multidimensional information available in cubes.

Reporting Architecture

Many reporting technologies required a client application to be installed on every user's computer. Reporting Services is different: It is a fully server-based application built around web services, as shown in Figure 2-10, which can render and deliver the same report in whatever format the user requests. The report can be an HTML page that is displayed using a browser, a PDF file that uses Adobe Acrobat Reader, an Excel spreadsheet, or one of several other formats.

Report developers can design a report on their workstation and then publish the report definition to the reporting server. When a user makes a request for a report, the Reporting Services web service is responsible for querying the underlying data sources, rendering the report in the necessary format, and returning the information back to the client for display. Reports can also be configured so that the data is cached to improve performance.

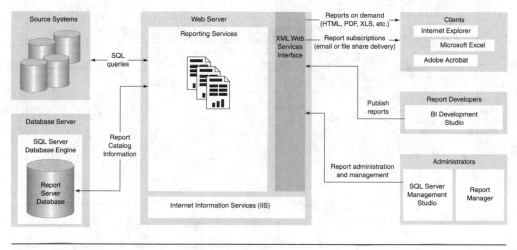

Figure 2-10   Reporting Services architecture

Reporting Services requires Internet Information Services (IIS) to be installed on the server, and in common with many Web applications, it is usually installed on a separate server from the database server.

Designing Reports

BI Development Studio includes a Report Server project type for building reporting solutions. Reports are developed using a drag-and-drop report layout and query designer, as shown in Figure 2-11, and the report can also be executed within the designer to preview the results. The report designer is flexible and not restricted to "bands" (in contrast to many other reporting environments). You can combine tables, lists, and text boxes in a single report that may have multiple data sources.

You can add parameters to the reports so that users can select the data that they are interested in seeing before running the report. You can link each parameter to a query so that a list of possible values is presented to the user. Reports can also include complex expressions using the VB.NET syntax, to provide totals or more complex calculations. For more complex applications, you can add functions to the report's code section or even register a .NET assembly and make calls to it from within report expressions.

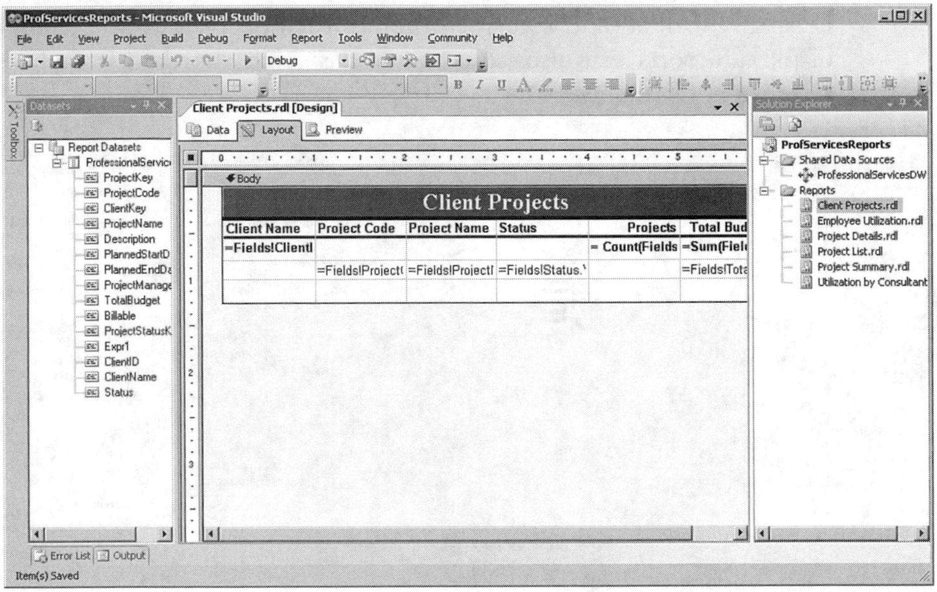

Figure 2-11 Designing reports

Report solutions that you create in the BI Development Studio environment consist of RDL (Report Definition Language) and other files on your development machine. After you have finished designing the reports, you can deploy the solution to a server running Reporting Services so that users can access the reports.

Accessing Reports

Because Reporting Services is essentially a web service that delivers reports on request, you can integrate reports into your Web-based or Windows client applications easily. Visual Studio 2005 includes a ReportViewer control that you can use to display server-based reports within a Web-based or Windows client application. Reporting Services also includes two Web parts that enable you to display reports in a Windows SharePoint Services (WSS) team site.

You can also access every report via a simple URL, so the easiest way to integrate reports into your own Web applications is just to supply a hyperlink that the user can click to display the report in his browser. Alternatively, one of the most common ways that users access reports is via a Web application called **Report Manager** that is installed as part of

Reporting Services, as shown in Figure 2-12. Report Manager enables users to browse a list of reports that they have access to, enter parameter values, and view the reports in the browser.

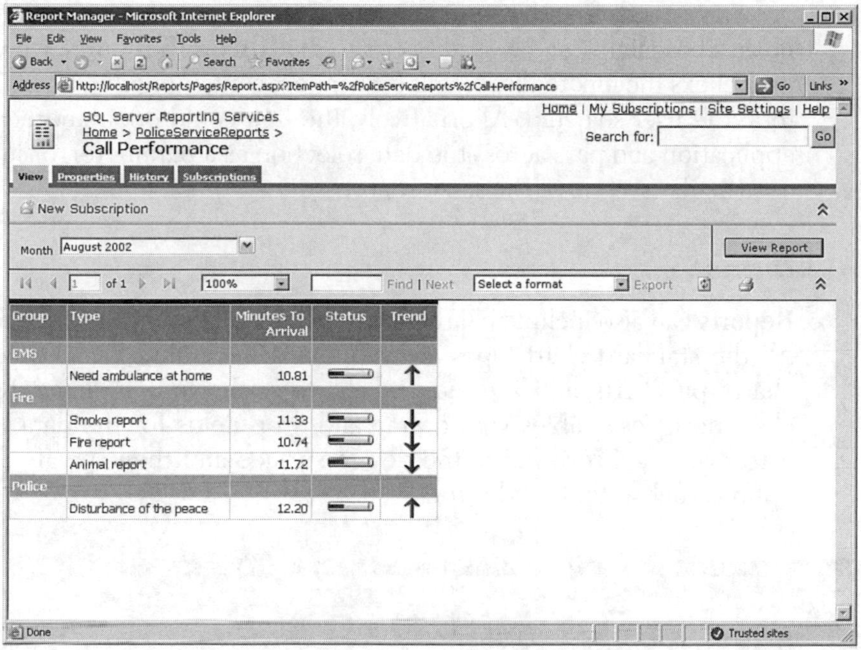

Figure 2-12 Viewing reports using Report Manager

Reporting Services Features

One of the most interesting features of Reporting Services is that a single report can include information from different queries, which are available as datasets in the report designer. Each dataset can be associated with data regions in the report to display the information. The data region could be a simple table, a flexible list that gives you more control over the formatting, or a matrix, which is similar to a table but with dynamic columns determined at runtime.

Interactive Reports

Rather than just statically presenting a list of information, you can also configure reports to include some interactivity. For example, in a report that shows revenue by product with subtotals for each product category, the report could be designed so that only the summary data is initially displayed and the user can **drill down** to see the detailed product-level information for a particular category.

You can also configure data elements in reports to include hyperlinks. These links can be used to create **drillthrough** reports, where the user clicks the link to display another report containing the details of the total the user selected. Alternatively, the link could open another Web application and pass across the data selection as a parameter, or jump to a particular section of the same report.

Charts

Reports can also include charts to graphically represent data in a report. All the standard chart types are supported, including bar and column charts, pie charts, and line and area charts, as shown in Figure 2-13. The chart designer enables you to drag and drop fields for the data values, categories, and series onto the design surface and then specify display options such as fonts and colors.

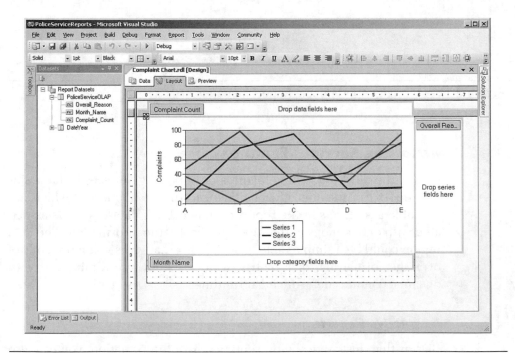

Figure 2-13 Charts

End-User Reporting with Report Builder

Access to predefined, parameterized reports suffices for many users, but most organizations have a number of people who need more flexibility in reporting but who don't have the technical background to be comfortable with BI Development Studio and SQL or MDX query syntax. **Report Builder** is a component of Reporting Services that enables business users to create their own ad-hoc reports against a more user-friendly view of the data called a **report model**.

Report models can be built on top of SQL Server relational or Analysis Services databases using BI Development Studio, or a complete report model can be generated from an Analysis Services data source in one step using the Report Manager or SQL Server Management Studio tools. After the report model has been deployed to the reporting server, business users can launch the Report Builder application to create reports, as shown in Figure 2-14.

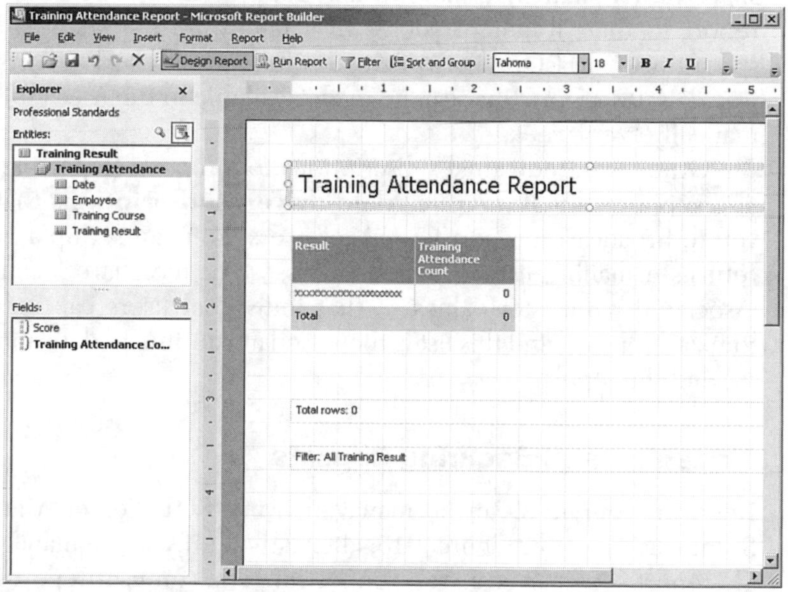

Figure 2-14   Using Report Builder for end-user reporting

Report Builder is designed along the same lines as other Microsoft Office applications (although it is a click-once application that doesn't require a complex client installation before use). Users start by selecting the area of the model and a standard layout, and then they can drag and drop fields onto the design surface and specify filters. Reports are then published to the Reporting Services server, either to the user's personal "My Reports" folder or to more widely available folders if the user has the appropriate level of access.

Subscriptions

So far we have looked at how users can view reports when they want, but Reporting Services also enables users to subscribe to a report and have it delivered to them via e-mail on a periodic basis. Users can specify parameter values for the report so that they receive the information relevant to their job, such as for a particular sales region or product group. Users can manage their subscriptions using the My Subscriptions feature in Report Manager, which allows them to modify or delete subscriptions.

A subscription can also be set up to send the report directly to a file share rather than by e-mail, which enables users to send a copy of a report to their folder of choice in a handy format such as an Excel spreadsheet or PDF. This proves useful for standard reports such as weekly sales reports that can be made available in the user's folder automatically every week.

Other than individual subscriptions to a report, Reporting Services also supports a feature called **data-driven subscriptions** that enables you to broadcast a report to a list of users. You can set up a query that returns a mailing list of e-mail addresses (or file share locations) and associated parameter values so that individual users can receive customized reports, and this list is then used at runtime to determine where to send the report.

Managing and Securing Reports

Reporting Services can be managed using SQL Server Management Studio, as shown in Figure 2-15; alternatively, if you are managing a single report server over a Web connection, you can use Report Manager. Many of the report properties are defined in BI Development Studio, but you can use the management tools for tasks such as changing the data source connections to point to production servers or modifying the parameters that are shown to the user.

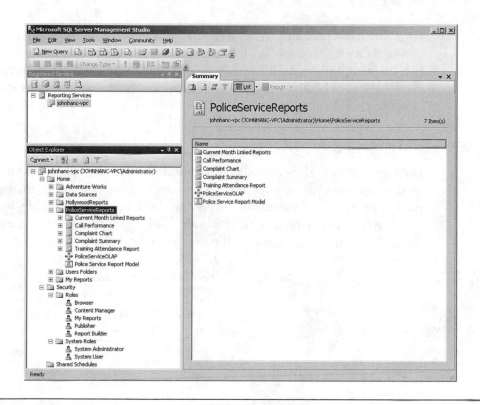

Figure 2-15 Managing reports using SQL Server Management Studio

Reporting Services has a number of settings that you must define, such as the location of the catalog database and the credentials used to access it, as well as the virtual directories for the web service and Report Manager Web application. SQL Server 2005 has a tool called the **Reporting Services Configuration Manager** that enables administrators to specify these settings and test the results.

Access to reports is based on the users' Windows account credentials and the groups that they belong to. Using the management tools, a single report can be secured so that only specific users or groups can access the report, or the security can be defined at the level of a folder containing multiple reports.

Data Mining

As you have seen, Analysis Services enables you to build powerful BI solutions that enable users to really understand the business. However, many business problems rely on the ability to spot patterns and trends across data sets that are far too large or complex for human analysts. Data mining can be used to explore your data and find these patterns, allowing you to begin to ask why things happen and to predict what may happen in the future.

Data Mining Architecture

Data mining in SQL Server 2005 is integrated into the Analysis Services engine, as shown in Figure 2-16. The information derived from data mining can be made available as part of Analysis Services cubes and Reporting Services reports so that users can apply the groupings and predictions from data mining to the existing data.

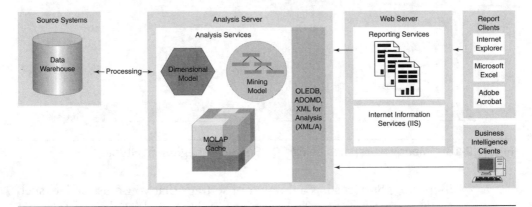

Figure 2-16   Data mining architecture

Preparing the Data

Data mining and data warehouses go well together because using clean, validated information is vital to the successful use of data mining. Just like most Analysis Services features, you can use data mining against almost any source of information, including transaction systems, but as usual we recommend starting from a data warehouse as the best source of data.

One of the great features of data mining in SQL Server 2005 is that you can either use relational tables as the source data for the models or you can build models on top of multidimensional cubes. The advantage of using cubes as the source is that the models can use any complex calculations that you may have added and can also sometimes benefit from the query performance increase for aggregated information.

Building Data Mining Models

You can use the BI Development Studio to design and validate data mining models by adding them to an Analysis Services project, as shown in Figure 2-17. After deciding whether to use a data source or the current cube as the source, you can select an **algorithm** and then supply the relevant information to set up the model. A data mining algorithm is the mechanism that actually creates the mining models by looking for specific patterns in a data set. The model created can be validated and tested within the same development environment and then deployed to an Analysis Services server.

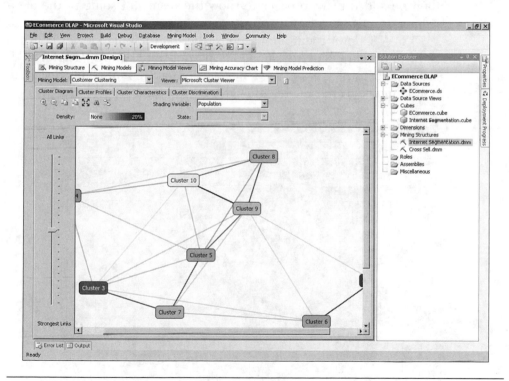

Figure 2-17 Building data mining models

Using the Information

After your model has been deployed on a server, you can use it to make predictions using a query language called **DMX** (Data Mining Extensions), which is somewhat similar to SQL. The process for querying a mining model is similar to querying other Analysis Services objects and uses the OLE DB Provider for Analysis Services. For example, when customers on your e-commerce site adds a DVD to their online shopping basket, you could submit a DMX query to use a mining model to predict which other titles a specific customer might like to purchase.

If you want to display the data mining models in your application, two different viewer libraries are available depending on whether you are building Web-based or Windows Forms applications. The Web-based controls are included with SQL Server 2005 as a sample project that you will need to compile using Visual Studio. These controls can then be added to Web pages to show the results of some of the algorithms.

For Windows client applications, the data mining viewer controls shown in Figure 2-18 are shipped as part of the Feature Pack for SQL Server 2005, which is a collection of add-ons and components that were only completed after the release of SQL Server 2005.

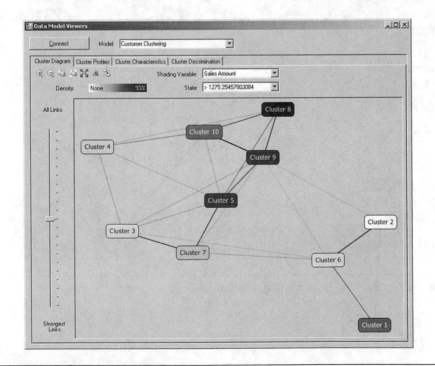

Figure 2-18   Data mining viewer controls

Data Mining Features

SQL Server 2005 ships with many Microsoft data mining algorithms in the box and also supports "plug-in" algorithms from third-party vendors. The algorithm that you decide to use will depend on the task you are trying to accomplish. For example, some algorithms such as Microsoft Decision Trees are good for predicting the expected value of a numeric attribute such as sales revenue, or predicting the category that a particular record may fall into. Other algorithms are used to group records together into similar categories, such as using the Microsoft Clustering Algorithm to segment customers by demographic information.

Using Data Mining in ETL

One of the most innovative aspects of data mining in SQL Server 2005 is the incorporation of data mining features into Integration Services. Data quality is one of the main concerns in BI projects, and Integration Services includes a **Data Mining Query** transformation that you can use to redirect or modify a row depending on the results of a data mining prediction. For example, data that is outside the normal range could be flagged for review or could be categorized using the mining model, as shown in Figure 2-19.

Integration Services also has some transformations that take advantage of data mining, such as **Fuzzy Lookup**, which can be used to return "close" rather than just exact matches from a reference table, and **Fuzzy Grouping** to help identify possible duplicate rows.

Managing and Securing Data Mining Models

Because SQL Server's data mining features are provided by Analysis Services, the security and management for data mining models work the same way as for cubes and other Analysis Services objects. You can add users to roles, which control their ability to access data mining models, and you can use SQL Server Management Studio to reprocess the models to load new data.

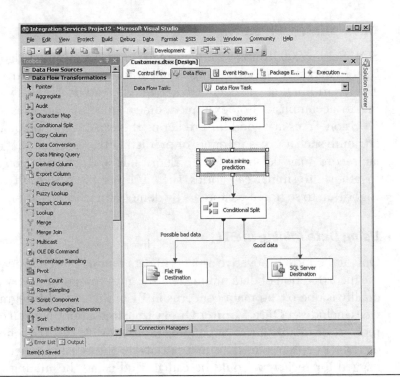

Figure 2-19   Data mining integration in Integration Services

Other Technologies

Here are some other components of SQL Server that you might find useful, although they aren't commonly used in standard BI applications.

Full-Text Search

Full-text search enables you to index and search text fields in a database, as well as to search text in various types of files on disk, such as Word documents or PDF files. The search uses word stemming and fuzzy matching to return a ranking of how well each document or row in a table meets the search criteria. An example of the use of full-text search is to allow customers to search an online product catalog. Full-text search supports multiple languages.

Notification Services

Notification Services enables you to notify a large number of users with personal messages of some data event, such as a stock exceeding a preset value or a delay of a flight. Subscribers to notifications can set the criteria, and event providers provide event notifications. Standard event notification sources include file system changes, SQL Server queries, and Analysis Services queries. In addition to e-mail, you can send notifications to a variety of other devices.

Service Broker

If you need to send an asynchronous message between two applications using SQL Server, with guaranteed delivery, Service Broker can provide that capability. It is similar to the intent of a message queuing service, although without some of the administrative requirements. Service Broker is integrated with the SQL Server database engine service and can be used effectively in the development of distributed applications.

Summary

This chapter examined the various components that make up the SQL Server 2005 BI platform. You can decide where you want to install the SQL Server components based on the particular environment that they are deployed into. SQL Server Management Studio enables you to administer all the different components, and the BI Development Studio enables you to design BI solutions.

The SQL Server database engine is a highly reliable, available, and scalable database server used to store the relational data warehouse. Integration Services provides the data ETL services that you use to deliver clean, validated data to your data warehouse.

Analysis Services is an OLAP engine designed to support storing and querying large amounts of data based on dimensional models and also includes integrated data mining features. Analysis Services can obtain data from almost any data source with an OLE DB provider, such as SQL Server, Oracle, DB2, and Access. Reporting Services is a server-based platform for designing, managing, and delivering both interactive reports and traditional printed reports. Like Analysis Services, Reporting Services can produce reports from a wide variety of data sources, including Analysis Services cubes.

CHAPTER 3

Building a Data Warehouse

Before companies can even begin to obtain some of the benefits of Business Intelligence (BI), they must first accept the fact that their disparate transaction systems cannot support the complex, integrated view of the business that is required. What is needed is a consistent store of up-to-date information that can be made available to the business—the data warehouse.

In this chapter, we cover the design and implementation of a data warehouse to support BI. We take a detailed look at the data modeling process and discuss the implementation of the relational tables using SQL Server features. We also give you guidance on securing the database and describe how to deploy and maintain the database.

Business Problem

Our customer for this chapter is a mid-size company that manufactures sporting goods and related accessories and, more recently, sports-related clothing. Their customers are large retail companies around the world.

Problem Statement

The information available is restricted by the current enterprise resource planning (ERP) systems' functionality, and it is difficult for end users to access operational information. Building new reports to answer business questions is a slow and costly process, and the promise of "end-user reporting" has never been realized because there are multiple systems, and in each system information is spread across multiple tables and requires expert knowledge to answer simple business questions.

This has led to the following issues:

- The manufacturer is falling behind competitively because business processes cannot keep up with change. Initiatives such as improvements in on-time deliveries and understanding the real impact of complex customer discounting structures are information intensive and are almost impossible to achieve across the business in a timely and cost-effective way.
- IT is finding it difficult to give people the information that they need to keep up with a changing business environment, and with the complexity of the different ERP systems, it is taking longer to deliver solutions. It is also expensive to answer simple one-off, what-if type questions.
- Using the ERP systems for reporting is adversely affecting the transaction systems' performance during peak reporting periods.

Solution Overview

We will build a data warehouse that consolidates the data from the ERP systems and other sources to enable new types of analyses and reduce the cost and complexity of delivering information. With our business value-based approach, we will focus on building the necessary functionality to support the highest-priority business objectives while providing a platform for future enhancements.

Business Requirements

The high-level requirements to support the key business objectives are as follows:

- **Sales reporting and performance tracking**
  The business needs timely and flexible access to sales information such as units shipped and revenue, including the ability to understand sales performance by territory, by product, and by customer.

Ultimately, the goal is to track the actual sales achieved against the targets for each sales territory.

- **Profitability**

  A key business driver is that the solution needs to include enough information to enable profitability analysis. This comprises information such as manufacturing and shipping costs and any discounts offered to customers. This will enable the business to understand profitability of product lines as well as types of customers and to optimize the mix of products and customers.

High-Level Architecture

The primary component of our solution is a data warehouse database that receives information from the source systems, as shown in Figure 3-1. We will focus in this phase of the project on building a database to support the requirements, and we will build the data integration process and more complex analytics in the following chapters.

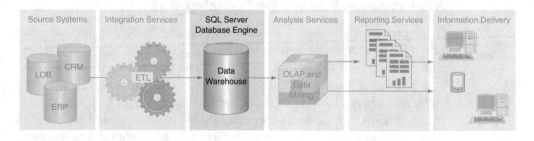

Figure 3-1   High-level architecture

Business Benefits

The solution will deliver the following benefits to the client:

- IT will be better able to support business objectives by delivering new types of information and analyses quickly and cost-effectively.

■ The solution will provide better performance for the ERP systems by moving reporting to the data warehouse.

Data Model

The primary goal of dimensional data modeling is to produce a simple, consistent model that is expressed in the users' own language and will enable them to easily access information. A common challenge when building BI solutions is that there are often so many areas in the business that have interesting information, you really need to resist trying to produce an initial data model that covers everything in the whole business. The key tenet of our approach is that you should carefully define the areas you will be focusing on delivering so that they align with the objectives and can deliver actual business value (something that has been in short supply in many large data warehouse projects).

What Process Will We Be Focusing On?

The business requirements describe our area of focus as sales and profitability reporting. We will deliver the data model to support these requirements, but design the dimensions so that they can become the "one version of the truth" that is eventually used in other areas of the business such as analyzing manufacturing scheduling or loss analysis.

As it turns out, defining the exact business process that we need to model is a bit tricky. To handle sales reporting and profitability, we need to know information from manufacturing (what is the actual cost of the manufactured products), ordering and invoicing (how much did we charge this customer taking into account discounts and other contract terms), and delivery (did the goods arrive on time and in good condition). This data is almost certainly stored in different tables in the transaction systems, and in fact may be in separate systems altogether.

TIP:

Do Not Constrain the DW Design by the OLTP Design

Designing data warehouse fact tables that do not necessarily map to a single transaction table (such as InvoiceLineItem) is a common feature of data warehouses and shouldn't worry you. The trap to avoid is designing your data warehouse schema by looking at the transaction systems. You should first focus on the end users and how they understand the information.

The business process that spans all these areas is often known as "shipments," and it includes so much useful information that having shipments data in the data warehouse is one of the most important and powerful capabilities for manufacturing.

What Level of Detail Do We Need?

Now that we have identified the shipments business process, the next question that we are faced with is the grain of information required. Do we need daily totals of all shipments for the day, or would monthly balances suffice? Do we need to know which individual products were involved, or can we summarize the information by category?

In some ways, this data modeling question of granularity is the easiest to resolve because the answer is always the same: You should strive to always use the most detailed level of information that is available. In the shipments example, we need to store a record for each individual line item shipped, including the customer that it was shipped to, the product UPC, the quantity shipped, and all the other information we can find in this area.

In the bad old days before technology caught up with our BI ambitions, a lot of compromises needed to be made to avoid large data volumes, which usually involved summarizing the data. A lack of detailed information leads to all kinds of problems in data warehouses—for example, if we store the shipments summarized by product group, how do I find out whether yellow products are more popular than green ones? We need the product detail-level information to figure that out. Today, modern hardware and SQL Server 2005 easily support detail-level information without special handling in all but the most demanding of applications. (See Chapter 11, "Very Large Data Warehouses," for more information on dealing with very large data warehouses.)

Different developing
Granularity Require
Different fact table

Do Not Mix Granularities in a Fact Table

This is probably the most important dimensional modeling lesson that we can share: A single fact table must never contain measures at different levels of granularity. This sounds like it should be easy to achieve, but some common pitfalls can trip you up, usually related to budget or forecast information. For example, business users often want to compare the actual measure (such as actual quantity shipped) with a forecast or budget measure (such as budget quantity). Budgets are usually produced at a higher level of granularity (for example, planned monthly sales per product group), and therefore should never be put into the same fact table that stores the detail-level transactions. If you find measures at different levels of granularity, you must create a separate fact table at the right level.

What Are the Ways of Looking at the Information?

As discussed in Chapter 1, "Introduction to Business Intelligence," the heart of the dimensional approach is to provide information to users in the ways they would like to look at it. One of the best ways to start identifying dimensions is to take note every time anyone says the word *by*. For example, we need to see sales by manufacturing plant, and we need to look at deliveries by the method they were shipped to see which method is more cost-effective. Each of these "bys" is a candidate for a dimension.

Out of the interviews with the business users, we can so far add two dimensions to our data model, as shown in Figure 3-2: Plant, which identifies where the product in a shipment was manufactured and shipped from; and Ship Method, which indicates the method used to ship the product.

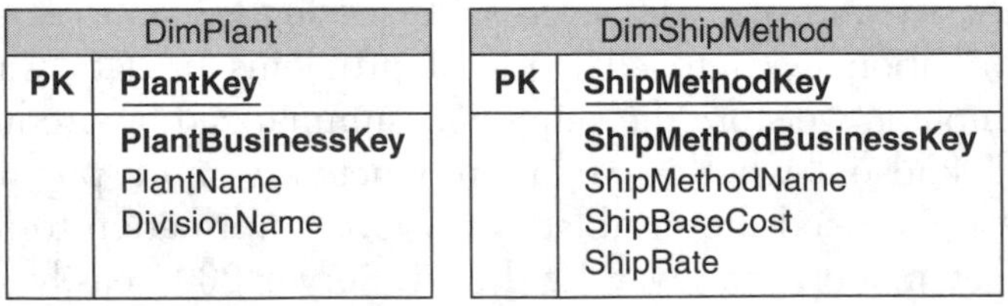

DimPlant	
PK	**PlantKey**
	PlantBusinessKey
	PlantName
	DivisionName

DimShipMethod	
PK	**ShipMethodKey**
	ShipMethodBusinessKey
	ShipMethodName
	ShipBaseCost
	ShipRate

Figure 3-2   Plant and Ship Method dimensions

Product Information

One of the main dimensions in this data warehouse contains the Product information. Products can be grouped into subcategories and categories, and each Product record can contain many descriptive attributes that are useful for understanding sales and profitability, such as Color or Size. To make it easy to load the Product information and to improve the efficiency of the queries used to load the cube, we will "snowflake" the dimension and create three separate tables, as shown in Figure 3-3. This is the first example of the design decision-making process that we outlined in Chapter 1; that is, when we have a dimension table with an obvious hierarchy, we can renormalize or snowflake the dimension into a separate table for each level in the hierarchy.

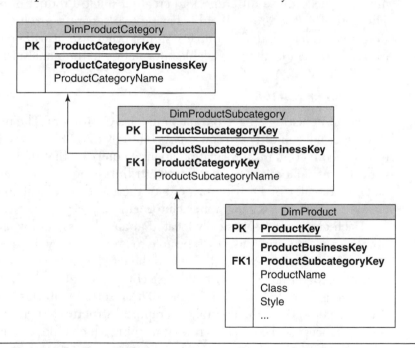

Figure 3-3   Product dimension

Note that every snowflake dimension table still follows the rule for surrogate keys, which is that all primary keys used in a data warehouse are surrogate keys and these are the only keys used to describe relationships between data warehouse tables. In the case of the Product Subcategory table, you can see that we have used the ProductCategoryKey for the relationship with the Product Category table.

The manufacturer in our example has an interesting issue with Products—their original business was the manufacture of sporting goods and related equipment, but several years ago they acquired another company with several plants that manufacture sports-related clothing. The two divisions in the company have separate ERP systems and totally separate product lines. In a data warehouse, we want a single Product dimension that is the only version of the truth.

Even though the two ERP systems might have different ways of storing the product information and we will have to perform some calisthenics in the extraction, transformation, and loading (ETL) process, we must reconcile these differences to create a single Product dimension. The design that we must avoid is having two separate product dimensions that map back to the source systems; otherwise, it will be difficult for users to include all the available information in their analysis.

Customer Information

The next interesting area in our data model is Customers. The manufacturer does not sell direct to consumers but only to retailers, so each customer record contains information about a company that does business with the manufacturer. In addition to attributes such as customer type (such as Retailer or Distributor), one of the most important sources of customer attributes is geographical information.

Each customer is physically located at an address, and you can see how users would find it useful to be able to group data by the customer's state or province, or even drill down to the city level. In addition to this natural "geographical" hierarchy, most companies also divide up geographical areas into "sales territories." These sales territories might not translate perfectly to the natural geographical structures such as state or province, because a company's rules governing which cities or customers fall into which sales territories may be complex or arbitrary. So, sometimes end users will want to see information grouped by physical geography and sometimes grouped by sales territories.

In our data model, we will extract the physical geographical information from the customer record and move it a Geography dimension, which will have one record for each Zip/Postal Code. This dimension record will contain all the natural geographical information such as state or province name, and each Customer record will have a GeographyKey column that contains the surrogate key of the appropriate Geography record. We will also create a separate Sales Territory dimension, and extend the Geography dimension so that every record relates to a particular sales territory, as shown in Figure 3-4.

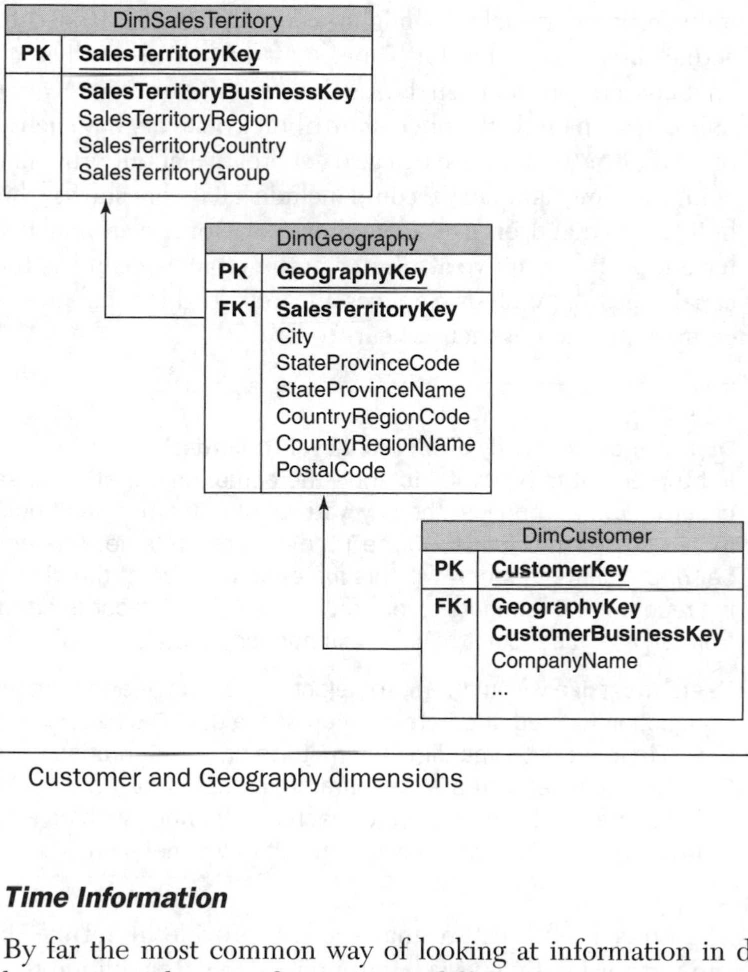

Figure 3-4   Customer and Geography dimensions

Time Information

By far the most common way of looking at information in data warehouses is analyzing information in different time periods. Users might want to see shipments for the current month, or year-to-date shipments, or compare the current period with the same period last year. Every shipment transaction has one or more dates associated with it (such as date ordered and date shipped), and we need to allow these dates to be used to group the shipments together.

The first thing that we need to determine is the level of detail required for our fact table. The shipments fact includes the actual date of the transaction, so we need day-level information rather than just weekly or monthly summaries.

Because most modern applications include extensive functions for interpreting date fields, it might seem that we don't need to create an actual dimension table for Time. As it turns out, a physical table that contains a record for each day, as shown in Figure 3-5, is very useful. Not only can we include the obvious attributes on every day such as the name of the day or the year; we can also get creative about providing analytical columns. For example, we could include a flag that shows which days are holidays so that users can select those days for special analysis. When we have lots of descriptive attributes in the table, we can use the analytical capabilities of Analysis Services to provide the capability of selecting complicated ranges such as year-to-date.

TIP:
Do Not Include Hourly or Minute-Level Records
If it turned out to be useful to know the actual time that a transaction occurred rather than just the day, you might think that we should just add more detailed information to the Time dimension table. This entails a number of problems; not only will this increase the size of the dimension (storing records at the minute level would mean 1,440 records per day!), but from an analytical point of view, it is not very useful.

Users most likely would want to select a date range and then see how transactions varied at different times of the day. The best way to support this is to leave the Time dimension at the day level (probably renamed Date for clarity) and create a separate dimension for Time Of Day. This would contain only one record for each time period, such as a total of 1,440 records for a minute-level Time Of Day dimension.

The other useful feature that you can provide in a Time dimension is support for multiple ways of grouping dates. In addition to looking at a natural calendar hierarchy such as year or month, most businesses want the ability to see fiscal periods. We can accommodate this by including the fiscal year (which usually starts on a different day to the natural calendar) and fiscal month on every daily record in addition to the standard calendar year and month. This could also be extended to support manufacturing calendars, which consist of 13 periods of exactly the same size made up of four weeks each.

DimTime	
PK	**TimeKey**
	CalendarYear
	CalendarQuarter
	CalendarMonthName
	DayNumberOfMonth
	DayNumberOfYear
	FiscalYear
	FiscalQuarter
	FiscalMonthName
	ManufacturingYear
	ManufacturingQuarter
	ManufacturingMonthName

Figure 3-5   Time dimension

Now that we have identified the different ways that users will want to see the information, we can move on to our next modeling question: What numbers will the user want to analyze?

What Are We Measuring?

All the information that we want to analyze, such as sales amounts, costs, or discounts, will end up on our fact table. Now that we have identified the grain of this fact table and designed the dimensions that we will be using, we can move on to building a list of numeric measures for the table. At this point in the design process, the fact table looks like Figure 3-6.

TIP:

The Importance of Clarifying Terms

Most data modelers find out early on that trying to do data modeling without a good understanding of the underlying business is a risky undertaking. People often tend to use different terms for the same concept depending on their specific area of the business, or use the same terms for very different concepts in different business areas. It is important to recognize this and take extra care to clarify terms even if they sound like commonsense concepts.

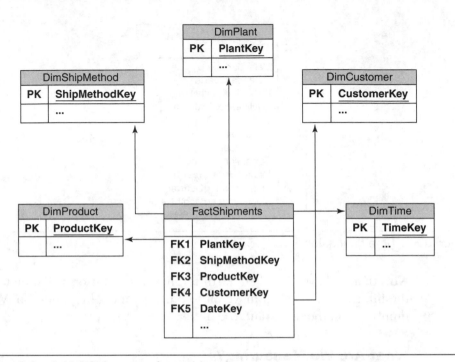

Figure 3-6 Initial Shipments fact table

Ultimately, the source for all the measures in a fact table will be a transaction table in the ERP systems, but it would be a mistake to start from the ERP schema to identify measures. As previously described, on-line transaction processing (OLTP) systems have normalization as a primary driver of their designs, whereas much of the information in data warehouses is derived. A better approach is to start from the business questions that the users need to answer and then attempt to build a list of measures that will be required to provide the answers. Some of this information might turn out to not be available in the ERP systems, but at least these issues can then be identified to the ERP team.

For example, an obvious candidate measure is the quantity of the product item that the customer ordered, but equally important for analysis is a measure that describes the actual quantity that was delivered, taking into account any breakages or errors in the shipping process. We can add both Quantity Ordered as well as Quantity Delivered measures to the fact table. The business requirements also lead us to add other numeric columns to support profitability analysis, such as discounts and manufacturing costs.

Numeric Measures That Can't Be Summed

All the measures that we have looked at so far are fully additive—that is, whether we are looking at a product group total for the last year or a single customer's transactions in a week, all we have to do is sum up the numbers on the fact table to arrive at the correct answer. Not all numbers are quite so obliging, however; for example, whereas the quantity of product sold in a shipment record is additive, the unit price is not. If you imagine what would happen if we looked at a year's total of all the unit prices in the Shipments table, you can see that this would not produce a sensible measure. In the case of unit prices that might increase or decrease over time, and other "rate" types of measures, the usual way of looking at the information is by taking an average over the time period we are querying.

The same logic usually applies to "balance" types of measures such as inventory balances, where either the average balance or the latest balance in the selected time period is much more meaningful than a total. These measures are known as partially additive or **semi-additive**, because we can sum them up along dimensions such as Customer or Product, but not across other dimensions such as the Time dimension.

It is often possible to transform "rate" measures into fully additive measures just by multiplying by the corresponding measure such as quantity. This will produce a fully additive measure such as Revenue rather than a semi-additive measure such as Unit Price. If you want to actually include a semi-additive measure, you can simply add the numeric column to the fact table—Analysis Services cubes can be set up so that the appropriate summary calculation is performed for semi-additive measures.

Handling Complex Relationships with Dimensions

Most of the relationships between dimension tables and the fact table are simple and easy to model. For example, every shipment has a method of shipping, so we can just add the ShipMethodKey to the fact table. Not all dimensions are quite so easy to handle, however; the Customer and Time dimensions in the manufacturing solution have more complex relationships with the fact table.

Every shipment that we make is sent to a specific customer, so we could just add a CustomerKey column to the fact table. However, because of the intricate corporate hierarchies that the manufacturer needs to deal with, the bill for the shipment might be sent to a different corporate entity (such as a parent company) than the customer that received the shipment. It is easy to find business requirements that would require both of these concepts, such as a financial analysis by the billing customer and a logistics or shipping analysis by the shipping customer. To accommodate this, we can simply add both ShippingCustomerKey and BillingCustomerKey columns to the fact table and populate them accordingly.

The Time dimension has a similar requirement. Depending on the analysis, users might want to see the shipments by the date that the order was placed, or the date that it was shipped, or even to compare the date actually shipped with the date that the shipment was due to take place. Each of these requires a new dimension key column on the fact table, as shown in Figure 3-7.

Fields on the Fact Table That Aren't Measures

The columns that we have added to the fact table so far are either dimension keys or numeric measures. Often, you must include some columns in an analysis that do not fall into either of these neat categories. A common example of this is Invoice Number. It would make no sense to consider this a numeric measure because we cannot sum or average it; and because there are probably many thousands of invoices and no real descriptive attributes to group them by, it is not really a dimension either. All the interesting information on an invoice has already been added to the fact table in the form of dimensions such as Customer and Product.

The Invoice Number would still be useful in many analyses, however, especially when a user has drilled down to a level of detail that includes only a few invoices and wants to see the full details of each. Adding this kind of column to a fact table is usually known as a **degenerate dimension**, because it is basically a dimension with only one column, which is the business key.

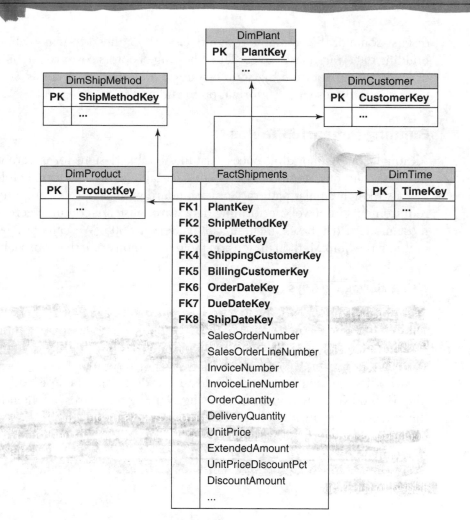

Figure 3-7   The completed Shipments data model

Technical Solution

In this section, we focus on building the relational tables to support the dimensional model that we have designed in the previous section and discuss some of the common design decisions you need to make when building data warehouse tables. The following chapters cover the details of loading the data from the source systems and building Analysis Services cubes to present the information to end users.

Building Dimension Tables

Although some minor differences exist in the table designs for different business solutions, most dimension and fact table structures usually follow a strikingly similar pattern. Some standard ways of approaching the requirements for a well-performing data warehouse are common across most modern databases, including SQL Server 2005. We can start by building the Ship Method dimension table to demonstrate the approach.

Using Surrogate Keys

As described in Chapter 1, every dimension table has a surrogate key column that is generated within the data warehouse and uniquely identifies the dimension record. In SQL Server databases, we can implement surrogate keys using a concept called **identity columns**.

The first column that we will add to the dimension table is called ShipMethodKey (see the sidebar "Using Naming Standards"), which is the surrogate key for the table. All surrogate keys in our databases are declared as integer fields with the IDENTITY property turned on. This means that there is no need to specify a value for this column. The database will generate a unique incremental value every time a new row is added to the table.

Adding the Business Key

The manufacturer has assigned a code for every method of shipping products to their customers, such as OSD for Overseas Deluxe shipping. Although we are internally using the surrogate key as the only identifier for shipping methods, we still need to store the original shipping code along with every record. This code will be used to translate the shipping codes in information received from source systems and is known as the business key.

Unlike surrogate keys, every business key in the data warehouse may have a different data type, so we must make a decision for each dimension table. The shipping method codes are currently three-character identifiers in the source systems, so char(3) would probably be a good candidate here. Some data warehouse designers like to add some additional space into codes to cater for any future systems that might need to be integrated that use longer codes; but because it is generally a trivial exercise to change this size if it becomes necessary (especially in dimension tables, which are usually much smaller than fact tables), this is certainly optional.

Business keys tend to have a wide range of names in source systems (such as CustomerNumber, ShippingMethodCode, or ProductID), so we will pick the nice consistent naming convention of using ShipMethodBusinessKey and follow this for all our business keys. When creating the column, remember that business keys should generally not allow nulls.

We will also add a unique key constraint for the ShipMethodBusinessKey column and for all the business key columns in our other dimension tables. Because we will be using the business key to look up records from the source system, the unique key constraint will ensure that we don't have any duplicates that would make this process fail. (See Chapter 8, "Managing Changing Data," for a common exception to the rule for unique business keys.)

Adding Indexes to the Dimension Table

The unique key constraint that we added to the business key will also provide an index on the column, and we will pick this index as the **clustered index** for the dimension table. This means that the data in the table will be physically arranged in order of the business key, which will improve performance when we need to fetch the dimension record based on the business key. For example, when a dimension record is received from the source systems, the ETL process will need to do a lookup using the business key to determine whether the record is new or is an existing record that has been changed.

Data warehouses that are used primarily as a consistent store to load Analysis Services cubes actually need little indexing because all the end-user querying takes place against the cube, but a careful indexing design that includes the surrogate keys used for relational joins will improve the performance for applications that run queries directly against the data warehouse, such as relational reporting.

Adding Descriptive Attributes

All the other columns in our Ship Method dimension table are descriptive attributes that can be used to analyze the information. During the data modeling stage, we will always try to include as many of these attributes as possible to increase the usefulness of our data warehouse. Attributes have different data types depending on the type of information (such as the currency shipping cost and rates on the Ship Method dimension), but many of them contain textual information.

When you are building a new data warehouse, you will often find patterns in the data types you are using for attributes, such as having some columns with a short description of up to 50 characters and other columns with a longer description of 100 characters. A useful technique is to take advantage of SQL Server's **user-defined types** feature to create special data types for common categories of columns, such as Short-Desc and LongDesc. This will standardize your approach for creating attributes, and make it easier to change the columns if the approach changes.

QUICK START: Creating a Dimension Table

As discussed in the Preface, the Quick Start exercises are intended to get you started with using the SQL Server tools to implement the technical solution we are discussing. In this Quick Start, we create a new data warehouse database and add the first dimension table, DimShipMethod.

1. Open the SQL Server Management Studio.

2. If you are prompted to connect to your database server, select your authentication type and click Connect. If this is the first time you are opening the Management Studio, choose Connect Object Explorer from the File menu, choose Database Engine as the server type, and select your database server name.

3. To create a new database, right-click the Databases folder in the Object Explorer and select New Database; then specify a name for your database, such as ManufacturingDW, and click OK to create it.

4. In the Object Explorer pane, expand the Databases folder and find your new database; then expand the database folder to see the object type folders, such as Database Diagrams and Tables.

5. To create the new dimension table, right-click Tables and choose New Table. A new window will open up in Management Studio to allow you to specify the columns and other settings. (You are prompted to name the table only when you save it.)

6. For the first column, specify ShipMethodKey as the name and int as the data type, and uncheck the Allow Nulls box. In the column properties, open up the Identity Specification section and set the (Is Identity) property to Yes.

7. To specify the new column as the primary key, right-click the Ship-MethodKey column and choose Set Primary Key.

8. In the next grid row, add the ShipMethodBusinessKey column with a data type of char(3), and uncheck the Allow Nulls box.

9. Right-click the table and choose Indexes/Keys. You need to change the Create As Clustered property of the existing primary key to be No, because each table can only have one clustered index, and we will be adding one for the business key instead.

10. To add a unique key constraint for the business key, click the Add button to create a new index. For the Columns property, select Ship-MethodBusinessKey, change the Type property to Unique Key, and change the Create As Clustered property to Yes. Click the Close button to return to the table designer.

11. Add the other descriptive attributes columns for the Ship Method dimension (see the data model), using varchar(25) as the data type for the ship method name and money for the other columns, as shown in Figure 3-8.

12. Click the Save button on the toolbar and specify DimShipMethod as the table name.

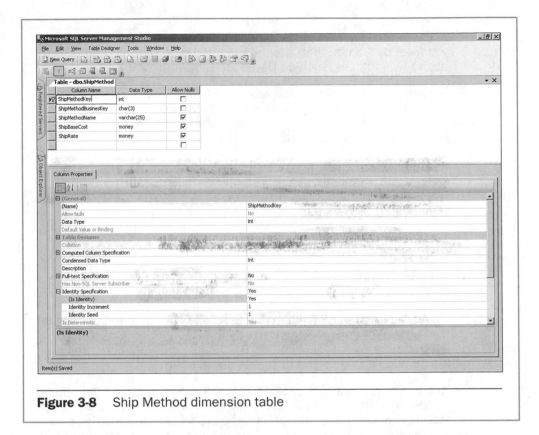

Figure 3-8   Ship Method dimension table

Using Naming Standards

Consistently applying a standard approach to naming the database objects you create will help administrators and developers to more easily work with your data warehouse. It is not really important which naming standard you pick, as long as you apply it consistently. Here are some examples that we have applied in the solutions in this book:

- **Tables.** Because we will be using views to provide access to the data, we have named the table with a prefix that describes the type (such as DimShipMethod or FactShipping) and the corresponding view with the real dimension or fact name (such as ShipMethod or Shipping).

- **Name style.** We have capitalized each word in a column or table name, rather than using spaces or other separators such as underscores (so, ShipMethod rather than ship_method or ship method).

- **Surrogate key columns.** We have used <<dimension>>Key as the name, such as ShipMethodKey.

- **Business key columns.** We have used <<dimension>>BusinessKey as the name, such as ShipMethodBusinessKey. We apply this consistently, even when there is another obvious candidate such as ShipMethodCode or CustomerNumber.

- **Primary and unique key constraints.** We have used <<dimension>>_PK for primary keys, and <<dimension>>_AK for unique keys such as the business key (the *A* in AK stands for alternate key).

Building the Time Dimension Table

As discussed in the "Data Model" section, the Time table has a record for each time period that we are measuring, which is per day for the manufacturing example. The table consists of descriptive attributes to support the various hierarchies such as Calendar and Fiscal, as well as other descriptive attributes such as the day number of the year or whether the day is a public holiday.

Although we could follow the usual convention of using an automatically generated integer surrogate key, it is often convenient for Time dimension tables to use an actual DateTime column as the primary key. Because the actual date is the value that is known to the source systems, this is basically the equivalent of using the business key rather than a generated surrogate. This violates the design guideline of always using a surrogate key, but does make some processes such as loading the fact table easier by avoiding the need to lookup the surrogate key for every date that you encounter.

To support the Analysis Services dimension that we will ultimately build from the Time table, we also need to add an additional unique column for each level in the hierarchies. For example, the Quarter Name attribute contains values such as Quarter 1 and Quarter 2, which are not unique because each year has the same four quarter names. We will add a Quarter key column using the date of the first day in the quarter to provide a unique value for each quarter, such as 01/01/2006, and take the same approach for the other levels such as Year and Month.

After we have finished designing all the dimension tables in the data warehouse, we can move on to the fact tables.

Building Fact Tables

As we have seen in the "Data Model" section, the fact table consists of a column containing the surrogate key for each dimension related to the fact table, as well as columns for the measures that we will be tracking. For the Shipments fact table, we need to add the ProductKey, SalesTerritoryKey, PlantKey, and ShipMethodKey columns. The fact table has two relationships with the Customer dimension, so we need to add separate ShippingCustomerKey and BillingCustomerKey columns to represent this. We also need three date keys (OrderDateKey, DueDateKey, and ShipDateKey) to represent the different dates for each shipment fact.

Most fact tables contain a single record for each distinct combination of the key values, so the logical primary key of the fact table is usually all the dimension keys. However, most information is analyzed with some level of summarization (especially BI solutions using Analysis Services), so it often does not matter whether you have multiple records for the same combination of keys because they will be summed except in some relational reporting scenarios. For this reason, a primary key constraint is usually not added to fact tables, and any potential requirement for avoiding multiple fact records is handled in the data loading (ETL) process.

As described for dimension tables, BI solutions that use Analysis Services cubes to query the information require little indexing in the data warehouse. It is worthwhile, however, to add a clustered index to the fact table, usually on one of the date keys. Because the data will often be queried by a date range, it will be helpful to have the fact data physically arranged in date order. For the Shipments fact table, we will use the earliest date, which is the OrderDateKey, as shown in Figure 3-9. If you are also doing relational reporting from your data warehouse tables, it will probably prove to be beneficial to add indexes for the dimension keys in the fact table because this will speed up joins to the dimension tables.

After the keys, we can add the remaining measure columns using the smallest data type that can contain the measure at the detail level. It is worth being careful with this process because the fact tables are the largest tables in the data warehouse, and properly selected data types can save a lot of space and lead to better performance. The downside of picking a data type that is too small is that at some point, your data loading process will probably fail and need to be restarted after increasing the size of the column.

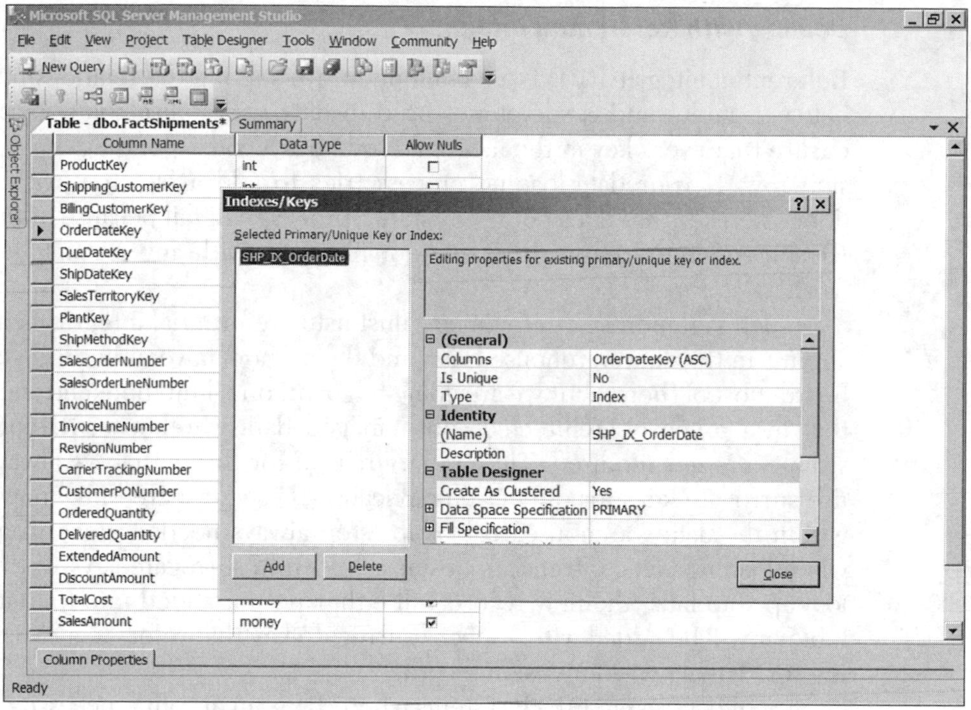

Figure 3-9 Shipments fact table

Using Views to Encapsulate Database Objects

If we allow client applications such as reporting tools or Analysis Services cubes to directly access the tables in our data warehouse, we run the risk that any future changes that we make might break these applications. Instead, we can create a view for each dimension and fact table in the data warehouse, which makes it easier to change or optimize the underlying database structure without necessarily affecting the client applications that use the database.

You can design views using SQL Server Management Studio, by right-clicking the Views folder under the database and selecting New View. The query designer allows you to add the source tables to the view and select which columns to include, and specify a name when you save the new view.

Dealing with Referential Integrity

Referential integrity (RI) is a technique for preserving the relationships between tables and is sometimes used in data warehouse solutions to ensure that every key in the fact table rows has a corresponding dimension row. If your data-loading process tries to add a fact row with a dimension key that does not yet exist, the process will fail because of the RI constraint and ensure that you don't end up with any mismatched facts.

Good arguments both for and against using referential integrity constraints in the data warehouse exist (and the authors have either used or heard most of them), but we are going to go out on a limb here and state that in a properly architected and managed data warehouse, RI constraints are not required. The primary reason for this is that we always use surrogate keys for dimensions. Because these keys are only known within the data warehouse, a "lookup" step always needs to take place when loading facts to translate business keys into surrogate keys. If this lookup step fails, the new record will either not be added into the fact table or will be added with a special surrogate key that refers to a "Missing" or "Unknown" dimension record.

So, in contrast to OLTP systems where RI is an absolute necessity, a major characteristic of data warehouses that strictly use surrogate keys is that RI is enforced through the data loading process. For this reason, it is not necessary to declare foreign key constraints in the data warehouse. The advantages are that load performance is improved, and the data loading sequence can sometimes be more flexible. The one potential disadvantage is that any errors in your data-loading process are harder to catch until you try to validate the numbers in your data warehouse, so it sometimes proves useful to turn on foreign key constraints during the development process.

It is only when you have exceptions to the rule of always using a surrogate key that you get into trouble, and an especially alert reader might have noticed that we have already broken this rule for one of our tables—the Time dimension. The date keys in our fact table are Date-Time columns and do not need to be looked up in the dimension table during load. This means that we will have to add some processing in the data-loading process to check that all the data in the new fact records falls into the date range contained in the Time dimension table, and to trigger a process to have more dates added if not.

Securing the Data Warehouse

If the company you are working with has a database security policy already, you will be able to follow the rules that have been laid out. This section lays out some guidelines for the security decision-making process as it applies to data warehouse databases, but security decisions should always be made with the context of the whole system in mind.

When you connect to a database, SQL Server can either validate your current Windows user account to see whether you have access (which is known as **Windows authentication**) or prompt you to supply a separate SQL Server login account and password. Windows authentication is usually recommended because it has increased security and it does not require maintaining a separate set of accounts.

Providing Access to Database Administrators

We have managed to create a database, add some tables, and specify columns for them, all without worrying about security. How did we manage to have permission to do all of that? If you have installed SQL Server 2005 onto a new server, the reason is probably that you are signed on to the database server as a member of the Administrators group on that machine. When SQL Server is installed, all local Administrators are granted a special right to administer the SQL Server instance, called sysadmin.

Because companies usually don't want every administrator to have complete control of all the databases on that server, a common approach is to create a new Windows group for database administrators only. SQL Server Management Studio can then be used to add the new database administrators group (under the Security, Logins folder) with the sysadmin role turned on, and then to remove the Administrators group.

TIP:
Log Off After Adding Yourself to a Group
A common mistake that can lead to a moment of panic after making the preceding change is when you have added your own user account to the database administrators group that you created. Just after you remove the Administrators group, you could suddenly be unable to access your databases.

The reason for this is that your Windows group membership only gets refreshed when you log on. To be able to access the database server after you have added yourself to the new database administrators Windows group, you need to log off and back on again so that your credentials are picked up.

Allowing Users to Access the Data Warehouse

The SQL Server security model is flexible and provides extremely granular control over the permissions that users have. You can control which users or groups can view information in a table, whether they can update the information, and other rights such as the ability to execute stored procedures. In all scenarios, we follow the principle of "least privilege," meaning that we will make sure that users only have the minimum level of permissions that they need to accomplish their tasks.

In the manufacturing data warehouse, we have created views for every dimension and fact table, and most of the data warehouse users will only need to have access to read the information in these views. Because we are using Windows authentication, we can create a Windows group for all users who need read access to the data warehouse's views. Using groups is much more flexible and easier to maintain than setting up permissions for individual user accounts.

QUICK START: Providing Read Access to Data Warehouse Views

After you have created a Windows group, such as Manufacturing DW Users, you will need to use SQL Server Management Studio to set up the group's permissions:

1. Open SQL Server Management Studio and connect to the database server.

2. In the Object Explorer pane, find the Security folder and right-click it. Select New Login.

3. Type the name of your group in the Login Name box, or use the Search button to locate the group (for searching, click the Object Types button and include Groups to make sure your group shows up). Select the data warehouse database as the default database.

4. Click the User Mapping page on the left side of the dialog. Check the Map box next to the data warehouse database and click OK.

5. Now that we have created the login, we need to assign the permissions to enable the members of the group to access the views. In the Object Explorer pane, find your database under the Databases folder and open up the Security, Users subfolders.

6. Right-click the name of your group and select Properties. Select the Securables section on the left side of the dialog.

---

7. Click the Add button and then select Specific objects and click OK. In the Select Objects dialog, click the Object Types button, select Views, and click OK.

8. Click the Browse button to display a list of all the views in your database. Check all the dimension and fact views, and then click OK to close the Browse dialog. Click OK again to close the Select Objects dialog.

9. Now that we have added all the views to the list of objects in the Securables section, we need to assign the permissions. Highlight each of the views in turn and check the Grant box for the Select permission (see Figure 3-10). Click OK to close the dialog.

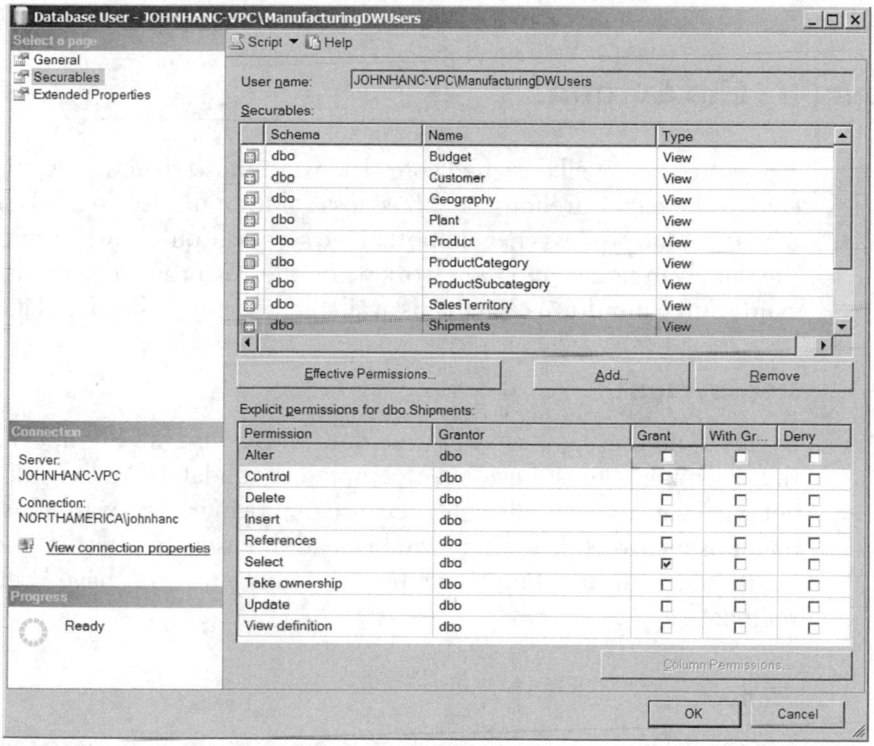

Figure 3-10   Data warehouse user permissions

Providing Access to Applications

In many BI solutions, users do not access the data warehouse database directly but through an analytical engine such as Analysis Services. In that case, the user account used to connect to the database for the purpose of loading data is often the service account that Analysis Services is using. You can cater for this by adding this service account to the data warehouse users group that you created previously.

Another application that needs access to the database is Integration Services. You can use some flexible options to select which user account is actually used when an Integration Services package is executed to load data, but whatever account is used will need more than just read access to the views. You could use a similar approach to the Quick Start to create a Windows group for data warehouse data loaders, and then instead of granting SELECT permission on individual views, you could add the login to two special database roles: db_datareader and db_datawriter. These roles will allow the data-loading process to read and write data.

Managing the Solution

No matter how well designed your data warehouse structure is, the success of the data warehouse as a business solution mostly depends on the management process that supports it. Users will only start to integrate the data warehouse into their work when they can rely on a consistently valid source of information that is available whenever they need it.

Deployment

By the time users get access to the data warehouse, all the information that it contains must have been completely validated. You usually only get one chance to get this right, because deploying a data warehouse that contains incorrect data will inevitably lead the users to question the reliability of the information long after any initial problems have been corrected.

Planning

Your development and deployment plan must include testing and an extensive audit of both the numbers and dimension structures. Dimension hierarchies are just as important to validate as numeric measures because incorrect structures will lead to invalid subtotals, which are as damaging as missing or incorrect source data.

If you cannot verify and correct the integrity of some of the data, often the best solution is to leave it out of the data warehouse completely for this release and continue to develop a "phase 2" that contains the additional information. The closer you are to launch, the more politically tricky cutting features in this way becomes, so you should start the auditing process early in the project to identify any potential problems as soon as possible.

Specifying the Database Settings

In general, SQL Server's default settings work well for data warehouse databases and don't require many changes. However, a few areas benefit from adjustment.

Recovery Model

Each database has a "Recovery Model" option that you can use to configure how transactions are logged, which can have a major impact on performance. Because most databases are used for capturing transactions, SQL Server defaults to the **Full** recovery model, which ensures that all transactions are kept in the log, allowing administrators to restore a failed database to any point in time.

For data warehouses, there is often only one large periodic update happening, and the database administrators are in control of when it occurs. For this reason, it is often possible to use the best performing **Simple** recovery model for data warehouses. In the Simple recovery model, only the data files need to be backed up and not the transaction logs, and log space is automatically reclaimed so space requirements may be reduced. However, databases can only be recovered to the end of the latest backup, so you need to synchronize your backup strategy with your data loads, as described in the "Operations" section.

Disks

The issue of where to put the database files can get complicated, especially now with the wide availability of SAN (storage area network) technology. In general, however, a good strategy is to store the data files and log files on physically separate disk drives. For data warehouses, this will improve the performance of your data-load process. It is easier to set the locations of files in the dialog when you first create the database because moving them afterward will require some knowledge of the ALTER DATABASE command.

Maintenance

SQL Server 2005 is generally self-tuning and performs many maintenance tasks automatically. However, you will need to schedule some maintenance tasks yourself, such as backups, checking database integrity and index maintenance tasks such as rebuilds. You can include these tasks in a **maintenance plan**, which can be scheduled to run automatically.

Setting Up a Maintenance Plan

Maintenance plans in SQL Server 2005 are built on top of Integration Services, which means you have a lot of flexibility when it comes to designing the flow of events. You can also use maintenance plan tasks in regular Integration Services packages, so you could include them as part of your daily or weekly build processes.

You can design a maintenance plan from scratch, but SQL Server 2005 includes a Maintenance Plan Wizard (see Figure 3-11) that walks you through most of the options to create a fully functional plan. You can access the wizard in the Management Studio's Object Explorer by right-clicking Maintenance Plans under the Management folder. Before you run the Maintenance Plan Wizard, the SQL Server Agent service must be running, so you might need to run the Surface Area Configuration tool to enable and start this service; by default, it is not enabled.

Versions of the Data Warehouse

Because a data warehouse consists of just a database and a set of processes to load the data, it is tempting to ignore all the versioning headaches that application developers have to suffer and just make any required changes directly to the production system. These changes could take the form of adding new columns, modifying the data load procedures, or even adding brand-new business processes.

The problem with that approach is that unless you stick to a clearly defined cycle of develop, test, and release, your data warehouse quality will inevitably suffer. Even when you need to perform the occasional high-priority fix to data loading routines when a bug is identified, this should still be tested in a development environment before deployment.

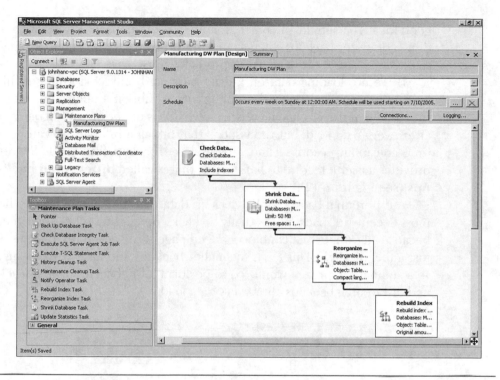

Figure 3-11   Maintenance plan editor

Operations

The so-called backroom activities of loading data, monitoring the database, and performing backups are the key activities required to keep the data warehouse operational. Chapter 4, "Building a Data Integration Process," covers the load process in detail.

Backing Up the Database

Using the Simple recovery model for our databases means that the transaction logs only contain currently executing transactions, so we only have to concern ourselves with backing up the data files. Because in a data warehouse we are usually in complete control of when data is changed, we can arrange the backups as part of the load process.

Backing up all the data in a database is known as a full backup, and scheduling a full backup on a periodic basis (such as once a week) is a good idea. You should, of course, follow the commonsense rules of handling computer backups, such as making sure they are stored in a separate location from the database to protect against drive failure.

If we are loading data on a daily basis and only performing a full backup once a week, we risk running into trouble if a failure occurs in the middle of the week. One way to solve this is to perform a full backup after every data load, but the issue is that taking a full backup can be a time-consuming exercise and creates large backup files. SQL Server provides a useful feature to handle this that is called **differential backups** (see Figure 3-12).

A differential backup only backs up data that has changed since the most recent full backup. (Actually, it backs up slightly more than that because all extents that contain changed pages are backed up, but this is just a technicality.) This leads to smaller backups and faster processing, so a standard approach would be to perform a full backup once a week and differential backups after every data load.

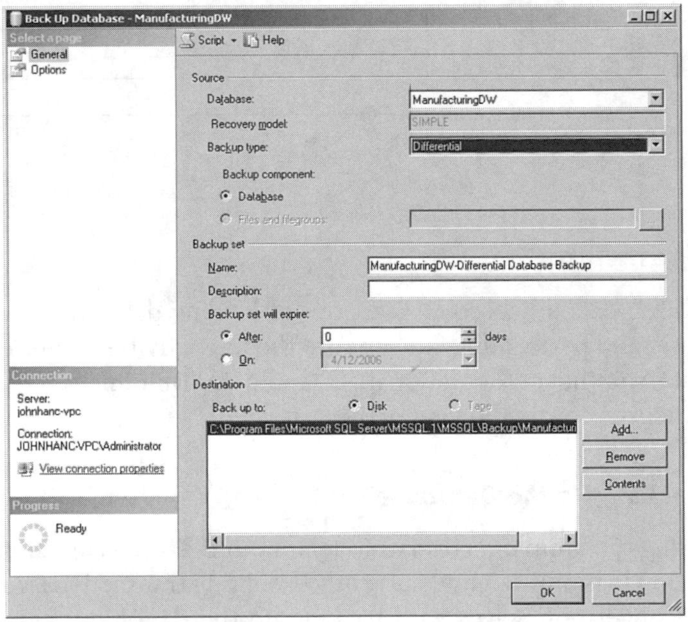

Figure 3-12   Differential backup

Restoring the Database

An up-to-date database backup is a valuable tool in case of system failure but also when an issue with the load process occurs. Many data load processes do not operate in a single transaction, so any problems with the load could leave your database in an inconsistent state. To recover the data, you will need a full backup as well as a differential backup that brings the database back to the point just after the most recent successful load.

Database operations staff should also periodically practice restoring the database as a test of the backup procedures, because you don't want to find out that there is a problem with the procedures when you are facing real data loss.

Are Backups Really Required?

The data warehouse contains a copy of data from the source systems, so could you just reload all the data into a blank database and avoid the need to backup the data warehouse? This is a bad idea for a couple of reasons, the first being that a full reload of all historical information will usually take much longer than simply restoring a backup, even if you include the time taken to make the backup in the first place.

The second and most important reason is that the source systems will almost certainly not retain history. This is sometimes misinterpreted because many OLTP systems keep transactions going back several years. However, there is more to this issue than transactions: The source system will rarely keep a copy of all the dimension records as they were at the time the transaction occurred. As you will see in Chapter 8, these "slowly changing dimensions" are valuable to analyze information and will only exist in the data warehouse.

Next Steps

Now that we have created a well-structured data warehouse database, we need to look at techniques for loading data from the source systems (covered in Chapter 4) and providing the information to users in a meaningful way (Chapter 5, "Building an Analysis Services Database").

Extending the Manufacturing Solution

We have really only scratched the surface of a full manufacturing data warehouse in this chapter, but remember that our goal is to achieve business value by focusing on delivering solutions that work, not by trying to model the entire business in one project. Based on the business problem described at the beginning of the chapter, we can include some new and interesting subject areas in the next versions of the data warehouse. One valuable area is to include quota or budget numbers so that users can track their performance against their targets. Also, we can look at adding information and calculations to support business objectives such as improving on-time deliveries.

Using the BI Development Studio to Generate the Data Warehouse

We will be using the BI Development Studio extensively in the next couple of chapters to develop the ETL process and to build some Analysis Services cubes. Instead of starting by manually building the data warehouse database as we did in this chapter, we could have started by defining our dimensions and facts at a logical level in the BI Development Studio, and then have generated the corresponding database tables.

This is a useful technique that enables you to use the BI Development Studio as a rapid prototyping tool to develop cubes and dimensions without an underlying data source. However, if you have experience in building data warehouse schemas by hand, you might find this approach somewhat limited in that you don't have complete control over the table structures and data types generated. BI developers who are not comfortable with building databases directly might find it much more intuitive, however, and then an experienced database designer could adjust the tables after they are generated.

To use the BI Development Studio in this way, you can create a new Analysis Services project with no data source, and then when adding dimensions, select the "Build without using a data source" option. After you have added attributes and hierarchies to the dimensions, you can select Generate Relational Schema from the Database menu to create the database.

Summary

In this chapter, we built a data warehouse that consolidates information from ERP systems and other sources. The data warehouse acts as a central repository that can support information-intensive business initiatives with reduced cost and complexity.

In this first phase of development, we focused on the shipments business process to provide sales and profitability analysis. We established the grain of the Shipments fact table and identified the key dimensions and attributes that will be used to analyze the information. The Product dimension has a natural hierarchy with three levels, so we used a snowflake design to make the ETL process easier and to improve performance of Analysis Services dimension loading.

The Customer and Time dimension tables both have multiple relationships with the Shipments fact table, so we added a column to the fact table for each relationship, such as ShippingCustomerKey and BillingCustomerKey. The Shipments fact table also includes several degenerate dimension columns such as InvoiceNumber.

We implemented surrogate keys for every dimension table using SQL Server's IDENTITY columns, and added a clustered index on the business key to improve the performance of key lookups in the ETL process. We used a clustered index on the order date key for the fact table. We created views for all fact and dimension tables and granted read access to these views to Windows groups for direct user access and the Analysis Services service, and set up another Windows group with read and write access to the tables to support the ETL process.

For deployment, we used the Simple recovery model for the database and set up a backup process synchronized with the data load cycle. We also defined a maintenance plan for the database and scheduled it to run automatically.

CHAPTER 4

Building a Data Integration Process

I t is easy to see the potential benefits of having a well-designed data warehouse that provides a single, consistent view of the information in a business. However, in today's business world, rapid growth, acquisitions, and mergers lead to multiple source systems and different ways of representing information within most businesses. Before we can reach the goal of a consistent data warehouse, we need to bring together the many different data sources that contain all your business data.

In this phase of developing your Business Intelligence (BI) solution, your task is to populate the dimension and fact tables in your data warehouse. Integrating all your data sources into the data warehouse is not always as straightforward as you would hope. You might be surprised by the many different ways the same data is stored by different departments. Some data may be in spreadsheets, some in text files, and some in various relational databases. The schema probably won't be in the shape you would like for the data warehouse. You will find that some developers have creative ways of representing various bits of information.

The interesting part of integrating data is really more about transforming data into a consistent model than it is about moving data between sources and destinations. In this chapter, we show how you can build solutions to bring data out of almost any data source, but more importantly how you can massage or transform that data so that it all converges and becomes compliant with your dimensional model.

Business Problem

The customer for this chapter is the same manufacturing company that we discussed in Chapter 3, "Building a Data Warehouse." We will be looking at the broader integration issues underlying the data warehouse solution, taking into account the sources of information and other business processes.

Problem Statement

The manufacturer has grown partly by acquisition, and the need to integrate multiple disparate systems is proving costly and difficult to achieve. Due to the high cost and risk of moving each of the businesses to a single enterprise resource planning (ERP) solution, two systems with different reporting capabilities are currently used. Also, additional information such as budgets and forecasts is generated outside the ERP systems.

This has led to the following problems for the business:

- Managers at every level aren't getting the information they need to run the enterprise effectively. Producing information that describes the business as a whole is difficult to achieve and requires extensive manual processes, which increases costs to bring the two sets of accounts together. To further reduce the effort required, many levels of detail were omitted, leaving the corporation with only a high-level view of operations.
- Information is stale by the time it reaches the readers. Manually consolidating information takes time, leading to the process being initiated only once per quarter.

Solution Overview

In our solution, we'll create a conformed data warehouse that can logically accommodate the information available in each of the sales systems. Our extraction, transformation, and loading (ETL) process will transform the data from each data source into the shape needed for the data warehouse. The ETL process can be run on a weekly (or more frequent) basis to keep the information current. The budgeting information will be integrated into the warehouse, eliminating the manual process of tracking sales to budgets. Users will continue to be able to use familiar Excel spreadsheets to enter their budget figures.

Business Requirements

The high-level requirements to support the business objectives are as follows:

- **Present a consolidated view of the information.**
  The information from the two source ERP systems needs to be consolidated, taking into account differences in product and territory dimensions and differences in representing transactional sales measures.

- **Present a comparison of budget versus actual sales.**
  The business creates budgets using an Excel spreadsheet for each region to understand sales performance. The budgets are created at a higher level than the detailed level transactions, specifically region by product by quarter.

High-Level Architecture

We will use SQL Server Integration Services (SSIS) to read data from our data sources, perform any data transformations we need, and then store it in the data warehouse. Integration Services will also be used to control the sequence of events and processes, such as emptying tables, loading data in the proper order, and generating audit logs of the operations. The tasks and transforms necessary for each of these processes are stored in Integration Services **packages**. You develop packages using the graphic designer for SQL Server Integration Services projects in BI Development Studio. You can test and debug your packages in the development studio. Once your packages are ready, you deploy them to the Integration Services server, where they can be executed directly, or they can be invoked by a job step in a SQL Agent job.

We will load the full set of dimension data into our warehouse on a daily basis. This data has the business keys from the original companies. We will use our own surrogate keys to uniquely identify the products and regions and create a uniform model across the business. A result of reloading the dimensions is the surrogate keys can change, invalidating the facts previously loaded. For this example, we will reload all the sales for each company so the new surrogate keys will be reflected in the fact table. This works if the volume of data is small enough that the processing fits within your time constraints. We show you how to properly update existing dimensions and incrementally load facts in Chapter 8, "Managing Changing Data."

The cube data will remain available to users during the rebuild process through the built-in caching facilities of Analysis Services. During the loading of sales data, we will translate business keys into the new surrogate keys. We will load budget data quarterly from Excel spreadsheets from each company and perform the same business key translations as we do for sales. This will allow us to directly compare sales and budgets. We'll use the capability of Integration Services to loop through the filenames in a directory to automate the loading of the budget spreadsheets. Figure 4-1 illustrates the flow of data in our ETL process.

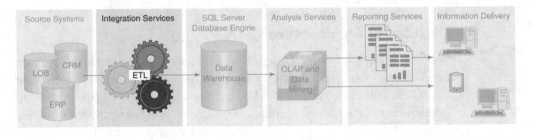

Figure 4-1   High-level architecture

Business Benefits

The solution will deliver the following benefits to the client:

- The automation of data integration will lead to lower costs and improved awareness of business performance and provide a solid platform for future growth and acquisitions.

■ Access to more up-to-date information will improve the business' agility and responsiveness to changing market conditions.

Data Model

We are extending the data model that we created in Chapter 3 by adding support for budgeting. The first question that we normally ask about a new business area is "What is the grain of the fact data?." You might remember from Chapter 3 that the grain of the Shipments fact data was customer by product, by day, by plant, and by ship method. The grain is defined by the lowest level of each dimension used in the fact table.

Now we'll look at the grain of the budget facts. You will see that although some of the same dimensions are used, the level differs for budgets. Specifically, the Time dimension goes down to the level of day, but budget grain is only at the level of a quarter. You don't need to define a new Time dimension to handle this. You can always support less grain with the same dimension.

The Budget Data

In our budget, we want to predict what we are going to sell, where it will be sold, and over what period of time.

We want to support the planning process of the manufacturing plants by providing estimates for each product, so Product is one component of the grain of the budget. We also want to show the commitments made by each sales territory to support these sales, so Sales Territory is another component of the grain. Finally, in contrast to the Shipments data, which is at a day level, it would be unrealistic to produce a budget that tried to predict for each day of the upcoming year exactly what products we would ship to our customers. The budget numbers need to be at a much higher level, such as quarterly. Our grain then is by product, by territory, and by quarter.

Figure 4-2 shows a sample of a budget spreadsheet that we will use as the source for the budget facts. There will be one spreadsheet for each sales region.

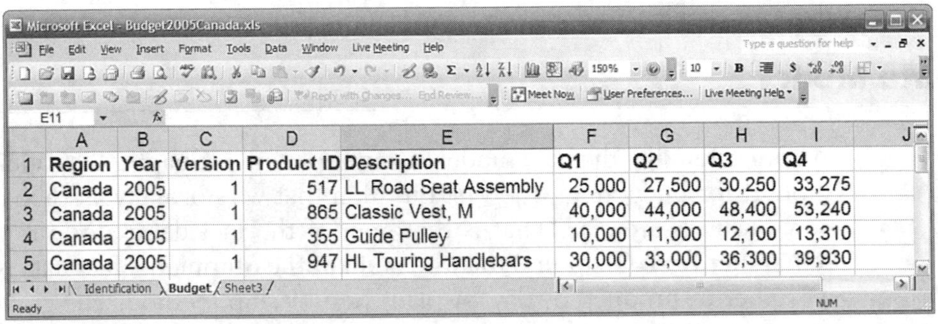

	A	B	C	D	E	F	G	H	I
1	Region	Year	Version	Product ID	Description	Q1	Q2	Q3	Q4
2	Canada	2005	1	517	LL Road Seat Assembly	25,000	27,500	30,250	33,275
3	Canada	2005	1	865	Classic Vest, M	40,000	44,000	48,400	53,240
4	Canada	2005	1	355	Guide Pulley	10,000	11,000	12,100	13,310
5	Canada	2005	1	947	HL Touring Handlebars	30,000	33,000	36,300	39,930

Figure 4-2 Budget spreadsheet

Working with Extended Measures

The budget spreadsheets express everything in terms of number of units. This is convenient in some ways because unit is a nice, additive measure that is very simple to model. However, we also want to use the price and cost to compute expected revenue, cost, and profit. Because the budget numbers are at the Product level, these additional measures can be calculated by looking up the appropriate selling price, cost, and profit amount on the relevant product record and multiplying by the number of units. By having the ETL process look up these numbers and store them on the fact table, we reduce the chances of a transcription error in the spreadsheet.

Instead of physically storing the extra columns in the Budget fact table, you could instead create a view over the fact table that joins to the Product table and calculates the revenue, cost, and profit. A side effect of this approach is that the values on the Product dimension record, such as standard cost, can change over time. If we calculated the revenue, cost, and profit in a view, this information could change through the course of a fiscal year, and we won't be able to go back and see the historical values. Of course, if this is the behavior you are after, using a view is a good solution.

Figure 4-3 shows the data model we will use to support the budgets. We will store the extended revenue and cost in the fact table. This will give us better performance and will retain the revenue and costs current at the time of the budgeting.

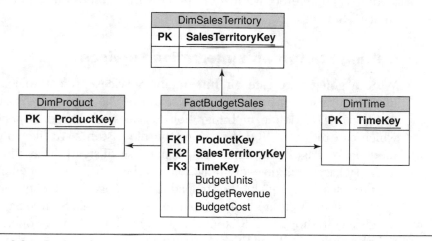

Figure 4-3   Budget fact table

Technical Solution

SQL Server Integration Services is the tool we will use to bring in our dimension data and our sales and budget facts from the source systems. Integration Services will also be used to transform the data into the shape we want before it is loaded into our data warehouse.

At a high level, all you want to do is copy some data from one or more data sources to the data warehouse. However, we are at the point now where you need to specify in detail just how to do that, and there is more to this than simply copying the data.

The sales and budget facts depend on the dimension data, so we must load the dimensions first. For simplicity, we have elected to reload all the data in our dimension and fact tables rather than trying to determine what has changed. Our data volume is small enough that we can get away with this. We address how you can load only the changes to the dimensions and facts in Chapter 8.

We need to accomplish several things in our ETL process. We need to load the dimensions, and then the sales facts can be loaded. Annual forecasts are prepared toward the end of each year, and these facts are loaded independently of the other dimensions or facts. When the data loading is completed, we need to process the dimensions and cubes in Analysis Services.

Getting Started with Integration Services

We are going to create an Integration Services project to load our dimensions and facts into the data warehouse. The sequence of tasks and transforms you define in Integration Services are saved in *packages*, which can reside in SQL Server or the file system. We like to create modular packages that have a single purpose, instead of creating very large packages that do everything. Later, we will add a package for loading the sales data, and another to load the budgets. We strongly encourage the use of integrated source control, such as Visual Source Safe 2005 or Visual Studio Team System, to prevent multiple developers from inadvertently modifying the same package.

Data Sources and Destinations

An Integration Services project usually needs one or more sources of data and a destination for the transformed data. In our project, we want to populate our data warehouse with data from a number of data sources: the dimension data and the sales from our on-line transaction processing (OLTP) systems, and the budgets from spreadsheets. Integration Services uses connection managers to connect data with tasks and transforms in Integration Services. Connection managers specify a database in an instance of SQL Server or other relational database such as Oracle or DB2, a file, a spreadsheet, or one of several other data sources. We find it useful to define these as soon as we create a package. We'd like to clarify a potential area of confusion about Data Source objects. These are not connection managers, but you can create a connection manager from a data source object. The advantage of a Data Source object is that it is visible to all packages in a project, and any connection managers based on a Data Source object are synchronized. If you change where a Data Source object points, all connection managers based on that data source will change to the new location. Note that this only applies during design. It is the connection manager that is exposed for configuration at runtime. This is discussed later in the section on deployment.

You don't need to have all your data in one source, or even one type of source—it can come from any number of different sources. If you don't see a data provider for your particular data source, there is usually one available from third parties. A quick search for "ole db providers" using your favorite search engine should locate what you need.

For our customer, we'll need a connection to the data warehouse on SQL Server, a connection to each of the sales databases, and a connection to the file location where the Excel budget data is kept.

If you are looking down the road to deploying your solution to another environment, rest easy. You can dynamically change where a connection manager points to at runtime by assigning a variable to the appropriate property of the connection manager, such as the Server-Name property. You can also set up an external runtime configuration that will set any property of a connection manager. We'll look at how to do that in a later section on deployment.

QUICK START: Setting Up Connection Managers

We're assuming at this point that you have set up your data warehouse in the previous chapter and that your source data is accessible via the network from the machine running SQL Server 2005. Our example uses data from a SQL Server database:

1. In the BI Development Studio, select New Project from the File menu, and choose Integration Services Project from the Business Intelligence Projects subfolder.

2. Name the project Manufacturing and click OK. Click Next to skip the first page.

3. Create a new data source by right-clicking Data Sources in the Solution Explorer.

4. Skip over the welcome page. Click New on the How to Define the Connection page.

5. On the Connection Manager form, choose the provider (Native OLE DB\SQL Native Client for our example).

6. Type or select the server name. Remember to specify the \Instance name if you are referring to a named instance of SQL Server.

7. Choose the method to log on to the server. (We prefer Windows authentication.)

8. Select a database to connect to that contains one or more of the source tables for the dimensions and click OK. Rename the connection manager to SalesTracking.

9. Repeat this process to create a data source for the data warehouse. Note that in Step 8, you will choose the data warehouse database, rather than the source database, and rename it to DataWarehouse.

10. At the bottom of the Control Flow tab, right-click in the Connection Managers area, select New Connection from Data Source, and choose the Data Source you just created.

Now we are ready to start defining our ETL process.

TIP:
Be Consistent in Naming Connection Managers
When it comes time to deploy your solution from development to other environments, you will want to redirect your data sources and destinations. The configuration for each connection manager is usually stored by name in a SQL Server table or an XML file. If you use the same name in each Integration Services package for connection managers that refer to the same database, you will only have to change a few rows in a configuration table or an attribute in a few XML configuration files. Note that connection manager names are case sensitive.

Loading the Dimensions

We are going to create one package for each dimension we want to load. All these packages will be part of the project we just created.

Integration Services explicitly separates the design of the process flow from the design of the data flow. This separation simplifies the creation of ETL processes, and makes the process you implement much more understandable to others who might have to maintain the application. You first define the sequence of events that need to take place in order to populate the data warehouse. This is called the **Control Flow**. Separately, you define how each table in the data warehouse is populated from the data sources and what transformations the data must go through before it is ready for the data warehouse. This is called the **Data Flow**. Each package has one control flow. You can have multiple data flows in a control flow, and you will have a data flow for each entity you are populating in the data warehouse.

Defining the Control Flow

We'll start by loading the Sales Territory dimension table. In this section, we create an Integration Services package you can use as a model for loading dimension tables from any source. We hasten to point out that we will deal with what are called slowly changing dimensions (SCDs) in a separate chapter because of the extra complexity needed to handle them. Right now, we're just going to ease into loading what we will assume to be static dimensions. This is appropriate for simple dimensions such as status, condition, or gender. It is also appropriate for situations where you don't care about the historical values of a dimension and will be reloading all your data when you update the data warehouse, or for when you are just working on a proof of concept. In our experience, most applications have an implicit requirement to maintain history, so you should plan on accommodating this in your designs.

Because our control flow for loading a dimension consists of just copying data from a source to a destination, simply drag a Data Flow task from the Toolbox onto the surface of the Control Flow tab, as shown in Figure 4-4. Click the label to rename the Data Flow task to Load Sales Territories.

Finally, you are ready to build the piece of the puzzle that you originally set out to do: moving some data into the data warehouse.

Defining the Data Flow

Data flow processing is initiated when a Data Flow task is executed in a control flow. In a Data Flow task, for one entity in the data warehouse, you define the flow of data from source to destination and the transforms needed along the way. The other streams required to populate other tables in the data warehouse will be handled by other Data Flow tasks. You can apply as many transformations as needed to prepare the data for the data warehouse. In this initial example, we just copy a subset of the columns from the source to the data warehouse.

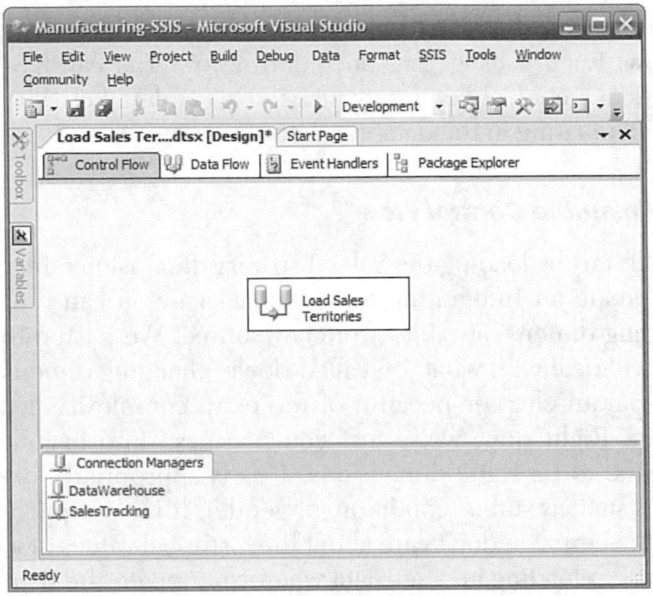

Figure 4-4 Initial control flow

QUICK START: Configuring a Simple Data Flow

Now we'll continue on with designing a package to load a dimension. In this example, we copy a subset of the columns of the Sales Territory table from our OLTP source system into a table in our data warehouse.

1. Drag a Data Flow task from the Toolbox onto the surface of the Control Flow tab, as shown in Figure 4-4. Click the label to rename the Data Flow task to Load Sales Territories.

2. Double-click the new Data Flow task to open the data flow design surface. Drag an OLE DB Source from the Toolbox onto the pane and change the name to Sales Territory.

3. Drag an OLE DB Destination data flow destination from the Toolbox onto the pane and change the name to DW SalesTerritory.

4. Click Sales Territory and drag the green arrow onto DW Sales Territory. You can't configure the data destination properly until it has data flowing into it.
   You will notice in the Sales Territory data flow source that there is a small red circle with an X in it. This is because it is missing some information. You can hover the mouse over the X to see what the problem is. We need to tell it where to find the source data, which table it is in, and which columns we want to copy.

5. Double-click the Sales Territory OLE DB Source to open the OLE DB Source Editor.

6. Set the OLE DB Connection Manager setting to SalesTracking.

7. Set the data access mode to Table or view, and select [Sales].[Sales Territory] from the list of tables. Click Columns.

8. We only want to copy TerritoryID, Name, CountryRegionCode, and Group, so check those columns. Uncheck the others.

9. Double-click the DW Sales Territory SQL Server destination to open the OLE DB Source Editor.

10. Set the Connection Manager to DataWarehouse.

11. Select [dbo].[dimSalesTerritory] from the list of tables.

12. Click Mappings.

13. Drag and drop each input column onto the corresponding destination column. The TerritoryID input column is mapped to the business key, not to the SalesTerritoryKey. SalesTerritoryKey is an internally generated surrogate key. (The editor does try to map the columns based on the name, but none of our names match. If there are any automatic mappings, it is a good idea to review them.)

14. Click OK to save the configuration. This would be a good time to save the whole solution, too.

Your data flow should now look like Figure 4-5.

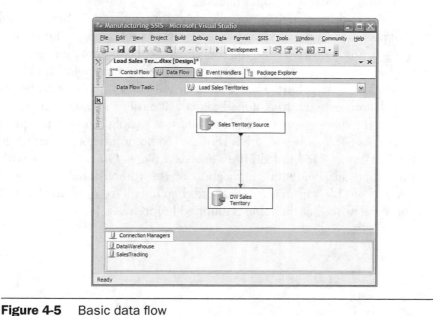

Figure 4-5   Basic data flow

TIP:

SQL Server Destinations Only Work on a Local Server

We did not choose the SQL Server Destination in the Quick Start because it will only work when the database is on the same server that the package is running on. If you know you will always be running on the same server, you should definitely choose the SQL Server Destination, because it is faster than the OLE DB Destination.

Testing Your Package

To try out your package, simply click the green Play button (or press F5, or choose Debug/Start). The data flow between the source and destination will show you how many rows were sent to the destination. You should see the task turn green when it has completed. The package is still in debug mode. To continue to work with the package, you need to stop debugging by pressing Shift+F5 or choosing Debug/Stop debugging.

You're so excited that it actually worked, you call the boss over to see it go, and press Play again. After what seems to be an interminable delay, the source task turns green, but the destination turns *red*. It didn't work the second time. You claim it is just the demonstration effect, but deep down you know something is missing.

Where do you look to see what went wrong? Click the tab labeled Progress to see a detailed list of the results of each step, as shown in Figure 4-6. Scroll down to find the row with an exclamation mark and hover the mouse over the line to view the entire error message. The message autohides after a short time. You can right-click it, copy it to the clipboard, and paste it into Notepad to make it easier to read the message.

In the message, you'll see that there is a violation of a unique key constraint. The business key is required to be unique, and that's a good thing. We just tried to load the same data twice. One of the constraints prevented an accidental duplication of the dimensional data, but we need to be able to run this task more than once! We need to change the control flow so that the table is emptied before we reload.

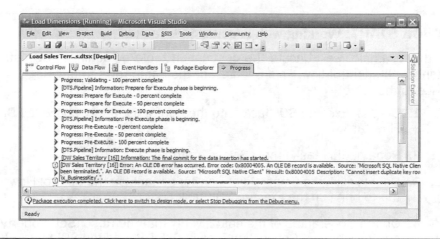

Figure 4-6   Examining the progress log

Constraints and the Data Warehouse

We strongly encourage you to implement constraints (such as uniqueness) at the beginning of the project. This is the time when the system is most exposed to data errors, so why not catch them early? It helped us detect a problem very early in a recent example in this chapter. You can spend a considerable amount of time wondering why the answers are wrong when it's really the data in your warehouse that's wrong. How to validate the data is discussed further in Chapter 7, "Data Quality."

Making Your Package Repeatable

The problem with the task we just created is that the data in the destination is not overwritten. Instead, we are inserting additional data even if it's the same data. A simple fix for this is to delete the data at the destination just before we insert the new data. All we need to do is issue a Truncate Table SQL statement. We can do this by modifying the control flow, adding a simple Execute SQL task before the Load Sales Territory task.

QUICK START: Working with Execute SQL Tasks

In this example, we truncate the destination table by adding a SQL statement to the control flow. This will prevent the same rows from being added twice to the table:

1. Drag an Execute SQL task onto the Control Flow tab, above the Data Flow task.

2. Rename this task Empty Sales Territories.

3. Double-click the Empty Sales Territories task on the Control Flow tab to bring up the Execute SQL Task Editor.

4. On the General tab of the editor, verify that the ResultSet property is set to None, the Connection Type is OLE-DB, and the SQLSource-Type is Direct input.

5. Click in the Connection property and choose the DataWarehouse connection manager from the list.

6. In the SQL Statement property, enter the following SQL command:
   `Truncate table dbo.DimSalesTerritory`

7. Click Parse Query to check for syntax errors. Note that this does not check to see whether the tables and columns exist! Your query may still fail at runtime if you made a spelling mistake in the table name.

8. Click OK to save the definition of this task.

9. Set the execution order of the two tasks by dragging the green arrow from the Empty Sales Territories task onto the Load Sales Territories task. This causes the Load Sales Territories task to wait for the successful completion of the Empty Sales Territories task before beginning execution. You can right-click the green arrow and set the condition for starting to failure of the previous task or any completion status.

Your new control flow will now look like Figure 4-7.

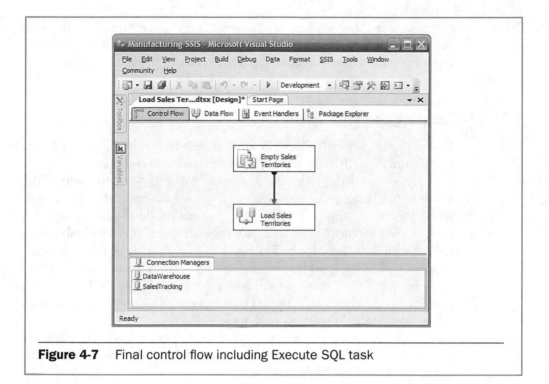

Figure 4-7   Final control flow including Execute SQL task

Now you can bring back the boss and click Play with confidence. The table will be emptied first, and then repopulated with the current contents of the source, so there will be no problem rerunning this task.

Inspecting the Data Flow

Sometimes, your transforms don't work as you expected, and the problem is more complex that forgetting to empty a table. If you want to see what data is flowing between two data flow components, you can add a Data Viewer to monitor the output of a task. Simply right-click the flow line you want to examine, and click Add. Choose Grid to show a table of the rows being passed between the data flow components.

The Data Viewer shows you a batch of rows, not a continuous stream of data. The size of the batch depends on the size of the rows. The data flow pauses at the end of a batch, allowing you to inspect the data in that batch. Press the Play button (green arrow) to continue.

Completing the Dimensions

You've now got a general idea how a simple data flow is built. You can now go ahead and build packages for loading the rest of the dimensions.

Use the same Integration Services project for these dimensions; just create a new package by right-clicking the Packages node in the Solution Explorer pane. After you have the dimensions in place, you can load the facts.

Loading the Fact Table

Unlike our dimension tables, the source records for the Shipments facts come from more than one table. The sales data is in two major tables: the SalesHeader and the SalesDetail tables. We also need to include the ProductCostHistory table so that we'll know how much the items cost when they were shipped. The header contains the business keys for sales-person, territory, the dates, and the customer. The detail table contains the business keys for product and special offer, as well as the measures for quantity shipped, unit price, and discount. To answer questions such as "Where do we ship each of our products?" and "What was our cost for the products we shipped?," we need to have columns from all three source tables in our Shipments fact table.

The other transformation that we need to perform is to translate the business keys in the incoming source records to the corresponding surrogate keys used by the dimensions.

Working with Multiple Source Tables

You have several choices about how to create this denormalized view of your shipments that joins the three source tables together. You could create a view in the original data source and directly query this view through the data source in your data flow. But often, you can't make any changes or additions to the source database, so you need to have an alternative method for loading this data. You can either load each table independently and denormalize later with a view, or you use a SQL query in your data source that joins the tables you need. For demonstration purposes, we're going to load from multiple tables using a SQL query into a denormalized table.

In our previous example where we loaded a dimension, the OLE DB data source Data Access Mode property was set to Table or view. To specify a query that we will build ourselves, you need to set the Data Access Mode to SQL Command. If you click the Query Builder button, you will see a fairly familiar graphical query designer. Use the Add Table icon (plus sign over a grid) to select the three tables we need (SalesOrderHeader, SalesOrderDetail, and ProductCostHistory) and create the joins by dragging SalesOrderID from the Header to the Detail table, and ProductID from the Detail to the CostHistory table. Finally, qualify which time frame in CostHistory we are referring to by adding a where clause:

```
WHERE OrderDate >= ProductCostHistory.StartDate and
➥OrderDate < ProductCostHistory.EndDate
```

Check off the columns we want to use. (We won't talk you through checking off each one; you can decide what you need.) Now you can click OK twice, and you have a multi-table data stream in your data flow (see Figure 4-8).

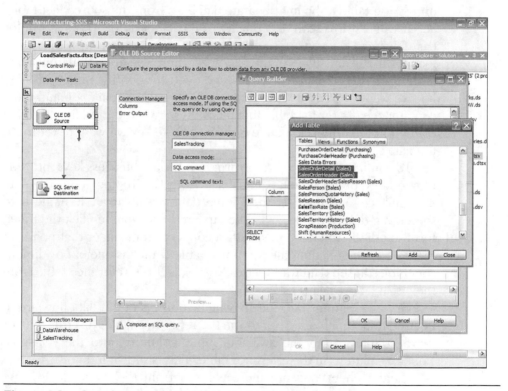

Figure 4-8 Creating a multiple-table query in a data source

Looking Up the Dimension Keys

The next step is to translate the business keys in the data stream from our data source into the surrogate keys used by the dimension tables in the data warehouse. The process is simple: Using the business key, look up the corresponding row in the dimension table. Sounds like a join, so why not use a join? We want to avoid hardcoding any database names in a query. Another reason is to ensure data quality by ensuring that we have a matching dimension member. We discuss this in Chapter 7. Another reason is to avoid hardcoding any references to databases on other servers. You would not be able to change the server name to use the package in another environment without editing the package. This only invites maintenance headaches.

Integration Services has a Lookup transform that can translate business keys into surrogate keys, and also meets both criteria of allowing the dimension table to be in a separate database from the source fact table, and it will assist us with data quality. You use one Lookup transform for each business key you are translating, so you will end up with a series of lookups in the data flows of the packages where you are populating a fact table. For each lookup transform, we need to identify which business key we want to translate into a surrogate key, which database and table contains the dimension table that maps these two keys, and finally which column in the dimension table is the surrogate key we want to return to the data stream.

To configure a Lookup transform to translate business keys into surrogate keys, drag a Lookup transform from the Toolbox onto the data flow surface, and connect the source data stream to it. Rename it to something descriptive such as Lookup Product. Double-click the transform to edit it. You need to specify a connection manager that points to the database containing the reference table, which is one of our dimension tables in the data warehouse. Next, select the reference table from the Use a table or view list.

On the Columns tab, specify which columns in the data flow are to be used to uniquely specify a row in the reference table. Just drag one or more columns from the available input columns onto the Available Lookup Columns in the reference table. This is shown in Figure 4-9.

Finally, check one ore more column from the Available Lookup Columns that you want to have joining the data flow. This is usually the surrogate key column in the dimension table.

A word of caution applies to Lookup transforms. The matching columns or join criteria is case sensitive, unlike a join in SQL. You might need to create a derived column to set the case of the business keys to a known state—for example, all uppercase.

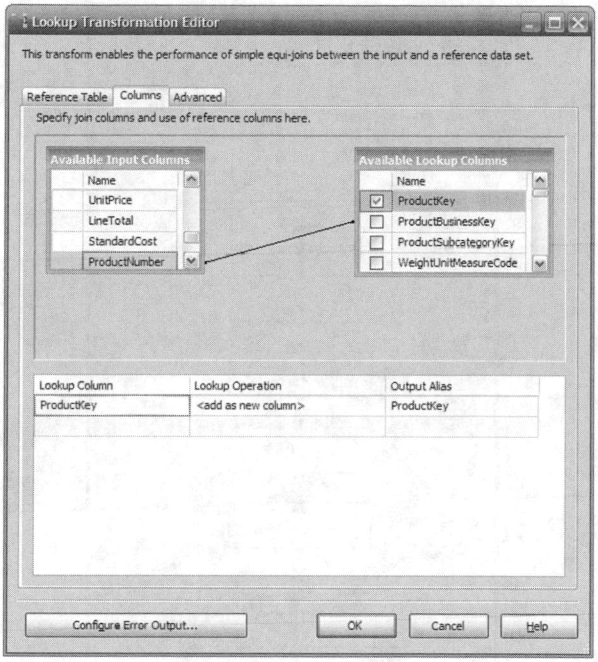

Figure 4-9 Configuring a Lookup transform

Add a Lookup transform for each of the other dimensions using the same pattern we used for the Product dimension.

To complete the data flow, drag an OLE DB Data Destination from the Toolbox onto the dataflow surface. Rename this destination to Sales Data. Reuse the Data Warehouse connection manager and set the table to your sales data table. (If you haven't created this table in the data warehouse yet, you can easily do so by clicking the New button beside the table field.)

You should end up with a data flow that looks like Figure 4-10.

Loading the Budget Information from Excel

The previous examples loaded data from relational tables. Now, let's look at loading data from an Excel spreadsheet. We want to be able to import the budget figures into the data warehouse so that we can compare them with the actual results.

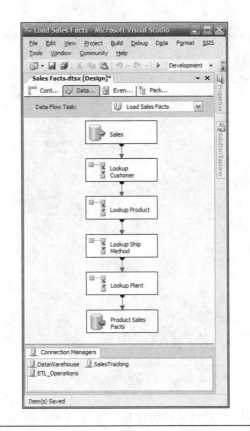

Figure 4-10 Fact table data flow

The company creates sales forecasts for each of the four quarters in a year, for each region and product. These forecasts are at the product level because they are used for plant capacity planning as well as revenue forecasts.

Budgeting will need its own package. You add a new package to a project by right-clicking on Packages in the solution explorer, and choosing New Package. Rename the package to Load Budgets. You will follow the same pattern of adding a data flow task to the control flow, along with any other tasks you need, such as one to empty the budget table in the data warehouse.

For the data flow, you start with an Excel data source. When you edit the data source and click New to create the connection manager, you will see that the dialogue is different than for a database source. You browse to the Excel file containing your budget, and specify which sheet in the workbook you want to use.

Excel Layouts for Importing Data

Users like to see some things on a spreadsheet that don't work well when you are trying to import data. For spreadsheets that we will be importing into the data warehouse, we only have a single row of headings because the Excel connection cannot handle more than one row of headings.

Empty rows left at the bottom of the spreadsheet are another thing that can cause problems. They will appear as rows with null values. To get around this, in the Excel data source we can add a filter "where Region is not null." To implement this, we needed to switch the data access mode from Table or view to SQL Command, and build a SQL query by clicking Build.

Matching Source and Destination Data Types

One important thing you need to do is set the true data types of each column. Excel chooses a type for each column based on an examination of the first eight rows. That choice doesn't always match the data warehouse requirements. For example, numeric columns come in as float, whereas general comes in as nvarchar(255). We recommend using a Data Conversion transform right after the Excel data source to set the data types to what you really need.

Reshaping the Data

Fact tables, such as the budget forecasts we are working with, need to have exactly one occurrence of each measure per row, along with one member of each dimension. This isn't always the way people like to see the information presented to them on a spreadsheet.

Looking back at the spreadsheet we are importing, shown in Figure 4-2, you see that the rows aren't normalized. Four forecasts for each region and product category repeat on each row; and the time dimension is not a value in the row, it is a column name. We really need the forecast on one row for each quarter. This will allow us to create a cube to compare the forecasts with the actual revenue. Fortunately, we can use an Unpivot transform to transpose these repeating fields onto a row of their own. In our case, one row from the spreadsheet will become four rows after the Unpivot transform.

QUICK START: Working with the Unpivot Transformation

To use the Unpivot transform, you need to specify which columns should be repeated on each row (passed through) and which columns are the repeated columns of the row and should generate a row for each of the columns. You also need to provide a value for a new column that denotes which column is on the new row:

1. Drag an Unpivot transform onto the data flow pane, below the Excel source.

2. Connect the Excel Source to the Unpivot transform.

3. Double-click the Unpivot transform to open the editor to set the configuration.

4. Check Q1, Q2, Q3, and Q4 for the columns to unpivot. These names will also be used in the Pivot Values, which will be an additional column used to identify which column a new row represents. Think of the names as an additional component in the compound key for this row. We change them later in Step 7.

5. Uncheck the Description column from the Pass Through check box. We don't need the description, because we have the description code. It was just there to help the users understand which product they were budgeting for. Columns Q1 to Q4 are automatically passed through to the output stream, on separate rows.

6. Set the Destination Column for each row to Units. This is the name of the new column that the value in Q1 to Q4 will be placed in. You could use different names for each column, but that isn't appropriate for normalizing this spreadsheet.

7. Set the Pivot Value column to 1, 2, 3, and 4, corresponding to Q1 to Q4.

8. Set the Pivot Value Column Name to Quarter. This column will take on the Pivot Values corresponding to columns Q1 to Q4 we set in Step 7, based on the column that is on the current row.

9. Click OK to save the configuration.

In the Unpivot transformation, we created a new column for Quarter. Whenever a transform creates a new column, check that the column has a data type compatible with the column it is mapped to in the next step in the data flow. You can check and set the data type for a new column created in a transform by using the Input and Output Properties tab on the Advanced Editor for that transform. Start the Advanced Editor by right-clicking the transform. The Unpivot transform configuration should look like Figure 4-11.

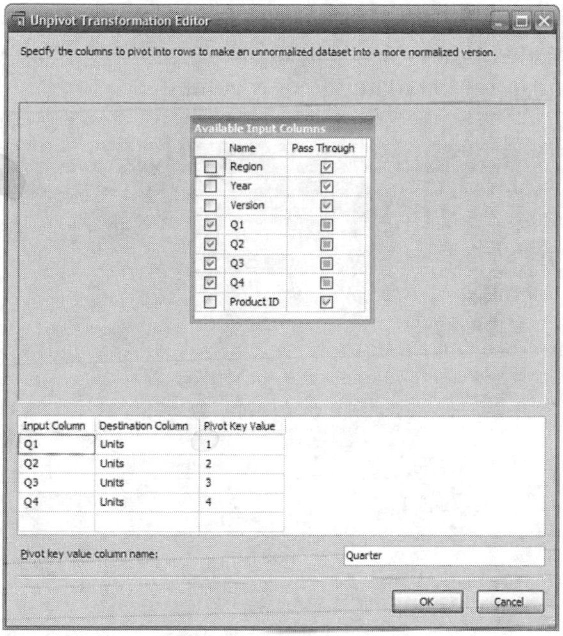

Figure 4-11　Transposing column values to rows

We have a couple of small tasks remaining before we can save the data into the warehouse. We need to use the Lookup task to find the Territory surrogate key for the region in the budget, and another Lookup task to find the product record to give us the product surrogate key, unit price, and unit cost. Finally, we want to compute the total price and cost for this product for this region and quarter.

Adding New Columns for Total Cost and Price

To create the two new columns for the total cost and total price, we'll use a Derived Column transform. This transform enables you to specify a name for the new column, define an expression for the value of the column, and to set the data type. Drag a derived column transform onto the data flow panel and give it a name like Compute cost and price.

　　Double-click the Derived Column transform to open it for editing. Enter a new column name for the derived column, such as TotalCost.

Provide the formula for the column. In our example, drag Budget Units from the available columns into the Expression field, enter an asterisk (*), and then drag in Product Cost. Check that the data type is correct. It should be Currency. You can create multiple new columns in one Derived Column transform, so just repeat this procedure for BudgetRevenue. Figure 4-12 shows how you would configure a derived column transform to create the new columns.

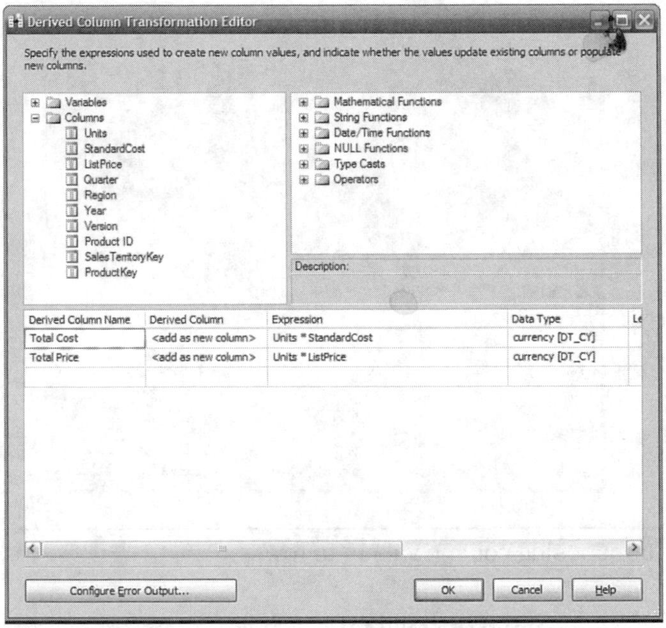

Figure 4-12   Adding new columns with a Derived Column transform

Saving the Budget into the Data Warehouse

The output of the Compute cost and price transform is now ready to be saved to the data warehouse. This output contains all the columns we've defined. You have done something similar when you saved the SalesTerritory dimension into the data warehouse. All you need to do is drop an OLE DB Destination onto the data flow, drag the green arrow from the Derived transform onto the destination, and map the columns from the stream onto the destination table. Your data flow for budget loading should now look like Figure 4-13.

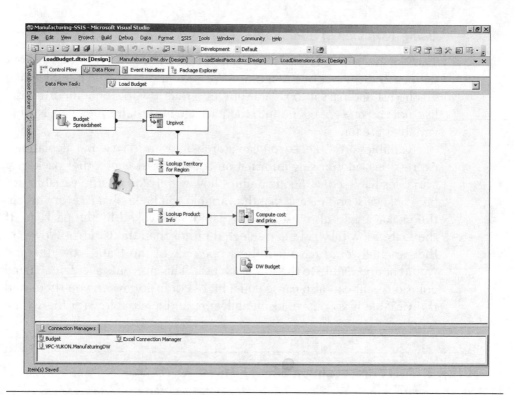

Figure 4-13 Final budget data flow

Loading Multiple Sets of Data

In our example, we have individual budget spreadsheets submitted from each region, so there will many spreadsheets and we don't want to have to change our package to specify the name of each spreadsheet. You can use the For Each Loop Container task to enumerate the file names in a directory that match a specific pattern. If we establish a convention that all our budgets will have filenames that start with Budget and have .XLS extensions, and we put them in a fixed directory, we can easily load every budget regardless of any other distinguishing parts of the name. For example, the name for the Canadian budget for fiscal year 2006 would be Budget-CAD-2006.XLS. This fits the pattern and distinguishes it from the Southwest budget.

Using Variables in a Package

The For Each loop gives us back a list of filenames; but how do we work with each filename, one at a time? We need a way to take one filename off the list and pass it to a data source so that it works on a file from the list, not the one we coded into the package at design time. This is what variables are for.

Variables are objects you can store values in for use in calculations, expressions, and passing information between tasks and other packages. Variables have scope. Scope defines how widely known the variable will be. Package scope means that the variable will be known to every task in the package, and also inside every data flow invoked by the package. If the Data Flow tab had been selected rather than the Control Flow tab, the variable would have had the scope only of the Data Flow task and would not be visible to the For Each task. This prevents accidental name collisions, but can also cause you a bit of confusion when you try to find the variable if you have accidentally created a variable with the wrong scope.

QUICK START: Processing a Set of Files

1. Go to the Control Flow tab, select Variables from the Integration Services menu to show the Variables window, and click the Add Variable icon. Give the variable a name, such as BudgetFileName. Select String as the data type.

2. You want to specify an initial Value for this variable that points to a valid Excel spreadsheet so that you can work with the data flow in design mode. Without a value, the Excel data source will complain; so, specify a full path such as C:\Budget-CAD-2006.xls.

3. Drag and drop a new For Each Loop Container onto the Control Flow tab, and double-click it to configure the properties.

4. On the Collection section, specify the folder name that contains your budget spreadsheets and the filenames to search for (such as Budget*.xls).

5. On the Variable Mappings section, select the variable created in Step 1 (BudgetFileName) from the list and specify 0 as the Index to map. As the For Each loop iterates through the filenames, each will be assigned one at a time to the variable. Click OK.

6. Drag your existing data flow task on top of the For Each Loop Container. If the Data Flow task has a preceding task, such as one to empty the table, you must disconnect the two tasks and make the connection to the For Each Loop Container. This will let Integration Services know that the data flow needs to be executed for every file that is retrieved in the loop.

7. You need to configure the Excel connection to pick up the filename from the variable. Right-click the Excel Connection Manager in the Connection Managers area at the bottom of the package designer and open the Properties window. Click the ellipsis button (...) next to the Expressions property.

8. Select the ExcelFilePath property and drag the variable BudgetFileName into the expression area. Click OK.

Your control flow for loading the budgets should now look like what is shown in Figure 4-14.

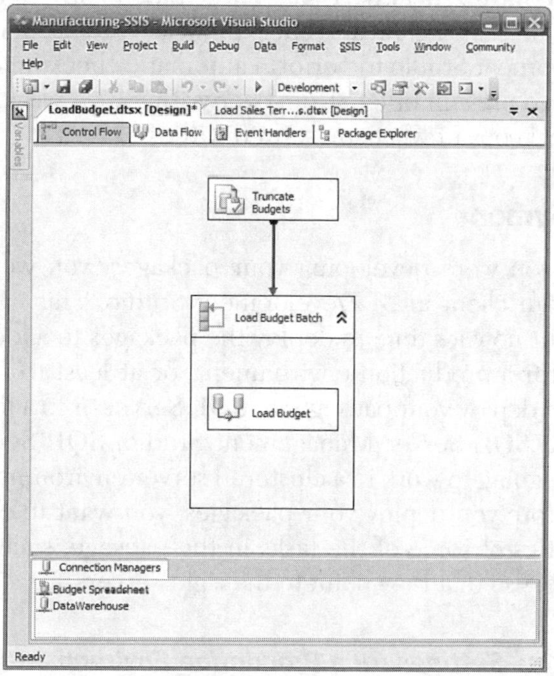

Figure 4-14   Control flow for iterating budget files

Managing the Solution

During development, you should be taking periodic checkpoints of your development so that you have a point to go back to should something go seriously wrong with the design or coding of one of your packages. When your packages are through the development stage, you will want to deploy them to the test and production environments and be able to configure them appropriately for that environment.

Protecting Your Source Code

The packages you create are XML files, and you can consider them to be source code for Integration Services packages. Throughout the development cycle, you will reach stages where a component is running well, perhaps not perfectly, but it is worth saving as a checkpoint before you continue to modify it. We highly recommend you use some form of source control, such as Visual Source Safe (VSS), to save copies of your source files at significant checkpoints. VSS 2005 integrates with BI Development Studio to perform automatic checkout of any package you modify to prevent others from overwriting your work, as well as saving a historical copy of what you started with.

Deployment

When you were developing your packages, you were executing them from your client in BI Development Studio. This was great for debugging, but now it's time to deploy the packages to a location more appropriate for a production environment, or at least to a test environment. You can deploy your packages to SQL Server or to a file system managed through SQL Server Management Studio. SQL Server is preferred if you are going to work in a clustered server environment.

Before you deploy your packages, you want to change some of the properties of some of the tasks in the package, such as the connection managers so that they point to the right servers.

Changing Settings for a Production Environment

Packages include a lot of information that may differ between development and production environments, such as the names of servers, database names, and input file paths. In Integration Services, you can specify which properties should be configured at runtime and where to obtain the values for those properties. The values can be stored in an environment variable, an XML file, or a table in SQL Server, or some combination of all three sources.

You specify a configuration file for a package by selecting Package Configurations from the SSIS menu. The dialog includes a wizard that walks you through the various options, such as selecting which properties of your package you would like to read from the configuration file at runtime. You can reuse the same configuration for multiple packages in your solution, meaning that a value for a property such as a ServerName can be specified in one place, but applied to all packages launched from the same location.

A common scenario is to store configuration settings in a table in SQL Server. A connection manager is used to specify which server to use, but one of our goals here is to be able to pick up different settings depending on the environment—how do we change this connection manager to point to another server? This is where an environment variable or an XML file in a fixed location is used. An environment variable proves very useful if you cannot guarantee that the XML file will be in the same location in each environment. Here is one way to set this up.

First, you need to add a new connection manager to each package you want to configure. Use a consistent name for the connection manager throughout your solutions. We use one named ETL_Operations. It should point to a SQL Server database that will contain tables used for managing your ETL tools, auditing, and operational statistics, not one used for the data warehouse. We'll create a new database named the same as the connection manager, ETL_Operations.

Next, we'll create an XML configuration file that will contain a connection string that will specify where the ETL_Operations connection manager should point to. Using the Configuration Wizard, choose a configuration type of XML configuration file and specify a fully qualified file name to contain the configuration settings. This file will reside in the same location on every server where you want to use this configuration (for example, development and production environments). We used `C:\SSISConfigurations\Manufacturing.dtsConfig`. Figure 4-15 illustrates what this looks like in the wizard.

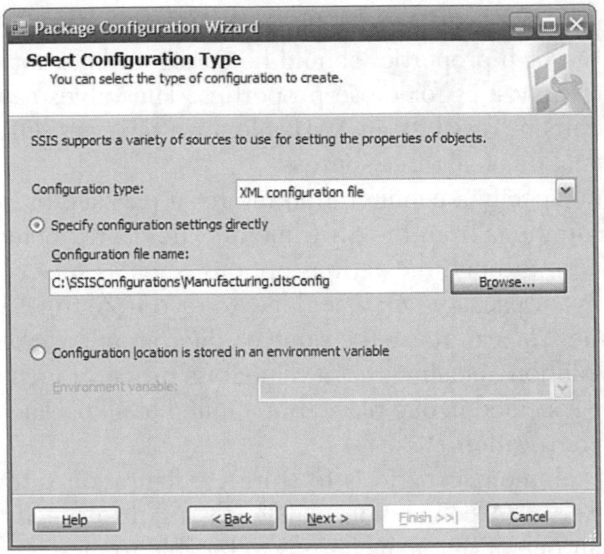

Figure 4-15   Setting the configuration pointer

Click Next. Now you can specify the properties of the ETL_Operations connection manager that will change as you move through different environments. In our example, it's just the server name. We consistently use the same database name and Windows authentication to keep things simple. Expand the Connection Managers node, and the ETL_Operations properties, and then check the ServerName property, as shown in Figure 4-16.

Click Next. Give the configuration a name. We'll use ConfigurationReference. Click Finish to save the specifications into the package. The configuration now appears in the Package Organizer.

Now you can add the other properties you want to configure to the configuration table in SQL Server referenced by the ConfigurationReference configuration file we just created. Click Add to add another configuration, but this time choose a type of SQL Server. For the Connection, choose the ETL_Operations connection manager we created just for this purpose. We don't have a table yet, so click New. This will create a table called [SSIS Configuration]. We'll use this table from now on for all our configurations stored in SQL Server. For the Configuration filter setting, choose a name related to the application, not the environment. We'll use Manufacturing. This will distinguish our configurations from others that could be set up independently for other applications (see Figure 4-17).

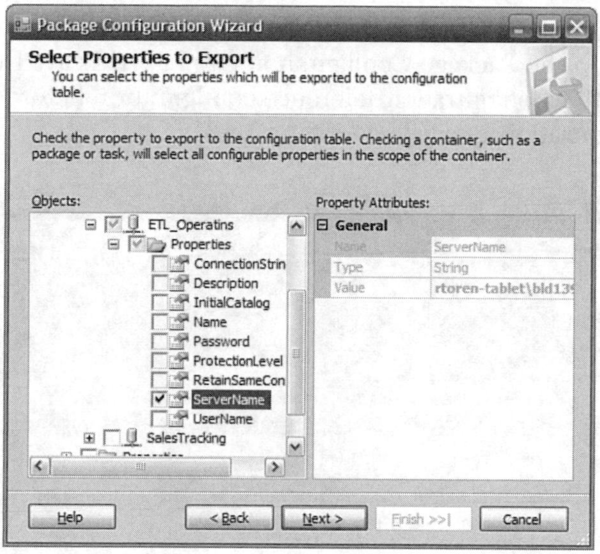

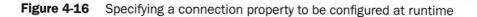

Figure 4-16   Specifying a connection property to be configured at runtime

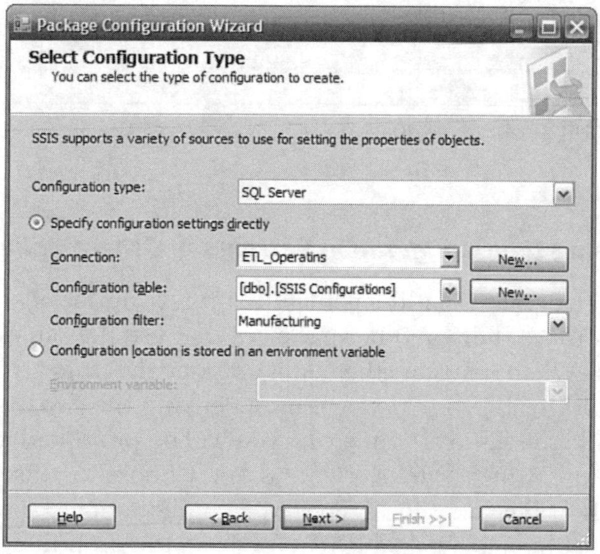

Figure 4-17   Defining configurations stored in SQL Server

Now, just as you did for the ETL_Operations connection manager, select the ServerName property from all the connection managers you want to reconfigure at runtime. Click Next and provide a name for the configuration, such as Connections. You should now see two configurations in the Package Configuration Organizer. Leave them in this order, with the ConfigurationReference configuration before the Connections configuration, as shown in Figure 4-18.

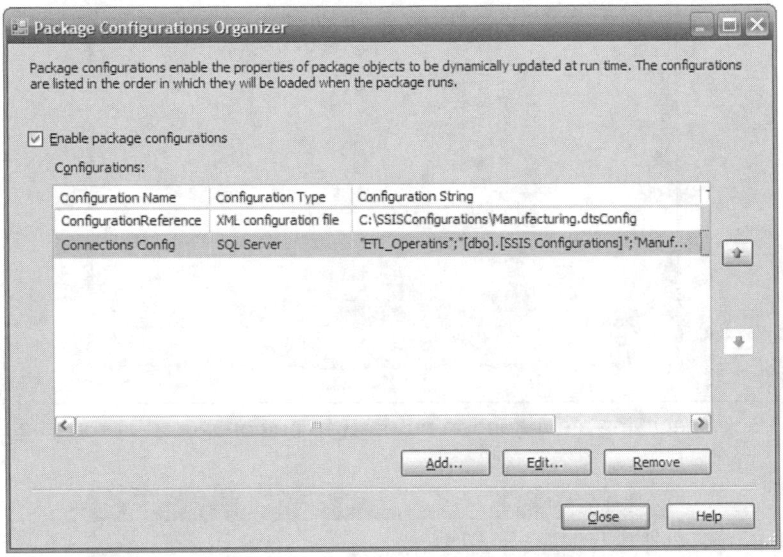

Figure 4-18   Configuration Organizer

Reusing the Configuration Settings in Other Packages

Now that you've got the configurations set up for one package, you can easily reuse them in other packages that use the same connection managers. When you start the configuration wizard for a package, begin as you did for the first package by specifying the XML configuration file. Provide the same filename, and you will be prompted to either reuse the existing settings or to overwrite them. Choose to reuse existing settings. Do the same for the SQL Server configurations, specifying the same connection manager, table (choose from the drop-down list), and filter.

It is important to note that to reuse existing configurations, you must use the same names for the connection managers, including case, and you must have the same number of connection managers. If you open the configuration for a package that is missing a connection manager (even if it doesn't use it), that connection manager will be dropped from the configuration.

Using the Configurations in Multiple Environments

We have defined the configurations for one environment, but our goal was to be able to use them in several environments. This is easy to accomplish. First, copy the XML file to the new environment, putting it in exactly the same drive and directory. Edit the file with Notepad and change the server name to the new server name. Then use the Copy Database Wizard in SQL Server Management Studio to copy the ETL_Operations database to the new server. Open the [SSIS Configurations] table and change the ConfiguredValue column for each of your connection managers to point to the new server(s).

Deploying Packages to a New Server

After you have set up the package configuration, the next step is to move the packages to the targeted environment.

Deploying a Single Package

You can move the packages one at a time, as they are completed, using the File/Save copy as menu option. Choose SQL Server as the location and specify which SQL Server instance you want to use to store the package. At the Package path: prompt, click the dot (.); under Stored Packages, select the folder where you want to save the package (usually MSDB, but you can create your own), and type in the name you want to store the package under, without the .dtsx extension. Click OK to set the location and name, and OK again to complete the save.

Deploying All Packages in a Project

You can also move all the packages in a project to SQL Server or the file system on a server using the manifest and Deployment Wizard. The manifest is a file defining what is to be deployed. You need to enable a project setting to create a deployment manifest. This is done through the Project/Properties menu. On the Deployment Utility node of the Configuration Properties, set the CreateDeploymentUtility property to True. Doing so causes the manifest to be created when you build the project. To launch the Deployment Wizard, double-click the manifest, which is located in the \bin directory of your solution.

Creating Integration Services Subfolders on SQL Server

Using SQL Server Management Studio, you can organize your packages stored on SQL Server by connecting to an Integration Services service. (Note that you do not specify an instance name for Integration Services, just the server name.) You will see two nodes in the tree: Running Packages and Stored Packages. Open the Stored Packages node. If you have many packages, it is convenient to create subfolders under the MSDB folder. To create a subfolder, just right-click the parent folder and choose New folder. When you deploy a package, or choose File\Save a copy as, you can specify the path to the subfolder you want to store it in.

Security

Package security is managed by specific roles for Integration Services created and managed by the SQL Server engine. Unless a user is a member of one of these three roles, that user will not be able to work with packages stored in SQL Server, or even store a package there. The three roles are as follows:

- **db_dtsadmin.** Can add, remove, and execute any package.
- **db_dtsltduser.** Can add, remove, and execute its own packages.
- **db_dtsoperator.** Can view and execute any package directly or as a job.

You assign Windows groups or users to these roles through the Security node of the msdb database in SQL Server Management Studio.

You can also change the roles that can run or replace a package. In SQL Server Management Studio, right-click a package and choose Package roles. You can set each of the read and write permissions to any SQL role defined for the msdb database.

Maintenance

You can also use the deployment utility to create a new installation routine when you have made changes after the packages have initially been installed, which will replace the existing packages in production. Because you probably don't want to overwrite any configuration changes that were made in production, you should set the AllowConfigurationChanges project property to False.

Operations

After you've completed your packages and they've been promoted to production, you are in a completely different environment from BI Development Studio. Your connection managers need to know where production servers are, you'll want to log progress information if a package fails, and you may want to be able to restart from a known checkpoint.

Running Packages in Production

After the packages have been deployed on the production server, you can use the Package Execution utility (available from the Integration Services folder on the Start menu) to select a package, set options and configurations, assign variable values, set connection properties, and, of course, run the package. You can also right-click a package and choose Run to execute a package. Both of these methods execute the package on the machine you are working on, not the server containing the packages.

Instead of running packages manually, in a production environment it is usually better if the packages are automatically executed at a certain time or after some event, such as every Sunday night at 10 p.m., with someone being notified only if they don't succeed. You can use the SQL Server Agent service introduced in Chapter 2, "Introduction to SQL Server 2005," to schedule packages; with the Agent, you can specify package logging options, select which configuration file to use, and notify an operator via e-mail or other device if the job fails.

Execution Location of Packages

Packages run through jobs started by the SQL Agent are executed on the server, as you would expect. You can run packages from a client machine using SQL Server Management Studio, but you need to be aware that the package will run on the client, not on the server that displays in the Object Explorer. If you use environment variables or XML files to set runtime configurations of packages, you must create those variables and XML files on the client, too.

Packages running on the client may increase the network traffic, or may execute slower than on the server, depending on the capacity of the client. Some packages may fail if the Integration Services runtime isn't installed on the client.

Running Packages within a Transaction

Many packages contain multiple steps that need to succeed or fail as a single unit. For example, in the Sales Territory dimension package that we created earlier, if the truncate step succeeds but the import from the source database fails for some reason (such as the source database not being available), we would be left with an empty Sales Territory table in the data warehouse.

Integration Services deals with this issue by allowing you to set up the whole package to run in a transaction so that it succeeds or fails as a unit, or to explicitly select which tasks need to share the same transaction. If you have packages that call other packages, they can also share the same transaction. If any task that is part of the transaction fails, all the preceding tasks in the transaction will be rolled back.

To set up a transaction for a package, right-click anywhere in the Control Flow view and select Properties. Change the TransactionOption property from Supported, which means that if the package is called from another package, it participates in the other package's transaction, to Required, which creates a new transaction for this package if one doesn't already exist. All the tasks that need to participate in the package's transaction also need to have their individual TransactionOption property set to Supported, which is the default setting for tasks.

Building Restartable Packages

Some packages include really long-running tasks such as downloading a file from an FTP server. If a subsequent task fails for some reason, such as loading the data into a table when the database server is not available, you might prefer not have to run the whole package again, but just the steps after the download.

Integration Services uses a concept called **checkpoints** to support this. When checkpoints are enabled for a package, a checkpoint file is created while the package is executing that keeps track of the last step that successfully executed. When a step fails and you have to restart the package, Integration Services can use the checkpoint file to restart from the point of failure rather than from the beginning.

To enable checkpoints, right-click anywhere in the Control Flow view and select Properties. Change the SaveCheckpoints property to True, specify a CheckpointFileName, and set the CheckpointUsage property to IfExists to make the package restart from the checkpoint if a checkpoint file exists.

TIP:
Designing Packages for Restartability
A package can only be restarted from the task level; so if, for example, you have multiple steps within a single Data Flow task, you can only restart the package at the beginning of the data flow. If you split up complex Data Flow tasks into multiple simpler tasks, the package can be restarted at a more granular level.

Logging Package Information

It often proves useful for operations staff to have access to a detailed execution log in case a package fails and they need to discover the cause. You can set up logging for Integration Services packages either in the Visual Studio designer by selecting Logging from the Integration Services menu or when you execute the package using the Package Execution utility or SQL Server Agent.

Logs can be written to multiple destinations including a simple text file, a SQL Server trace file for integrated debugging of the database and Integration Services package, or the Windows event log. The level of detail that you want to include can also be specified, so that you can limit the amount of information that is included. We recommend logging these events: OnError, OnPostExecute, OnPrevalidate, OnTaskFailed.

Next Steps

In this introduction to Integration Services, you've learned how to copy and transform data in a number of different ways. Integration Services has many additional aspects, and we want to draw your attention to a few of them.

Data Quality

For purposes of clarity in introducing Integration Services, we have assumed in this chapter a rather ideal world where there are no errors in the data. This is rarely the case, and in Chapter 7 we discuss techniques for detecting and correcting bad data. All the tasks and transforms we used have an error output you can use to divert the process or data flow in case of an error.

Scaling Your Solution

The techniques shown in this chapter work well for moderate to high volumes of data. If you have a very large database, or very high rates of new data, you should read Chapter 11, "Very Large Data Warehouses." This addresses design and management issues relating to Integration Services packages, the data warehouse, and the on-line analytical processing (OLAP) databases. Integration Services packages are typically stored in the msdb database in SQL Server. This means that if that SQL Server instance is clustered, the packages are accessible even if a cluster node fails. Integration Services itself is not cluster aware and doesn't really need to be, because it is really just a service available on any machine it is installed on. In a cluster, you can only store Integration Services packages on one instance of SQL Server. If you are using Integration Services packages stored on a clustered instance of SQL Server, be sure to use the virtual server name, not the physical server name, when referencing a package.

Other Transformations

Our goal in this chapter was to get you familiar with the structure of Integration Services packages, not necessarily to explain each transform or task. A number of other transformations are not covered in this chapter. One set of transformations controls how rows flow between source and destination, such as Union All to merge multiple data sets with the same set of columns, and Merge Join, which allows you to perform database-style joins between two data streams. You can also Sort data, or use the Aggregate transformation to perform functions such as sum or count.

Another set of transformations allows you to transform column values, such as converting data types using Data Conversion or performing string manipulations using the Character Map transformation. There are also transformations for working with Analysis Services objects, such as the Dimension Processing and Data Mining Model Training transformations.

The Script transform is extremely useful for creating complex transforms because you can code in a flexible language.

Finally, one important transformation called the Slowly Changing Dimension transformation is covered in detail in Chapter 8.

Control Flow Tasks

We have focused our attention mostly on the Data Flow task in this chapter because this is the most commonly used task. Other tasks include Data Preparation tasks that prepare data for loading, such as copying or downloading files using FTP or MSMQ, and Bulk Insert.

You can also add a great deal of flexibility to your packages by writing custom .NET code using a Script task, execute other packages or Windows applications using Execute Package or Execute Process tasks, or even call Web services to perform a function or return data using the Web Service task.

Summary

ETL processes are defined in Integration Services packages. A package consists of a control flow definition, which describes the high-level flow of a process. A process flow can invoke a data flow, which describes the details of any transformations a data source must go through before being stored in a destination. Packages make it easy to intercept and redirect bad data, and simplify maintenance by making it easy to see what processes and transforms the data is undergoing. You use the BI Development Studio to create and debug your packages and to deploy your solution to other environments such as test and production. In those other environments, connections to data sources and destinations, as well as variables and other parameter settings, can be set at runtime through environment variables, XML files, and database tables.

CHAPTER 5

Building an Analysis Services Database

Now that we have invested the time and effort to build a robust data warehouse and data-integration process, we can add the final piece to the solution: the on-line analytical processing (OLAP) database. Flexible analytical capabilities are required to really take advantage of the integrated information in the data warehouse and move beyond a simple level of understanding such as measuring the increase in income received.

In this chapter, we extend the manufacturing solution from the previous two chapters by building an Analysis Services database to enable users to flexibly access the information in the data warehouse. We describe how to adjust the data model to better support cubes and show you how to define and manage cubes on top of the relational structures you have already created.

Business Problem

For this chapter, we return to the sporting goods manufacturing company one last time to show you how to add analytics to the complete Business Intelligence (BI) solution.

Problem Statement

Management needs to be able to determine what impact their decisions will have on overall profitability and customer satisfaction. In particular, the manufacturer wants to address the following issues:

- Customer satisfaction levels are down because of problems with delivering goods on time. The consolidated data warehouse is an obvious source of information to help find out why this is occurring, but the users need a flexible analytical capability that is easy to use. They need to be able to discover the underlying reasons for the delivery issue, and then track the performance as they introduce improvements to the process.

- The business has been tasked with improving profitability across all product lines and customers, and they need to be able to discover which types of customers and products are least profitable. Reports and queries against the data warehouse do not perform well enough to support these ad-hoc queries because of the huge data volumes.

Solution Overview

We will use the data warehouse as the source for a new Analysis Services database that the users can query to support their business initiatives. The database will include dimensions that are structured to make it easy to do different kinds of analyses and will include measures that are based on the relational fact tables as well as more complex calculations.

Business Requirements

The high-level requirements to support the business objectives are as follows:

- **Profitability analysis.** The primary requirement here is query performance and flexibility. Profitability analyses generally need to look at huge amounts of information, and using relational reporting in this area has not worked well because of the time taken to run reports against detail-level data. Users need a solution that enables them to easily access the information to identify opportunities and problem areas. In addition, the system needs to provide very fast (subsecond, if possible) response times so that users are free to explore the data.

- **On-time shipments analysis.** An "on-time" shipment is defined as a shipment that was shipped on or before the due date that was promised to the customer. Users need to be able to see the on-time deliveries as a percentage of the total deliveries and to track how this changes over time as they introduce new techniques to improve performance. They also need to understand aspects, such as how many days late shipments are, as well as potentially interesting factors such as how much notice the customer gave and how long from the order date it actually took to ship the products. They need to be able to change the product and customer mix they are looking at and generally to be able to understand what kinds of shipments are late.

High-Level Architecture

We will build an Analysis Services database on top of the data warehouse and add a cube and dimensions to support the business requirements. The data will be loaded into the Analysis Services database on a regular basis after the data warehouse load has completed. Our approach will ensure that only the most recent data needs to be loaded into the cube, to avoid having to reload all the fact data every time new data is available.

From an architectural point of view, the relational data warehouse is supplying the data storage and integrity, and the Integration Services packages are providing the data consolidation and cleansing. The Analysis Services database will extend the picture shown in Figure 5-1, providing the rich analytics and sheer performance that is required. Because we have defined views in the data warehouse for all facts and dimensions, the Analysis Services database can use these views as its source rather than accessing the physical data warehouse schema directly.

The users will connect to the Analysis Services cube using client tools such as Excel, which provides a drag-and-drop metaphor for easily accessing the information. Also, reporting tools such as Reporting Services can access the information in the cube, making it easier to publish the information to end users.

Although many people think of OLAP technology or cubes as restricted to being used for drilling down and pivoting through data, Analysis Services 2005 databases will generally remove the need for reporting directly from the relational data warehouse database. The reason for this is that Analysis Services uses an "attribute-based" model, meaning that all the columns in the underlying data source can be made available for analysis if required, instead of having to go back to the relational data for detail data.

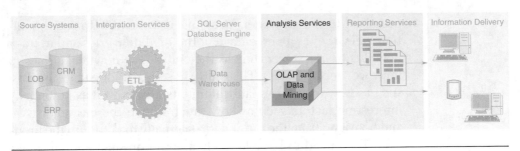

Figure 5-1   High-level architecture

Although you can use Analysis Services databases to add analytics to most data structures, the best solution to some calculation issues is to modify the underlying database. We make some changes to the fact views in the data warehouse to present information to Analysis Services in the way we need it for this solution.

Alternative Solution: Analysis Services Database over Source Systems

Analysis Services databases can be used to create a Unified Dimensional Model (UDM) directly on top of the source systems (the two enterprise resource processing [ERP] systems and some spreadsheets in this example). Because we can get many of the benefits of a complete BI solution using a UDM, including combining information from multiple systems in an easy-to-use and well-performing format, this could potentially save us all the effort required to build a data warehouse and associated extraction, transformation, and loading (ETL) process. This sounds like a great idea!

The reality is that although the UDM is a convenient and flexible solution when you need to build a departmental BI solution and don't have the time to do it right, a data warehouse is always the best long-term solution. Analysis Services is the best technology for providing information to the user and providing the performance for ad-hoc queries, but there are still areas where the data warehouse and associated ETL process will be the best bet.

Data quality is probably the most important reason for a data warehouse, because real-world source systems are never going to contain completely clean data. As you have seen in previous chapters, you can use a relational database and Integration Services to get around some thorny issues in the data, such as unpivoting columns into rows. Another important reason is to allow additional systems to be easily integrated—when half your sales fact records need to start coming from the new ERP system that your company has just acquired, an adjustment to the Integration Services packages is all that is required.

Business Benefits

The solution will deliver the following benefits to the client:

- The solution will support the on-time delivery and profitability business initiatives by providing flexible analytical capabilities with the required subsecond response.
- Allowing end users to directly access the information they need will reduce the pressure on IT to deliver new reports all the time and will free up valuable resources to work on other projects.

Data Model

The data warehouse that we built in the previous two chapters already contains all the dimensions and fact tables that we need to support the business requirements, and most of the measures. In this section, we look at how the data model needs to be extended to more easily support building Analysis Services cubes.

How Do We Handle "On-Time" Shipments?

The business requirements tell us that the users are interested in finding out how many (or what percentage) of shipments are on time, meaning that they were shipped on or before the due date. Because we already have ShipDateKey and DueDateKey columns that contain the relevant dates on the Shipments fact table, we should be able to calculate this without any problem.

In a relational reporting environment, we might add a where clause to our query that selected those records where one date was less than the other. It turns out that this approach is somewhat tricky to replicate in an OLAP environment, so we need another approach that can take advantage of the fact that cubes are very, very good at handling additive measures because of the power of precalculated aggregates.

We can start to solve the problem by realizing that each fact record is either "on time" or "not on time," depending on the date values. If we have a Boolean value such as this in our data model, the best approach is to model it as a numeric field with a 0 or 1. For example, we could add an OnTime column to the fact table that contains 1 for an on-time delivery and 0 for a late delivery.

This works great for cubes, because then we can add a measure that simply sums the column to return the number or percentage of on-time deliveries. No matter how you slice the cube, whether you are looking at the total for the whole cube or just a specific customer's shipments in the past week, the measure can simply sum the OnTime column.

TIP:
Transforming Logic into Additive Measures
Cubes are great at handling additive measures, so a common technique is to transform complex logic into a nice simple column. Logic that returns a true or false value is commonly expressed as a numeric column with a 0 or 1, or with a value such as a sales amount for some records and a 0 for other records.

This is especially true for logic that needs to be evaluated for every record at the detailed, fact-record level. Calculations that work well with totals (such as Profit Percentage defined as the total profit divided by the total sales) can more easily be handled with calculations in the cube itself.

Of course, because we have defined views over the fact and dimension tables and the views are going to be the source for the Analysis Services database, we don't actually have to create a physical OnTime column. Instead, we can just add the calculation to the Shipments view using the following expression:

```
CASE WHEN ShipDateKey <= DueDateKey THEN 1 ELSE 0 END AS
OnTime
```

If you don't have access to the views or tables in the source system, you can define the preceding SQL calculation in the Analysis Services database's data source definition, but it is more flexible and easier to maintain if you define SQL expressions in the views. The performance penalty that some people associate with SQL date calculations isn't particularly important in this case because the query will only be executed to load the data into the Analysis Services database.

An alternative approach to modeling this is to add a new On Time Category dimension that has two records, On Time and Late. This has the advantage that users could select a dimension member and restrict their analysis to only those shipments that fall into that category. Which of these options (or both) that you choose will depend on your users' preferences, underlining again the benefits of prototyping and involving the users in design decisions that they will ultimately end up living with.

How Late Were These Shipments, Anyway?

Another area that users will want to explore is the time periods for the shipments. For example, users need to know how many days late shipments were. They could perform some interesting analyses with this information, such as the average days late for a specific product or time period.

In a relational report, we could add an expression that calculates the number of days between the ShipDateKey and DueDateKey, which would give you the number of days late. This is another example of logic that needs the detail-level date keys to return a value, so we can add another calculated column to the view. Because we are trying to figure out how many days late the shipments are, and number of days happens to be a nice additive value, we can add an expression that returns the days between the two keys:

```
DATEDIFF(dd, DueDateKey, ShipDateKey) AS DaysLate
```

Actually, this expression turns out not to work so well because some shipments are early, so you will have negative DaysLate values that will tend to reduce the apparent lateness. This will require you going back to the users for clarification, but in the manufacturing example they don't want to get credit for those shipments that happened to be early. (In fact, that might be another area they are interested in analyzing further because it has interesting business implications.) We need to adjust the expression so that shipments that are on time or early do not contribute to the Days Late value:

```
CASE WHEN (ShipDateKey < DueDateKey) THEN 0
  ELSE DATEDIFF(dd, DueDateKey, ShipDateKey) END
AS DaysLate
```

We can handle the other business requirements in this area in the same way, such as calculating the number of days notice that we had by subtracting the due date from the order date and calculating the number of days it took to actually ship the product by subtracting the order date from the ship date.

What Doesn't Work Well in a Cube?

If you add columns to your fact table that aren't fully additive, such as Unit Price or Product Standard Cost, when you build your cube, you will start to realize that they don't work very well. A cube generally sums up the values for the records that the user is looking at, based on their dimension selections. Analysis Services 2005 has some other ways of aggregating numbers beyond a simple sum such as Max or Min, and even supports some advanced scenarios for dealing with data that behaves strangely over time; by and large, however, most measures are summed.

Unit Price doesn't work when you sum it. Although the Quantity Shipped sums very nicely under all conditions, the sum of the Unit Price for all shipments last year is meaningless. That is why the data model instead has an Extended Amount column, which contains the quantity multiplied by the unit price for the product. You can add up all the extended amounts for all shipments and come up with a useful number.

On the other hand, if the users needed to see the *average* unit price for the shipments, you can easily add a calculated measure to the cube that divides the total Extended Amount by the total Quantity, which is probably what the users wanted all along.

Technical Solution

In contrast to a relational database, which is solely designed as a reliable data storage engine, you can think of an Analysis Services database as a rich semantic layer that provides information to users in the way they like to think about it, and which also loads data into a cache with some precalculated summaries to increase performance.

Getting Started with Analysis Services

We start by using the BI Development Studio to create a new Analysis Services project. This will create a new local folder on your development machine that will contain the definitions for the Analysis Services objects that we will be creating. Later when we have finished designing the objects, we can deploy the project to a server that is running Analysis Services to create the cube and allow users to access the information.

You will notice that this is a different approach from working with normal relational databases. So far, when we have used the SQL Server Management Studio for tasks such as defining the data warehouse database, any modifications that we made to objects such as tables or indexes were immediately updated to the live database when we clicked the Save button.

Defining the Logical Data Model

All Analysis Services databases have one or more data sources that contain the information that will be loaded into the cubes. In our example, the source will be the manufacturing data warehouse database. The first step for creating an Analysis Services project is to add a data source and specify the type of database and connection information, using the same techniques we used for Integration Services projects in the previous chapter.

Most source databases contain a large number of tables and views. You can select the parts of the source database that will be used for analysis by defining a logical view of the database called a **data source view** (DSV), so we will be focusing this logical view on the dimension and fact views that we created when we set up the database. The DSV can also be used to define relationships between objects and to implement business logic by adding calculated columns to the logical view.

The DSV acts as an abstraction layer over the source system and can prove useful when you are building cubes over legacy data sources where you don't have access to add simplifying views over the normalized underlying schema. When using data warehouses as the source, it is usually better to add any required business logic or calculated columns into the underlying views rather than using the DSV. As discussed in the "Data Modeling" section, we can add calculated columns to the underlying views in the database. These views can then be managed along with their corresponding tables and can be made available for other applications, too.

Defining the Relationships Between Dimension and Fact Views

After we have added all the dimension and fact views to the DSV, we need to create the relationships between them. If we were using physical tables rather than views, the wizard that created the DSV could detect these relationships based on the primary key and any referential integrity constraints, but this doesn't work for views, so we need to create the relationships manually.

The simplest approach is to arrange the dimension tables roughly around the fact table, as shown in Figure 5-2, and then drag each key column from the fact table to the corresponding dimension table primary key column. We also need to create the relationships for any snowflake dimensions such as Product. Similar to the fact columns, you drag the foreign key to the primary key (such as dragging the Product-CategoryKey column from Product Subcategory to Product Category).

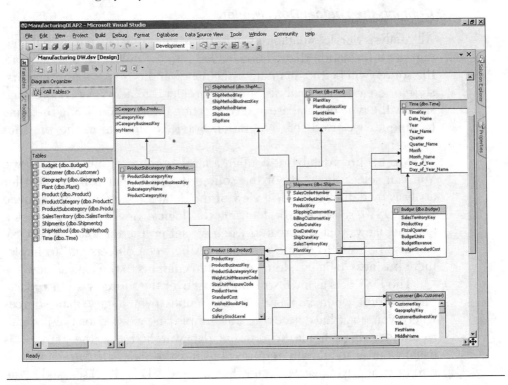

Figure 5-2   Data source view

For dimensions such as Customer, there may be multiple relationships with the fact table. You can simply repeat the drag-and-drop process for each column on the fact table, such as ShippingCustomerKey and BillingCustomerKey. This is referred to as a "role playing dimension" in SQL Server Books Online.

TIP:
Dealing with Multiple Date Relationships
Fact tables frequently contain multiple date columns, which are often used to calculate values such as the total time taken to move from one state to another. When you are defining relationships in the DSV, you may decide to create relationships between the Time dimension and the fact table for each of the date columns. This makes sense as long as users are going to expect to be able to analyze the information by each of the different dates. So, when the users are looking for year-to-date sales, they would need to decide which kind of date analysis they would use, such as by order date or ship date.

For the Time dimension in the Manufacturing database, we will create relationships for the ShipDateKey, OrderDateKey, and Due-DateKey columns on the Shipments fact table. This decision (like many decisions in BI) will make some things easier and others harder. If we had defined a single relationship with the ShipDateKey column on the Shipments fact table, this would have made things simpler for the user. There would be no ambiguity about which Time dimension to pick, but users would not be able to perform certain analyses such as the number of orders placed last month versus the number of orders shipped.

Building the Initial Cube

Now that the logical data model has been defined in the DSV, we can create a cube. BI Development Studio includes a wizard that will analyze the relationships that you have defined, as well as the actual data in the tables; the wizard usually produces a pretty good first pass for a cube design. The wizard makes suggestions for which tables are probably facts and which are probably dimensions, and also looks at the data in your dimension columns to try and come up with some reasonable attributes and hierarchies where possible.

A single cube can contain many different fact tables with different granularities and different subsets of dimensions. Each fact table that you include in a cube becomes a **measure group**, with a corresponding set of measures based on the numeric fact columns. This allows users to easily compare information from different fact tables, such as comparing Actual Revenue from a Sales measure group with Planned Revenue from a Budget measure group. This may trip you up if you are familiar with other BI technologies that had one separate cube per fact table—in

Analysis Services 2005, the most common approach is to have only one cube in the database with multiple measure groups.

QUICK START: Creating an Analysis Services Cube

Before you can create a cube, you need to use BI Development Studio to create a new BI project with a data source and DSV. You also need to use the DSV to define the relationships between the tables:

1. Select New Cube from the Project menu, and click Next to skip over the welcome screen.

2. We will be using the wizard to recommend the cube structure, so leave the Auto Build checked and select Create attributes and hierarchies. Click Next.

3. Click Next again to select the Manufacturing data source.

4. The wizard uses the relationships you have defined in the DSV to identify fact and dimension tables. Click Next to see the results (see Figure 5-3).

5. Make sure to select the Time dimension table from the drop-down list at the top of the page. You can now review the list of tables and check which were identified as facts or dimensions. If there are any strange selections, you can either fix them manually or return to the DSV to define relationships correctly. Click Next.

6. Because you selected a Time dimension in the previous step, you now need to let the wizard know the contents of the columns in the table (that is, which column contains the Year, which contains the Month, and so on). Make sure to select the TimeKey column as the Date selection. Click Next.

7. You can use the Select Measures step to rename measures or measure groups and to select any numeric columns that the wizard identified that are not actually measures. A good example of this is the Invoice Line Number and Revision Numbers column, which need to be unchecked because they are not measures. Click Next.

8. The wizard now reads the data in the dimension tables to see whether it can detect any hierarchies. Click Next to review the hierarchies that the wizard detected, along with the attributes found. You can use this step to uncheck any attributes or hierarchies that you don't want to include in the cube. Click Next.

---

9. Give the cube a name that will be meaningful to users, such as Manufacturing. You may be tempted to use the name of a fact table here, but remember that later versions of your cube may include other business areas, so it is better to be quite general. Click Finish to create the cube and dimensions.

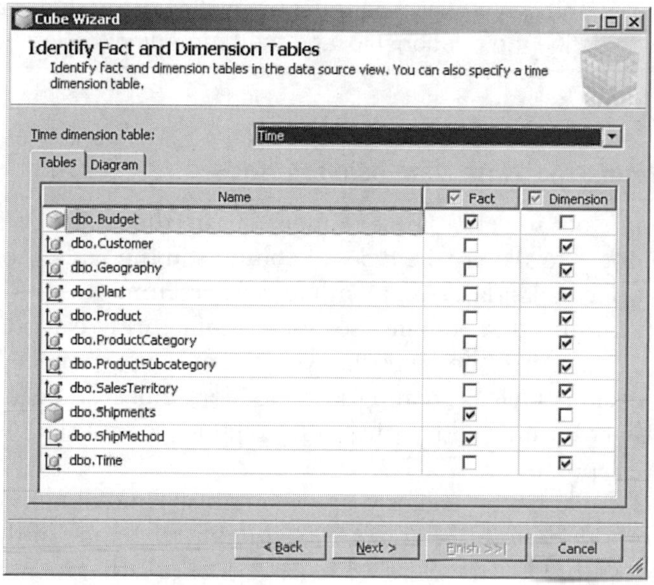

Figure 5-3   Fact and dimension tables

You may have noticed that the Ship Method table was identified as both a dimension and a fact. This is because there are numeric or money columns on the dimension table, and the wizard is including the table as a possible fact because the users might want to include those columns as measures in a query. In addition to having a Ship Method dimension, the cube will include the numeric measures from the Ship Method table as part of a separate Ship Method measure group.

TIP:
Why the Wizard Sometimes Identifies Dimensions as Facts
When using the Cube Wizard, you will often get to the step that shows which tables were identified as facts or dimensions and see that one of your dimension tables is incorrectly showing up as a fact. This is often due to a missing relationship or a relationship defined in the wrong direction in the DSV, and can usually be fixed by canceling the wizard, returning to the DSV to define the relationship, and then rerunning the wizard.

Defining the Time Dimension Periods

When you select a Time dimension in the Cube Wizard, you are prompted to specify the types of columns in the table. For example, you can select calendar year, month and day columns, as well as the equivalent columns that contain fiscal or manufacturing calendar information. The wizard uses the types that you select to apply special logic for time dimensions such as creating sensible hierarchies, and calculation formulas that you may add to the cube, such as year-to-date values, also use these types.

For elements such as years or months, Time dimension tables often have both descriptive columns containing the name of the period (such as FY 05 or Quarter 2), as well as a key column that identifies the period. This key column may be unique, such as a datetime column storing the first day of the period as the key (for example, 1/1/2006 for the first quarter of 2006). Alternatively, the key column may be a repeating number, such as using the numeric index of the period (for example, 3 for March).

When designing the Time dimension table, it is better to use the first approach (that is, create unique keys for periods), and then select these unique keys when specifying Time dimension periods in the wizard. Using the unique keys rather than the descriptions (such as selecting Year rather than Year_Name) will result in more efficient storage and avoid any problems with hierarchies that may be caused by nonunique keys, such as strange-looking hierarchies with members in the wrong places.

Loading Data into the Cube

When the wizard has finished creating the cube, it will be opened up in the cube designer. You can use the Cube Structure tab shown in Figure 5-4 to view the dimensions and measures in the cube, and to add or remove new measures and dimensions. Before we start changing the structure of the cube, however, we should probably take a look at how the cube would look when a user browses it.

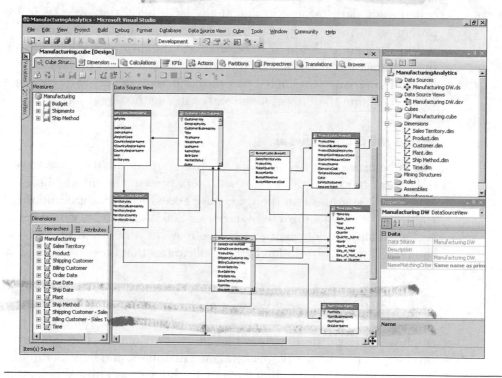

Figure 5-4   Cube designer

If you click the Browser tab after creating a cube, you get an error message that "Either the user does not have access to the database, or the database does not exist." The problem is that although Visual Studio has created the files on your local PC that describe the definition of the cube and dimensions, we have not yet deployed these definitions to the server or loaded data into the objects. If you have a background with relational databases, you can think of our progress so far as similar to having used a fancy designer to generate a bunch of CREATE TABLE SQL statements, but not having executed them on the database server to create the tables, or loaded any data into them.

You can fix this problem by selecting Process from the Database menu. Visual Studio will detect that the definitions that you have created on your development PC differ from the definitions on the server and prompt you to build and deploy the project to the server first. When this deployment has been completed, the server will contain the same cube and dimension definitions that you designed locally, but they will still not contain any data. After the definitions have been deployed, you are prompted to process the database. This executes queries against the source database tables to load the cube and dimensions with data. Note that this might take a while when you have large volumes of data.

You can change to which server the database is deployed by choosing Properties from the Project menu and changing the target server.

Using the Cube Browser

The cube browser in BI Development Studio is intended to show developers how the cube will look when users browse the information. Of course, this assumes that the users have access to a BI application that supports the new features in SQL Server 2005, such as measure groups and attributes. If not, their experience may be very different, and you should test your cube design in the applications that they will ultimately use.

To use the browser, just drag and drop the measures that you want to analyze on to the center of the display, and then drag any hierarchies or attributes on to the columns and rows (see Figure 5-5). You can start to see how some of the decisions that the wizard makes show up in the browser, such as names of measures and attributes, and how hierarchies are structured. After building the initial cube, you will probably want to spend some time trying out different combinations and taking note of aspects that you would like to change.

For example, you may notice that the wizard has not created any hierarchies for the Plant dimension, even though it would be useful for users to be able to drill down through divisions to plants. Because Analysis Services 2005 is attribute based, users could actually build this hierarchy dynamically at runtime by simply dropping the Division Name on to the rows, followed by the Plant Name. Still, it is usually helpful for users to see some prebuilt hierarchies, so we will go ahead and add some in the next section.

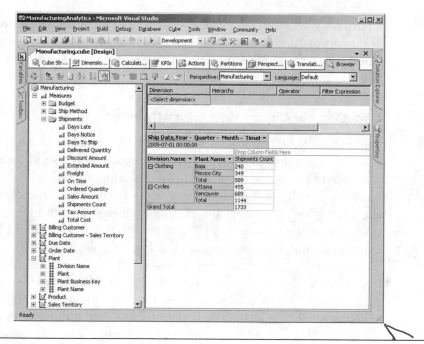

Figure 5-5   Cube browser

If you are building a cube that doesn't have much data in the fact table yet, you might have difficulty figuring out how your attributes and hierarchies will look because the browser by default only displays rows and columns that actually have data. If you want to include the rows with no associated fact data, select Show Empty Cells from the Cube menu.

Setting Up the Dimensions

After we spend some time browsing through the data in the Manufacturing cube, we can see that we need to change a number of areas. This is where developing BI solutions gets interesting, because there are probably no clear requirements that you can turn to that say things like "the users would probably prefer to have a Divisions hierarchy to pick from rather than selecting two or three plant attributes manually." There is a lot to be said for an iterative approach to developing cubes, where you build prototypes and show them to users for feedback, and then release versions of the cube to allow the users time to explore the system and give more feedback.

Because many dimension tables contain a lot of fields that are not particularly useful for users, you should exercise some care about which attributes you create rather than just creating an attribute for every field. Too many attributes can be confusing to users, and for very large dimensions, it may impact query performance because each attribute expands the total size of the cube.

Changing the Display Values for Attributes

When the Plant dimension was created, the wizard created separate Plant Name and Division Name attributes. There is also a special attribute called Plant based on the PlantKey column. Each dimension has one attribute like this that has its Usage property set to Key, usually based on the surrogate key, which uniquely identifies a dimension record but doesn't actually contain any information that the user would be interested in seeing. If a user includes the Plant attribute in the browser, the user will see meaningless integer values.

What we can do to fix this is to change the Plant attribute so that the plant name is displayed rather than the surrogate key. This can be accomplished by clicking the Plant attribute in the dimension designer, going to the NameColumn property in the Properties window, and selecting the Plant Name column. This means that having a separate attribute for Plant Name is now redundant, so we can remove it by selecting the attribute and clicking the delete button.

Also, now we have one attribute called Plant and another called Division Name, which is somewhat inconsistent, so it's probably a good idea to change the attribute name to Division because you are not restricted to using the original source column name for an attribute (see Figure 5-6).

Adding Hierarchies to a Dimension

A **hierarchy** is a way to organize related attributes, providing a handy way for users to navigate the information by drilling down through one or more levels. Although users can define their own drilldown paths by dragging separate related attributes onto the browser, providing a sensible set of hierarchies for each dimension will help them to get started with common analyses.

The next change we make for the Manufacturing cube is to add a hierarchy to the Plant dimension that drills down through Division and Plant (see Figure 5-6). To set up our hierarchy, you can drag the Division attribute on the hierarchies and levels area of the dimension designer, and then drag the Plant name underneath it to create two levels. The name will default to Hierarchy, but this can be changed by right-clicking the new hierarchy and choosing Rename to change the name to something more meaningful.

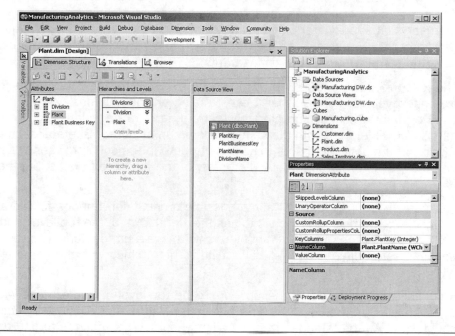

Figure 5-6 Defining a Plant hierarchy

Usually when you define a hierarchy, the bottom level contains the key attribute for the dimension (Plant, in this case) so that users can drill down to the most detailed data if they want to; this is not mandatory, however, and you can create hierarchies where the lowest level is actually a summary of dimension records.

Another area of the dimension that you might sometimes want to change is the name of the All level. When you include a hierarchy as a filter in the cube browser, the default selection is the top of the hierarchy, which includes all the data in the dimension. The name that displays for this special level can be changed for each hierarchy using the AllMemberName property of the hierarchy, such as All Divisions for the hierarchy we just created. You could make a similar change to the dimension's AttributeAllMemberName property, which affects the name used when any simple attribute is used as a filter.

Naming Conventions for Hierarchies

When you were creating a hierarchy for the Division and Plant attributes, you might have been tempted to use the name Division for the hierarchy because the user will be looking at plants by division. If you gave this a try, you would have received an error message that let you know that a hierarchy cannot have the same name as an existing attribute.

The reason for this is that behind the scenes, each attribute actually has its own one-level hierarchy so that it can be used on the columns or rows in a cube browser. Because the hierarchy name needs to be unique, you can't name a new hierarchy with the same name as an attribute. One approach is to turn off the ability for users to use an attribute in the cube browser by setting the AttributeHierarchyEnabled property of the attribute to false, but that is usually not what you want.

Alternatively, you could adopt some possible naming conventions for hierarchy names. A simple approach is to use the plural form of the top level, such as Divisions for the Division/Plant hierarchy. This is a bit restrictive, however, because some dimensions will have multiple hierarchies with the same top level.

A similar issue occurs if you simply prefix the top-level attribute name with By, such as By Division, but with a bit of creativity either of those options could work. A more standardized but slightly clumsy approach is to use the name of each level in the hierarchy name, such as Division Plant or Category Subcategory.

Declaring the Relationships Between Attributes

One of the most important steps you need to take when working with dimensions is to correctly define the **relationships between attributes**. For example, in a typical Geographic dimension, city is related to state, and state is related to country. These relationships are used by Analysis Services to figure out which aggregates would be useful, so they can have a big impact on the performance of your cube and also affect the size of your dimensions in memory.

Setting Up the Relationships in the Time Dimension

If you look at the structure of the Time dimension that the wizard has created, you can see that we can clean up a few areas. When we set up the Time dimension in the Cube Wizard, we specified the key columns such as Year and Quarter rather than Year_Name or Quarter_Name, so we also need to change the NameColumn property for each of the attributes to point to the corresponding text column containing the name of the period. We can also rename the hierarchies and some of the attribute names.

If you expand the key attribute in the Dimension Structure tab, you will notice that the wizard created a relationship between the key attribute and every other attribute. The reason is that each attribute needs to be related to the key in some way, and it is technically true that every attribute can be uniquely determined by the key. When you think about how calendars actually work, however, you can probably see that there are other potential ways of defining these relationships. Each month belongs to one quarter, and each quarter belongs to a single year.

Because strong relationships exist between the time period levels, we should define the attribute relationships accordingly so that each child attribute has a relationship with its parent. Starting with the regular calendar periods of Year-Quarter-Month-Date, we can expand each of the attributes in the attributes pane on the left, and then drag the Year attribute onto the *<new attribute relationship>* marker under the Quarter attribute, and drag the Quarter attribute onto Month. The final level of relationships between Month and Date is already defined by default, so we don't need to create this, but we do need to delete the existing Year and Quarter relationships under the Date attribute because these have been defined in a different way (see Figure 5-7).

The same approach applies to the Fiscal and Manufacturing attributes because they also have strong relationships, so we can repeat the process of relating Fiscal_Year to Fiscal_Quarter, Fiscal_Quarter to Fiscal_Month, and Fiscal_Month to Fiscal_Day. However, every attribute needs to be related in some way to the dimension key, whether directly like Month or indirectly like Year. So, we also need to create a relationship between Fiscal_Day and Date so that all the fiscal attributes also have a relationship with the key.

Modifying the Cube

Now that we have the dimensions looking more or less the way we want them, we can turn to setting up the cube itself. The Cube Structure tab in the cube designer shows the measures and measure groups that have been defined, as well as a diagram that shows the underlying parts of the data source that make up the cube.

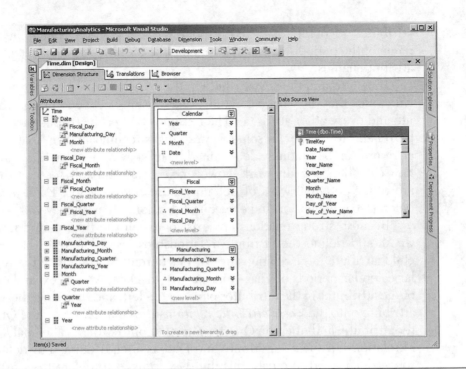

Figure 5-7   Defining Time attribute relationships

Numeric Formats for Measures

One of the areas that you probably noted when browsing the cube was that the numeric formats of the measures didn't really match up with how users would want to see the information. For example, currency measures are shown with many decimal positions. You can change the display format by selecting a measure in the Cube Structure tab and modifying the **FormatString** property. The formats that you can specify are based on the Visual Basic syntax, which basically consists of a set of special named formats such as Percent or Currency, as well as characters that you can use to build user-defined formats.

If you have a lot of measures, changing the formats one at a time is painful, and the standard view of measures doesn't allow you to select more than one measure at a time. A feature can help with this, as shown in Figure 5-8: Select Show Measures In Grid from the Cube menu, and you can then select multiple measures at a time and set all their formats simultaneously.

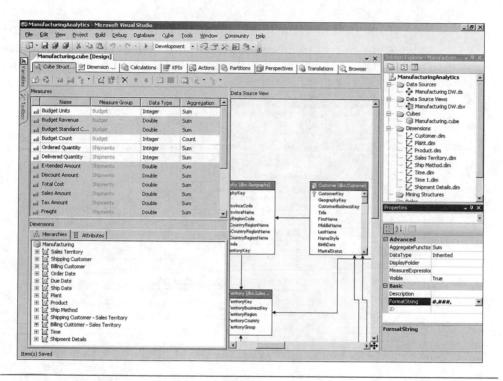

Figure 5-8   Setting numeric formats

Adjusting the Relationships Between the Cube and the Dimensions

When the wizard was creating the cube, it looked at the relationships that you had defined between the fact and dimension tables in the DSV to determine how to add the dimensions to the cube. You can adjust the results using the Dimension Usage tab in the cube designer, which shows the grain of the different measure groups (see Figure 5-9).

We need to modify a few things to get the cube to work the way we want. As you can see, a dimension such as Time or Sales Territory can be used multiple times in a single cube. The names that are shown to the user for these **role-playing dimensions** are based on the column names from the fact table. For example, the names that were created for the Time dimension are Due Date, Ship Date, and Order Date. You can modify these names by clicking the dimension on the left side of the Dimension Usage tab and then changing the Name property.

Usually, the order date is used as the standard way of analyzing a date, so we can name this relationship Date and rename the others to Date Due and Date Shipped so that they are listed together in the users' tools.

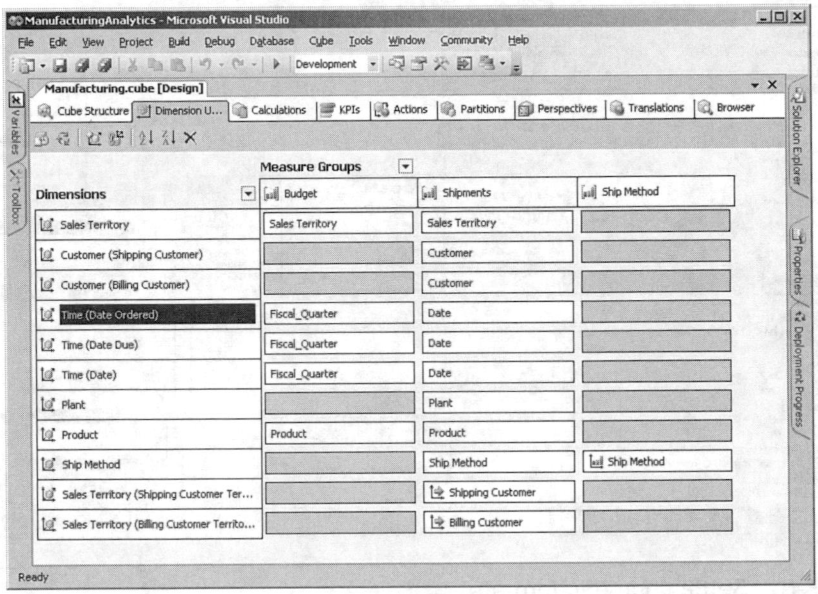

Figure 5-9 Dimension Usage tab

Adding Calculations to the Cube

Many of the key measures that are part of our manufacturing solution are just pulled directly from the fact table, but a lot of the really interesting information that the users need is derived from the basic data. Cubes can contain **calculated measures** that take data from the physical measures and apply complex logic. These calculated measures are computed at query time and do not take up any disk space; and because they are based on the Multidimensional Expressions (MDX) language, you can create sophisticated metrics if necessary.

On-Time Delivery Analysis

One of the major business requirements is to analyze how the company is doing when it comes to delivering shipments on time. We have already added some physical measures such as On Time Count that can help with this, but we need to add more to the cube to really allow the users to make decisions. For example, it's probably more important to be able to see the percentage of shipments that were on time rather than just a count.

To add the calculated measure, switch to the Calculations tab and click the New Calculated Member button (see Figure 5-10). The formula for this measure is simply the number of shipments that were on time, divided by the total number of shipments:

```
[Measures].[On Time Count]/[Measures].[Shipments Count]
```

The major rule that you need to follow when naming calculated measures is that if you include spaces in the name, you have to surround the whole name with square brackets, such as [On Time Percent]. Because the name inside the brackets will be shown in the users' analytical tools, it's a good idea to use spaces and try to make the name as meaningful as possible. This may be counterintuitive for database designers who are used to avoiding spaces in names, but it is important to remember that the names in an Analysis Services cube are shown to users and need to make sense to them.

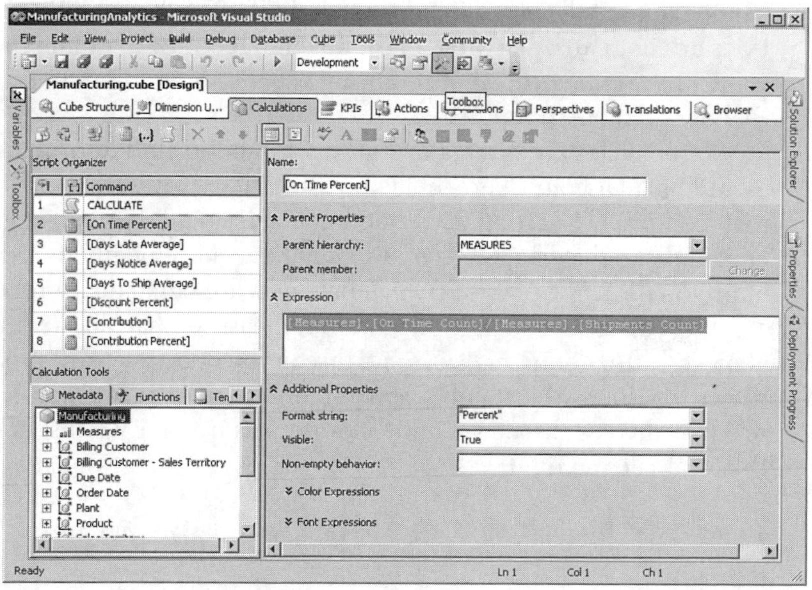

Figure 5-10   Defining calculated measures

If you tried to use the Days Late or similar measures that we discussed in the "Data Model" section in a query, you will probably have realized that they are not useful at the moment because they just give the total number of days late for whatever filters you specify. A much more useful measure is the average number of days late for whatever the user has selected, whether that is, for example, a certain type of product or a date range such as the past three months.

The formula to express the average days late is to divide the total number of days late by the number of shipments in question:

```
[Measures].[Days Late]/[Measures].[Shipments Count]
```

Because the three physical measures (Days Late, Days Notice, and Days To Ship) aren't really useful, we can switch back to the Cube Structure tab and change the Visible property of each of the three measures to False after we have created the equivalent average calculations. This is a common approach for measures that need to be in the cube to support calculations, but should not be shown to users.

Profitability Analysis

We have some helpful measures such as Total Cost and Discount Amount in the cube, but the other business requirement that we need to support more fully is profitability analysis. Although profitability calculations are not particularly complex, it is much better to define them centrally in the cube instead of requiring users to build them in their client tool or add them to reports.

Percentages are often a useful way to understand information, such as adding a Discount Percentage measure that expresses the discount as a percentage of the total sales amount. Users could then select groups of customers to see what kinds of discounts they have been offered, or look at product categories to see which products are being discounted.

We can also add a Contribution measure that shows the profit achieved after deducting costs and discounts. Because it will probably be useful to also see this number as a percentage, we can add another measure that divides the new Contribution measure that we just created by the total sales amount:

```
[Measures].[Contribution]/[Measures].[Sales Amount]
```

Testing Calculations

You can use the Browser tab of the cube to test the calculated measures that you have defined. It's a good idea to try different filters and combinations of dimensions on the rows and columns to make sure that your new measures make sense in all the circumstances that the user will see them. Because adding a calculation is a change to the structure of the cube, you need to deploy the solution again and click the Reconnect button in the cube browser to make the new measures show up.

The first thing you will notice is that your new measures are not grouped under the existing measure groups such as Shipments or Budget, but are at the bottom of the list. Because the users probably don't care which measures are calculations and which are physical measures, you should go back to the Calculations tab and select Calculation Properties from the Cube menu and specify an associated measure group such as Shipments for each of the calculations.

Showing Order and Invoice Details

Several columns on the fact table contain potentially useful information that we cannot define as measures because they have no meaning when they are aggregated. For example, if users are looking at all the shipments for the past year, there is no point in showing them the total or average of all the thousands of Carrier Tracking Numbers or Customer PO Numbers.

This kind of column is often referred to as a degenerate dimension, because you can think of it as a dimension with only a key (like Order Number) and no descriptive attributes. Analysis Services 2005 instead uses the term **fact dimension**, meaning a dimension that is based on a fact table.

QUICK START: Creating the Shipment Details Fact Dimension

We will create a fact dimension based on all the interesting columns from the Shipments fact table that only make sense at the detail level, such as Carrier Tracking Number:

1. Select the Cube Structure tab in the cube designer for the Manufacturing cube.

2. Select Add Cube Dimension from the Cube menu and click the New Dimension button. Skip the first screen of the dimension wizard by clicking Next.

3. The Manufacturing DW data source will be selected by default. Click Next.

4. Select Standard Dimension and click Next.

5. From the Main table list, select the Shipments table. The primary key columns (SalesOrderNumber and SalesOrderLineNumber) are selected as the key columns by default. Change the member name column to SalesOrderNumber and click Next.

6. Click Next to skip over the Related Tables page.

7. Uncheck all the columns except Invoice Number, Invoice Line Number, Revision Number, Carrier Tracking Number, and Customer PO Number. Click the Finish button to skip all the remaining steps.

8. Specify the name Shipment Details and click Finish to create the dimension. Click OK to close the Add Cube Dimension dialog.

Figure 5-11 shows how a user can see the invoice and carrier tracking numbers for a set of shipments by selecting attributes from the Shipment Details dimension that we just created.

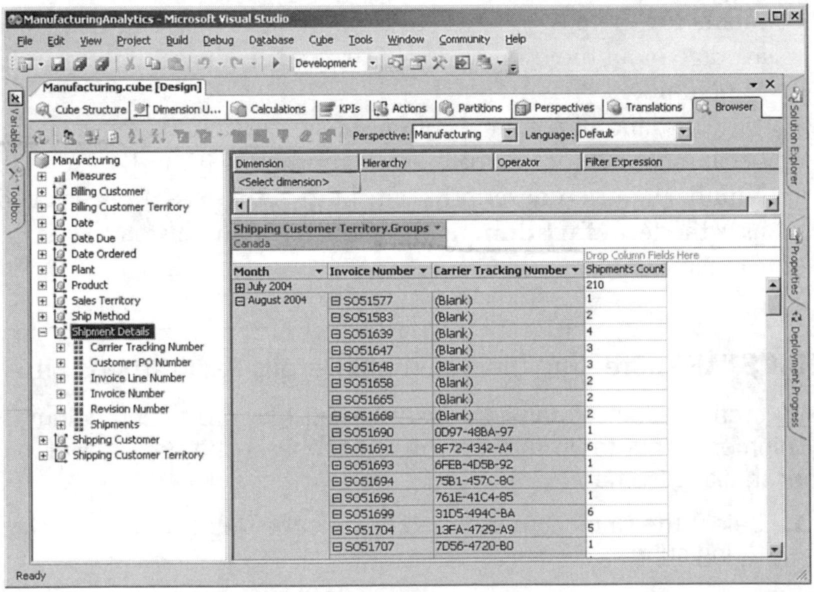

Figure 5-11   Shipment Details dimension

Managing Security for Users

The last step before we can deploy our solution is to figure out which users will need to have access to the database and whether they will need to see all the information or just parts of it. You can develop sophisticated security schemes by adding **roles** to your Analysis Services project, by selecting New Role from the Database menu.

Each role defines which cubes and dimensions users will have access to, and can even restrict the data that they will see (for example, limiting the Sales Territory dimension to show only North American territories for U.S. sales reps). Dimensions or measures with potentially sensitive information can be turned off completely for some groups of users.

After the role has been defined, you can set up the membership by adding Windows groups or specific user accounts to the role. You can test that the role is working the way you intended using the cube browser, by clicking the Change User button on the left of the toolbar and selecting the role.

Managing the Solution

We have so far been using the BI Development Studio to develop the project and deploy it to the server. After the database has been deployed, the emphasis switches from developing a solution to managing the deployed database, and you will be using the same SQL Server Management Studio that you used to manage SQL Server databases.

To connect to an Analysis Services database from SQL Server Management Studio, select Connect Object Explorer from the File menu, choose Analysis Services as the server type, and select the server name before clicking the Connect button.

Deployment

As you have seen while developing the cube in the "Technical Solution" section, you can deploy an Analysis Services database directly from within the BI Development Studio. This proves to be very useful during the development phase; when you need to move the database to a test or production environment, however, a more structured approach is required.

Using the Analysis Services Deployment Wizard

Analysis Services 2005 includes a Deployment Wizard that can either interactively deploy the database to a specified server or create a deployment script that can then be executed on the target server using SQL Server Management Studio. You can access the Deployment Wizard from the Start menu, under the Microsoft SQL Server 2005, Analysis Services folder (see Figure 5-12). The source file that the wizard uses is a file with an .asdatabase extension that is created in your project's bin folder when you build the project in BI Development Studio.

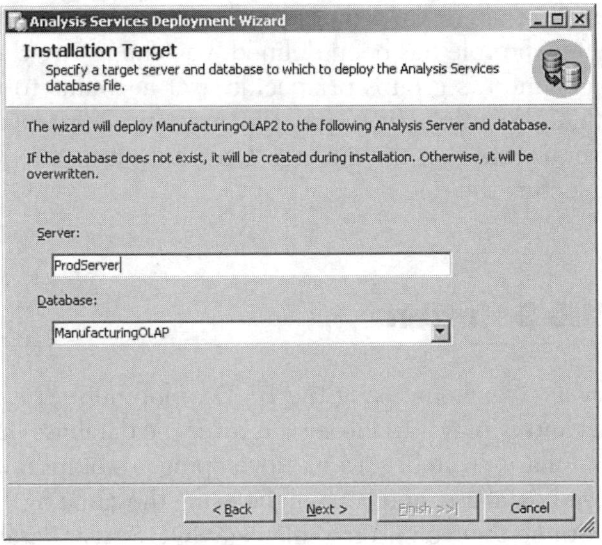

Figure 5-12   Deployment Wizard

The wizard also gives you control over the configuration settings for your Analysis Services database. For example, if you are deploying to a production server that uses a different database from development, you can specify a different data source connection string and impersonation setting for the deployment. You can also choose not to overwrite any settings such as role members or connection strings (in case these have been modified on the target server by the system administrator).

That takes care of getting your new database definitions on to the target server, but what about initially loading the data? The wizard also enables you to specify that objects must be processed after they have been deployed, including an option to use a single transaction for processing objects and roll back all changes if any errors are encountered.

Managing Security for Administrators

Analysis Services server administrators can perform any task on the server including creating or deleting databases and other objects, administering roles and user permissions, and can also read all the information in all the databases on the server. By default, all members of the server's Administrators group are Analysis Services server administrators, and you can also grant additional groups or individual users server administration rights by right-clicking the server in SQL Server Management Studio, selecting Properties, and then adding them to the server role in the Security section.

You can change the default behavior that grants local administrators full Analysis Services administration rights by changing the BuiltInAdminsAreServerAdmins setting to False, but this is not a worthwhile exercise because this setting is stored in the configuration file for Analysis Services, which local administrators would probably have access to anyway. Also, because you can actually have multiple Analysis Services instances on a single server, technically speaking a server administrator is actually an "instance administrator" because the permission is granted for an instance, not necessarily the whole server.

If you have an environment where you want to grant administrative privileges only to specific Analysis Services databases rather than all of them, you can create a role in a relevant database and select the Full Control (Administrator) permission, as shown in Figure 5-13. The groups or specific users who need to administer that database can then be added to the role. Database administrators can perform tasks such as processing the database or adding users to roles.

If you add roles to a database using SQL Server Management Studio, you need to be aware that they will get overwritten if you redeploy the project from BI Development Studio. You must either add the roles to the project in BI Development Studio so that they always exist, or deploy the project using the Deployment Wizard with either the "Deploy roles and **retain** members" or the "Retain roles and members" option selected. If you select "Deploy roles and members" in the wizard, any roles that you manually created using SQL Server Management Studio are removed.

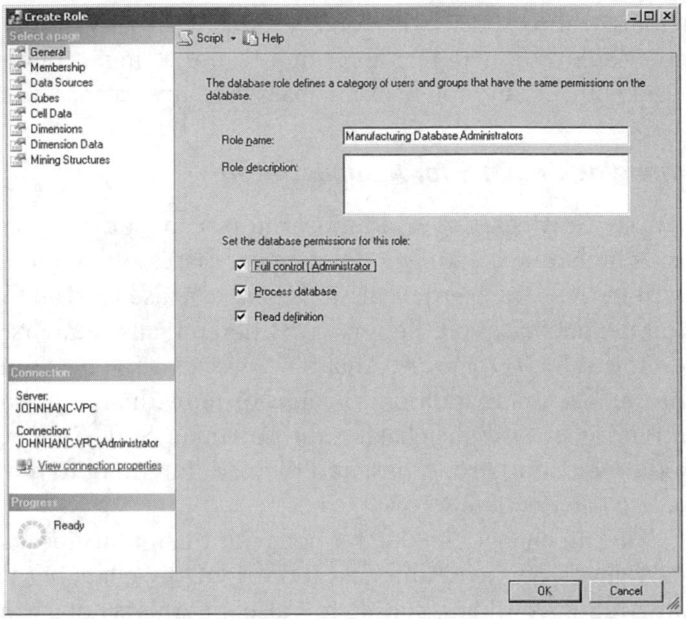

Figure 5-13   Creating a database administration role

Maintenance

Every BI solution that we have ever delivered has required some enhancements, usually soon after deployment. The reason for this is intrinsic to the way people use BI applications, in that every time you show them some interesting information, they immediately come up with a specific aspect that they would like more detail on.

Using Source Code Control

You can use the BI Development Studio to make changes to the project files and redeploy them to production using the method described in the "Deployment" section, but it is a great idea to start using a source code control system for these files. In addition to making it easier to work in a team environment, source control enables you to keep track of the versions of the solution that you have created.

Changes to the Underlying Data Sources

At some point, you are probably also going to have to r
the underlying source database, such as adding new colu...... .. ..
and dimension tables. Because we have recommended that you build
the Analysis Services databases from views rather than directly on the
tables, this will probably provide you with some protection because you
can make sure that the same schema is presented if required.

However, if you want to include these new database objects in your
Analysis Services project, you must update the database views and then
open the relevant DSV in BI Development Studio and choose Refresh
from the Data Source View menu. The Refresh feature has a nice user
interface that shows you what (if anything) has been changed in the
source objects, and then fixes up the DSV to match.

One important caveat applies, however: Any objects based on the
changed database object will not automatically be fixed, and you need to
manually address these. For example, if you changed the name for a
database column, the corresponding attribute will still have the old column name and must be updated manually.

Operations

The major operations tasks that you need to perform for Analysis Services are processing the databases and making backups.

Processing the Cube

As you have seen when using the BI Development Studio to create a
cube, after Analysis Services objects have been deployed to a server, they
need to be processed before users can access them. This kind of processing is known as **full processing**, and it will usually take some time in
production systems because all the data for dimensions and facts is read
from the source systems and then used to create the Analysis Services
databases.

Full processing must be performed whenever you have changed the
database definition in certain ways, such as adding an attribute hierarchy. In most cases, however, you only really need to load the new data for
the period, such as changes to the dimension records or additional fact
rows. For dimensions, you can select the Process Update option to read
all the dimension records and create any new members, or update existing ones when they have changed.

Measure groups are a bit more complex because you usually only want to add the new records from the fact table, so you need to supply a way to enable Analysis Services to identify those records. The Process Incremental setting shown in Figure 5-14 enables you to either select a separate table that contains the new records you want to load or to specify an SQL query that only returns the relevant records.

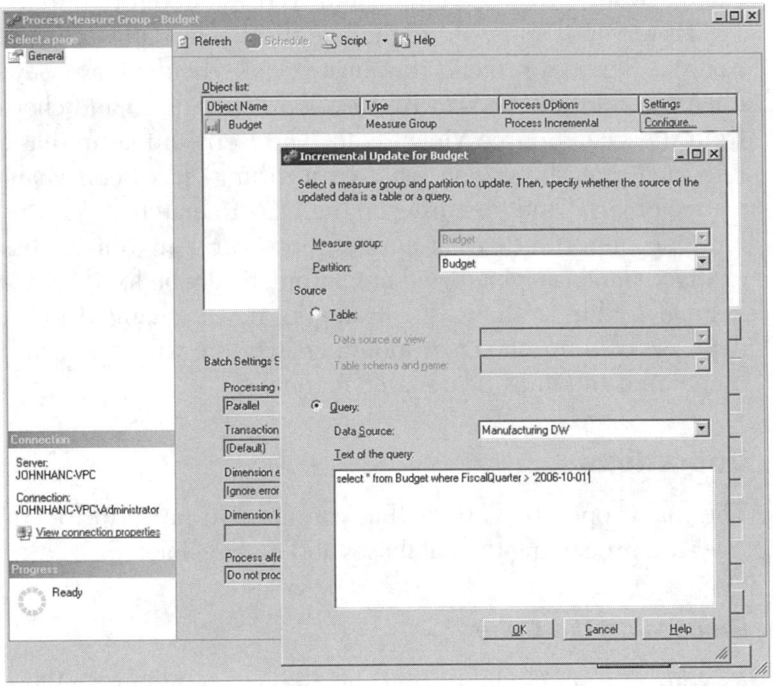

Figure 5-14   Incremental processing options

Because the Analysis Services processing usually needs to be synchronized with the ETL routines that load the data warehouse, a common approach is to add an Analysis Services Processing Task into the Integration Services packages for the load process.

Backing Up the Analysis Services Database

If a disaster happens to your Analysis Services database, one way of recovering is to redeploy from the original project source code and then reprocess the database. So, a key part of your backup strategy is to always have an up-to-date backup of the solution files or the source control repository. However, reprocessing can be very time-consuming, so the usual approach is to make a backup of the Analysis Services database, too.

You can back up the database from SQL Server Management Studio by right-clicking the database and choosing Back Up. Figure 5-15 shows the options that you can specify. The backup process creates a single .abf file containing the metadata and data for your database, and this can optionally be compressed.

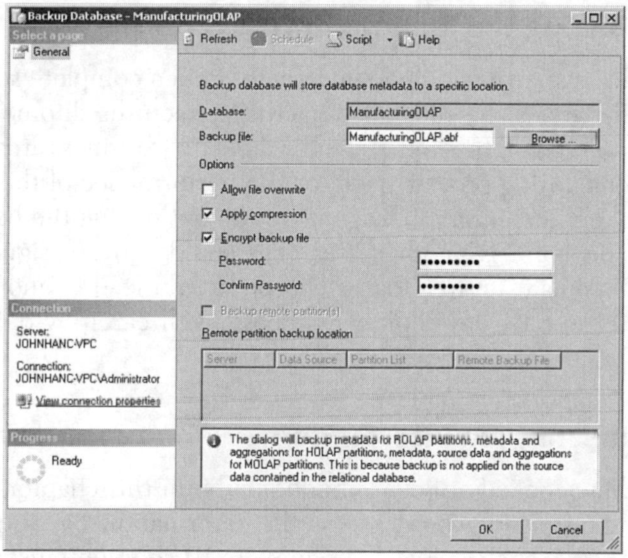

Figure 5-15   Backup Analysis Services database

Because these databases often contain sensitive information, you can also specify a password that is used to encrypt the file. It is worth being careful with this password, however, because you will need it to restore the backup if necessary and the file cannot be decrypted if you lose the password.

If you need to recover the database, you can restore the backup by right-clicking the Databases folder in SQL Server Management Studio and selecting Restore.

Next Steps

The previous three chapters showed how to build the foundation of a complete BI solution, including a data warehouse, ETL process, and Analysis Services database. These are really the basic building blocks that we use as the basis for the rest of this book, which covers the other areas that you need to understand to start building valuable BI solutions. From now on, each chapter covers a specific solution for a single customer from end to end to demonstrate one specific aspect of BI in detail.

Extending the Manufacturing Solution

We have shown you in detail how to build a complete solution to a very small part of the total manufacturing picture: shipments. Real-world solutions could be extended into whole new business areas to analyze the manufacturing process itself, or the performance of the manufacturer's suppliers. Inventory management and optimizing the balances of products on hand is another area that could provide significant business value. Whatever area that is chosen should lead to another small iteration of our BI development process, with carefully defined objectives leading to a new release.

Accessing the Information

We have looked at how to build a cube in this chapter, but we glossed over how users would access the information by simply referring to client tools such as Excel. A complete BI solution must supply information to users in whatever ways are most suitable for them, including Excel or other "slice-and-dice" client tools, but also other mechanisms such as web-based reporting or dashboards that show summary information and support drilldown for more details. Chapter 9, "Scorecards," describes the approach to provide complete access to the information in your databases.

Using BI Development Studio in Online Mode

In this chapter, we used BI Development Studio in **project mode**, meaning that we worked on a set of project files that were stored on the developer's workstation, and then we selected Deploy to update the definitions on the corresponding Analysis Services database on the server.

BI Development Studio can also be used in **online mode**, by connecting directly to a live Analysis Services database.

You can access a database in online mode by selecting File, Open, Analysis Services Database, and then specifying the server and database name. Any changes that you make are immediately saved to the database. Be cautious not to mix project mode and online mode, however, because you could easily overwrite any changes you made in online mode by deploying a project.

Summary

In this chapter, we built an Analysis Services database using the data warehouse as the source. The key goals were to support flexible analysis of the profitability of various customer groups and products, and to support the company's On-Time Delivery improvement initiative. The Analysis Services database can be directly accessed by the users using tools such as Excel, reducing some of the pressure on IT to deliver standard reports.

We extended the fact table views in the data warehouse to provide the information in the best format for Analysis Services, such as transforming logic about which shipments were on time into an additive OnTime column with a 0 or 1 value. We also used the various dates in the fact table to calculate quantities such as the number of days a shipment is late.

In the Analysis Services project in BI Development Studio, we created a data source view and defined all the relationships between the fact and dimension tables, and then used the Cube Wizard to produce a first pass at the cube and dimension design. For the Time dimension attributes such as Year and Quarter, we used the unique columns that we defined in the dimension table rather than the descriptions, because this is more efficient and avoids problems with duplicate members in hierarchies.

We changed some of the attributes to use descriptive names such as Plant Name rather than the surrogate key and defined some hierarchies. One of the most important steps in the design process was to set up the attribute relationships for every dimension, because the relationships between attributes can have a big impact on the performance of the cube. We also added some calculations to the cube, such as On-Time Percent, and picked suitable formats for all the measures.

We used the Analysis Services Deployment Wizard to create a script that was executed on the production server to create and process the database. The operations team is now also managing the processing of the Analysis Services database, and the backups (which include both the metadata definitions and the data that has been loaded).

CHAPTER 6

Reporting

The Microsoft Business Intelligence (BI) strategy is based on the idea that everyone in an organization can benefit from information. Although data warehouses and BI in general are a great way to serve the needs of analysts, an opportunity exists to get even more value by including all the users. Web-based reporting allows you to present information in a useful way without requiring extensive training or complex client software. Reports can be published in Web portals, sent to users via e-mail, or included in applications and dashboards to allow all users to benefit from the information in a data warehouse.

In this chapter, we cover Reporting Services, which is a server-based platform for designing and delivering reports. We look at some of the kinds of business benefits that can be realized by getting specific information to users at the right time, in the format they need.

Business Problem

Our customer for this chapter is a mid-sized professional services company, with several hundred consultants who work on projects at various large corporate clients. Most of the work they do is on a time and materials basis, with every consultant keeping careful track of the hours he or she has spent working on a project and submitting detailed weekly timesheets.

Problem Statement

The customer's timesheet system was developed in-house several years ago, and the primary issue with the system is that it has no flexible reporting features. To work around this problem, they have developed some ad-hoc solutions to connect to the application's database and query the information. The business operations team is using several complex Excel spreadsheets that run queries against the database and supplements this information with manually captured information such as forecasts. Some of the project managers have also built queries to manage the hours that consultants are billing against their largest projects.

This has led to the following problems:

- Lack of project information is leading to customer dissatisfaction. Because project managers don't have a clear indication of how many hours consultants are billing until the invoice is ready to submit to the client, in many cases projects have been over budget because the project has not been closely managed.

- With no standardized key business metrics and consistent categories, different teams are unable to agree on the current state. (Every meeting starts with the question "Where did you get that number from?.")

- The custom-built solutions need a lot of manual care and feeding especially around month ends, and this is mostly a burden on administrative staff that should be focusing on things such as sending out the bills on time.

Solution Overview

We will consolidate the data from the timesheet system and other sources into a new SQL Server data warehouse, and use Reporting Services to deliver predesigned reports. Users can access the reports from the intranet either on-demand using a Web browser or subscribe to the reports so that relevant reports are e-mailed to them automatically when the data is ready.

Business Requirements

The high-level business requirements to support the objectives are as follows:

■ **Managing projects**

Each project that this company undertakes has a budget that is agreed up front with the customer. Project managers need up-to-date weekly reports so that they can ensure that the project is delivered within budget, which will increase customer satisfaction and lead to the most profitable type of work, namely contract extensions and repeat business. Also, project managers must ensure that they are on target to hit the planned budget by the end of the project, to ensure that the services business meets its forecasted revenue.

■ **Managing utilization**

All consultants have target utilization levels that they must meet for the business to succeed. Consultants and their managers need to see up-to-date information on their utilization levels so that they can take action early enough to hit their goals.

■ **Managing the business**

The business operations team needs access to strategic business measures so that they can report monthly information to management. They urgently require information on billed revenue versus planned revenue, utilization, average billing rates (ABR), sales pipeline, and backlog, with a need for more measures in following phases of the project.

High-Level Architecture

The solution has two main components: the data warehouse database and the reporting server to publish reports. We will be loading the data from the timesheet system on a periodic basis using Integration Services, and the data warehouse will also include information from other sources such as forecasting spreadsheets. The reporting server will run Reporting Services, which is essentially an ASP.NET application and web service.

Unlike older client/server reporting environments that require a client application to be installed on every machine, Reporting Services is a server-based reporting solution, as shown in Figure 6-1. One way to understand this approach is by comparison with ordinary Web development. For regular Web applications, HTML and ASP files are created using a designer and then published to a Web server, which then executes any server instructions in the files and serves up the resulting information to client machines' Web browsers. Similarly for Reporting Services, reports are designed using a graphical designer such as the report designer in BI Development Studio, and then published to the reporting server. When a request for a report is received by Reporting Services, the reporting server then retrieves any data required and renders the results for display on the client.

Users can access reports using a Web browser and can also export reports into other Office applications such as Excel to work with the numbers, or export to printable formats such as PDF. Although Reporting Services is designed so that reports can be integrated into other applications such as intranet portals (see the sidebar "Integrating Reports into Other Web Sites or Applications"), we will be using the Report Manager Web-based application that ships with SQL Server. It provides all the features we need, such as browsing a list of reports and securing reports for specific audiences.

Building standardized reports against a properly architected data warehouse has many advantages and is usually the best solution for the long-term information requirements of a client. The solution can be extended in future iterations to include information from more data sources in the data warehouse or to provide information in more flexible ways for users or applications that require it.

Typically for this kind of solution, we would suggest building an Analysis Services database and then writing reports against the cubes as described in Chapter 9, "Scorecards." However, because this customer doesn't have any experience with building or managing Analysis Services databases, we focus on providing some high business-value reports against the relational data warehouse and leave the more flexible Analysis Services approach for a follow-up phase.

Alternative Solution: Reporting against the OLTP Timesheet System's Database

One option that is often popular with clients is to build reports directly against the existing application database, under the mistaken assumption that by skipping the step of building the data warehouse they could drastically reduce the cost for the project. Unfortunately, it's never that simple— one issue is that the time to develop even the initial set of reports would be increased quite considerably because the report developer would need to

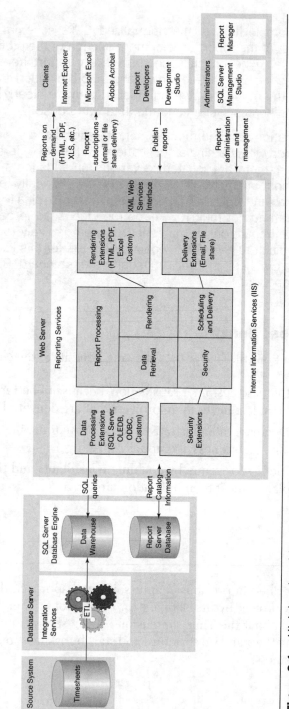

Figure 6-1   High-level architecture

deal with the complexities of the normalized OLTP schema, which would increase the cost of the report development section of the project. This cost increase would also be ongoing, because every report developed in the future would face the same issue. Any changes to the underlying source system may affect the reports rather than just affecting a clearly defined interface between the source system and the data warehouse.

Also, the information required to make sensible decisions about a business is rarely contained within a single application; in this case, forecasting numbers and sales targets are located in various spreadsheets and can't be included. And most important of all, report queries typically reference large amounts of data, and because OLTP databases are typically optimized for single-row writes and not multi-row reads (as discussed in early chapters), the performance impact on the timesheet system is likely to be too great. (Although it's difficult to give good impact estimates for this kind of question when pressed, the best answer is usually the standard BI consultant's response: "It depends.")

Business Benefits

The solution will deliver the following benefits to the client:

- Increase customer satisfaction, because of better project management leading to more projects that are delivered within budget
- Decrease administrative costs by automating time-consuming manual business operations reporting
- Increase revenue by enabling consultants and their managers to plan to meet their utilization targets

Data Model

As described in previous chapters, we will approach the data modeling for this project by first looking for dimensions. There is nothing really unusual about the Time dimension for the services business, so we will be using the standard structure and start by asking some questions about the business.

Who Does the Work?

The obvious place to start for this model is with the people doing the work—consultants and project managers. In the professional services business, the reality is a little more complex (different types of consultants, engagement managers as well as project managers, people managers, sales executives, administrative staff), but these are just extensions to the simpler model we are looking at.

We could take the approach of having separate Project Manager and Consultant dimensions, but because people can change positions over time, it seems more natural to model this as an Employee dimension, with each employee having a position such as consultant. On a related note, because consultants can change to project managers over time, we need to be careful here that we don't lose the capability to analyze history by overwriting an employee's position—this is a complex topic usually handed by a technique called slowly changing dimensions (SCDs), which is so common that we have written a whole chapter on it—see Chapter 8, "Managing Changing Data."

The other attributes for the Employee dimension are the usual ones such as Name (see Figure 6-2), but we also want to include the employee's network user ID so that report content can be tailored to the individual user (described in "Giving Users What They Want" in the "Technical Solution" section). We can also include their e-mail address so that reports can be e-mailed to them. The other interesting aspect is the Reports To relationship—employees have managers who are also employees. This is an example of a self-referencing dimension (called a Parent/Child dimension in Analysis Services).

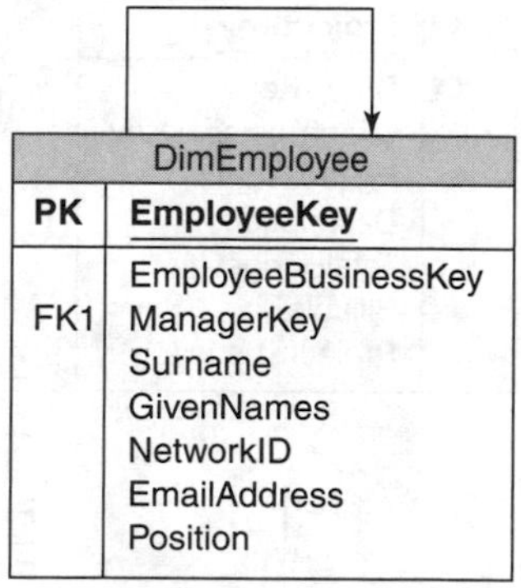

DimEmployee	
PK	**EmployeeKey**
	EmployeeBusinessKey
FK1	ManagerKey
	Surname
	GivenNames
	NetworkID
	EmailAddress
	Position

Figure 6-2   Employee dimension

TIP:
Avoid Object-Oriented Designs in a Data Warehouse
Those of us with a strong object-oriented design (OOD) background may be tempted to model the Employee structure using an inheritance-like structure rather than a star or snowflake design; that is, with an Employee base table and two specialized Project Manager and Consultant tables.
Although there are occasions when this type of design is appropriate (usually in OLTP systems where it matches up well with the application code), this approach is usually not appropriate for a DW because of the complex ETL that results, as well as the performance impact.

What Are They Working On?

We know that there is ultimately a client paying the bills, so this is an obvious candidate dimension, but because there may be multiple projects for a client each with its own attributes such as start dates, project manager, and budget, we will also include a separate Project dimension, as shown in Figure 6-3. We will also keep a list of the major Project Tasks, which is useful for project analysis to understand which areas of a project are going over budget.

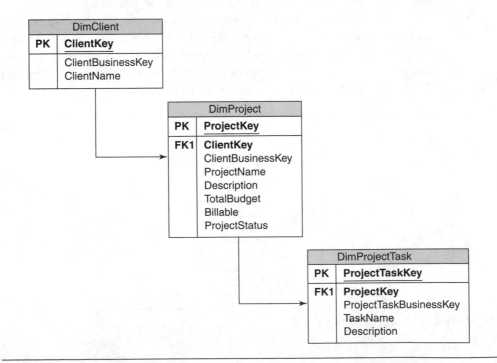

Figure 6-3   Project dimension

One area of complexity is billing rates. Consultants will have different standard billing rates depending on their position, and may even be allocated to projects at different positions than their employee record suggests (such as assigning a senior consultant to a project at a lower consultant-level rate). The current rate information needs to be stored in the timesheet system, but it's debatable whether this information makes it into the data warehouse in that format. What we are really interested in is how much money we actually charged the customer for the work and the average billing rates over time, not what the current standard rates are. One exception to this is when services businesses are interested in finding out which employees are not billing at their standard rates—this could be modeled by either adding a standard hourly and overtime rate to the Employee table based on their position, or by creating a separate Resource table that links a specific employee to a specific project along with the agreed rates.

How Do We Measure What Work They Are Doing?

The professional services business is built on a simple principle—hours billed means money earned. The central fact table to measure the business' performance has a record with the hours billed and the revenue earned for every piece of work that a consultant performs on a project, with a key of Time, Employee, and Project Task, as shown in Figure 6-4.

FactWorkCompleted	
PK	TimeKey
PK	EmployeeKey
PK	ProjectTaskKey
	StandardHours
	OvertimeHours
	NonBillableHours
	StandardRevenue
	OvertimeRevenue
	TotalRevenue
	LostRevenue

Figure 6-4   Work completed fact table

Because hours can be translated directly to revenue by applying the appropriate rate, OLTP systems would usually only store the hours and calculate the revenue on demand; in a data warehouse, however, this would miss the opportunity to have well-performing fully additive measures that are stored directly in the database. We can also extend the columns to enable interesting analysis on all kinds of measures, such as overtime revenue versus standard revenue, or billable hours versus non-billable (such as administrative time that consultants spend on tasks like filling in timesheets).

The business requirements for this solution make frequent reference to utilization, which shows how much billable time an employee has spent as a percentage of the total time available for the month. In practice, the "available time" is often not as simple as multiplying the working days for the month by eight hours—what about vacation, for example? If the employee's vacation is not included in the total available time for the year, a consultant can achieve 100 percent utilization for the month just by taking a month off. On the other hand, if vacation is included, an incentive exists for employees to manage their vacation time so that they don't lower their utilization for an important period such as the last month before year-end. A simple approach may be to use 52 standard 40-hour weeks for all the available time and adjust the consultants' percentage utilization targets to match.

Also, utilization is a percentage, so we won't store this in the fact table because it is not additive. Because this business only looks at utilization at a month level, the total hours available are stored on each Month record, and utilization can be computed easily by summing the billable hours from the fact table and dividing by the total for the selected periods.

How Much Work Will They Be Doing in the Future?

Although the Work Completed fact table is crucial for understanding the business, trying to manage using only measures of the past is like trying to navigate using your rear-view mirror: At some point, forward-looking measures will be required. In the services business, these measures are typically called something like delivery backlog and sales pipeline.

The delivery backlog is the work that has been sold but that hasn't been delivered yet, and gives us measures of how busy our consultants will be in the near future, as well as how much money we will be making. The sales pipeline is information on potential future sales. Because we can't be sure that these sales will actually get signed (and become part of the backlog), there is a probability percentage assigned to each possible sale, which is increased according to business rules as the sales process progresses and is used to adjust the expected revenue measure.

Both of the preceding are "moving targets" in the sense that the business will need to see how the numbers progress over time. ("What was our sales pipeline at the end of this month compared with the same period last year?") The fact tables shown in Figure 6-5 are both snapshots, where we load all the records at the end of a period, which represents the current view. We can see historical views by selecting prior periods, but because these are snapshots, we cannot add the numbers across time periods. (For example, there is no sense in looking at the total of sales pipeline for January, February, and March because we will triple-count any potential sale that was in all three periods.) This is a clear example of a fact table with "semi-additive" measures, which add up across any dimension except Time in this case.

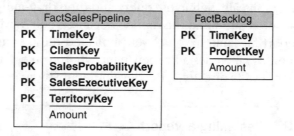

Figure 6-5   Backlog and Sales Pipeline fact tables

Now that we know what kind of information we are using, we can move on to building the solution.

Technical Solution

We are focusing on developing the reporting piece for this solution, so we have already implemented the data model and loaded the data warehouse database (ProfessionalServicesDB) following the guidelines and best practices we presented in previous chapters (if only it was that easy in the real world!).

Getting Started with Reporting Services

We start by using the BI Development Studio to create a new Report Project. The project will be created in a folder on your development machine and will contain a set of Report Definition Language (RDL) files, which will eventually be published to the reporting server.

The BI Development Studio includes a Report Wizard to walk you through the steps for defining a report, which consist of the following:

1. Selecting a data source.
2. Defining the query that will be executed.
3. Selecting the layout, fields, and groups.
4. Choosing a style for the report.

The resulting RDL report design files are based on XML and are usually edited using the graphical report designer. This designer enables you to graphically define the query and then drag-and-drop fields onto a design surface to build the report. Because you are working locally with the report files and have not yet published them to a report server, the designer also includes a Preview pane where you can run the report and view the results directly in the development studio.

QUICK START: Designing a Report

Now that you have some background on the BI Development Studio, we can walk through the steps to develop the first report for the customer's solution, which is a Project List. We will be using the Report Project Wizard, which walks you through the steps to create a project, data source, and a single simple report:

1. Open the Business Intelligence Development Studio.

2. Select New Project from the File menu, and choose Report Server Project Wizard from the Business Intelligence Projects subfolder.

3. Name the project ProfServicesReports and click OK. Click Next to skip the first page.

4. On the Select the Data Source page, click the Edit button to specify the connection information.

5. Type the name of your database server (or localhost if you are working on a single machine), select Use Windows Authentication, and select the ProfessionalServicesDW database from the list of database names. Then click OK.

6. Check the "Make this a shared data source" check box, and then click Next.

7. For the Query string on the Design the Query page, type SELECT * FROM Project. Click Next.

8. On the Select the Report Type page, choose Tabular and then click Next.

9. Select all the fields on the Design the Table page and click the Details button to add them to the report. Click Next.

10. Select Slate on the Choose the Table Style page and click Next.

11. The Choose the Deployment Location page allows you to specify the location of your Reporting Services server where the reports will eventually be published. If you are working on a single machine, you can leave the default settings; otherwise, you need to modify the report server URL. For example, if your server is named MyServer, type http://MyServer/ReportServer. Click Next.

12. On the final page, type Project List as the name of the report and click Finish (see Figure 6-6).

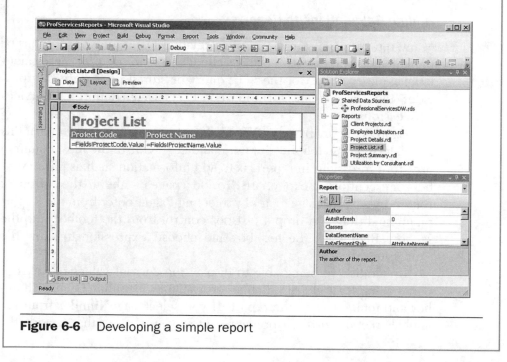

Figure 6-6   Developing a simple report

The wizard creates the report project files, including the shared data source and Project List report, and opens the report in the report designer. You can adjust the design of the report on the Layout tab, modify the query on the Data tab, or use the Preview tab to see the report with data.

TIP:

Use Shared Data Sources

Every report needs a **data source** that defines the database connection information, including the name of the database server and the credentials that will be used to connect. Although you can define this information separately for each report, a much better option is to use a shared data source. Doing so enables you to define the database connections to be used for the entire project, which will be referenced by the individual reports. The advantage of this approach is that you can change the connection information for all the reports in a single location, which proves useful, for example, when you move from development to production servers.

Adding Calculations to Reports

Many reports need some form of calculation logic, such as subtotals or percentages. You have two choices about where to perform these calculations: either as part of the SQL query or stored procedure that provides the source data for the report or using Reporting Services **expressions**.

Expressions are based on VB.NET syntax, so some knowledge of this language is always helpful, but not mandatory. One of the most common uses for expressions in reports is to add information such as page numbers or execution time to reports. To add a page number to the bottom of report, turn on the page footer by selecting Page Footer from the Report menu, and drag and drop a text box control from the toolbox into the section. Right-click the text box and choose Expression to show the expression editor.

In addition to being able to display the current values of fields or parameters, some global variables are available, including the page number and total pages in the report. If you select PageNumber from the Globals section in the expression editor, you will see that it adds the expression =Globals!PageNumber. You could also use string concatenation and multiple variables in an expression. For example, to display "Page 3 of 10" at the bottom of the report, use the following expression:

```
="Page " + Globals!PageNumber.ToString() + " of " +
Globals!TotalPages.ToString()
```

Notice that because we are concatenating strings and numbers, we had to convert the page numbers to strings using the ToString() syntax.

Deploying Reports to the Server

When you have finished developing the report in this section, you can publish the project by selecting Deploy Solution from the Build menu. The report will be available to users when we have configured the security in a later section.

When you deploy a solution from Visual Studio, the reports and data sources are published to the server that you initially specified in the Report Project Wizard. You can change this server using the project properties dialog (select Properties from the Project menu), which allows you to specify the URL for your report server and also the name of the folder to publish the files into. Because you may be deploying to a server that has different source databases than your development environment, you can also choose not to overwrite any data sources that have already been set up on the server by making sure the OverwriteData-Sources setting is false.

Accessing Reports

As mentioned in the "High-Level Architecture" section, end users will be using the **Report Manager** Web-based tool to access reports. Now that we have published the reports, it would be a good idea to get familiar with this tool.

To use Report Manager, open a Web browser and navigate to http://MyServer/Reports, where MyServer is the name of your report server. Reports on the server are grouped into folders, such as a ProfServicesReports folder for the project that you just deployed. Click this folder to view the list of reports and data sources. To run a report, click the link and it will be executed and displayed in the browser, as shown in Figure 6-7.

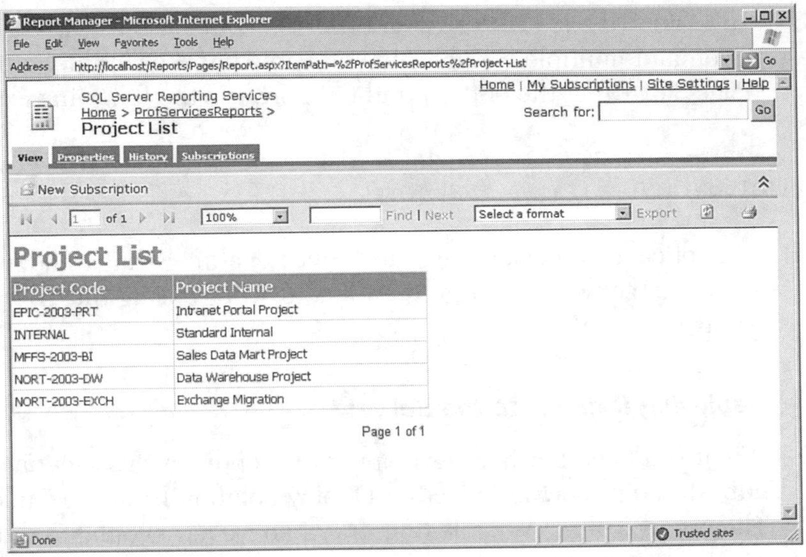

Figure 6-7   Viewing a report in Report Manager

The report displays in HTML format initially, but users can select another format and click Export to view the report in Excel, Acrobat (PDF), CSV (comma-delimited), or even XML. Users can also print the report using the Print button on the toolbar, which uses an ActiveX control downloaded to the computer when the user first selects this option. All printing happens on the client machine itself because there is no facility to print directly from the server.

Integrating Reports into Other Web Sites or Applications

The Web-based Report Manager installed with Reporting Services provides all the features that our report users will need, such as providing a list of reports and viewing reports in a Web browser or other formats such as Excel. However, many companies already have an intranet portal that they use to publish information to their user community, or a rich-client desktop application that is widely used. The good news is that Reporting Services reports can easily be integrated into these existing systems.

Each report that is published to a server has a unique URL that can be used to access the report, such as http://MyServer/ReportServer?/ Sample+Reports/Products+Report. You can use this URL to add a hyperlink to your Web site that opens up the report and can also append other settings to this URL to allow you to control properties including the format (such as HTML or PDF) that is initially displayed or even pass report parameter values.

If you would like to actually embed reports into your Web pages rather than opening a separate window, you can use a simple technique such as using an IFRAME tag in your HTML that points to the preceding URL, or use the ReportViewer Web control in Visual Studio 2005. If you have deployed Microsoft SharePoint Portal Server or Windows SharePoint Services (WSS), you can take advantage of the Reporting Services Web parts to add reports to your portal or team sites, as described in Chapter 9.

Finally, to integrate reports into rich-client Windows applications, you can either use the extensive XML Web services API for Reporting Services or use the ReportViewer control in Visual Studio 2005 to display reports.

Giving Users What They Want

Now that we have completed a simple report and seen how the user will ultimately access the reports, we can move on to developing some of the more complex reports for the solution. The report that we have looked at so far has just presented a list of information to the user, but most reports are usually targeted to the individual user's needs.

The most common approach to handling this is to add **parameters** to the report. When users run the report, they are prompted to specify some values for the parameters, which are then used to limit the data that is displayed.

QUICK START: Adding Parameters to a Report

Project managers who will use our solution need a report that shows a summary of all the projects they are responsible for, so we will build a new parameterized Project Summary report. The report will be based on an SQL query that includes a parameter, @PMKey. We will then add an additional data set to the report that lists all the project managers so that we can present a list to the user:

1. Open the BI Development Studio, and then open the ProfServices-Reports project that you created in the previous Quick Start.

2. Right-click the Reports folder in the Solution Explorer on the right side and select Add New Report.

3. Follow through the wizard as before, but for the query specify
    ```
    SELECT * FROM ProjectSummary WHERE ProjectManagerKey =
    @PMKey.
    ```

4. Name the report Project Summary and click Finish.

5. If you preview the report now, you will notice that you are prompted to enter a numeric value for PMKey. Enter a value such as 9 to view the data.

6. To present a list of project managers instead of requiring the user to type a value, we need to specify a new query for a list of project managers. Select the Data tab and choose <New Dataset> from the Dataset list.

7. Name the query ProjectManagersList, and for the query specify `SELECT * FROM DimEmployee`. Click OK. Run the query using the ! button to see the results.

8. On the Report menu, select Report Parameters.

9. Change the prompt from PMKey to Project Manager, as shown in Figure 6-8.

10. Under Available values, select From query, and then select the Project Managers dataset from the list.

11. For the Value field, select EmployeeKey—this will be used to supply a numeric value to the @PMKey SQL parameter.

12. For the Label field, select FullName—this will be used to build the list for the user. Click OK, and then preview the report to see the results.

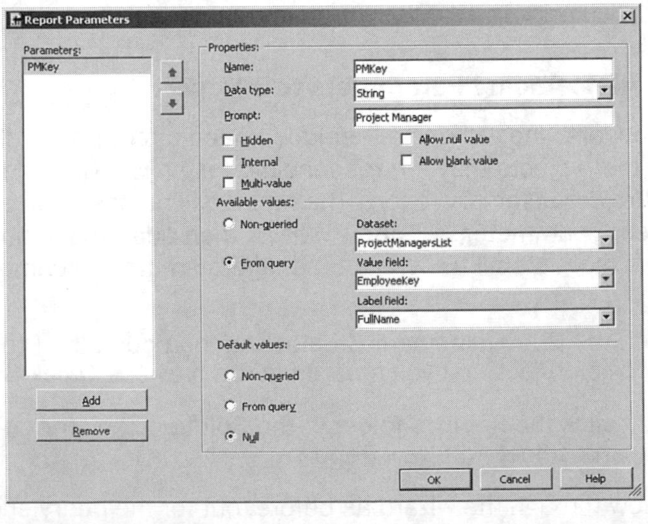

Figure 6-8   Specifying report parameters

Using the User's Identity

Another approach to tailoring report content is to use the user's network ID to retrieve data specific to the user. For example, the Project Summary report could retrieve the network ID of the user who is running the report using the User!UserID expression as the default value of a parameter, and then display the relevant information. For this to work correctly, you need to have a column in the Employee table that maps an employee's record in the database to the employee's network ID, such as MYDOMAIN/JSMITH, where MYDOMAIN is the name of your domain.

Presenting Information

With the huge amount of information available in most companies today, most reporting solutions need to include ways of summarizing information and allowing the user to learn more information as required. The reports in our Professional Services solution achieve this by presenting summarized information and using other report formats or providing drilldown to show more detailed information.

Adding Groups and Subtotals

One of the most common ways of presenting summary information is to add **groups** and subtotals to a report, as shown in Figure 6-9. Detailed report data can be grouped by fields in the report, such as client name or month, or by more complex expressions that you define. For calculating subtotals, Reporting Services expressions can include functions such as Sum, Avg, Min, or Max, which can be used with numeric fields and added to the grouped row. You can also include more complex calculations such as running totals or row numbers using the RunningValue and RowNumber functions.

For example, because our solution includes some clients with many projects, we will design a Client Projects report that shows a list of projects by client, along with a subtotal of the current project budgets. The report expression to calculate the sum of projects for a client would be =Sum(Fields!TotalBudget.Value).

Groups are really easy to achieve in Reporting Services: If you are using the wizard to create a report, you can specify that the Client Name field is a separate Group rather than in the Details with everything else.

If you miss this step in the Report Wizard, you can create a group within a table by selecting the Detail row in a report table, right-clicking and choosing Insert Group. You can then drop the columns that you want into the new group header—the designer is smart enough to specify a sum expression if you drop numeric fields such as the project budget into a Group section.

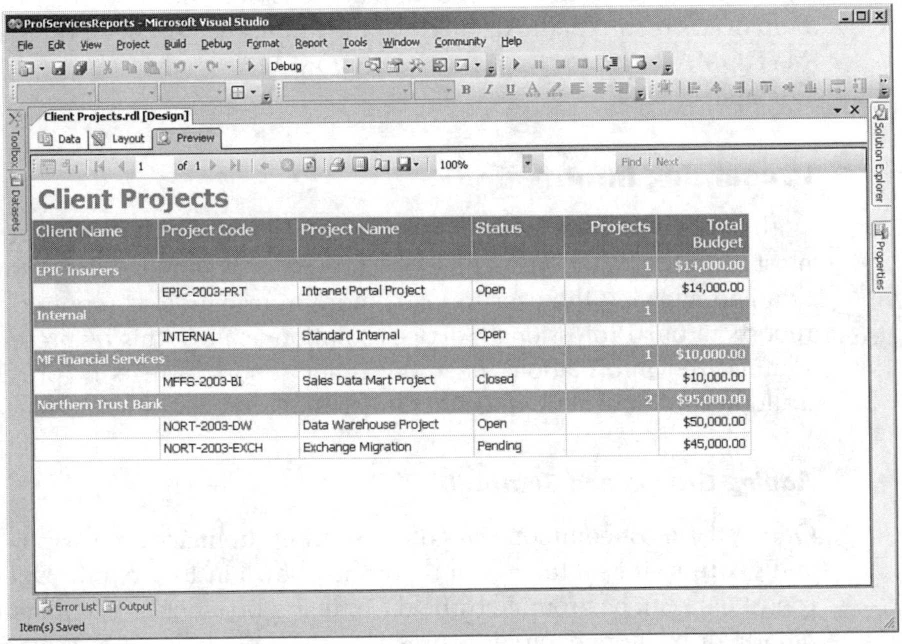

Figure 6-9 Groups and subtotals

Using Different Types of Reports

The reports that we have looked at so far have all been based on table layouts, each with a fixed set of columns. Many of the reports in our solution are time based and show performance over time, so it would be useful to be able to show one or more columns for each month in a report. Reporting Services supports this kind of reporting using a report item called a **Matrix**, which can include column groups as well as just row groups.

We can use a Matrix report to build the Employee Utilization report that shows utilization percentages over the months of a fiscal year, as shown in Figure 6-10. Managers can use this to track the performance of the consultants that report to them. Matrix reports can be created either by selecting the Matrix report type in the Report Wizard or by opening a report and dragging a Matrix on to the report, and then dropping appropriate fields into the Rows, Columns, and Data areas.

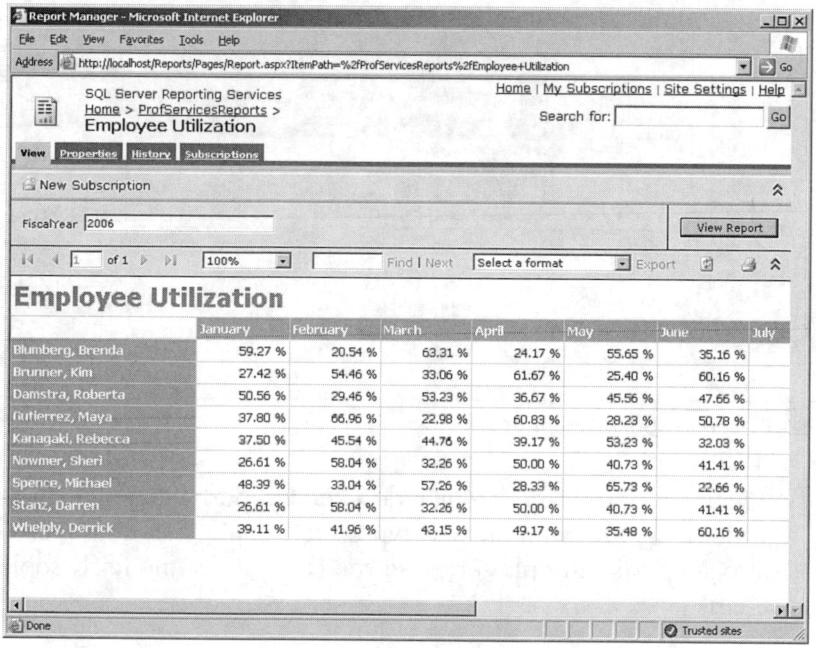

	January	February	March	April	May	June	July
Blumberg, Brenda	59.27 %	20.54 %	63.31 %	24.17 %	55.65 %	35.16 %	
Brunner, Kim	27.42 %	54.46 %	33.06 %	61.67 %	25.40 %	60.16 %	
Damstra, Roberta	50.56 %	29.46 %	53.23 %	36.67 %	45.56 %	47.66 %	
Gutierrez, Maya	37.80 %	66.96 %	22.98 %	60.83 %	28.23 %	50.78 %	
Kanagaki, Rebecca	37.50 %	45.54 %	44.76 %	39.17 %	53.23 %	32.03 %	
Nowmer, Sheri	26.61 %	58.04 %	32.26 %	50.00 %	40.73 %	41.41 %	
Spence, Michael	48.39 %	33.04 %	57.26 %	28.33 %	65.73 %	22.66 %	
Stanz, Darren	26.61 %	58.04 %	32.26 %	50.00 %	40.73 %	41.41 %	
Whelply, Derrick	39.11 %	41.96 %	43.15 %	49.17 %	35.48 %	60.16 %	

Figure 6-10 Matrix report

Reports also often need to include information that is not arranged in either tables or matrices. The **List** report item is used for reports that have flexible layouts, such as order reports that have a free-format header section containing customer information, then a table containing all the order details. The Project Details report is an example of this kind of report; the project information fields such as name, start date, and total budget are at the top of the page along with captions, and there are also two matrices containing work completed by employee and task, as shown in Figure 6-11. To create this type of report, drop a List item onto the report, and then drop fields and text boxes in the List area.

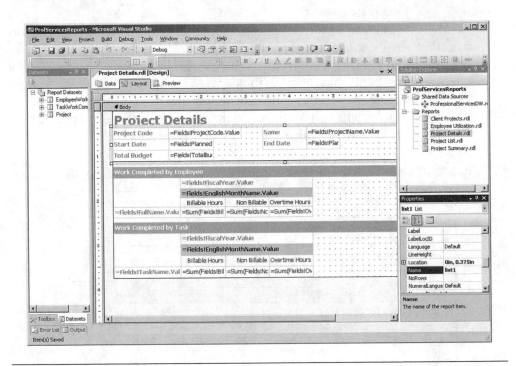

Figure 6-11 List report designer

Finally, reports can also include **Chart** report items, which support a wide range of common chart types such as pie, bar, and line. The chart also supports multiple series, so you can build some fairly sophisticated charts.

Drilling Down to See More Details

To avoid swamping users with long, multi-page reports, we can also design reports so that they present a short summary of the information to the user when they initially view the report, and then they can click links in the report to **drill down** to see more information. The Client Projects grouped report that we built previously would end up displaying a large amount of information. So instead of just showing a list of projects with subtotals, we could initially just show a list of clients along with a total of their current project budgets, and then allow the user to click the client name to see the breakout of individual projects, as shown in Figure 6-12.

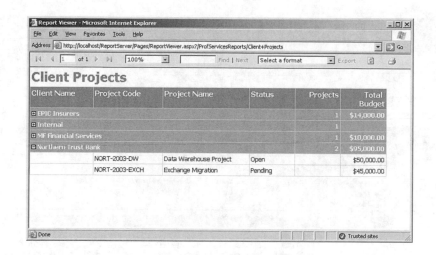

Figure 6-12   Drill down to show details

To implement this, first we need to define a group on Client Name, which will be the summary level for our report. To specify that the details of each client's projects are hidden at first and then displayed when the user clicks a client name, select the Details row in the table and then look in the Properties window for the Visibility section. Specify a Hidden value of True to hide the details section initially, and then for ToggleItem, select the field that you want the user to click (in this case, the Client Name field). This idea is applied all over the place in Reporting Services and is a powerful way to show the user what they want.

Drilling through to Detailed Reports

Another approach to dealing with presenting large amounts of information is to show the user a summary report that contains hyperlinks that launch a separate report with the detailed information—this approach is known as **drillthrough**. For example, project managers who are using the Project Summary report that we built earlier will need to be able to run a Project Details report that prompts for a specific project and shows detailed information such as the hours that consultants have billed to the project, remaining budget, and tasks completed, as shown in Figure 6-13.

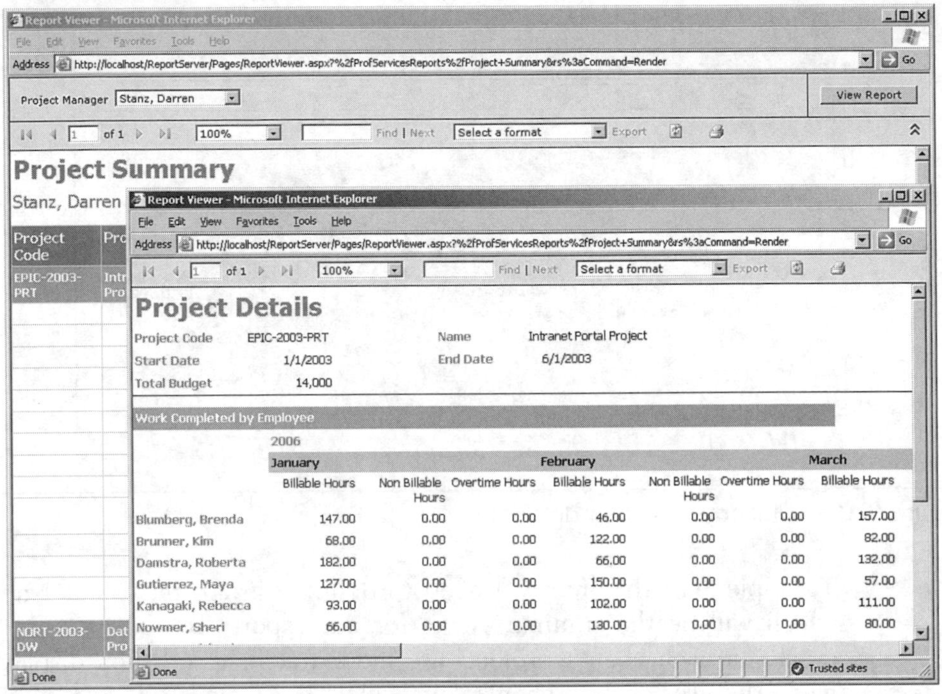

Figure 6-13   Drill through to detailed reports

To set up the hyperlink, open the Project Summary report that we built in the previous Quick Start and right-click the Project Code field to open the Properties dialog, and go to the Navigation tab. If you select the Jump to Report radio button, you will be able to select the Project Details report and also specify that the Project Key field value should be used for the ProjectKey parameter for this report.

Securing the Information

The users of the professional services reporting solution can be categorized into three groups—consultants, project managers, and business operations staff. Each of these groups needs different information, and we would like to prevent some users from seeing certain information. For example, consultants should be able to see their own utilization and billing performance, but not the performance of their colleagues. Managers, on the other hand, should be able to see the utilization of all consultants that report to them.

Restricting access to information is a common requirement in most reporting solutions, and Reporting Services has a flexible model to support it. In addition to controlling who can access a report, Reporting Services also allows administrators to control who can perform tasks such as uploading new reports. Permissions can be granted at a folder level rather than just individual reports, for example, so that you can allow users in a specified Windows group to access all reports in a folder.

For our solution, we start by creating three Windows groups and adding the Windows accounts of the users to the appropriate groups. Most users can see all the reports, so with Report Manager, we will open the Properties for the report folder and add all three groups with the Browser role. This will set the default security for all reports in the folder, and then we can override the security settings for specific reports, such as removing the Consultants group from the Business Operations reports.

Using Linked Reports to Present Limited Views

One specific requirement for our solution is that consultants can only see their own utilization report. We could just build two separate reports, one report that only managers could see that contains a parameter to allow any consultant to be selected, and another report that uses the User!UserID expression to only display the user's own utilization. However, Reporting Services includes a feature called **Linked Reports** that we can use for this requirement without having to build and maintain two separate reports. These have a link to an existing underlying report, but can hide parameters and supply specific parameter values, as well as have a different set of security permissions than the original report.

We can start by creating a Utilization by Consultant report with a parameter that presents a list of consultants but defaults to the current user's record. In Report Manager on the Properties tab for this report, click the Create a Linked Report button. You can change the name to something like My Utilization and click OK, and the new linked report will display. You can then change the parameters for the linked report by unselecting the Prompt User check box so that the user is not prompted to select a consultant for the My Utilization linked report.

Finally, secure the reports by only permitting members of the Manager role to view the Utilization by Consultant report but allowing all three groups to view the My Utilization report. Managers will then be able to choose any consultant for the report using the parameter, but everyone else will only be able to see his or her own utilization.

Accessing the Database

Now that we have secured the reports for our solution, we can move on to the topic that generally has the most effect on performance and scalability for reporting: controlling how and when the source databases are accessed.

Credentials Used to Access Database Sources

At some point before a report can be displayed for a user, Reporting Services connects to the data source and executes the queries required for the report. When you create a new data source, Windows integrated security is used by default, which means that the **credentials** of the user running the report are used to access the database. However, if the source database is on a separate server, Kerberos will need to be enabled to allow the user's credentials to be passed from the reporting server to the database server. (Talk to your friendly network administrator for more information on this topic.) Unlike client/server applications, Web applications usually avoid this approach of using the user's credentials to access the database, because this means that connection pooling is ineffective and expensive database connections cannot be reused.

The most common approach is to use Windows security to restrict users' permission to access the reports, as described in the previous section, and then use specific credentials to allow the reporting server to access databases. These credentials are stored securely on the reporting server (meaning they are encrypted and can only be read by the Reporting Services service) and consist of either a Windows username and password or a SQL Server username/password. We will be using a specially created Windows account for our reporting solution that has the minimum possible permissions required to access the database. You must avoid using powerful accounts such as administrator-level Windows accounts or the SQL Server sa account for this purpose.

Controlling When Database Queries Are Executed

If users always require the most up-to-date information, report queries need to be executed every time a user views a report. This can place a huge burden on database servers and is not usually a recipe for scalability. Most reports don't require data to be quite so current, especially when those reports are built on a data warehouse that is only updated periodically. You can get a lot of performance improvement by turning on **report caching** using the Report Manager execution properties for the report. This caches a format-neutral combination of the data and report layout, so the same cached data can be used whether the user requests the report in HTML or any other format.

The cached information can be set to expire either after a specified number of minutes or by using a schedule (for example, to expire caches every night). If a report uses parameters, a separate cache is created for every combination of parameter values that is used. One problem with the caching approach is that the first user who requests the report must wait while the data is fetched, whereas all subsequent users who request the same report and parameter values get the benefit of caching.

To avoid this problem, Reporting Services enables you to control when the queries are executed using **snapshots**, which are executed at a specific time and cache the resulting data. These settings are also controlled using execution properties in Report Manager. This is useful in data warehouse scenarios because we can schedule the report snapshots to be created after the nightly batch processing. Multiple snapshots can also be stored so that a history is created, and the user can easily see how the report looked at some time in the past.

A few caveats apply to snapshots, however. Because the report is not executed by a user, any parameters defined for the report will use the default values. Also, for both cached and snapshot reports, credentials to access the database must be stored with the data source. You can work around the default parameter issue by defining separate linked reports for every parameter combination that you want to cache, but, of course, this approach is limited to specific types of reports.

Subscribing to Reports

Most users really like the idea of having some reports e-mailed to them on a regular basis, especially now that so many people manage their whole life through their inbox. Reporting Services allows users to set up their own **subscriptions** using Report Manager and also enables administrators to set up a data-driven subscription that sends reports to a whole list of users, with the parameters set up so that relevant information is e-mailed.

QUICK START: Subscribing to a Report

The Project Summary report that we created earlier is a great candidate for a subscription because the content is tailored to a specific project manager. Before we can set up a subscription to the report, we need to change the data source so that the credentials used to access the database are stored:

1. In Report Manager, select the data source.

2. Under the Connect Using section, select the Credentials stored securely in the report server radio button.

3. Specify a Windows username and password that has access to the database. You could also use a SQL Server login instead.

4. If you specified a Windows account in Step 3, check the Use as Windows credentials check box.

5. Click Apply, and then open the Project Summary report.

6. If you have followed the preceding steps to store the credentials, you should now see a New Subscription button for the report. Click this button.

7. Specify the e-mail address to send the report to in the To section, as shown in Figure 6-14. (Note that if you don't see Report Server E-Mail as an option in the Delivered By section, you probably did not set an SMTP server when you installed Reporting Services. To fix this, search Books Online for the "Configuring a Report Server for E-Mail Delivery" section.)

8. Set the render format that you would like to receive as an attachment to the e-mail, such as PDF or Web Archive.

9. Set up a schedule to e-mail the subscription, such as 8 a.m. every Monday.

10. Select a value for the Project Manager parameter.

11. Click OK.

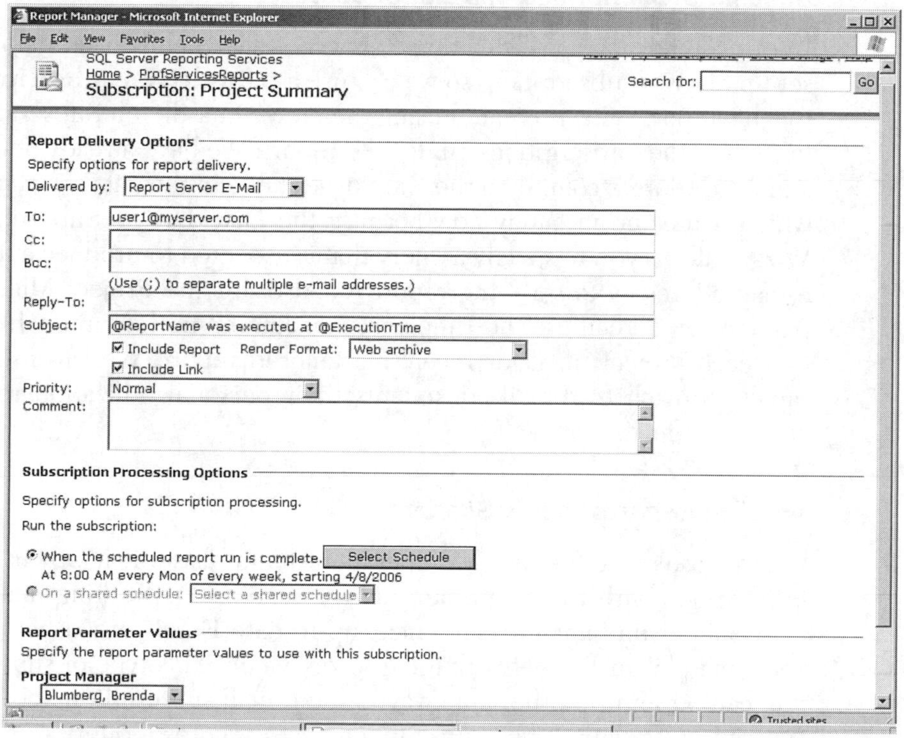

Figure 6-14 E-mail subscription

TIP:

Testing Subscriptions

Unless you want to wait until next Monday to see whether the subscription works the way you want it to, it helps to know something about how Reporting Services handles scheduling. A SQL Server Agent job is created for the subscription, named with a GUID that is used by Reporting Services to keep track of the job. Right-click the job in SQL Server Management Studio and choose Start Job, which will trigger the start of the subscription processing. In Report Manager, you can go to the Subscriptions tab for the report and refresh the view a few times to see how it proceeds.

Sending Subscriptions to a List of Users

In our solution, we probably don't want to make each project manager set up his own subscription, so we can use a **data-driven subscription** for this report. This is created using the New Data-driven Subscription button on the Subscriptions tab for the report. We have already defined an EmailAddress column in the Employees table in the data warehouse, which will come in handy now because the Data-Driven Subscription Wizard allows you to specify a query that is executed to produce a list of e-mail addresses to send the report to. Also, for the Project Manager parameter, you can use the EmployeeKey column in the same table, so that each project manager receives a tailored report. We can use the same approach to e-mail consultants their personal utilization report every month.

Sending Reports to File Shares

We can also make the business operations team blissfully happy using a subscription with the File Share delivery extension. Nothing makes a financial person happier than a nice, up-to-date Excel spreadsheet that appears in his or her network folder every week. This type of subscription can be set up in the same way as the e-mail subscription above, so you can use a data-driven subscription that executes a query to determine information such as a list of network locations to write reports to. This is also commonly used for financial reports that show a current position, because you can set up the subscription to use a different filename for each file that uses the current date. Over time, this will produce an archive of files that show the changing positions.

Managing the Solution

So far, we have been using the Web-based Report Manager tool both for viewing reports and for management purposes such as setting up report properties and security. Report Manager is a convenient management tool if you are managing one report server at a time over a Web connection, but otherwise you can use SQL Server Management Studio to connect to report servers and manage all aspects of your BI solutions (including database, Analysis Services, Integration Services, and Reporting Services) from within one tool.

Deployment

As described in the "High-Level Architecture" section, we will be using separate report and database servers. Deploying Reporting Services is similar to deploying many ASP.NET applications. You need to configure the server as an application server and enable IIS and ASP.NET.

The database server has no special requirements; the ReportServer and ReportServerTempDB databases are created when you set up Reporting Services. To deploy the reports and data sources that you have created, you can use the BI Development Studio as we have already described. If you want to create a repeatable, easy-to-deploy package containing all the reports and data sources to be deployed to production, however, unfortunately it is not going to be as easy as the Analysis Services or Integration Services deployment wizards.

Currently, no tool enables you to package up a report solution for deployment. If you can't use BI Development Studio because you want something that an operations team can use, you will have to get them to either deploy the report files one at a time using Report Manager or SQL Server Management Studio. Alternatively, you can write a custom script to deploy the solution following the techniques in the PublishSampleReports.rss script that ships as a sample with Reporting Services. You can execute scripts using the **rs** command-line utility, for example:

```
rs -i PublishSampleReports.rss -s
http://myserver/reportserver -v parentFolder="Professional
Services Reports"
```

Alternative Deployment: Database and Reporting Services on the Same Server

One option frequently used is to install both the SQL Server database and Reporting Services on the same server. The best reason to do this is the traditional one: cost. Because Reporting Services is a component of SQL Server just like Analysis Services or Integration Services, that means that every server running Reporting Services needs a valid SQL Server license, even if the report definitions are being stored in a separate, licensed SQL Server catalog database.

Because there will probably be moderate use of this particular application and the database is not very large, you might be able to get away with using a single server for both database and reporting servers in this case. If the application starts to suffer from performance problems, it is easy to add an additional reporting server, or even a Web farm to handle large numbers of concurrent users.

One area to be careful of is corporate server standards. Large enterprise companies often specify that database servers cannot run additional Windows services that are typically not required for databases for security reasons, and IIS is usually not enabled on database servers. Because Reporting Services requires IIS, they will either need to make an exception in this case or run Reporting Services where it belongs (on a Web server).

Maintenance

After the initial euphoria from a user community accustomed to struggling to get information has worn off, it is likely that they will quickly come up with requests for changes in the form of new reports that present the information in different ways, or request new measures to understand different areas of the business.

Adding New Reports

Using the Visual Studio report designer, you can easily add new reports or modify existing ones, and then publish them to the server. Because the operations staff may have modified the data source connection information, the OverwriteDataSources project setting is useful as it allows developers to redeploy report projects without overwriting data sources.

In a production system, however, the usual approach is for the developers to publish their changes to a test server, which are then deployed to the production reporting server, as described in the "Deployment" section.

The Long-Term Outlook for Standard Reporting

Publishing a set of standard reports usually has the most benefit to an organization when the solution is initially deployed. In the long run, requests for minor changes, which will inevitably accumulate from the user community, can quickly drive the cost of the solution up beyond the point where any real return on investment is possible. The most practical answer to this problem is to introduce some form of "self-service" reporting and analysis after the initial standardizing of reports. This could take the form of building Analysis Services cubes to enable users to use tools such as Excel to analyze their information or using the end-user reporting features of Report Builder.

Operations

Mission critical is a term usually associated with line-of-business systems such as payroll and ERP. When users become accustomed to easy access to information through a reporting solution, however, there will be a lot of pressure on operations teams to ensure that the system is reliable. In addition to the usual operations tasks associated with servers and databases, a few additional areas are required for reporting solutions.

Long-Running Report Jobs

This is a common issue that operations staff must address. Reports could start taking a long time to complete for various reasons, such as an increased load on the source database server or an increase in the amount of data for a report. The best approach is to set sensible timeouts on the server or specific reports so that Reporting Services can automatically cancel any reports that are taking too long to complete.

Alternatively, administrators can see which jobs are running and cancel them if necessary using the Manage Jobs section under Site Settings in Report Manager, or the Jobs folder in SQL Server Management Studio. However, reports are usually waiting for the data source to return data, so a common approach is to cancel the long-running query on the database server.

Backing Up Information

Backing up a Reporting Services solution covers several areas. First, all the catalog information such as reports, security settings, and snapshots are stored in the ReportServer SQL Server database. This database needs to be backed up using standard SQL Server backups, along with the ReportServerTempDB database. Second, because all configuration information such as database connection strings is stored in an encrypted format in the ReportServer database, you need to back up the encryption keys for your server using the rskeymgmt utility.

Finally, the report projects and solution files that you used to develop the reports also need to be backed up. The best approach for this is to use a source control solution such as Visual Studio Team System's version control or SourceSafe.

Next Steps

In this solution for professional services, we focused mainly on solving the most important business need, which was tracking the resource utilization. Other areas that we would need to add in future iterations would probably include tracking customer satisfaction, which is one of the most important metrics because it is a great predictor of likely future revenue. The business operations side of professional services also needs information on cost factors such as travel and expenses to be able to manage the business successfully. These measures would all prove useful for analytical purposes, too (for example, tracking trends and breaking down costs), so an Analysis Services cube is another likely addition to the solution.

Adding Code to Reports Using .NET

In our solution, we managed to implement all the required calculations using a combination of SQL and Reporting Services expressions. Some reports will need more than that; for example, your reports may require complex mathematical or financial calculations. You can achieve this in Reporting Services by adding a reference to a .NET assembly containing your code, and then call this assembly from report expressions. Also, if you need to reuse the same code fragment a few times in a report, you can add custom VB.NET functions to the report that can be called from expressions. See "Using Custom Assemblies with Reports" in Books Online for more information.

Using Report Builder for End-User Reporting

Many of the users of the information in the data warehouse will be "power users" who would benefit from the capability to create their own queries and reports. Report Builder is a simple, Microsoft Office-like report design tool that allows users to connect to a user-friendly view of the data called a report model. You can design a report model in BI Development Studio using the Report Model project type, using either the relational data warehouse or an Analysis Services database as the source.

One possible approach for the professional services solution is to create an Analysis Services database that could be accessed by the user's client tool of choice, and then create a report model from this Analysis

Services database for those users who want to use Report Builder to create custom reports. You can easily generate a report model by creating a new reporting folder using Report Manager or SQL Server Management Studio, adding a data source that points to the Analysis Services cube, and then clicking the Generate Model button or context menu item on the data source. This creates a new report model in that reporting folder, and users can immediately launch Report Builder using the button on the Report Manager toolbar.

Supporting Multiple Languages in a Report

One area that will be important in many solutions is localization, or providing the same report in multiple languages. This area involves a few complexities, such as whether just report captions need to be language specific, or data such as product names also needs to be localized. One simple solution to this problem is just to rewrite the report for different languages and provide the correct reports to different audiences. This may not work well where you have a large number of reports that often need to be modified, because you will be maintaining more than one copy.

When a user views a report, the browser passes the user's preferred language to the server; this can be accessed in a report expression using the User!Language syntax. You can localize data and captions by using this language as a parameter to either SQL queries or a .NET assembly referenced in the report. Another powerful technique often used to localize .NET applications is using resource files. Because Reporting Services will correctly set the language of the thread used to process a report, you can build .NET assemblies that use the ResourceManager class to return the appropriate string for a specified key. See the MSDN documentation on localizing applications for more information.

Summary

In this chapter, we built a new data warehouse focused initially on the key areas of the professional services business, with data loaded from the timesheets system and forecasting spreadsheets, and provided the information to users through a set of Web-based reports. The business operations team now gets reports delivered to them weekly rather than spending time using spreadsheets to manually produce information from various sources. Project managers and consultants use the Report Manager Web-based application so that they have easy access to reports that show the current situation; they can also print the reports or export them in formats such as Excel or PDF.

We decided to build a data warehouse instead of reporting directly against the OLTP timesheets system because the reports need additional information from other sources, and to reduce the complexity of report designs and avoid any performance impact on the timesheets system. We decided to use the standard Report Manager Web-based application to publish reports because it provides all the features required for this solution without doing any additional Web development.

We used a shared data source definition in the report project so that it can be changed in one place for all reports if necessary. The data source was configured with a specific Windows account with the minimum permissions required to access the database, because this approach works well for accessing data on different servers and also for automated processes like report snapshots and subscriptions.

We secured the reports by restricting access to specific groups of users, including using linked reports to provide more limited views of data for some groups. Report caching was used to improve the performance by avoiding the need to hit the data warehouse every time, and we also used report snapshots to run some key reports overnight and provide a historical view. We used the subscriptions feature to send Excel versions of the reports to a file share, and a data-driven subscription to e-mail tailored reports to all project managers and consultants.

We deployed the reports to a separate reporting server rather than using a single combined database and reporting server, using the rs utility and a custom script. Key operations tasks now include managing long-running reports and backing up the report server databases in addition to the data warehouse.

CHAPTER 7

Data Quality

The data warehouse is expected to be the authority for any data it provides. To gain and maintain this position of authority, a data warehouse should only contain data that is complete, correct, and consistent. If you are the manager of the data warehouse, you may not be responsible for the quality of data sources, but you are responsible for ensuring that only quality data reaches the data warehouse.

It seems that regardless of how much care is taken with an OLTP database, data quality issues arise when data reaches the data warehouse. When your data warehouse is receiving data from a multitude of independently managed sources, problems are compounded. Data "managed" locally by users is often deemed good by them, and any errors don't appear as a problem to those users because they make ad-hoc adjustments and allowances. Even well-managed local data likely isn't directly compatible or consistent with other local data. Industry estimates are that close to half the data quality issues must be resolved at the source. A much smaller number of the issues can only be resolved in the ETL process. This chapter is about the techniques available to you to detect and correct bad data, merge multiple data sources into a consistent model, and keep track of the successes and failures of the processing.

Business Problem

Our customer for this chapter is a bricks-and-mortar retailer who has recently acquired an online competitor. The companies have many customers in common, and both companies sell similar products. The bricks-and-mortar stores have a loyalty program that they use to profile their customers' buying habits, and the online company tracks their active members using customer account numbers.

Problem Statement

The company wants to have a unified view of sales from both sources. They are also experiencing problems with analytic reports being inaccurate and incomplete. Sales results are always lower than expected. The problems have been traced to poor quality source data.

It isn't possible to get a combined view of a customer's activities in the store and on the Web. The Internet customers do not have a loyalty card that they can use at a store, and the loyalty card is not recognized by the online checkout. The two customer lists have not been successfully combined into a common list. An attempt was made to merge the customer lists, but customers who were patrons of both stores were never resolved to one customer. Minor differences in the customer records caused a significant number of matches to be missed.

Detailed customer data is sometimes missing because a new customer can obtain and use a bar-coded loyalty card by filling out a form at the cashier, but the data on the form may not be entered into the system for several weeks afterward.

Some product sales data is missing from regular reports, and the totals from the data warehouse do not always agree with what the stores report. When the two product catalogs were merged, they tried to match every product stock-keeping unit (SKU) between them and assign a new SKU to every product. However, this was a semi-manual process, and it seems some products were missed. Cashiers simply key in the SKU and the price marked on the packaging. Customers are returning some goods with the old SKUs marked on the packaging. None of these SKUs show up in the analysis because the SKUs aren't in the catalog.

Finally, the two sales projection systems haven't been integrated yet, and some budgets are being entered via spreadsheets. Through misspellings, the product categories can't always be determined.

Solution Overview

Our solution uses patterns that can be repeated for many commonly occurring data cleansing requirements. We will merge two partially overlapping lists using fuzzy matching, detect facts that refer to missing dimension members and re-route them appropriately, create placeholders for delayed dimension members, and implement an ETL audit process. The entire solution is implemented in the ETL phase, using SQL Server Integration Services (SSIS, or Integration Services).

Business Requirements

The customer lists from the two stores must be merged, and duplicates should be eliminated. When duplicates are encountered, the most recent customer information should be retained. All sales data must be accounted for. Valid records must be placed into the data warehouse, and records with any faults must be redirected for corrective action. Where possible, fact records should be included in the data warehouse even if they can't be completely assigned to standard categories. Those incomplete fact records must be assigned to well-known special categories such as "unknown" or "missing."

High-Level Architecture

Our goal is to load only clean data from the source systems into our data warehouse. The ETL process will move valid data directly into the data warehouse without using an intermediate staging database. A new management and auditing database will be used to hold data that needs remedial action and data that tracks and traces the flow of data into the data warehouse. Resolving issues with the rejected data will typically require a solution tailored to your specific subject area to present the rows to a user for correction and subsequent resubmission to the ETL process. We leave building that application to you as an exercise because it is not directly related to SQL Server 2005.

Before we can load any operational data, we need to clean up the existing customer data by merging the lists from the two companies. This one-time process removes duplicate customers from the merged list, while retaining the most recent customer data. To accommodate the free-form entry of names and addresses, we will use **fuzzy matching** techniques available in Integration Services to achieve good duplicate detection in spite of small differences in formatting or spelling between some of the common fields of the same customer.

In production, we will use Integration Services to perform the normal ETL processes necessary to deliver the data from the source to the data warehouse. During this processing, errors such as **missing dimension members** will be automatically detected by the Integration Services transforms. Most transforms have at least two output paths: one for success, and one for the failing rows that we will use to redirected problem fact records for alternate processing. We'll use additional transforms to count the records moved along each path and record the counts in an audit table. As shown in Figure 7-1, source data will be routed using Integration Services data flows either to the data warehouse, to a process for automatic correction, or to a queue for manual correction.

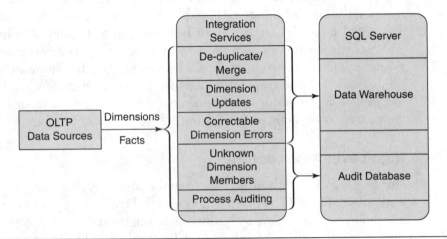

Figure 7-1   High-level architecture

Business Benefits

Users will be able to rely on the data they obtain from the data warehouse. Reports will be available sooner and will be more accurate because errors will be detected before they find their way into reports, and systemic processing errors in the data sources can be more readily identified and corrected, further reducing the effort necessary to produce reports.

Data Model

We will modify the dimension tables in the data warehouse to support what are known as late-arriving dimension members. Each dimension table needs a status column, which we'll call IsInferred. If a fact record shows up with a business key that we do not yet have in our dimension, and we have to create a dimension record as a placeholder, we will set IsInferred to true. **Inferred members** are described in detail later in this chapter. In Figure 7-2, an example using the Customer dimension table is shown with the added column. This column is also used by the Slowly Changing Dimension Wizard described in Chapter 8, "Managing Changing Data."

We also will create a new database to contain tables related to monitoring the ETL operations. We've named this database ETL_Operations. We will use a table named PackageExecutionLog to track the execution of each package and record when each package is run, how long it ran for, and how many rows were received from the source, written to the destination, or rejected as errors. For each fact table we load, we'll create a new table to hold the rejected facts and the reason for rejection. The schema for each reject table matches the input schema for the source records, with the addition of the error reason and date of rejection. There are no constraints on these reject tables because some portion isn't valid, so a constraint would just get in our way of determining what is wrong with the record contents. An example of a table for rejected facts using the Sales facts, named RejectedSales, is shown in Figure 7-2.

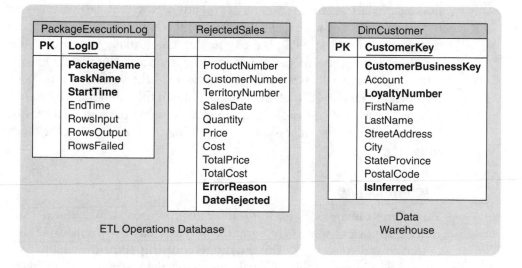

Figure 7-2   Data model

Technical Solution

We will be able to use Integration Services to accomplish the entire process of data extraction, error detection, data routing, and loading into the data warehouse. Independent Integration Services packages will be used to perform one-time merging of the customer lists, loading and cleansing of the facts, and updating of the dimension tables. The special features of Integration Services that are important to these processes are fuzzy lookup of rows using a similarity measure, and the ability of most transforms to direct rows to different data flows based on results of the transform.

Merging and De-Duplicating Customer Data

We have a problem with our customer list that is preventing a complete view of our customers' shopping patterns. The customer lists from the two companies are in good shape in the context of the individual companies, but they were never merged, so we don't have a single consistent list of who our customers are. Creating the single list isn't easy because the information is essentially unreliable. It is entered by customers, either on a hand-written form or over the Web in free-form text. Getting exact matches that return only one identical customer from each list doesn't provide accurate content. If you attempt to match by name, you likely will get many false matches, which will combine some distinct customers into one. Including the city in the match likely won't solve the problem. Using the street address might be tempting, but matching with street address usually is not effective because of the variety of ways people enter street data. Street, St., and St all mean the same thing to us, but will obviously not be considered equal in any comparison in the SQL language. What we really want is a matching process that is a bit more forgiving.

Fuzzy Matching

Fuzzy matching looks for the similarities between strings, but doesn't require a perfect match. Integration Services has two transforms that employ fuzzy matching. The **Fuzzy Grouping** transform helps you detect duplicates within a single table or data stream. The **Fuzzy Lookup** transform helps you find duplicates between two separate tables or between a data stream and a table. Rather than returning true or false as a match indicator, both transforms return a **similarity rank** between zero and one to indicate how good a match two rows are.

We have two overlapping customer lists, so we'll use the Fuzzy Lookup transform to provide us with a list of probable matches between them. The transform requires a reference list and an input list. You can think of the reference list as the current "master" and the input list as a new set of customers. Because we are starting from scratch, we will arbitrarily choose one list to be the reference list and check the customers in the other list against it. The reference list will be directly added to the data warehouse as the initial customer list. We will then insert new customers from our second customer list. The new customers are ones that don't match any customers in the reference table. Our business requirement says we want to keep the latest customer information. That means for customers where we do find a match, we want to update customer rows that have a later LastUpdate date than those already in the reference table.

The most challenging part of fuzzy matching is deciding what fields to use for comparison, and then deciding what level of similarity you will accept as a match. Name is a good criteria, but isn't sufficient by itself because there will be many different customers with the same (or similar) name. Street address and city are good candidates to resolve this problem. Zip code would be good, too, but "close" in numbers has two meanings. 98109 and 18109 only differ in one digit, but are on different sides of the continent. The concept of "similarity" using strings is probably easy to grasp. It is simply a measure of how close we (or in this case, Integration Services) thinks the two rows are to representing the same thing.

Another measure provided by the Fuzzy Lookup transform, **confidence**, indicates how reliable Integration Services thinks the similarity measure is. You've probably heard of political pollsters providing an approval rating of a politician as "48 percent, 19 times out of 20." The 19 times out of 20 is a confidence rating—their prediction will, on average, be wrong one time in 20. You might need to experiment with the level of similarity and the confidence level to get the highest number of correct positive matches. It is important to realize that there almost certainly will be some false positives (that is, two customer records that matched within your constraints that are in fact two distinct customers). In an advertising campaign, this might not be too serious; if you are dealing with data that has privacy considerations, however, you might want to review all customer records that were merged to assure yourself that the correct decision was made.

QUICK START: Merging Lists Using Fuzzy Matching

This Integration Services package will merge our list of bricks-and-mortar customers into the list of online customers. First, we'll copy the online list into the data warehouse. Then we'll determine which customers are common between the lists and which ones are not on the online list. The process produces three intermediate tables, which will contain the customer IDs of the new customers, the existing customers that need an update, and existing customers that are current. We will use these tables later to drive the inserts and updates to the master customer list.

1. Create a new Integration Services package and name it Merge Customer Lists.

2. Create three connection managers: one for the online store source, one for the bricks-and-mortar data source, and one for the data warehouse. Name them OnlineSource, BricksAndMortarSource, and DataWarehouse.

3. Drag a Data Flow task from the toolbox onto the design surface and rename it Copy Online Customers. Edit the data flow task and create a simple copy of the online customer table to your master customer table in the data warehouse. (You already know how to do this from Chapter 4, "Integrating Data.")

4. Drag a Data Flow task from the toolbox onto the design surface, rename it Create Matching List, and connect it to the control flow from the Copy Online Customers task. Open the Create Matching List task for editing.

5. Drag an OLE DB Source onto the data flow design surface and name it Bricks and Mortar Customers.

6. Edit the data source, and specify the Bricks and Mortar connection manager for your source data.

7. Specify the table or view, or create a SQL query, that contains the primary key, all the columns you want to match on, and the last-modified-date column. In our example, we are going to match on First Name, Last Name, Street Address, City, and StateProvince. We built a view joining the Customer and Address tables on CustomerID, but a SQL command would work just as well.

8. Drag a Fuzzy Lookup transform onto the design surface and label it Match to Customer Master. Connect the Bricks and Mortar Customers data source output to the fuzzy lookup.

9. Edit the Fuzzy Lookup transform. On the Reference Table tab (see Figure 7-3), set the connection manager property to the DataWarehouse connection manager. This is where the master customer list is maintained. The data warehouse will already contain the online store customers when this step executes.

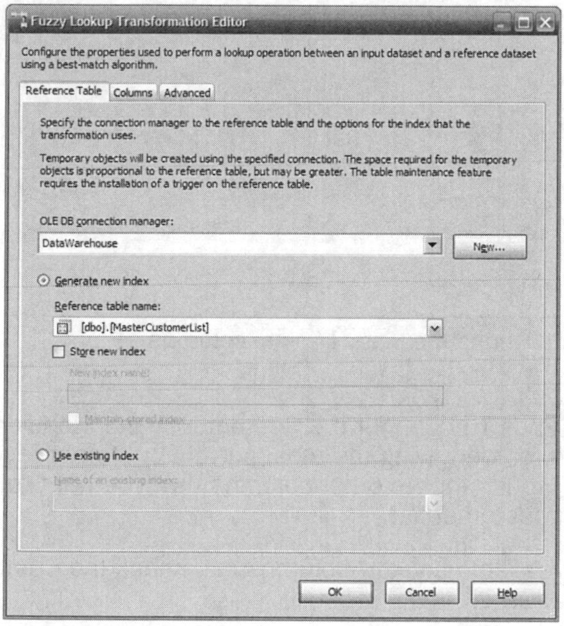

Figure 7-3   Configuring the Fuzzy Lookup inputs

10. Set the Reference Table to MasterCustomerList, which is our view in the data warehouse containing the data to be matched against the incoming customer list. (We created this view outside of this quick start.)

11. On the Columns tab (see Figure 7-4), set the mappings between the two lists so that only the columns we want to match on are mapped. This would be First Name, Last Name, Street Address, City, and StateProvince.

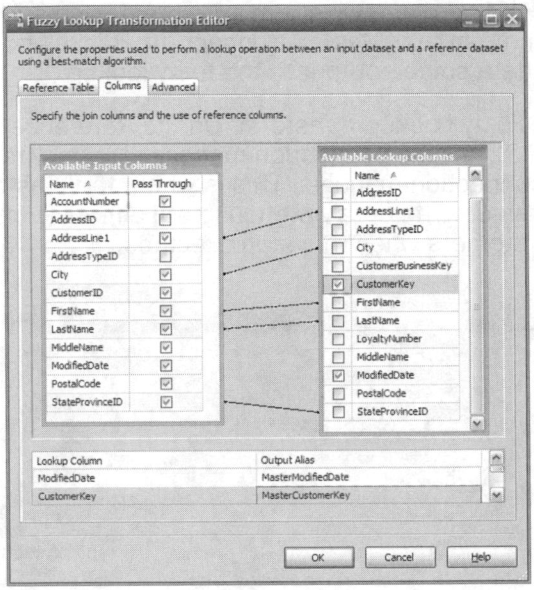

Figure 7-4 Configuring the Fuzzy Lookup columns

12. Check Pass Through for the CustomerID and ModifiedDate. They are needed for identifying the most current customer record. Also click Pass Through for the other columns that you want to store in the master customer list.

13. In the Available Lookup Columns list, check the CustomerKey and ModifiedDate.

14. The output of the fuzzy lookup will contain the customer business key from the Bricks and Mortar store, the customer surrogate key from the master customer list, and last modified date for both input tables. For clarity, provide an output alias for the reference (master) input to differentiate CustomerKey and ModifiedDate from the two sources, such as MasterCustomerKey and MasterModifiedDate.

15. On the Advanced tab (see Figure 7-5), check that the Maximum number of matches to output per lookup is set to 1. Because the data in each list is clean (no duplicates), we expect no more than one match to occur. The most similar match exceeding the overall Similarity threshold will be returned. We'll set the Similarity threshold to 0 to allow at least one row through for each input row. The conditional split following this lookup will then be able to examine the similarity of each column. This will give you the opportunity, if you choose, to weight the similarity of each column differently before deciding if a row is a good match. For example, we may choose to require a strong similarity on last name, with less emphasis on the similarity of the first name. The conditional split will redirect the row to the appropriate data flow based on the similarity and dates in the comparable rows.

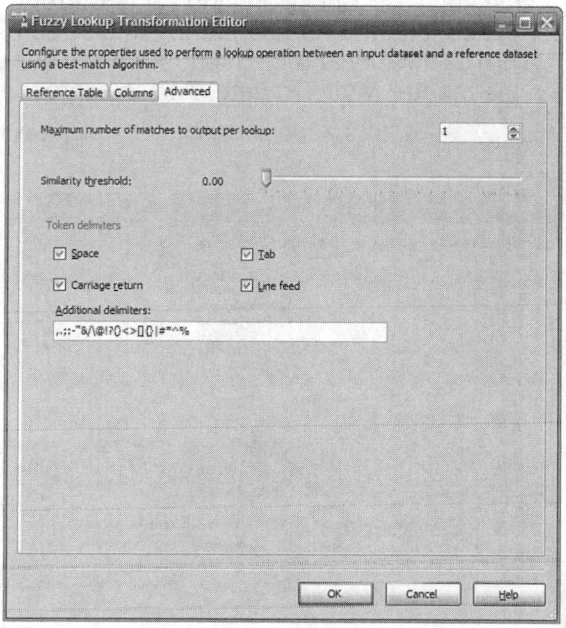

Figure 7-5 Configuring the fuzzy lookup threshold

16. Click OK to save this transform.

At this point, if you could run this transform by itself, you would get a list of the customer IDs of all rows in the input stream, the key of their best possible match in the reference table, and the similarity score of the possible match. Rows that have a good match will have a low similarity score. You will also know which row of the match is the most recent, because we included the ModifiedDate in the stream. For each input row, we want to insert it into the data warehouse if it is new (low similarity to the existing list), update an existing row if the input row is newer than the match in the data warehouse (high similarity and later ModifiedDate), or discard the input row if we already have the row in the data warehouse (high similarity but earlier ModifiedDate). A Conditional Split transform is exactly what we need to split our input stream into these three paths.

17. Drag a **Conditional Split transform** onto the design surface and connect the Fuzzy Lookup transform to it.

18. Edit the conditional split transform to create the three data flows we want, as shown in Figure 7-6. Click in the Output Name column, enter a name such as "Bricks and Mortar is Current," press Tab, and enter the condition for data entering this stream. In this case, we want a high similarity and the input stream ModifiedDate to be later than the master Modified date. This is expressed as follows:

```
(_Similarity > .75) && (ModifiedDate > MasterModifiedDate)
```

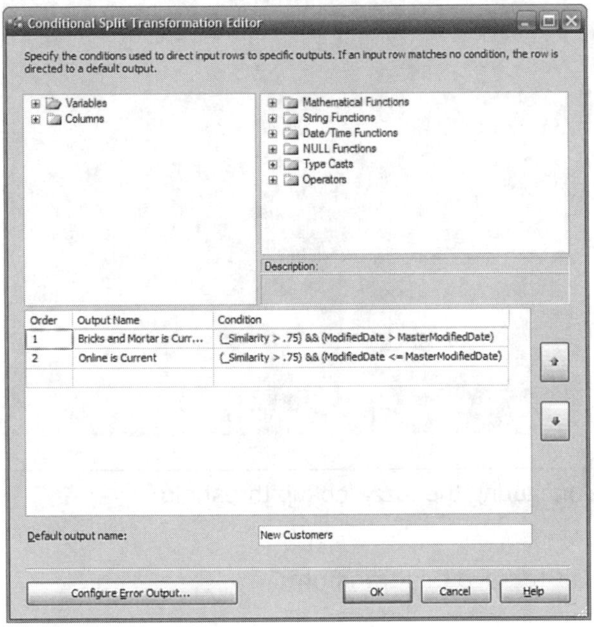

Figure 7-6 Configuring a Conditional Split transform

19. Repeat for the second output, where there is a match but the master is more current. Set the name to "Master is Current," and the condition for data entering this stream to this:

```
(_Similarity > .75) && (ModifiedDate <= MasterModifiedDate)
```

20. Set the Default output name to "New Customers." All rows that don't meet conditions one or two will flow through the default output stream. Click OK to save this transform.

21. Drag an OLE DB Destination onto the design surface, rename it Add Customers, and set the Connection property to the

BricksAndMortarDataSource connection manager and the table to CustomersToBeAdded. (Click New to create this table if you don't have it already.) Connect the conditional split transform to this destination and choose the New Customers output.

22. Drag an OLE DB Destination onto the design surface and rename it Customers to Update. Set the Connection property to the Bricks-AndMortarDataSource connection manager. Click New to create a new table, "CustomersToUpdate," to hold the rows you will use in a later update step. Connect the Conditional Split to this destination and choose the Bricks and Mortar is Current output stream.

23. Drag another OLE DB Destination onto the design surface so that you can save the rows that were marked as duplicates. Rename this destination No Action. Connect the Conditional Split transform to this destination and choose the Online is Current stream. This table is created to support auditing of the customer merge process.

24. Save this package. The completed data flow for fuzzy matching should now look like that in Figure 7-7.

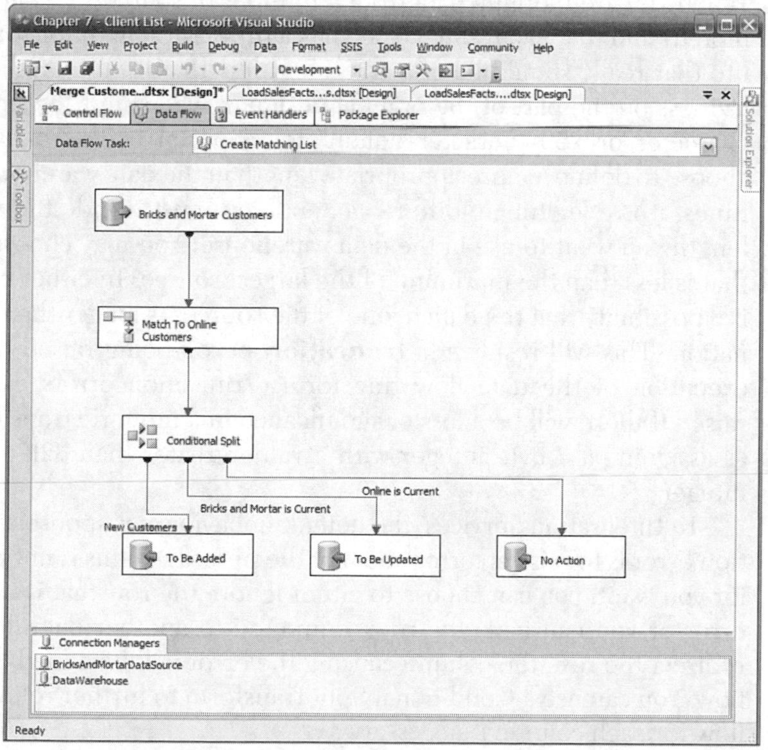

Figure 7-7 Data flow for merging members using fuzzy matching

We have created three tables, one for customers who were only in the Bricks and Mortar customer list and need to be added to the master list, one for customers who were on both company's lists but where the information in the Bricks and Mortar list is more current, and one where the Online store record is more current. The reason we created these tables, rather than immediately doing something with the data, is that we wanted an audit trail of how the data was handled.

Your remaining task is to append the "CustomersToBeAdded" rows to the master customer list in the data warehouse, and to update the rows in the master customer list using the data in the "CustomersToUp-date" table. We won't drag you through this step by step, since you already know how to build this kind of transform. You would use a simple copy data flow to move the new customers to the master list, and an Execute SQL task to execute a T-SQL Update statement to update the existing customers with the more current information.

Data Truncation Errors

When you are merging data from a number of sources, it is not uncommon to find that each source specifies a different length for some attribute that really should be of a consistent length. Often this is a result of laziness on the part of the original designer, who simply accepted a 50-character or 255-character default for a postal code. You will likely choose to define a more appropriate length in the data warehouse. Other times, it is a legitimate difference, and you must decide the maximum length you want to use in the data warehouse. You may choose a length that is less than the maximum of the largest source. In either case, there is a possibility that the data in one of the sources is longer than the destination. This will result in a **truncation error** being raised during the execution of the data flow transform. Truncation errors can also be raised if there will be a loss of significance in a numeric transform, such as assigning a 4-byte integer with a value greater than 32k to a 2-byte integer.

In Integration Services, the default behavior in response to a truncation error is to raise an error and halt the process. If this is not the behavior you want, you can choose to either ignore the row that is causing the error or you can have the row redirected to another data flow. If you redirect the row, the column causing the error will be added to the data flow. You can use a Conditional Split transform to further refine the data flow for each column if necessary.

In our example, we have set the target lengths to be large enough to accommodate the data from each source, and so have left the error handling for truncation to Fail component.

Dealing with Missing Dimension Members

Missing dimension members can cause fact rows to be omitted from the data warehouse. If this occurs, your results will be wrong, and there will be no indication of a problem, unless you are proactive in detecting and correcting the problem. We have deliberately encouraged you to use Lookup transforms rather than joins for a simple reason: Lookups raise a trappable error if a member is missing, whereas a join just silently ignores the row. A Lookup gives you a chance to do something about the problem when it occurs. In this section, we show how to configure a Lookup transform to redirect failing rows to a different data flow for remediation.

When you load facts into your data warehouse, they are expected to have a context provided by well-defined dimensions. For example, you expect to have a valid date, store, product, and customer for every sale fact, because you want to analyze your data that way. The dimensions contain members—the known set of possible values—for every day, store, product, and customer. If one of those is missing from a fact row, you can't analyze the data the way you would like because you don't know how to completely categorize the sale. Or, if we don't handle the problem well, the fact will not be included in the warehouse, and your sales totals will be wrong. Needless to say, most of our customers find this effect undesirable!

Regardless of why they are missing, your first task is to determine which incoming fact rows, if any, refer to dimension members that you don't have in your data warehouse.

Detecting Missing Members

Remember that when you first receive a fact row, it contains business keys. Part of the work of building a data warehouse is transforming the business keys into surrogate keys. The surrogate keys uniquely identify a member within a dimension. It is during this transformation that you are first going to know whether a member is missing.

In Integration Services, you use a Lookup transform to translate a business key into a surrogate key. You use one Lookup transform for each dimension related to the fact. You can control how each Lookup transform behaves when it doesn't find a matching business key. By default, an error is raised, and the Integration Services package stops processing any more data. Although this is effective in preventing bad data from reaching the data warehouse, it doesn't help you in identifying the problem, fixing it, or getting the good data through the process. We want to send the good data on and send the bad data down a different path. The Lookup transform can be configured to do exactly that.

QUICK START: Redirecting Failing Lookup Data

If a lookup of a fact row fails, we want to redirect the row to a separate data flow. In this example, we'll send the errant facts to a new table for later evaluation; otherwise, we'll just let the row continue on to the next transform. There is one Lookup transform for each dimension, and each transform will detect a different error. However, it is still the same fact that is causing the problem, so we'll put all failing rows of the same fact into the same table and add an indicator to the row that will identify the specific Lookup that caused the problem.

We skip the parts of the package design you already know—creating a data flow task, adding OLE DB source and destinations, and doing simple lookups. We instead concentrate on handling the error processing and assume you have a data flow from the source to the destination, including any lookups.

1. Open your SalesFact Integration Services package for editing.

2. Drop a Derived Column transform beside the Product Lookup transform. Rename it "Set reason code to Product."

3. Connect the red error output from the Lookup transform to the Derived Column transform. There will be a pop-up dialog asking you to configure the error output. Choose Redirect row under the Error column. Click OK.

4. Edit the Derived Column transform. Add a new column named Error-Reason, set the expression to "Missing product member," and set the Length to 50. Click OK.

5. Add additional Derived Column transforms, one for each Lookup transform, giving each a descriptive name and setting the expression to Missing … (according to what was missing).

6. Drag a Union All transform on to the design surface, underneath and to the right of all the Derived Column transforms. Connect each of the Derived Column outputs to the Union All transform. This gives us back one data flow instead of a separate data flow for each Lookup failure.

7. Drag an OLE DB Destination task onto the page and click New for the table destination. Change the table name to something like BadSalesFacts.

8. Check the column mapping to see that all the columns you want are copied to the table.

9. Click Finish. Your data flow should look like that in Figure 7-8.

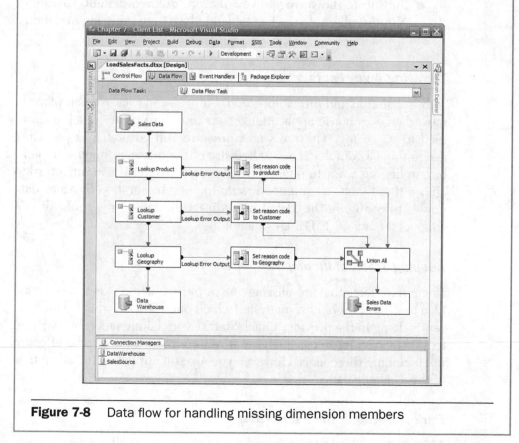

Figure 7-8   Data flow for handling missing dimension members

Now we have separated data that has valid business keys from data that has business keys that we don't know about. Let's see what our options are for fixing the initial problem and maximizing the quality of the data in the data warehouse. We could do one of the following:

- Throw away the fact.
- Throw away the fact but keep track of the number of those rows to provide an index of the completeness of the data.
- Park the row for later review and repair.
- Create a new temporary dimension member for the missing member.
- Substitute the surrogate key of a pre-defined default Missing or N/A member into the fact table in place of the missing member.

Throwing Away Facts

This is a simple and direct approach, but it doesn't have much place in most data warehouse applications. Your totals are pretty much guaranteed to be wrong. The row's measures are still correct; you just can't assign them a complete context because of the missing dimension member, so finding a way to retain the fact is worthwhile. If you can afford to ignore these facts, all you need to do to your Integration Services data flow is to configure the lookup to redirect the failing rows, but do not connect it to an OLE DB Destination.

Keeping Track of Incomplete Facts

If you have facts that are missing one or more business keys, it is a good idea to keep track of how many and which ones. That is what we are currently doing in the previous Quick Start. Every failing fact row is written to a table, which you can analyze for row count, or evaluate the effect of not including these facts. However, you are still not taking full advantage of the available data.

Park and Repair the Facts Later

This approach is good because all the data will eventually make its way to the data warehouse. It can be an essential step when the error is caused by misspelled business keys, which need some human intelligence to decipher and fix. In the meantime, the reports will show lower than actual values. You will need to create a simple application that presents each row to a user for repair and then inserts the row in a table or updates the source so the rows can be put through the ETL process again.

Inferring a Dimension Member

Remember our business problem where a customer fills out a loyalty card at the register at the time of a purchase? We now know the loyalty number of the customer but nothing about them (because their information is not yet entered into the system). This sales fact is a candidate for rejection because it refers to a customer not in the customer dimension. What if you want the correct totals in your reports, even if the details aren't correct? What if we don't care so much about a member's properties? At least we could include the fact in our analysis right now. If you are sure that the business key is valid, and not a misspelling, you can create a temporary placeholder record in the dimension table, or what Integration Services calls an **"inferred" member**.

We should only create inferred members for dimensions where we have a high expectation that the business key is correct. In our loyalty card example, the key is scanned in, so there is much less risk that it will be wrong than if it were keyed in by an operator. Why does this matter? Because we want to be able to come back and provide the detailed information when we finally get it. If there's a misspelling, we won't be able to match the business keys, and we'll have an extra member that has no real meaning.

What properties do we really need to create an inferred member? Well, the business key is important; that's what we use to find the surrogate key. The good news is that we have a business key given to us by the source fact row. The surrogate key is simply assigned automatically by SQL Server. Unless the source fact row contains some denormalized information about the member, we are unlikely to be able to supply a value for any other attributes. For example, if the customer is inferred, we will not know their name, address, or anything else about them, because that information is not collected at the point of sale.

Now for a little housekeeping. It is a good idea to mark your inferred members with a simple Boolean flag so that you know that they are incomplete. This flag will also prove to be useful in working with slowly changing dimensions, which are discussed in Chapter 8, "Managing Changing Data." When we receive the real dimension data for this member, if the flag tells us that the current row is an inferred member, we will just update the current row. This is particularly important for dimensions where we are tracking history because we don't want to create a new member if we just need to fill in the missing information for the current row. If the flag indicates the current row is not an inferred member, you simply handle the new dimension data as you normally would.

Data Flow for Inferred Members

We'll modify the data flow to detect missing members we created previously. Instead of sending the facts to a table for later processing, we'll first route them to an OLE DB Command transform. This will call a stored procedure to insert the business key into the Customer table and return the surrogate key. The stored procedure will also check that we haven't already added this customer since we started this package. If we have, the surrogate key is simply returned. Finally, the two data flows are merged with a Union All task. You might now be wondering why the customer would be not found by the lookup if we have just added it to the customer table. The reason is that the customer table is cached by the Lookup transform, and the new customer doesn't appear in the cache.

TIP:
Continuing the Data Flow After an SQL Operation
You can use an OLE DB Command transform rather than an OLE DB Destination to continue the data flow after executing an SQL command, such as an `Insert` statement. We need this capability here to allow the inferred Product member to be inserted and then continue the data flow to read the new surrogate key and rejoin the main data flow.

QUICK START: Implementing Inferred Members

If we know the member we are missing is just late arriving, we can create a temporary inferred member so that at least we have the surrogate key for that member.

1. Create a stored procedure to add the new customer and return the surrogate key:

```
create procedure AddCustomer
@LoyaltyNumber as nvarchar(12),
```

```
@CustomerKey as int out
as


—      Check if customer exists
SELECT        @CustomerKey=CustomerKey
FROM   dbo.DimCustomer
WHERE LoyaltyNumber=@LoyaltyNumber

if @@Rowcount > 0
begin          — Customer has already been inserted
       return       — @CustomerKey already set by SELECT
above
end


—      Insert inferred customer member
INSERT        dbo.DimCustomer
(LoyaltyNumber)
VALUES (@LoyaltyNumber)


—    Return new surrogate key
SELECT        @CustomerKey = SCOPE_IDENTITY ()
```

2. Delete the Derived Column transform connected to the Customer Lookup transform.

3. Drag an OLE DB Command transform onto the workspace. Name the transform Create Inferred Customer, connect the Error output of the Customer Lookup transform to it, and then edit it.

4. On the Connection Manager tab, set the Connection Manager field to the data warehouse connection.

5. On the Component Properties tab, set the SQL Statement property to this:

```
EXEC AddCustomer ?, ? OUT
```

The OUT option is important! The new surrogate key will not be returned if you leave it out.

6. On the Column Mappings tab, set the Parameters so the input column LoyaltyNumber is mapped to @LoyaltyNumber and CustomerID is mapped to @CustomerKey. Save this transform.

7. Drag a Union All task onto the workspace.

8. Break the normal data flow coming out of the original Customer Key Lookup transform.

9. Connect the output from the Customer Lookup transforms to the input of the Union All task.

10. Connect the output of the Union All task to the next task in the original data flow. Your updated data flow should now look like the data flow in Figure 7-9.

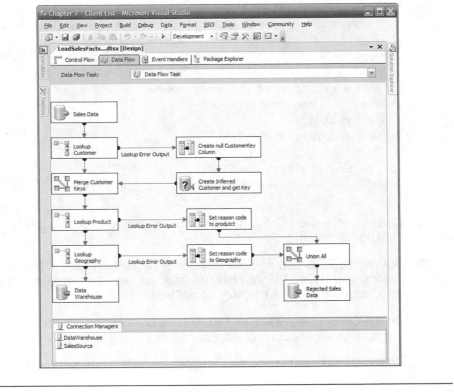

Figure 7-9   Data flow for handling inferred members

Legitimately Missing Data

The customer business key can be null in the fact records because not everyone has a loyalty card, so we couldn't capture the customer information when the transaction took place. The difference between this condition and a late-arriving customer member is that the customer business key is null, as opposed to a non-null value that isn't in the customer dimension table yet. We will never know who this customer was, and we have no way of distinguishing one missing customer from another. One thing is certain: We made a sale. If we ignore those records with null customer keys, however, the sales won't show up in the analysis. So, we have a new kind of subset of the facts to handle: legitimately missing data.

Define Special Missing Members

To keep these sales in the data warehouse, we could substitute the missing customer business key with the key to a pre-defined member such as Walk-in, Public, or simply Unknown. We could also just set the surrogate key for this customer to a standard value, such as zero, to indicate that it is missing (you will need to create a member with the surrogate key value of 0). Establishing standard members for the different types of missing members is considered a best practice. It demonstrates that we saw the missing data and consciously categorized it. We didn't just ignore it. You create standard members during the initialization of the dimension table by inserting them directly into the dimension table before loading the real dimension data.

Letting Analysis Services Handle Missing Members

You could also leave the surrogate key as null in the data warehouse. Analysis Services 2005 has added support for missing members. All you have to do is enable it in the properties of those dimensions that need it. Sounds easy. But before you reach for your mouse to enable this option, you need to ask whether users will access data only through Analysis Services, or whether they might use the relational data warehouse directly. Enabling support for unknown members does not change the null in the data warehouse, so inner joins will still fail, and this could continue to be a source of error in relational reporting.

Here's our take on this. The data warehouse may be used directly by some end-user tools for a while. Without any extra work, it should provide the same answers as you would get through Analysis Services. There also may be more than one reason that a member is missing, but you only have one kind of null to work with. On that basis, you should define members in a dimension for all the different reasons a member could be missing and always use a non-null surrogate key in the fact tables. Now Analysis Services will work correctly for you, and so will any query against the relational data warehouse. There is now only one possible answer for the same question presented to the relational data warehouse and the cubes. We do appreciate that you could make the data warehouse behave just like Analysis Services using views to deal with the necessary outer joins and substitutions, but now you have two places to maintain business logic, and that is a maintenance headache we prefer to avoid.

Data Flow for Legitimately Missing Members

Our approach for the customer dimension is to augment the data flow for when the business key is null, not just missing from the dimension table. We will add a Conditional Split task to the data flow that handles the inferred members. We'll route the fact rows with null business keys to another path where we will use a Derived Columns task to insert the Missing Member surrogate key into the data flow. Then we route this data flow back into the main flow with a Union All task and carry on with normal processing. As part of our initialization of our dimension, we inserted an Unknown member with a known surrogate key value. For our example, we set the surrogate key value to zero. Figure 7-10 shows the data flow.

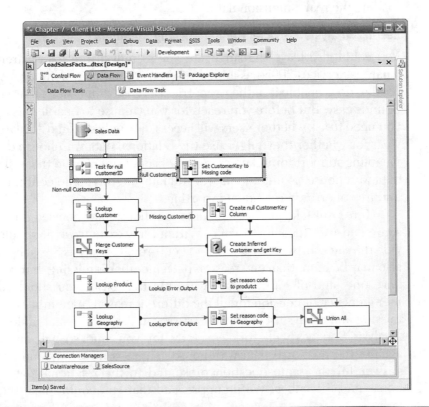

Figure 7-10   Data flow for handling legitimately missing members

Adding Row Counts for Auditing

One of the simplest and most effective audit controls you can have on the success of an ETL operation is to compare the number of rows input and the number of rows output. To do this effectively, you must have a simple query for the input to avoid the possibility that a join omits a row from the result set. Instead of joins, you would use a Lookup transform.

You use a **Row Count transform** to assign the number of rows that flowed between two transforms to a package variable. By using two or more Row Count transforms at the beginning and ends of the data flow task, you can determine whether the task has dropped any rows, or how many rows have been redirected for error handling, as shown in Figure 7-11. To track this information, you can insert a task to the control flow immediately after the data flow task that writes the package variables along with the package name and execution date to an audit table.

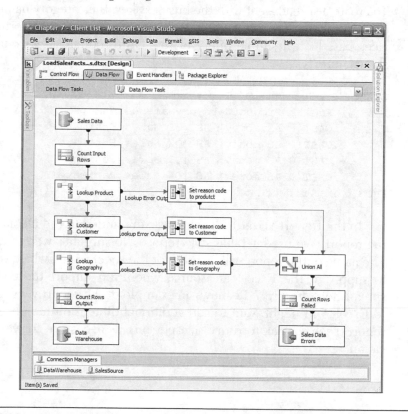

Figure 7-11 Auditing using the Row Count transform

Preventing Bad Data at the Source

One of the main sources of bad data is manually entered data. The business keys are rarely entered correctly—and why should a user have to remember the *exact* spelling of a business key in the first place?

If you are expecting users to enter data such as budgets into a spreadsheet, you can reduce their frustration and increase data quality by supplying them with a spreadsheet with the business keys already entered on the sheet, in protected columns. You can create the spreadsheet by either using MS Query from within Excel to directly populate the spreadsheet from a dimension table or use Reporting Services to create the empty report (except for the keys) and then save it as an Excel spreadsheet. You can also consider populating drop-down lists from the dimension table to assist the user in choosing the correct key.

In our example, sales forecasts are prepared at the Category level. To create a spreadsheet with the business key, the category name, and a column for the forecast amount, we created a report in Reporting Services based on a simple query of the DimProductCategory table, as shown here:

```
SELECT  ProductCategoryBusinessKey AS CategoryID,
        EnglishProductCategoryName AS Name,
        CAST(0 AS money) AS [Q1 Sales Estimate],
        CAST(0 AS money) AS [Q2 Sales Estimate],
        CAST(0 AS money) AS [Q3 Sales Estimate],
        CAST(0 AS money) AS [Q4 Sales Estimate]
FROM    DimProductCategory
```

In the Report Wizard, all columns were added to the Detail level of the report. We used a Table style report. No subtotals were requested. The name of the report will be used for the sheet name, which you need to supply to the Excel data source when you import the completed spreadsheet. Figure 7-12 shows an example of the report we will export to Excel. You might want to add additional dimension members to the report (such as year, territory, salesperson), as necessary, for your application.

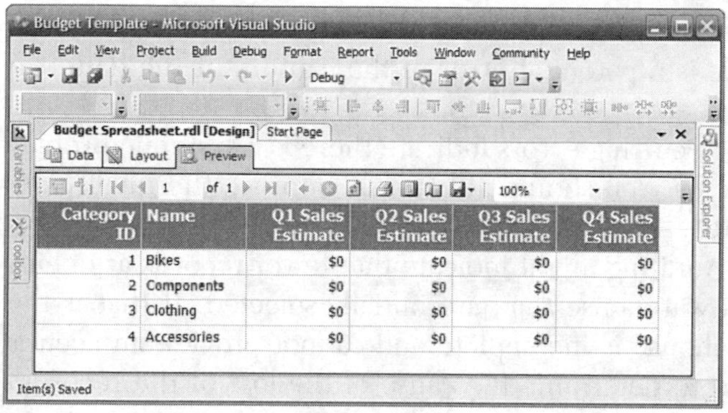

Figure 7-12 Sample Excel budget template report

Managing the Solution

Most of the additional management you need to implement for increased data quality is in the operations area. You will likely be capturing source data that is not clean and forwarding it to an external application or manual process for remediation. You also want to analyze the bad data to determine what you can do to improve the source applications so that they generate more reliable data.

Deployment

You deploy the Integration Services solution for data quality just the same way as you would any other solution for integrating data. Refer to Chapter 4 for a review of the deployment process for Integration Services. You will have the additional task of deploying the application that reviews the tables of rejected data and another database to handle the records generated by the ETL process auditing.

Operations

You might want to review dimension tables for late-arriving (inferred) members that have not been resolved for an extended period of time. If there are many unresolved members, this might indicate that there is a false assumption that the data fits the criteria as late arriving or that there is a potential error in the capture of the data leading to missing members.

Recurring errors indicate there is a systemic problem in the source systems. You should attempt to improve the quality of the data at the source.

Auditing might indicate that fewer records are being written to the data warehouse than are initially selected. If that is the case, the data warehouse is incomplete and cannot provide an accurate picture. You need to determine the cause of the loss of the records and design the ETL process to correctly handle these records so that they are either retained or redirected for review and correction.

Failing fact records or dimension records are redirected to one or more queue for manual correction. The records in the queues need to be promptly reviewed, corrected, and resubmitted for inclusion in the data warehouse. (The process and application that manages the error-remediation workflow is beyond the scope of this chapter.) It is important for these records to be handled rather than left in the queue, because they are not contributing to the analysis process in any way until they become part of the data warehouse. One approach is to have an application that presents a row to an operator for review and allows the operator to make corrections and put the row back into the data source for reprocessing by the ETL stage. In the event that the row can't be corrected because, for example, the product cannot be identified, the operator should substitute a well-known product code that has been defined to be the category for unknown products.

If you have deemed some errors to be so unlikely that they will rarely if ever occur, you should be prepared for the possibility that the ETL process or cube processing might fail. If you do not explicitly handle all potential errors, be sure at least to enable error handling in the cube to report the error and stop processing.

Next Steps

We have focused on dimension issues, which are a common cause of low-quality data. There are situations where the measures are of poor quality. Here are some tips that you might use to solve some of these problems.

Out of Range Values

Data quality might be affected by out-of-range values, but you need to have clear business rules regarding the ranges. You would use a Conditional Split transform to direct a fact row to the normal data flow or to a flow to handle the out-of-range condition. For an example of how to implement this, look at how the customer merge was handled, where we used a Conditional Split transform to decide whether a sufficient match existed between two customer records.

Unexpected Values

You might not necessarily know the true range for each measure, or the range might depend on some complex combinations of the values of some of the dimensions. Often the rules are far too complex to be explicitly stated. In these cases, using a data mining query to assess the probability of a value being correct based on known occurrences of good values and related dimension members is recommended. Because this only provides you with a probability, you will want to route low-probability rows through a manual process for review. The threshold of "low probability" should in most cases be fairly high to minimize false positives. Chapter 10, "Data Mining," provides an introduction to data mining techniques.

Null and Zero

A null measure is considered empty by Analysis Services. Depending on the settings of your cube browser, empty cells might not display. Zero values, on the other hand, are not empty and will display. You should consider whether to convert null measures to zero. You can use a Derived Column transform to check for and convert nulls to zeros.

Summary

It is almost a given that your source data will have errors. Your goal is to get as much useful data into the data warehouse without introducing incorrect data. If a fact isn't providing a business key for a dimension, the data is still useful in other dimensions, just not in that one missing dimension. You should make use of the error output of most of the data flow transforms to handle imperfect data. You can deal with imperfect data by rejecting it, creating an inferred member if you have a business key without a matching dimension member, or you can simply assign the fact to an unknown or miscellaneous category in the dimension. Fuzzy matching can help increase the number of facts successfully matched to known dimension members.

You need to track the quality of your data. Facts that you reject should be written to a reject table for later handling. Even if you can't fix them, you can gain an understanding of what needs to be fixed in the source systems. You can use a simple ratio of rows input from the source to rows output to the data warehouse to gauge the quality of your data. Place rejected and auditing data in a database that is separate from both the staging and data warehouse databases.

CHAPTER 8

Managing Changing Data

Many data sources are simply a snapshot of the current state of some part of your enterprise. If you reload the dimension tables of your data warehouse directly from these sources, all reports and cubes appear as if the current state is the way things have been for all time. This may be alright if you are recording birthdays, but it can seriously mislead you if you are looking at something such as a customer's credit rating or which salesperson is (or was) responsible for a given territory.

When some of the attributes of a dimension record change over time, the dimension is called a **slowly changing dimension** (SCD). For example, customers or employees change their names, the cost of production for a product changes, or a salesperson may become responsible for a different marketing region. Date, on the other hand, is an example of a dimension that is not a SCD because it has a well-defined and universally accepted structure (unless you happen to be modeling events around the time of Caesar, when February 29 and 30 were "repurposed" to lengthen the months of July and August!).

In this chapter, we explore how to model slowly changing dimensions and show how to design the extraction, transformation, and loading (ETL) process to support them. We also examine Analysis Services options that can optimize the processing of SCDs. We also build a solution based on a problem drawn from the financial industry to illustrate the key techniques in working with SCDs.

Business Problem

The customer is a large, progressive credit union with a growing personal and business client base approaching 100,000 members. They offer a full set of services including banking, loans, mortgages, retirement funds, brokerage, and financial planning.

Problem Statement

The customer relationship group in the credit union maintains their customer information in a commercial customer relationship management (CRM) system. They would like to track various pieces of information about their clients over time, but the CRM system maintains only a snapshot of the current status of their clients. Data is uploaded from the CRM system once per month into a data warehouse. The CRM system does not indicate what data has changed, and the data in the data warehouse is simply overwritten.

The credit union also receives monthly feeds of all the customer transactions for the preceding month from a central service provider. However, the CRM system and the financial transaction system feed are independent. The transactions contain an account number and a transaction date that could be used to determine the value of the client attributes at the time of the transaction, but this is of little analytic value because the data warehouse contains CRM data for only one period. No existing facility enables users to easily generate analytic reports that combine data from both systems and provide a view of any point in history. It is not even possible to reprint a previous report with the same data after more than one month, because the data has been replaced.

Solution Overview

The solution we are going to examine builds a data warehouse designed with the ability to correctly represent historical information. We will use Integration Services to manage the loading and updating of slowly changing dimension tables and Analysis Services to analyze the facts in the context of the time it was captured.

Business Requirements

The high-level requirements to support the business objectives are as follows:

- **Ability to track client history.** Some changes to a client's information are interesting and useful for analysis, other changes are not. Credit rating is interesting in analysis, phone number changes are not. The credit union needs the ability to know the state of their clients at any point in time, so that any analysis carried out in the client's context applies at that point in time. Any significant changes in a client's state should not overwrite existing values but should be added to the client's history. This means, for example, that when a client's credit rating changes, the periods of time when the old ratings are in effect and when the new rating is in effect are treated independently. Conversely, if the client's phone number changes, it makes no difference to any analysis, and there is no need to track old phone numbers.

- **Multidimensional transaction analysis.** The solution must allow the users to analyze the transactions using the dimension values from the CRM system that were in effect at the time of the transaction, as well as by other dimensions such as the type of transaction (withdrawal, payroll deposit, and so on) and channel (ATM, Branch, Internet Banking, and so forth).

High-Level Architecture

We will build a data warehouse based on a standard dimensional data model and periodically load the information from the CRM and other systems (see Figure 8-1). In common with most real-world solutions, many of the descriptive dimension attributes such as channel names or customers' credit rating can change over time, but usually these changes to a record will not happen frequently.

The dimension tables and ETL processes will be designed to support these changes, including detecting when records have been updated and making appropriate adjustments to the data warehouse records. Because ETL processes to support SCDs can be complex to implement properly, we will take advantage of the Integration Services Slowly Changing Dimension transformation to correctly process inserts and updates to the dimension tables.

Business Benefits

The solution will deliver the following benefits to the client:

- The effectiveness of planning and forecasting activities will be improved by having access to accurate data for all time periods, including historical data that was previously unavailable.

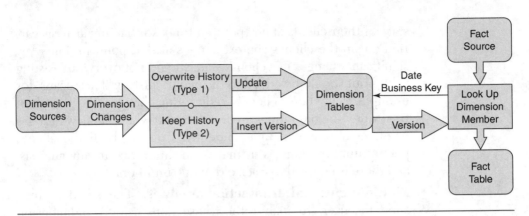

Figure 8-1 High-level architecture

- The ability to track changes in customer attributes will provide accurate models of customer behavior that can be used to develop more profitable products and services.

Data Model

The data model for credit union transactions is for the most part fairly standard. The transactions can be analyzed by the channel, type of transaction, and source of the transaction, and by the customer responsible for the transaction with extensive attributes from the CRM system, including credit rating information, as shown in Figure 8-2.

The main modeling decision that we will need to make is how to handle the effect of dimension data changes in our data warehouse design. The key is to look carefully at the business requirements for each of the dimensions. The question that we need to answer for each dimension is "If a change to an attribute occurs, will users always want to analyze data using the latest value for that attribute, or when they look back at historical data, do they want to use the value that was in effect at that time?" The approach that we will take depends on the answer to this question.

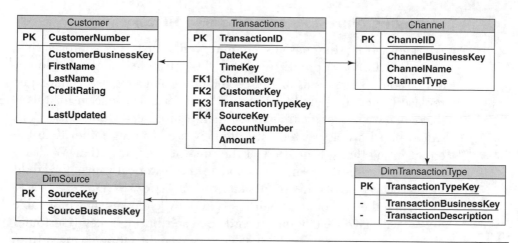

Figure 8-2   Credit Union Transaction data model

Managing Dimensions When History Doesn't Matter

If users always want to see the latest value for an attribute, we can just update the existing dimension record with the new value. This is known as a **Type 1 SCD**. This type of SCD is the easiest to implement because we don't have to make any changes to our standard data model for dimension tables.

For example, the name attribute in the Channel dimension may change over time, but users really only want to see the latest names for the channels. When an update occurs in the source system, we can simply use the business key (which is a channel code in this case) to locate the record in the Channel dimension and replace the name (for example, replacing **Internet** with **Internet Banking** for the *NET* channel code, as shown in Table 8-1). When this dimension is used in a cube, only the latest name displays.

Table 8-1   Channel Dimension Records

Channel Surrogate Key	Channel Code	Channel Name	Channel Type
1	ATM	ATM	Direct
2	BRN	Branch	Direct
3	NET	**Internet Banking**	Indirect

Managing Dimensions to Preserve History

We know from the business requirements that the approach just described is not appropriate for all the attributes in the Customer dimension. When a customer's credit rating changes, we cannot just replace the existing credit rating on the record. The reason for this is that when we look at the transactions in the cube, all the old transactions would be shown associated with the new credit rating rather than the credit rating that was in effect at the time of the transaction. What we need is a design that can accommodate the historical values for credit ratings. This type of dimension is known as a **Type 2 SCD**.

When the Customer dimension is initially loaded as shown in Table 8-2, it will have exactly one record for each business key (Customer Number in this case). If Emily Channing's credit rating changes from **High** to **Medium**, for example, we will need to insert a new record that has the same business key (1000) but a new generated surrogate key (see Table 8-3).

Table 8-2   Original Customer Dimension Records

Customer Surrogate Key	Customer Number	Customer Name	Credit Rating
1	1000	Emily Channing	High
2	1121	Roberto Berneman	Low
3	1212	Deborah Shaffet	Medium

Table 8-3   Updated Customer Dimension Records

Customer Surrogate Key	Customer Number	Customer Name	Credit Rating
1	1000	Emily Channing	High
2	1121	Roberto Berneman	Low
3	1212	Deborah Shaffet	Medium
4	**1000**	**Emily Channing**	**Medium**

Although the data model looks somewhat unorthodox because we have multiple records for the same customer number, we can reassure you that this design is a cornerstone of the dimensional approach and is used in most data warehouses of any significant size.

Some interesting questions arise now that we have multiple records for the same business key:

- How will we identify the current or latest customer record?
- More important, how will we make sure that users see the correct view of the information when looking at transactions?

The first question is fairly easy to handle. We have a few choices of how to approach this, such as adding a status column or date columns that represent the date range for which the dimension record is valid.

The second question is even easier to handle. The major reason that surrogate keys were introduced for dimensional models is to support SCDs that need to display historical information. Because we have used these surrogate keys in all our designs, there is actually nothing else we need to do as long as our ETL process is working correctly (and we will spend most of the technical solution stage explaining how this process should work). The following example helps illustrate this.

Suppose that Emily Channing's credit rating was changed from High to Medium on 3/April/2006. Before that date, there was only one dimension record for customer number 1000, and it had a customer surrogate key of 1. All the transactions in the fact table for Emily Channing that were loaded up until that point are associated with a surrogate key of 1.

After we add the new dimension record for customer number 1000 with a surrogate key of 4, any new transactions after that date will use the latest customer record and have a customer key of 4, as shown in Table 8-4.

Table 8-4   Transaction Fact Records for Customer 1000

Transaction Date	Customer Key	Channel Key	Amount
15/Dec/2005	1	2	4214.12
7/Feb/2006	1	3	213.11
12/Apr/2006	**4**	**2**	**3431.11**

You can see how this would work using an SQL query that shows the sum of amounts grouped by credit rating. If we were to execute the following SQL, the result would be as shown in Table 8-5:

```
SELECT C.CreditRating, SUM(Amount) AS TotalAmount
    FROM FactTransactions F
INNER JOIN DimCustomer C ON C.CustomerKey = F.CustomerKey
GROUP BY C.CreditRating
```

Table 8-5   Transactions Group by Credit Rating for Customer 1000

Credit Rating	Total Amount
High	4427.23
Medium	3431.11

Another common example of a Type 2 SCD occurs in Sales databases. If we were to update the sales rep name attribute on a customer record, all transactions for that customer would be assigned to the new sales rep. Because this would undoubtedly affect the sales rep's total bonus for the year, the business requirement would probably be to make sure that any transactions that occurred while the original sales rep was assigned to the customer are credited to that sales rep, and only the new transactions would be assigned to the new sales rep. This kind of situation occurs often enough that we can give you the following tip.

TIP:
Any Dimension Attribute That Affects Someone's Bonus Is a Candidate for Type 2 SCD
This is a somewhat light-hearted statement but is usually born out in practice. During the modeling phase, it is common for users to claim that they are not interested in tracking attribute history. If that attribute affects how important metrics such as revenue or risk (as in the credit union example) are assigned, give the user concrete examples of what the ramifications would be.

When an Analysis Services cube is used to analyze the data, it will also take advantage of the join on the surrogate key and present the information correctly. So as you can see, Type 2 SCDs are a simple and powerful way to correctly represent historical information in a data warehouse.

Technical Solution

The solution for the Credit Union data warehouse will focus on the ETL process required to handle SCDs and on the changes to the relational tables and Analysis Services dimensions required to support this.

Updating Dimensions with Changing Attributes

We will start with the Channel dimension, which does not track historical information because any new values for attributes will overwrite existing values. (This is a Type 1 SCD.) There will not be any changes required for the Channel dimension table because we have followed the best practices of using a surrogate key and creating a unique key constraint on the business key.

The **Slowly Changing Dimension transformation** in Integration Services automates much of what used to be a fairly complex and time-consuming job for ETL designers. In the past, you would usually need to copy all the source records into a staging area, compare the staging table to the dimension table and insert any new records, compare all the attribute values that might have changed, and then retrieve and update the record using the business key.

To use the Slowly Changing Dimension transformation, you need to specify the source of the dimension records as well as the destination table in the data warehouse. The wizard also needs to know information such as which column is the business key and which columns may have changed values.

QUICK START: Using the Slowly Changing Dimension Transformation for Changing Dimensions

We will be using the Credit Union sample databases for this chapter, which already has the required dimension and fact tables. To begin, create a new Integration Services project and open the default package:

1. Drag a new Data Flow task onto the control flow area and double-click it.

2. Drag an OLE DB Source onto the data flow area and double-click it to bring up the Properties dialog. Specify a connection to the Credit Union Source database, select the Channel table, and click OK.

---

3. In the Data Flow Transformations section of the toolbar, find the Slowly Changing Dimension transformation and drag it onto the data flow area.

4. Drag the green arrow from the OLEDB source to the Slowly Changing Dimension transformation.

5. Double-click the Slowly Changing Dimension transformation to start the wizard. Click Next to skip the Welcome page.

6. Specify a connection to the Credit Union data warehouse and select Dim Channel as the dimension table. In the input columns table, map the ChannelCode source column to the ChannelBusinessKey column and select this column as the Business Key. Click Next.

7. Specify ChannelName and ChannelType as **Changing Attribute**, as shown in Figure 8-3. Click Next and then Next again to skip the Fixed and Changing Attribute Options page.

8. Uncheck "Enable inferred member support" and click Next. Click Finish to complete the wizard.

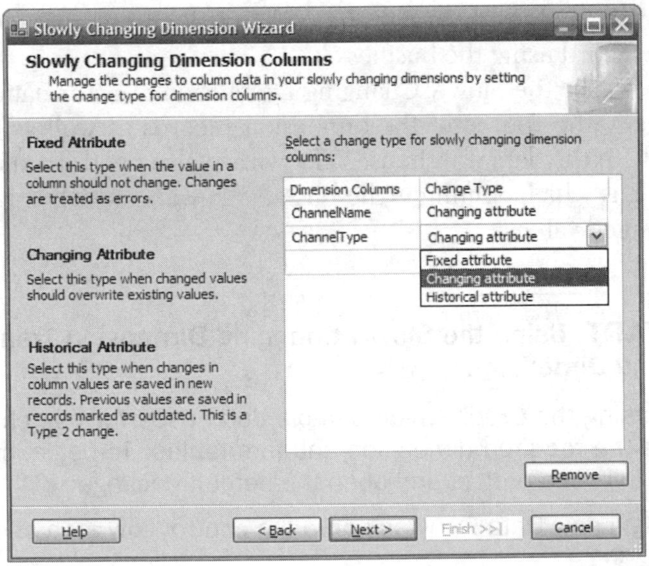

Figure 8-3   Selecting changing dimension attributes

The wizard will create two separate output destinations for new or updated records. Any new records that are not already in the dimension table (which is determined by looking up the record using the business key) are inserted into the table from the New Output data flow path. For dimension records that already exist, the Changing Attribute Updates Output path will execute an SQL command to retrieve the dimension record using the business key and update the changing attributes, which are ChannelName and ChannelType in our example. Because the SQL command uses the business key, it can take advantage of the clustered index that we recommended you create on all dimension tables, as described in Chapter 3, "Building a Data Warehouse."

TIP:

Deleted Members

You might notice that the outputs from the SCD transformation do not cater for deleted records. Remember that you are trying to track history in the data warehouse. Even if a member is no longer used in new activities or transactions, it is still used by facts in your data warehouse. For this reason, you normally don't want to delete any dimension rows from the data warehouse.

Rebuilding Dimension Tables

You might be tempted to simply truncate the dimension table and then re-import all the dimension data into the data warehouse, especially if you don't have to support any dimensions that track historical information. Two things can go wrong with this approach. Any physical deletes (or "hard deletes") from the source table will cause the record to be deleted from the data warehouse, and historical facts will no longer join to that record.

Also, if you have taken our advice to use surrogate keys, and the keys are generated automatically by SQL Server when the rows are inserted, there is no guarantee that the surrogate keys will have the same value for a corresponding business key. You have a substantial risk that the existing facts will now be linked to the wrong dimension member and you will get incorrect results for historical data.

Preserving Information for Dimensions with Historical Attributes

The next dimension that we will tackle is the Customer dimension. Even though some attributes, such as customer name, can be overwritten in the same way as channel, this dimension still needs to be able to preserve history because of the credit rating: Older facts still need to roll up under the correct credit rating, so we need to make some changes to the Customer dimension table.

Changing the Dimension Table to Support Historical Information

When a customer record has an updated value for credit rating, we will be inserting a new dimension record that has the same business key but a new surrogate key. The first table change we need to make is to remove the unique key constraint for the Customer business key column, because each business key may now have multiple records. As discussed in the "Data Model" section, any new facts that are added will be using the new surrogate key and so they will automatically link to the correct credit rating.

However, when we are processing the facts, we only know the business key, so how do we know which one of the two dimension records to pick? The answer is to add some columns to the dimension table that enable us to indicate which one of the records is the latest dimension record, so that we can look up the correct surrogate key. One possible approach to this is to add a Status column that contains a value such as Current for the latest record and Expired for all the older records.

The problem with this approach is that it only tells you which record is the latest one. If at any point you need to reload all your historical facts (which should not happen if you have good backups), you need to know which dimension record is appropriate for each fact record. For example, a transaction from January 12, 1998, should use the dimension record that was in effect at that point.

In our Customer dimension, we will be using the approach of adding StartDate and EndDate columns to the table. These are simply Date-Time columns, and only EndDate is nullable. When the dimension table is first loaded, all records will have the same initial StartDate and a null EndDate. When a changed dimension record is received, the existing record has its EndDate set to the date of the load, and a new record is created with a null EndDate and the StartDate set to the current load date, as shown in Table 8-6.

Table 8-6 Customer Dimension Records

Customer Key	Customer Business Key	Customer Name	Credit Rating	Start Date	End Date
1	1000	Emily Channing	High	1/Jan/2004	**18/Feb/2006**
2	1121	Roberto Berneman	Low	1/Jan/2004	NULL
3	1212	Deborah Shaffet	Medium	1/Jan/2004	NULL
4	**1000**	**Emily Channing**	**Medium**	**18/Feb/2006**	**NULL**

We can then see which dimension record is the "current" record for each business key by looking for all the records with null end dates. Also, we can reload historical facts by joining to the dimension table using the transaction date and selecting dimension records that fall into the correct range.

Loading Dimension Records with Historical Information

In Integration Services, the logic needed to detect changed attributes, to set the end date for the old record, and to add a new record is all provided for you by the same type of SCD transformation that we used for the Channel table. To implement the Customer load package, we can just follow the same steps as for the Channel table; but when the SCD wizard wants to know the type of changes that are required for Credit Rating, we can select **Historical Attribute** rather than Changing Attribute. This lets the wizard know that it will need to generate the steps that are required to support Type 2 dimension changes.

One thing to note is that we can still select Changing Attribute for the Customer Name column, which we always want to overwrite, even though the Credit Rating column has Historical Attribute. What will happen with this is that if the customer name changes, the Integration Services package will simply update the current dimension record with the correct customer name. However, if the credit rating changes, because it was marked as a Historical Attribute, the package will go through the steps required to expire the old record and create a new one with the changed credit rating.

Updating All the Existing Records with a Changed Attribute

By default, when a customer name or other field marked Changing Attribute changes, only the current dimension record is updated by the Integration Services package. This means that when you look at older facts records that link to expired dimension records, you will still see the old customer name. This is often not the behavior that you want—if an attribute is marked as Changing rather than Historical, the reason is usually that you always want to see the most current information for that attribute.

To make sure that the SCD transformation updates all the records for a changing attribute, when running the SCD wizard, you need to check the "Change all the matching records, including outdated records" check box in the Options page, as shown in Figure 8-4.

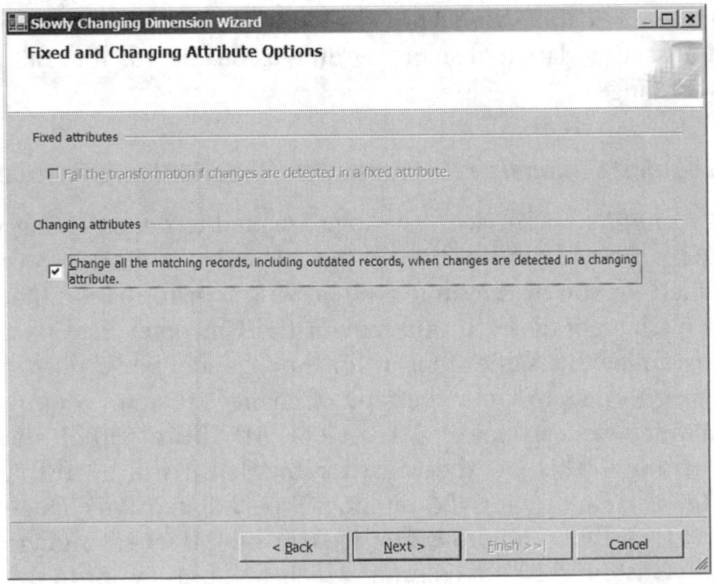

Figure 8-4   Change all matching records option

Running the Package

To understand how the SCD transformation for historical attributes actually works, it is helpful to load your dimension once and then go back and make a few changes to the source table to see what happens. For example, try updating a customer name on one record, changing a credit rating on another record, and adding a record with a new business key. When you run the Integration Services package, you can see the counts of records that flow to each of the steps, as shown in Figure 8-5.

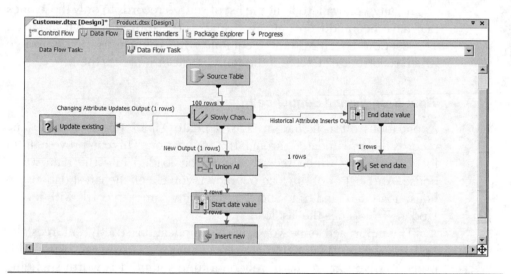

Figure 8-5 Slowly changing dimension package

All the records in the source dimension table flow from the source to the SCD transformation and then are split up depending on their characteristics. If changing attributes such as Customer Name have changed, the record is sent to the Changing Attribute Updates Output to update the existing customer record. If a historical attribute has changed, the record is sent to the Historical Attribute Inserts Output, which will set a variable to determine the end date and then update the end date on the current record. The record is then sent on to the Union All transformation, which combines any new records from the source and sets a value for the start date. Finally, one record is inserted for the new source record, and another record is inserted for the new version of the record with changed historical attribute.

Detecting Changes in Source Dimension Data

The packages that we have built so far have used all the records in the underlying source dimension tables as the input. This is easy to implement, and Integration Services provides good performance for most scenarios. However, if you have a large number of records in a source dimension that do not change often, it is inefficient to throw all the source records at the Slowly Changing Dimension transformation and let it figure out that almost none of them have been changed.

Ideally, you want to limit the list of source records to only those ones that have been added or changed since the last time you ran the load. This section describes some techniques that you can use to determine which records are affected if the source system supports them.

Time Stamps and Sequence Numbers

Applications often include a "Last Update Time" time stamp on any records that are updated through the application. This can prove helpful for determining which records should be loaded into the data warehouse. At the start of the load operation, you check the latest data warehouse load date and time and then load any source records with a Last Update Time since the last load.

This approach only works if the application strictly enforces the updating of the time stamp and no manual processes can bypass this process. If you are going to rely on a time stamp, it is worth spending extra time confirming the behavior with the owners of the source system. If there is any doubt at all, we recommend simply loading all records; otherwise, the "missing updates" will become a data quality issue for the data warehouse.

If an application database includes transaction sequence numbers such as automatically generated identity columns, these are an efficient method to detect additions to the fact tables. You can check for the highest sequence number in the fact table being loaded and then load any source facts with a higher transaction sequence number.

Triggers

A trigger on the source table is a good way to capture changes because it doesn't rely on developers to maintain time stamps or other indicators on the rows. They fire every time, regardless of which application loaded the data. Because every change is captured, even if your data source does not preserve history, your triggers can capture historical rows.

In the code for a trigger, you can insert the affected record into one of three tables depending on whether the operation is an insert, update, or delete. Or you can put all affected rows into one table with an operation type indicator.

Triggers can only be applied to data sources that are relational databases, not flat files or spreadsheets. Sometimes, the database administrator for the data source won't let you add triggers for a variety of reasons, including application performance, so a trigger isn't always an option.

Snowflake Dimension Tables and Historical Attributes

If you are working with Type 2 (preserve history) dimensions, snowflake schemas make the problem of managing the dimension table much more difficult. Each level in snowflake dimension tables contains a key that identifies the parent. If the parent changes in a way that its history must be preserved, its surrogate key will change because a new row is created. This change must be propagated down to its children, which will cause new child rows to be created, which also will have new keys. You can see that a simple change near the top levels of a Type 2 dimension can have a significant cascading effect on the lower levels. You aren't creating significantly more data than in a star because both schemas duplicate data, but you do have to manage the propagation of the changes at each level.

Inserting Facts with Surrogate Key Lookups from Changing Dimensions

The next area of the Credit Union solution that we need to look at is the fact records. Each transaction record from the source system has, as usual, the business key for dimension such as channel and customer. This is easy to handle for the Channel dimension because each business key maps to exactly one surrogate key, so it can be handled as described in Chapter 4, "Integrating Data," using the Integration Services Lookup transformation.

The lookup for the Customer dimension is more challenging. Because there can be multiple records in the customer table for each business key, we need to implement some logic that can locate the correct customer record for each incoming fact. If all the facts that we load are always new (that is, we never have to reload historical facts), we can simply use a query that returns only the current, unexpired customer records as the source for the Lookup transformation, as shown in Figure 8-6.

```
SELECT CustomerKey, CustomerBusinessKey
FROM DimCustomer
WHERE EndDate IS NULL
```

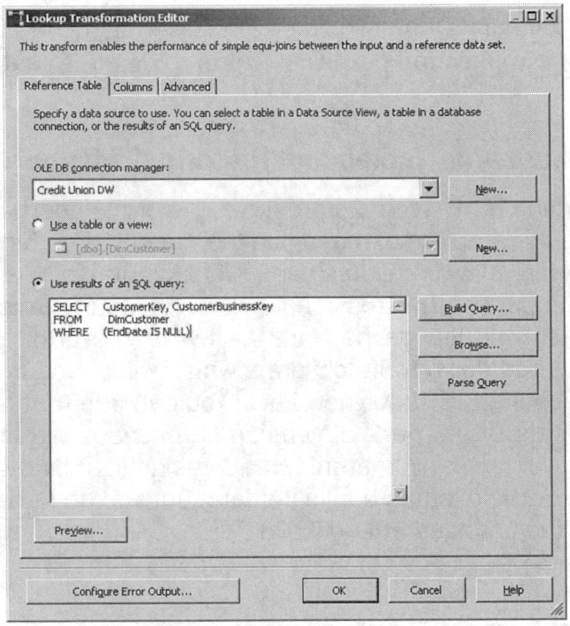

Figure 8-6   Specifying the source for the Customer lookup

Because this will return a single record for each customer business key, we can use this as the lookup source to translate business keys to surrogate keys. However, it is more likely that we will want to support reloading historical facts. In this case, we need to check the transaction date on each fact record and figure out which customer record was applicable at that time. Because SQL is the best performing tool for big joins such as this, the approach usually involves copying the source fact records that you want to load into the temporary staging area and then joining to the dimension table to retrieve the surrogate key in the data source query, rather than in a lookup transform. An example data source query is shown below:

```
SELECT C.CustomerKey, F.Measure1, F.Measure2, …
FROM FactStaging F
LEFT JOIN DimCustomer C
    ON C.CustomerBusinessKey = F.CustomerBusinessKey
   AND F.TransactionDate >= C.StartDate AND
(C.EndDate IS NULL OR F.TransactionDate < C.EndDate)
```

You need to explicitly check for null end dates in the join; otherwise, fact records for the latest time period will not be matched. You can see that we used a left-outer join to connect the dimension, so we will not lose any facts if the dimension member is missing. In a derived column transform, you can check to see if CustomerKey is null, and substitute a missing member key for CustomerKey.

Dealing with Very Wide Dimension Tables

In some CRM systems, you find a large number of attributes in a single table such as Customer. These attributes exist either because they came "out of the box" because the vendor wanted to cover as many situations as possible, or system owners kept adding attributes without much regard to an efficient data model. If you are trying to support a Type 2 changing dimension, a wide row can quickly inflate the space consumed by a dimension table. Not all dimensions will be a problem, but a dimension such as Customer can have millions of members and those members will have multiple rows. It is possible that each year each member will be updated several times, and each update will generate a new row.

Some of these attributes are only of interest for their current value. If they change, it is either to correct an error or the historical value isn't relevant. The history of other attributes will be of interest, which is what makes a Type 2 SCD. If you find that you have only a few attributes where tracking history is important, and many attributes where replacing history is acceptable, you might want to split the physical dimension table into two parts, one for the Type 2 attributes and one for Type 1 attributes. In this way, you will be creating multiple versions of a much smaller row.

Analysis Services Dimension Changes

The approach that we have followed in earlier chapters for creating Analysis Services dimensions works pretty well for slowly changing dimensions, too. Returning to the example shown again in Table 8-7, if a user is looking at all time periods that include transactions from when Emily Channing had a High credit rating, as well as transactions where she had the updated Medium credit rating, the query will return the information that the user usually is expecting to see.

Table 8-7 Updated Customer Dimension Records

Customer Surrogate Key	Customer Number	Customer Name	Credit Rating
1	**1000**	**Emily Channing**	**High**
2	1121	Roberto Berneman	Low
3	1212	Deborah Shaffet	Medium
4	**1000**	**Emily Channing**	**Medium**

For example, if a user drags the Credit Rating attribute onto the rows, he will see totals for both High and Medium credit ratings correctly allocated to the relevant credit ratings. This is essentially the point of SCDs: The revenue earned from this customer when she had a High credit rating is shown correctly, regardless of the fact that she currently has a Medium credit rating.

If we use the Customer Business Key attribute (which contains the customer number from the source system) in a query, everything still works perfectly. Even though there are now two physical dimension records for customer number 1000 with different surrogate keys, the transactions for Emily Channing are correctly grouped together into a single row for customer number 1000 in the results.

Things get interesting when we drag the Customer attribute onto the rows. Remember that in our usual approach for dimensions, we remove the separate Customer Name attribute that the wizard creates, rename the Customer Key attribute to Customer, and use the customer name as the NameColumn property setting. So, we have a single Customer attribute that is based on the unique surrogate key (that is, Customer Key) and displays the customer name when it is used in a query.

Because we now have two records for Emily Channing with different surrogate keys, when we drag the Customer attribute onto the rows, we get two separate rows, as shown in Figure 8-7. All transactions from the original when she had a High credit rating are allocated to the first row, and all the later transactions are allocated to the last row. This is actually technically correct, but because the user can only see the customer name and not the surrogate key (nor would the user understand the surrogate key if he could see it), the user is likely to complain that the dimension contains duplicates.

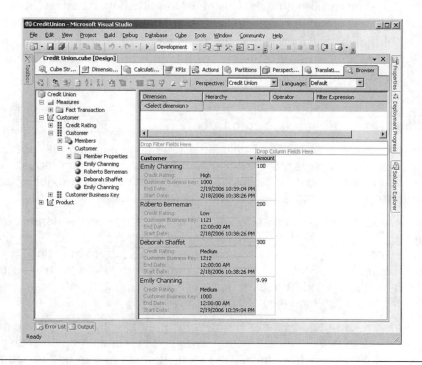

Figure 8-7   Multiple rows for a customer

This might be exactly the behavior that the users want, especially because they can disambiguate the apparently duplicate records by showing the member properties for that attribute if their client tool supports it, which will show them the changes in member property values that are the reason for the separate rows. However, if this behavior is not what they want, you can fix the issue.

The first change to make to the dimension is to change the name of the Customer attribute that is based on the surrogate key to something else, such as Customer Key. You can then drag the CustomerBusinessKey column onto the list of dimension attributes to create a new attribute. Rename this new attribute to be Customer and specify the CustomerName field as the NameColumn property for this attribute. Now when the user drags the Customer attribute onto a query, the data will be grouped so that there is a single row for each unique customer number rather than separate rows for each surrogate key.

You can also hide the Customer Key attribute based on the surrogate key if you want by setting its AttributeHierarchyVisible property to false, although that means that the users won't be able to use the member properties of this attribute to see the different states that the customers have gone through.

Adding Time Intelligence to a Cube

All of our solutions so far have included a Time dimension so that users can select specific years or months for their analysis. A common request is to also add more flexible date calculations to a cube, such as the ability to see "Month to Date" or "Month over Month Growth %" values.

The meaning of terms such as *Month to Date* depends on the context of the user's query, such as what member they have selected in the Time dimension. It's possible to manually add calculated measures to the cube for each of the necessary date calculations, but the MDX tends to be a little tricky (although it has the advantage of being similar for most cubes, so you would only have to master the calculations once).

BI Development Studio includes a wizard to automatically create some of the necessary date calculations for you, which you can launch by selecting Add Business Intelligence from the Cube menu. The wizard can add various calculations to the cube, including time intelligence such as Month to Date and a range of other options.

Managing the Solution

Deploying and operating this solution follows the usual model for Analysis Services, data warehouse, and Integration Services but with some additional steps to take the SCD loading and processing requirements into account.

Deployment

One area that we need to pay particular attention to is the initial load of data for dimension tables. If you initially load all your dimension records with the current system date at that time, the SQL for surrogate key lookups will not work correctly for older fact records. The easiest solution to this is to use an old date, such as 1900/01/01, as the start date for all the dimension records when you initially load the dimension. That way, there will be one dimension record with an appropriate date range for each of the business keys in the fact table. Of course, you need to check that your facts themselves aren't arriving with "special" dates that are even earlier—although these rarely represent the truth anyway, and so they should be replaced during the ETL process.

Operations

The daily processing for solutions using slowly changing dimensions is usually handled by a series of Integration Services packages to load the new and updated dimension data first followed by the fact data, and then reprocess Analysis Services objects as required.

Processing Slowly Changing Dimensions in Analysis Services

To handle any changes or additions to the dimension tables, the Analysis Services processing will need to include running a **Process Update** on the dimensions. This is usually performed using an Analysis Services Processing Task in an Integration Services package that is executed after the new data has been loaded into the data warehouse. Process Update will read all the data in the dimension table and add any new members to the dimension (as well as update any changed attribute values for existing members).

TIP:
Use the Summary Pane to Select Multiple Dimensions for Processing
If you are working on fixing an issue with SCDs' ETL and you need to reprocess several dimensions, you may have tried to select multiple dimensions at once in the free view in SQL Server Management Studio without any success. The trick is to click the Dimensions folder instead, which then shows the list of all dimensions in the Summary pane on the right, and then you can select multiple dimensions simultaneously in the Summary pane and right-click to select Process.

Permission to Process Objects

In an environment with specialized operations staff who perform daily tasks such as managing the overnight load process, there is often a requirement to create a role that only has permission to process some database objects but has no permissions to do anything else. You can create an Analysis Services role that has the Process permission for either the whole database or specific cubes or dimensions.

However, if you want to allow them to use the management tools such as SQL Server Management Studio, you also need to grant them the Read Definition permission, which means that they can see the metadata for all objects such as the data source connection string, which might not be what you want. A better choice is probably to grant them only the Process permission and then create an XMLA script that they can run that does the required job, as described in the following sidebar "Scripting Actions in SQL Server Management Studio."

Scripting Actions in SQL Server Management Studio

When you are working in a development environment, it's easy to connect to your Analysis Services database and run whatever tasks you like, such as adding users to a role or processing a cube. In a production system, this approach will probably not fit well because every action that needs to be taken should be tested first in a QA or test environment.

SQL Server Management Studio has a useful feature that can help make this easier: Every dialog box that you use to make changes to a database has a **Script** button, which will use the settings that you have specified in the dialog to create an XMLA script. This script can then be executed in the Test environment, and then moved to Production if desired.

For example, you can right-click a cube and select Process, specify the settings, and then click the Script button to create a new query window with the relevant XMLA command. This can be saved as a file and then executed in SQL Server Management Studio later. You can also edit the script file manually, if necessary, to make changes to accommodate differences between your development, test, and production environments.

Backups

It's important to regularly back up the data warehouse when SCDs are involved because you might not be able to rebuild the data warehouse from the source if the source is only a snapshot. However, even though this means that the data warehouse contains data no longer available anywhere else, you can still use the Simple recovery model rather than the Full recovery model because you are in complete control of when updates are made to the data warehouse, and can arrange your backup strategy to match. For example, you would typically back up the data warehouse as soon as a data load has been completed and checked to make sure that you could restore to that point in time. If you are not completely sure that there are no updates trickling in between batch loads and backups, you must use the Full recovery model; otherwise, you risk losing data.

Next Steps

In this chapter, we concentrated on the effects of changes to dimension data, but some solutions also need to support changes to the fact data.

Dealing with Updated Facts

Financial systems may restate the figures for historical time periods, or records in transaction systems occasionally need to be corrected. These applications may then retransmit the updated facts to the ETL process.

As we have seen for dimensions, there are a number of potential solutions depending on the business requirements. If each updated transaction has a unique key that can be used to locate the original record in the data warehouse, you could simply update the record in place. In this case, you need to reprocess any cubes (or specific partitions within a cube, as described in Chapter 11, "Very Large Data Warehouses") that reference those time periods. This approach would not be appropriate for applications that need to show that an update has taken place, because the original information is lost.

If users need to be able to see original versus updated facts, for each update that is received, you could work out the difference for each measure between the original record and the updated record and then append a new record that has the (positive or negative) adjustment required with a flag that states that this is an update.

If users need to be able to see multiple versions of the data such as for financial restatements, you could add a Version dimension to the cube. This is somewhat complex to model, however, because if a user selects a specific version, the only information they will see will relate to that one version. One technique is to combine the Version dimension with the Date dimension so that each period can have multiple versions.

Historical Snapshots for Reporting

As you saw in Chapter 6, "Reporting," Reporting Services enables administrators to store snapshots of reports at certain points in time, which can be retrieved by users. These snapshots are complete representations of the data required to display the report as it currently exists, even if the underlying data source is changed in the future.

This is a useful feature because we do not have to make any changes to the data warehouse to support it. For systems that have a high volume of fact changes and need to accurately reprint reports for historical periods, this might be the easiest approach.

Summary

Slowly changing dimensions occur in almost every application. Type 1 SCDs simply overwrite historical values. Type 2 SCDs preserve historical values, and you need to design the schema for SCDs to include a start and end date so the ETL process knows what time period each member is valid. Type 2 SCDs must be referenced using surrogate keys because the business key is no longer unique. If you have wide records, you can reduce storage costs by splitting the attributes into a single Type 1 SCD record and multiple Type 2 records so that the Type 1 attributes won't be repeated unnecessarily. Integration Services has a Slowly Changing Dimension Wizard that makes it easy to create the essential data flow transforms need to implement Type 1 or Type 2 dimensions.

CHAPTER 9

Scorecards

Many organizations are moving beyond managing their business by focusing completely on the bottom line to include a more balanced set of perspectives in their strategic management system. New management processes and books such as *The Balanced Scorecard* (Kaplan and Norton) are driving an increased interest in scorecard or dashboard applications to help achieve strategic goals.

In this chapter, we cover the tools needed to build an effective scorecard application, including the relevant SQL Server 2005 technologies as well as related tools such as Windows SharePoint Services and Office. We look at extending the cubes to provide more complex metrics required by the scorecard using some advanced Analysis Services features, including many-to-many relationships, perspectives, key performance indicators, and parent-child dimensions. We also look at building and publishing Reporting Services reports using the information in the cubes.

Business Problem

Our customer for this chapter is a regional police service with several thousand employees serving a metropolitan region. As with any large organization in the government sector, many stakeholders have an interest in their activities, including the public, the municipal government, and the police services board. They are continually challenged by the need to do more with less budget, which has led to a renewed focus on their strategic direction.

Problem Statement

The police service is looking for new and innovative ways to manage the service from many different dimensions to satisfy the different stakeholders and has been having difficulty aligning all the departments and initiatives around their strategic plan. Although they have a data warehouse and have started to build some reports that describe the types and frequency of crimes that are occurring, this is not sufficient to really effect change across the police service.

This has led to the following problems:

- Although management has spent a great deal of effort creating a comprehensive strategy for the police service, there is a lack of understanding across the organization of how the strategy applies to their particular job.

- Currently, no standard way to measure performance exists in the various key areas identified in the strategy, so it is difficult to establish whether meaningful improvements are being made.

Solution Overview

To address the police service's need to easily communicate their strategy across the organization, we will build an intranet-based portal to publish an up-to-date scorecard that spans all the business areas. The scorecard will communicate progress on all the key areas and allow management to publish related information.

Business Requirements

The high-level requirements to support the business objectives are as follows:

- **Communicate the strategy to all parts of the organization.** Building additional reports that simply include even more information is not sufficient to meet the police service's needs: To really be effective, the proposed solution must include a way to communicate the strategy across the whole organization and must enable every member of the police service to see the performance in the areas where they have an impact.

- **Include all aspects of the strategy.** The proposed solution must include all four main aspects of the police service's strategy:
  - **Crime reduction.** The primary goal is to reduce the levels of specifically targeted types of crime in certain regions of the city.
  - **Community relationships.** One clear measure of the condition of the police service's relationships with the various communities is the number and type of complaints that they receive.
  - **Internal processes.** A key focus area is how well they handle calls to the emergency 911 service, because this has a major effect on the way that the public views the police service. This includes everything from how long the operator takes to answer the call through to the arrival on scene of the dispatched employees.
  - **Professional standards.** To achieve their goals in the other three strategic areas, the police service needs to improve the training that they are providing to their officers.

High-Level Architecture

The existing data warehouse and Analysis Services database will be extended to cover the new subject areas outlined in the business requirements, and new Integration Services feeds will be built to load the information. Any common dimensions across different business areas will be identified and conformed to allow cross-functional reporting. Reporting Services will be used to create the components of the scorecard such as charts and other graphical reports directly from the Analysis Services cubes (see Figure 9-1).

Instead of using standard Web development tools such as HTML or ASP.NET pages to build the portal, we will use Windows SharePoint Services (WSS) both to reduce the complexity and cost of development and to provide a number of additional features. WSS is a server-based component of Windows Server 2003 and is used for building information sharing and collaboration applications.

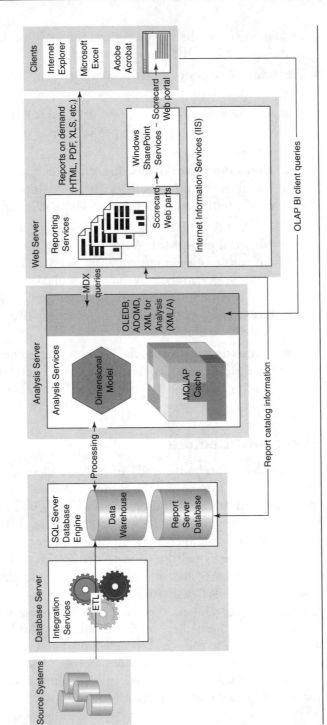

Figure 9-1 High-level architecture

WSS is based on the idea of **web parts**, which are reusable components that can be flexibly assembled on a page to build dashboards or scorecards without any programming. Reporting Services reports can be hosted in these web parts, along with other types of content such as announcements or other Web pages. Users can also publish documents to the portal from within Office applications, making it much easier to disseminate information.

Alternative Solution: Build Reports Directly on the Relational Tables

Instead of using an Analysis Services database as the source for the reports, we could have chosen to build the reports on top of the relational tables using standard SQL. In this solution, as in most Business Intelligence (BI) solutions, there are a number of compelling reasons to include an Analysis Services database. In addition to the performance increase from using on-line analytical processing (OLAP) rather than relational database technology, Analysis Services databases can include some flexible and advanced features, such as parent-child dimensions that can easily be queried, and key performance indicators (KPIs), as you will see in this chapter.

Business Benefits

The solution will deliver the following benefits to the client:

- Increase the ability to communicate their strategy across the organization, with enough flexibility that the information can easily be updated as progress is made
- Create a common set of measures that is understood across the whole police service, so that everyone has a clear and up-to-date understanding of his or her performance

Data Model

Scorecards are usually built on mature data warehouses with data models that span different areas of the business, and the police service scorecard is no exception. To deliver a comprehensive understanding of their police service and support their strategy, the business processes that need to be included in the data model are call handling, crime occurrences, training attendance, and public complaints.

How Good Are We at Handling Calls?

The Call fact table contains a single record for every call received. Because we are interested in what times of day calls are received as well as the date, we use two separate dimensions as described in Chapter 3, "Building a Data Warehouse": a Date dimension that has daily records; and a Time Of Day dimension that has a record for every minute of the day, or 1,440 records in total. When the call record is loaded into the data warehouse from the source system, we can extract the date portion of the call time stamp as the key for Date, and use the time portion of the time stamp to look up the Time Of Day key.

Measures of Elapsed Time

Because we are trying to measure aspects such as how quickly we can dispatch someone after receiving a call, the most interesting measures on this fact table are the ones measuring the gaps between dates and times, such as the time elapsed between dispatching a vehicle and arrival on the scene. We can take the same approach that we used for the manufacturing shipments and store the received, dispatched, arrived, and cleared values as datetime columns in the fact table. Then, we can add calculated columns to the fact view to return the information as useful measures in the form of a number of seconds elapsed between each status.

We could also have modeled this differently and inserted a separate fact record for every change in status, along with a dimension key that describes the event: for example, one fact record for the Call Received event, another record for the Call Dispatched event, and so on. This approach makes a lot of sense for some scenarios, but in our case it's much easier to have a set of additive numeric columns on a single fact record to work with.

One final note on the Time Of Day dimension: As you can see from the fact table in Figure 9-2, we received four different datetime columns from the source system. The modeling question is this: Do we need to add four different Time Of Day keys to allow the user to analyze the facts by any of the four times? The answer you choose depends as usual on the business you are working with. In this case, fairly short gaps occur between the four time periods, so we can just use the time that the call was received as the single Time Of Day key.

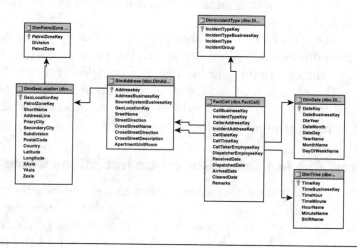

Figure 9-2   Call data model

Dealing with Address Information

Address information always presents interesting challenges in a data warehouse, not the least of which is the data quality issue. The possibilities for interesting analyses almost always outweigh the difficulty of dealing with addresses though, so sooner or later you will need to deal with this kind of information.

The major issue with addresses is that even after applying data cleansing and standardization techniques, the best you will end up with is a set of text attributes that hopefully roll up along some hierarchies such as Country, Province/State, and City. The most interesting analyses you can do with address information, such as looking at which areas in the city are experiencing the most crime, really require more than just street or suburb name matching—we often need to know where the address is physically located.

You have some options for finding the corresponding latitude and longitude from a textual address, such as using third-party geographical information systems or a Web service such as the Microsoft MapPoint service. The MapPoint Web service enables you to submit a text address during the data loading (even an untidy human-entered address) and returns the coordinates and standardized address information. However, geographical information never goes down to the level of detail that some addresses include, such as "Apartment 21B" or "corner of King and Bay St."

In the Call data model shown in Figure 9-2, we can create a GeoLocation dimension table that contains the physical geographical coordinates and description of a location, and an Address dimension table that has the extra information such as apartment numbers. Geographical locations can also be grouped into different patrol zones, each of which belongs to a division within the police service.

How Are Our Crime Reduction Initiatives Going?

Every time police officers are called to a scene, whether a crime has actually been committed or there is just a disturbance, this is known as an "occurrence." The police service is interested in a wide range of information about occurrences, including aspects such as the physical location, the kind of occurrence, whether weapons were involved, and what charges (if any) were laid as a result of the occurrence.

Fact Tables with No Measures

Unlike many of the fact tables we have worked with so far that related to some kind of "transaction," such as a product shipment or a call received, the Occurrence fact table is really modeled around an event. We are interested in what type of event occurred, when it happened, and who was involved; but there is no real "measure" that we can put our hands on. The kind of fact table that we need here really just has a set of dimension keys and no numeric measures, so the analyses that we can perform are mostly about the count of records for a particular selection such as the number of burglaries in the past two months.

Of course, we need to take great care with the concept of conformed dimensions here and make sure that common dimensions such as geographic locations are the same for all fact tables in the data warehouse to allow comparisons across different business areas.

Handling Multiple Charge Records

One interesting problem that we need to solve with this business area relates to the charges that can be laid as a result of the occurrence. Each charge has a number of different dimensions (such as Person and Charge Type) that don't belong with the occurrence as a whole. This means that Charge facts actually have a different granularity to Occurrence facts, and we need to model them with a separate table, as shown in Figure 9-3.

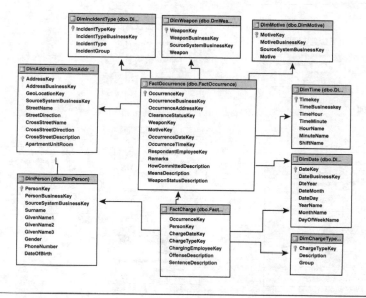

Figure 9-3   Occurrence data model

We could also include on the Charge fact all the dimension keys from the Occurrence fact, so that, for example, we could find out what types of charges were laid as a result of occurrences in a specific geographical area. However, this approach is a bit unwieldy to manage, so we will model a one-to-many (1:M) relationship between the two fact tables and then take advantage of some Analysis Services 2005 features described in the "Technical Solution" section to enable the user to analyze charges using occurrence dimensions.

How Are We Improving Professional Standards?

Every time an officer attends a training course, we add a record to the Training Attendance fact table, including the date, course, result (such as Pass or Fail) dimension keys, and the numeric score the officer received. The Employee dimension has a similar structure to the example in earlier chapters; every employee (except the chief of police) reports to somebody higher up in the chain. We can model this as shown in Figure 9-4 by adding a ParentEmployeeKey column to the dimension table, which contains the surrogate key of another employee record (or null, in the case of the chief). This is an example of a self-referencing dimension, called a parent-child dimension in Analysis Services.

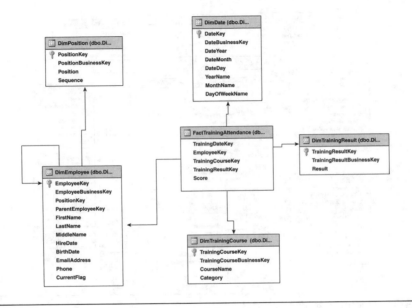

Figure 9-4   Training Attendance data model

What Does the Public Think?

When people call the police service to complain or send in a letter of complaint, we can create a new Complaint fact record with the date and time, as well as the complaintant's address so that we can match it up to the geography dimension and see which communities are having the most complaints. Of course, it would also be really useful to be able to analyze the reasons for the complaints they are receiving. However, the issue that we need to deal with is that complaints don't always neatly match up to a single record in a list of standard complaint reasons.

Some complaints will have more than one reason, so a possible approach is to create multiple fact records for each single complaint, one for each separate reason. This doesn't really match up to the business process, however, because one complex complaint that happens to match up to three different reasons in our dimension table isn't counted as three separate complaints.

We can resolve this dilemma by adding an additional fact table between the Complaint fact table and the Complaint Reason dimension, as shown in Figure 9-5. This is a common technique for resolving M:M (many-to-many) relationships in OLTP databases and works well in data warehouses, too, as long as it can be made transparent to the user of the information. Analysis Services does include features to handle M:M relationships, as you will see in the next section.

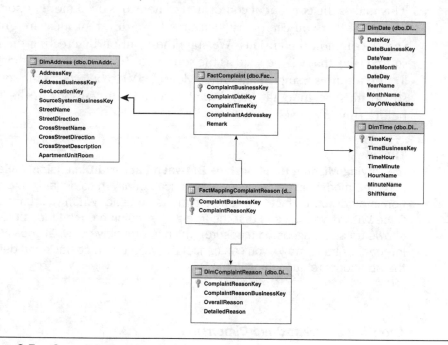

Figure 9-5   Complaints data model

Technical Solution

We will assume that the data warehouse and Integration Services packages follow the standard approach and focus in this section on the particular Analysis Services features that we need to build the solution, as well as on the reporting techniques and Windows SharePoint Services development.

Analysis Services Database

Because we have six fact tables and about 17 dimension tables in the police service data warehouse, the first question we have to answer is how many cubes we need to build. In previous versions of Analysis Services as well as other OLAP technologies, a cube is usually related to a single business area or granularity, meaning that we might have four or five different cubes for this model.

Analysis Services 2005 takes a much simpler approach to this. A cube can essentially contain all the facts and dimensions in a data warehouse, even though the different facts may have different granularities. This makes the concept of conformed dimensions even more important, to ensure that you can query measures from different measure groups across common dimensions. We start the solution by creating the data source view that will be used as the source for the cube. Remember that a cube requires a single data source view (DSV) to be used as the source, so we must include all the relevant facts and dimensions in the DSV before running the Cube Wizard.

TIP:
Identifying Missing Relationships Between Fact and Dimension Tables
For large models like this, it is easy to occasionally miss defining a relationship between a fact table and a dimension table. When you run the Cube Wizard, you will see that the foreign key column on the fact table shows up as a suggested measure, which is probably not what you intended. At this stage, you can cancel the wizard and go back and define the additional relationships in the DSV.

Creating a Parent-Child Dimension

The Employee dimension table contains a record for every employee in the police service, with a column that contains the employee key of the employee's direct superior. Analysis Services understands this type of relationship and lets you create a **parent-child dimension**, which will allow users to drill down through the levels defined by the employee key relationships.

One way that you can set up a parent-child dimension is to use the Dimension Wizard, which will pick up the self-referencing relationship that you defined in the DSV and suggest that the dimension supports parent-child. Alternatively, you can edit an existing dimension and change the Usage property of the parent key attribute to **Parent**. After you have specified this setting, the attribute will show up in client tools as a hierarchy, as shown in Figure 9-6, so you should rename the attribute from Parent Employee Key to something more meaningful, such as Direct Reports.

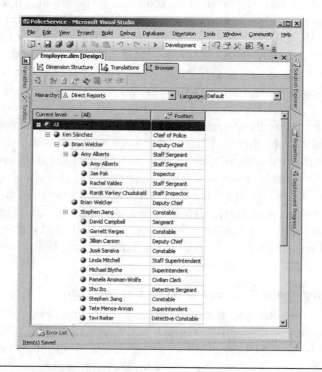

Figure 9-6 Employee dimension

The name that will be used for each member of the Direct Reports hierarchy is taken from the dimension's key attribute. And, because there are separate First Name and Last Name columns in the Employee table, we have added a FullName column to the Employee view in the database that we can use to provide a meaningful name for the key attribute (using the Name Columns property of the Employee key attribute).

Parent Members with Their Own Data

Usually when you use a hierarchy in Analysis Services queries, the numbers for the child-level members are summed up to produce the totals for the group that they belong to. For example, a Product Category total will show the sum of the individual products in that category. Parent-child dimensions make things a little more interesting—because all the members in the Employee dimension from the chief of police down all have an employee key, there can be fact records associated with parent records and their children.

This means that in the dimension shown in Figure 9-6, if Amy Alberts received some complaints and so did the people who report to her, should a query show Amy's total as the number of complaints that she personally received, or the total number of complaints that all her direct reports received? Analysis Services handles this by adding a special child to Amy Alberts that also has the same name, as you can see in the figure. Any complaints that Amy personally received would be associated with this special child, and then these personal complaints would be added to those of her direct reports so that the parent-level Amy Alberts total will include the complaints made to everyone.

For cases when you don't want to show the special child member, you can change the **MembersWithData** property of the parent attribute to be NonLeafDataHidden instead of the default setting, NonLeafDataVisible. In this case, the parent total will still be the same because it will still include the parent's own information, but the special child will not display.

Changing the Sequence of Dimension Members

Each attribute in a dimension has an associated key column and optionally a name column that contains the text to display. When you use the attribute in a query, the sort order of the members is controlled by the OrderBy property of the attribute, and you can choose to order by either the key or the name. This works well for most cases, but what about when you want special control over the order so that, for example, the Position attribute shows the chief of police first in the list and then sorts the rest of the members by their rank?

We can deal with this by adding a Position Sequence column to the Position dimension table, which will contain a number such as 1 for the Chief, 2 for the Deputy Chiefs, and so on. This sequence column can then be added to the Employee dimension as an attribute.

To use the new Position Sequence attribute to change the order of the Position attribute, you can change the OrderByAttribute property of the Position attribute to Position Sequence, and then change the OrderBy property to AttributeKey. If you deploy the changes and browse the dimension, you will see that the positions now show up in the correct sequence. One side effect that we didn't intend though is that we now have an extra attribute, Position Sequence, which doesn't really mean anything to the users.

You can hide the Position Sequence attribute by changing the **AttributeHierarchyEnabled** property to False for that attribute. This setting means that the attribute will not be available for users to select in a query, but can still be used in calculations or for purposes such as ordering other attributes and will still show up in client tools as a Member Property.

Setting Up the Complaint Reasons Many-to-Many Relationship

As you saw in the section "Data Model," each complaint may have many reasons so we have created an intermediary FactMappingComplaint Reason table to resolve the **many-to-many** relationship. When you use the Cube Wizard to create the cube, you must create at least one measure based on this mapping fact table (such as a count); otherwise, the cube will not create the relationship correctly.

This means that the users will end up seeing an additional Mapping Complaint Reason measure group, with a Mapping Complaint Reason Count measure. If this count does not make sense to the users, we can hide the measure by setting its Visible property to False, which will also hide the corresponding measure group. On the other hand, users may be able to use this count to figure out useful information such as the average number of reasons within a single complaint. If you decide to leave this measure visible, you will probably want to change the measure's Display Folder property to be Complaint because users may not consider Mapping Complain Reason a sensible measure group.

When you browse the cube, you will notice, as shown in Figure 9-7, that the number of complaints does not add up to the grand total when you use the Complaint Reason dimension. This makes sense because although we had 1,000 complaints in total, each may have had multiple reasons.

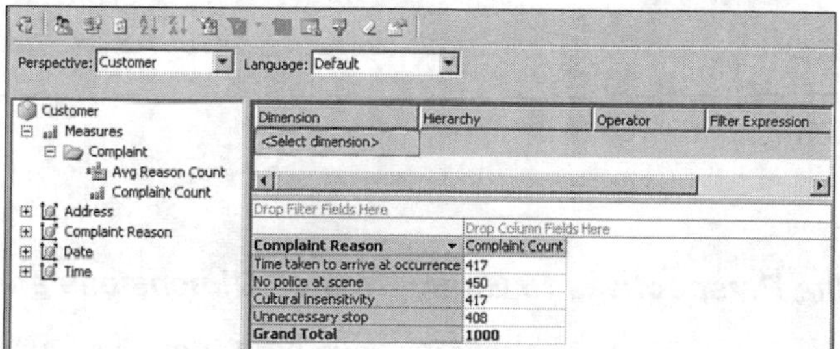

Figure 9-7 Complaint counts with reasons

Another design decision that you need to make during the Cube Wizard is whether you want the Complaint fact to also be available as a dimension. If you want people to be able to drag a Complaint Business Key attribute onto the rows of a query and then look at what reasons each individual complaint consisted of, you must mark Complaint as both a Fact and a Dimension in the wizard. This will create a Complaint "fact dimension," which is similar to the Invoice Details dimension we created in Chapter 5, "Building an Analysis Services Database." If you don't want to add this complexity, make sure to just select Fact and not Dimension in the wizard.

When the wizard has created the cube, you can see the results in the Dimension Usage tab, as shown in Figure 9-8. The Complaint measure group has a relationship with the Complaint Reason dimension, which is set up as M:M with Mapping Complaint Reason selected as the intermediate measure group.

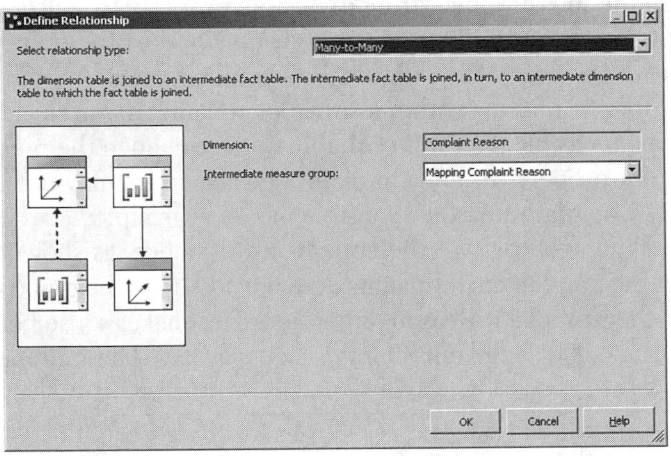

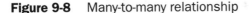

Figure 9-8   Many-to-many relationship

Using Perspectives to Group Related Dimensions and Measures

The police service cube that we have built includes four different measure groups and about 25 dimensions. This is helpful for building our scorecard, but will probably be somewhat overwhelming for users who connect to the cube using a BI client tool such as Excel 2003 or earlier.

One way to help users to navigate complex cubes is to use Analysis Services **perspectives** to collect related measure groups and dimensions into simplified, topic-specific views of the cube.

You can add perspectives to the cube using the Perspectives tab in the cube designer, which allows you to specify a name for the new perspective, as shown in Figure 9-9. For this particular solution, we will leave the default Police Service perspective, which shows everything in the cube, and add four new perspectives that cover the different business areas of Crime Reduction, Community Relationships, Internal Processes, and Professional Standards.

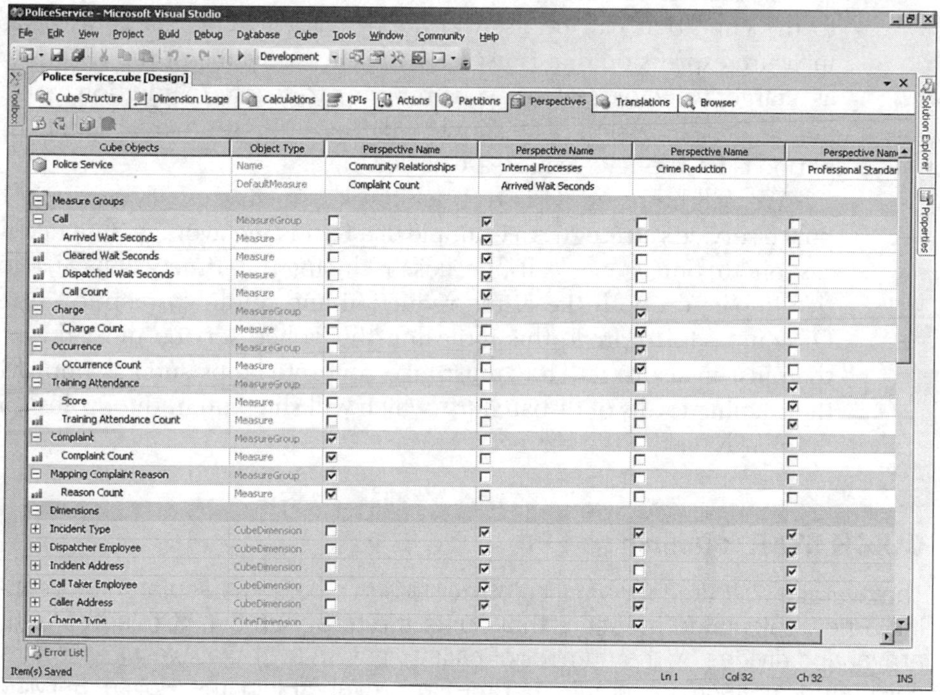

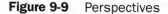

Figure 9-9 Perspectives

These different perspectives show up in client tools as different cubes when users connect to the database, but they are really just different views of the same cube. This is especially useful in client applications such as Excel 2003 and earlier that don't do a great job of displaying many attributes in a single cube. Note that perspectives cannot be used as a security mechanism to grant users access only to certain parts of the cube, because you can only permit or deny access to particular cubes, measures, and dimensions—not to specific perspectives.

Defining Key Performance Indicators

The term *key performance indicator* (**KPI**) can have different meanings depending on the context and the speaker, like so many concepts in BI. In the context of scorecards, it is usually used to refer to a measure that you are tracking, sometimes with an associated goal that you are trying to achieve.

In Analysis Services, a KPI is an additional feature that you can add to the cube that can be used in queries. Each KPI has an associated measure expression that is used for the current value of the KPI as well as a target value or goal that you are trying to reach. In addition, you can define an expression that shows whether the trend over some time period is for the KPI to increase or decrease.

We will be using KPIs to track the key measures of success in the police service's strategy. An example of a KPI is the average time taken to respond to emergency calls, because reducing that time will have a positive impact on both the crime reduction and public-perception fronts. Of course, to improve this indicator, the police service must do more than just measure it. They must take concrete steps such as improving the training levels of dispatchers (which will show up in the Professional Standards part of the scorecard).

QUICK START: Defining a KPI

The average wait time for a police officer to arrive can be calculated by defining a new calculated measure that sums the total number of minutes until arrival and divides by the number of calls to get an average. We will use this calculated measure to create a Time To Arrival KPI in the Police Service cube:

1. In the cube editor, switch to the KPIs tab and select New KPI from the Cube menu.

2. Type Time To Arrival as the name for the new KPI, and select Call as the associated measure group, as shown in Figure 9-10.

3. Enter the Value expression, which represents the current value of the KPI, by dragging the Avg Minutes to Arrival measure from the calculation tools area over to the value expression.

4. Enter a fixed goal of 10 minutes as the goal that the police service is trying to achieve for this KPI. We could use another measure to calculate an appropriate goal instead (such as a percentage improvement over the previous year), or a measure from a separate Goals fact table.

5. The Status indicator will graphically show how we are currently doing with this KPI, which can be represented in various ways such as by selecting a traffic light with red, green, and yellow.

6. Enter the Status expression below, which is an MDX expression used to determine whether to show a low, medium, or high indicator (often shown as red, yellow, and green) for the current status. The expression must return a value in the range from −1 to +1, where −1 indicates low, 0 is the midpoint, and 1 indicates high.

```
Case
    When [Measures].[Avg Minutes To Arrival]<10 Then 1
//early is good
    When [Measures].[Avg Minutes To Arrival]>10 Then -1
//late is bad
    Else 0
End
```

7. Select a trend indicator and enter the trend expression below to show whether the status for the KPI is improving or declining. This expression also returns a value in the range from −1 to +1, and is usually graphically displayed as an arrow showing the direction. For this KPI, we will compare the current value of the expression with the value for the previous calendar period.

```
Case
    When IsEmpty([Date].[Calendar].PrevMember) Then 1
    When [Measures].[Avg Minutes To Arrival] <
        ([Date].[Calendar].PrevMember,
    [Measures].[Avg Minutes To Arrival])
    Then 1 //less than previous period: improving
    When [Measures].[Avg Minutes To Arrival] >
        ([Date].[Calendar].PrevMember,
    [Measures].[Avg Minutes To Arrival])
    Then -1 //more than previous period: declining
    Else 0
End
```

> **8.** Save the cube definition, and select Show KPIs in Browser from the Cube menu to test the KPI.

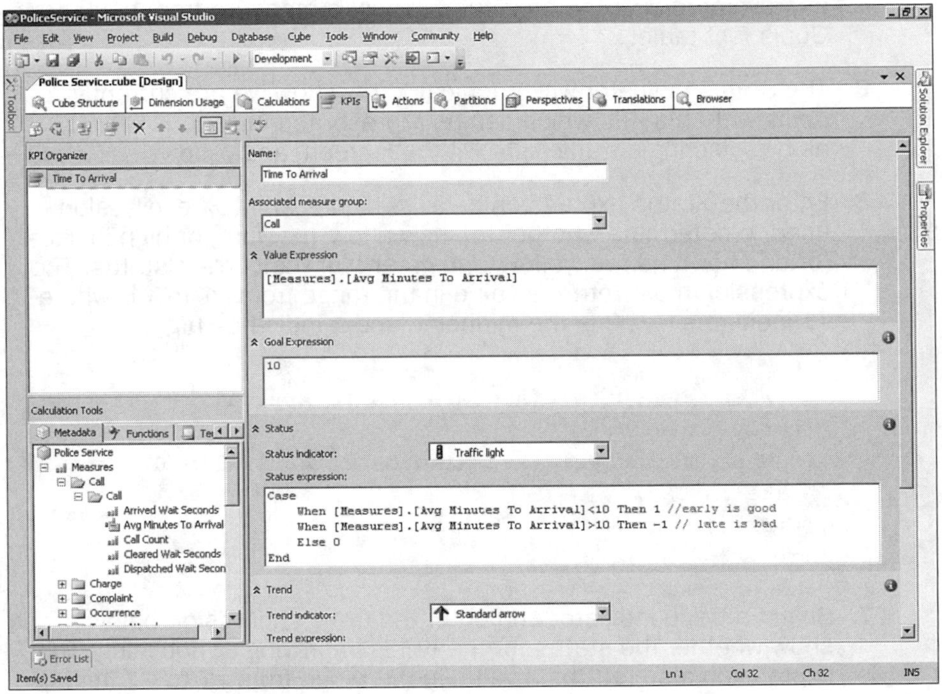

Figure 9-10   Key performance indicators

How the KPIs display to the user depends entirely on the client tool. The MDX language includes KPI functions that the client tool can use to get the different numbers associated with the KPI, such as KPIValue, KPIGoal, and KPITrend. For our police service solution, we will be using a Reporting Services report that uses these functions to display performance indicators, as shown in the next section.

Building the Reports

Now that we have built the Analysis Services database, we can create some Reporting Services reports based on the cube, instead of directly against the relational data warehouse as shown in Chapter 6, "Reporting." Reporting Services 2005 has really good integration with Analysis

Services, so building reports on top of cubes is similar to relational reporting. The report designer in BI Development Studio includes a graphical query designer that you can use to create queries without an in-depth knowledge of the MDX language.

Before we get started, we can add a new Report Server Project to the existing solution by selecting New, Project from the File menu. This makes it easier to work with the Analysis Services and Reporting Services projects in a single solution file. We will also add a shared data source to the report project that uses the Microsoft SQL Server Analysis Services provider and points to the Police Service OLAP database.

The first report that we need for our scorecard is a summary of the complaints that were received during the current month. If you create a new report using the data source you previously defined, the default query editor that will be used is the graphical MDX editor. As shown in Figure 9-11, you can design a query by dragging the Complaint Count measure and Complaint Reasons hierarchy onto the design area. If you want to see the MDX that is used, click the Design Mode button on the right of the toolbar.

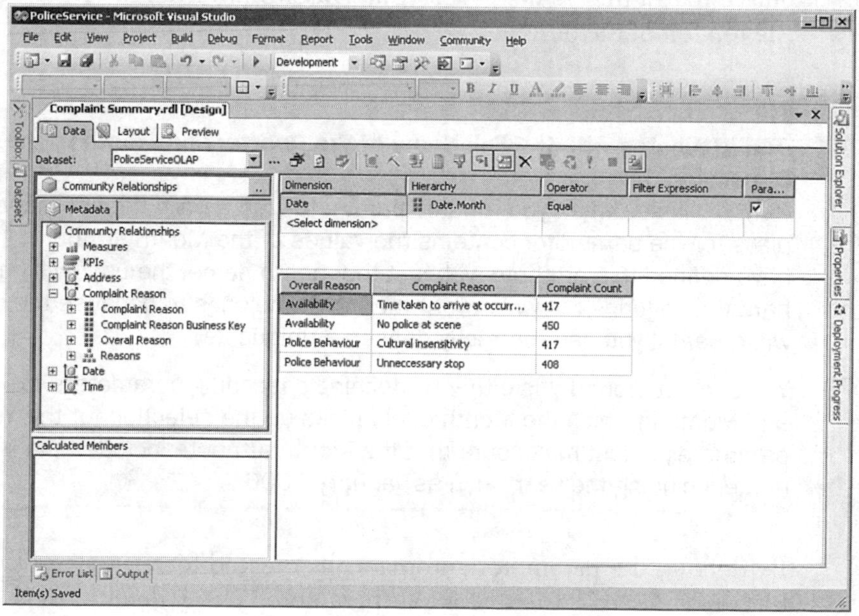

Figure 9-11 MDX query designer

Setting Up Parameters for Analysis Services Queries

We need to set up the report so that the user can select a particular month and show the number of complaints received in that month. This can be done in the same way as for relational reports, by defining a report parameter along with a database query that is used to populate the list of values that the user can choose from. It's a little tricky to write the correct MDX query to return this list, however, so the query designer includes a handy feature that helps you to create parameterized Analysis Services reports more easily.

We can define a filter on Month by selecting the Date dimension and the Date.Month hierarchy in the filter area at the top of the designer, as shown in Figure 9-11. You can enter a specific value or set of values in the Filter Expression area, or just select the Parameters check box to parameterize the MDX query.

When you select the check box, the designer automatically creates a new report parameter for you called DateMonth, and also creates a new dataset containing an MDX query that returns the list of all possible values for the Month hierarchy. You can see or modify this query and execute it to test the results by selecting DateMonth from the Dataset list at the top left of the designer.

TIP:

Add Attributes with the Full Name of the Quarter and Month to the Date Dimension

As you will see when you run this parameterized report, the list that displays for the parameter contains the values of the Month attribute. If you have defined this attribute with just the month name, the user will have a hard time figuring out which year the month belongs to because the month will repeat if you have correctly defined a unique key.

You can get around this either by defining cascading parameters for Year and Month in which the Month query picks up the selection for the Year parameter, or just make sure that the Month attribute includes the full name including the year, such as January 2006.

By default, the parameter automatically created for you allows the user to select multiple values for the parameter using check boxes. In our case, that is not required because we want the report to be run for a specific month, so we can modify the properties for the parameter by selecting Report Parameters from the Report menu, and unchecking the **Multi-value** check box.

Adding KPIs to a Report

We will be using the Time To Arrival KPI that we have defined in the cube to build a report that graphically shows the performance for the current month, across a number of different Incident Types. Although it is possible to build reports that show KPIs, you need to do some manual work because there is no automatic KPI display in the current version of the BI Development Studio report designer.

QUICK START: Adding a KPI to a Report

The query designer supports dragging and dropping a KPI onto a query in the same way that you would use a measure. This will create a column for each of the four KPI numbers, namely Value, Goal, Status, and Trend, which you can use in your report. However, this would just show the numeric values (–1, 0 or 1) for the Status and Trend, so we will use a report expression to figure out which image to display:

1. Add a new report to the project and select the shared Analysis Services data source.

2. In the query builder, select the relevant perspective and drag the Time To Arrival KPI, and the Groups hierarchy from the Incident Type dimension onto the query.

3. Group the data by the Incident Group attribute, and add the Incident Type and the four Time To Arrival columns to the details area.

4. In the report designer, select the textboxes for the Status and Trend columns and delete them. These will be replaced with images rather than just displaying the numbers.

5. Drag an Image item from the report toolbox onto the Status column of the report. The Image Wizard will display; click Next to skip the Welcome page. Select Embedded as the image type and click Next.

6. Click the New Image button and add the three Cylinder GIF files one at a time from the following folder, and then click Finish to exit the Image Wizard. Figure 9-12 shows the resulting images.

   ```
   C:\Program Files\Microsoft SQL Server\90\Tools\binn\VSShell
   \Common7\IDE\DataWarehouseDesigner\KPIsBrowserPage\Images
   ```

---

7. Change the expression for the Value property of the image to the following:

```
=IIF(Fields!Time_To_Arrival_Status.Value = 1, "cylinder2",
 IIF(Fields!Time_To_Arrival_Status.Value = -1, "cylinder0",
 "cylinder1"))
```

8. Change the Sizing property of the image from Fit to AutoSize so that the image displays correctly.

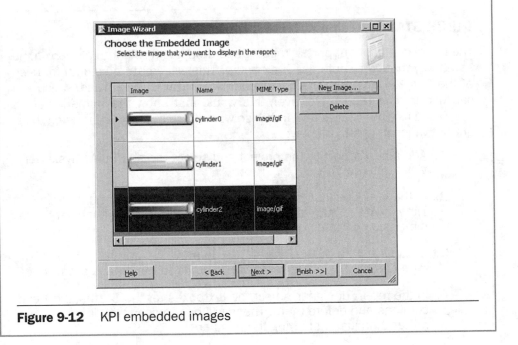

Figure 9-12   KPI embedded images

The process described in the Quick Start for the Status column can also be applied to the Trend column using the arrow images in the KPIs-BrowserPage folder. When you preview the report, you will see how the KPIs are displayed, as shown in Figure 9-13, although you will need to add a parameter to the report to select a specific month to be able to see some different results.

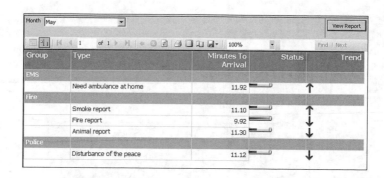

Figure 9-13   KPI report

Using Charts in a Report

Because a scorecard is meant to give people an overall impression of different business areas, you will often end up using lots of charts in the reports to make the information easier to understand. We will use the Chart component to build a complaints report that shows the number of complaints we are receiving every month, grouped by reason. The first step is to create a new report that contains a query that returns the Overall Reason attribute from the Complaint Type dimension, the Month, and the Complaint Count measure. You will also have to add a parameter for the Year attribute so that the user can select the year they are interested in.

When you drag a new Chart onto the report, you will see three different areas at the top, bottom, and right of the chart, as shown in Figure 9-14. The Data area is used to define the numeric measures (Complaint Count) that the chart will display, and the Category area is for the information that will be shown on the rows (Month). You can also show different series in a chart, which we will use to show different lines for each complaint type. You can specify values for each of these areas by dragging the relevant column from the Datasets toolbox.

Building the Scorecard Portal

The business requirement is to provide employees with easy access to the information that they need to understand the current state of the police service, and asking them to run reports periodically or set up e-mail subscriptions is not really an effective way to promote change. As described in the section "High-Level Architecture," we will be using WSS to build a portal that will be every employee's home page and use this portal to publish our scorecard reports and any other information that they need.

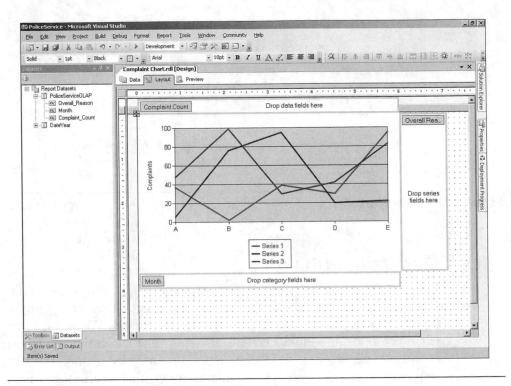

Figure 9-14   Setting up the Chart component

WSS is part of the Windows Server 2003 R2 installation, or for Windows Server 2003, you can download it from Microsoft's download site (search for WSS) and install it separately. Be careful to read the installation information before installing the technology on a Web server that has existing Web applications, because their behavior will be affected.

We will be using WSS to create the main scorecard portal, as shown in Figure 9-15, which includes the high-level information that everyone needs to be aware of. WSS is a large topic, and we could have devoted a whole book to working with it, but this chapter introduces some of the main areas that you need to consider to create a portal.

Creating a WSS Team Site

After you install WSS, any user who goes to the root Web (such as http://MyServer) will see the standard team site. This site includes a shared document library for publishing information, contact and task lists, and a discussion area. You can add additional types of lists or document libraries by clicking the Create button on the toolbar. WSS pages are built around the concept of web parts, which are components that you can arrange on the Web pages and configure to provide functionality such as displaying reports.

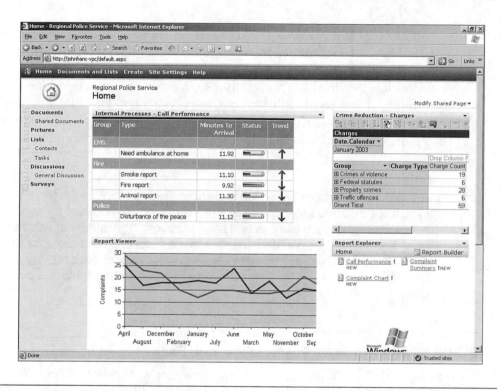

Figure 9-15   Scorecard Web portal

We can also use WSS to create separate sites for different teams such as particular divisions that show specific scorecards that relate to their area. For example, the main portal page could show the number of occurrences in the whole police service, and the team site for 42 Division could use a parameterized report to show only the occurrences within that division. You can create separate team sites by clicking the Create button and choosing Sites and Workspaces. The site will then be available to users by navigating to the address you choose, such as http://MyServer/42division.

Add Reports to the Site

Reporting Services includes two web parts for displaying a list of reports to select from and displaying the contents of a single report on a Web site, but these are not installed by default. Before you can use these web parts, you must run a WSS utility called STSADM.EXE that registers the web parts with the Web server. The detailed steps are described in the Books Online topic "Viewing Reports with SharePoint Web Parts."

The **Report Viewer** web part displays a report right in the Web page along with the other content, so it's a great way of integrating report content into the site. When you add the web part to a page, you can specify the URL of the report server and the path to the report. You can also decide whether to show the toolbar at the top of the web part to allow the user to select values for parameters or use actions such as printing. If you turn off the toolbar, the reports will look like a natural part of the page (see Figure 9-15), but you can't use this approach for reports with parameters because the web part needs to prompt the user.

TIP:
Use Linked Reports to Show Parameterized Reports in Web Parts
If you want to turn off the toolbar on the Report Viewer web part for parameterized reports, you can create a linked report that has default values for all the parameters and then use the linked report as the source for the web part. This allows you to control exactly what the user sees but does mean that the user can't override the default, because the toolbar is disabled.

QUICK START: Adding a Report to the Web Page

We created a Call Performance report that graphically shows the Time To Arrival KPI by Incident Type, and we will be adding this to the Scorecard site using the Report Viewer web part:

1. Open a browser and go to the scorecard site on the server with WSS installed (for example, http://myserver).

2. Select Modify Shared Page on the top right of the page, select Add Web Parts, and select Browse.

3. Select the Virtual Server Gallery option, which will show the two Reporting Services web parts that you have registered on the server.

4. Click the Report Viewer item, and click the Add button at the bottom of the dialog. This will add a new blank report viewer web part to the left pane.

5. Click the arrow at the top right of the new web part and select Modify Shared Web Part. This will show the web part's tool pane so that you can set up the properties.

6. Enter the URL of the report service as shown in Figure 9-16, such as http://myserver/reports, and the full path to the report that you want to display, such as /PoliceServiceReports/Complaint Summary.

7. If you want to hide the toolbar, select None as the toolbar size. As discussed earlier, you must use a report with no parameters such as a linked report with default parameter values if you want to use this option.

8. Open the Appearance region by clicking the plus sign (+) and specify a title for the web part, such as Complaints. If you want to increase the size of the web part, you can specify a fixed value for the height or width.

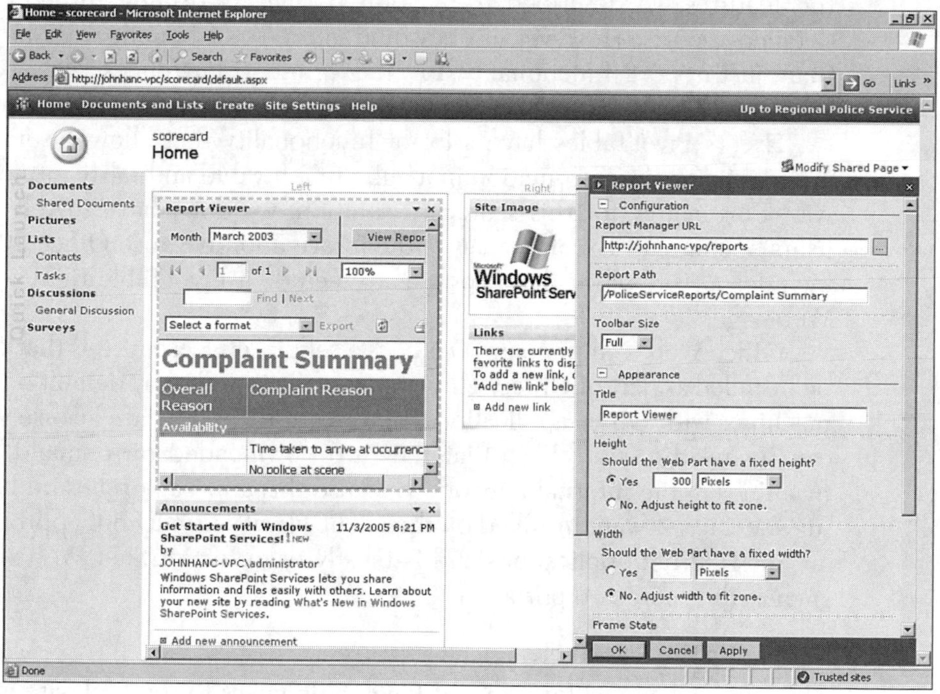

Figure 9-16   Adding a report web part

The **Report Explorer** web part can show a list of reports in a specified folder on the report server, as shown on the bottom right of the page shown in Figure 9-15. When a user clicks the hyperlink for a report, a separate browser window is opened to display the report. You can also add a Report Viewer web part to the page and then connect it to the explorer so that when the user clicks a link, the report displays within the Web page rather than a separate window.

You can connect the two web parts by clicking the arrow at the top of the explorer web part and choosing Modify Shared Web Part, clicking the arrow again when the web part is in design mode and selecting Connections, Show report in, and then selecting the report viewer web part.

Add PivotTable Views to the Web Site

The reports that we have added so far are pretty flexible, and we could extend them to give the users even more capabilities by adding some of the features we described in Chapter 6 such as drilling through to detailed reports. However, users would get a lot of benefit from more than just report functionality for the crime occurrences web part because there are so many different ways to understand the information.

Excel's PivotTables have a lot of functionality that allows users to slice and dice the information in a cube in a flexible and fairly intuitive way. Fortunately for this scorecard solution, we don't have to rely on users opening up Excel to analyze the information because Office 2003 includes a technology that allows us to include a PivotTable right on a Web page.

Office Web Components (OWC) is a set of ActiveX controls that can be installed as part of Office. These are usually installed by default on all machines with Office applications, but with the appropriate license you can set up the controls so that they are downloaded on demand for machines in the internal network. Because this approach relies on having specific software installed on the client PC, it's usually not appropriate for Internet applications and is mostly used for intranet Web sites such as this scorecard portal.

Setting Up the PivotTable

The approach we will use to add PivotTable views to the Web site is to first set up a PivotTable using Excel, and then save it as a Web page that includes the OWC control. From Excel, you can run the PivotTable and PivotChart Report Wizard from the Data menu, which will prompt you to connect to an external data source and use the OLAP cube as the source. Because we don't want to include all the dimensions and measures from the base cube, we can select the smaller cube based on the Crime Reduction perspective. After the wizard has completed, we can drag and drop the measures and dimensions to set up the pivot table view, including adding any filter dimensions such as Date to the page area.

When the view is set up correctly, we can select Save As Web Page from the File menu, and then click the Publish button on the save dialog. This allows us to choose the PivotTable we created and specify a filename to save the HTML file. The important step is to check the **Add interactivity with** box and select PivotTable from the list (see Figure 9-17). If you open the resulting file in a text editor, the HTML is fairly straightforward and basically consists of one big <OBJECT> tag and some page definitions.

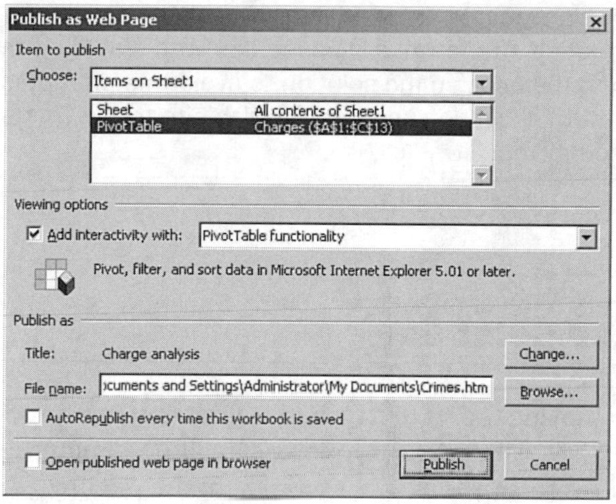

Figure 9-17 Publishing a PivotTable using OWC

Adding the OWC Control to the Portal

We can use a couple of different approaches to get the PivotTable definition we have just created into the portal Web page. The first is to publish the HTML page that was created on a Web server and then use the Page Viewer Web Part to include the page in a web part. This is a good approach when you are already managing a Web site and can just add your OWC pages; in our case, however, we will take advantage of WSS's ability to embed HTML fragments right in the WSS Web page.

If you add a Content Editor web part to the page, you can open the tool pane and click the Source Editor button, which allows you to type HTML that will show up within the web part when the page displays. If you open the PivotTable HTML page that we saved from Excel, you can copy everything from <OBJECT ...> to </OBJECT> and paste the text into the WSS dialog box. When the changes have been applied, you will see the PivotTable control displayed in the Web page, as shown on the top right of Figure 9-15, and the users will now have the ability to flexibly analyze the crime occurrences right in the scorecard site.

TIP:
Add the Scorecard Web Site to Trusted Sites for OWC to Work
If users go to a Web site that contains an OWC control and they are using a recent version of Internet Explorer, they may be prompted with the message "This Web site uses a data provider that may be unsafe." This gets very irritating after a while because this Web site is on their intranet and is known to the user, so the solution to avoid this prompt is for the user to open Internet Options and add the Web site to the Trusted Sites section of the Security tab.

Managing the Solution

When moving the system from development into production, the Analysis Services database and reports can all be deployed in the usual ways, but the WSS site adds a new wrinkle to the picture.

Deployment

If you are going to install Reporting Services and WSS on the same server, you must follow the instructions for configuring Reporting Services with WSS in SQL Server Books Online because WSS has a tricky way of jumping in when any IIS applications are created.

When you are initially moving the Web portal from development to your production environment, you can use the SharePoint Migration Tool (smigrate) to migrate the site over to the new server. Basically, that involves running smigrate on the development server to create a backup file and then copying the file over to production and running smigrate with the -r option to restore the site.

All the information about the WSS site is stored in a SQL Server database, much like Reporting Service's approach. When you install WSS on a server, by default it installs Microsoft SQL Server 2000 Desktop Engine (MSDE) to store the content information, but you can also use an existing database server, which is probably the best option because it will be easier to administer.

Security

Access to the Analysis Services database and Reporting Services report is controlled as described in previous chapters, so we focus here on setting up the security for the WSS portal as well as using some of the advanced security features available in Analysis Services.

More Advanced Cube Security

As you saw in Chapter 5, you can control the dimensions and measures that a user can access by adding roles to the cube and defining which users and groups belong to a role. Doing so proves useful for large complex cubes such as the police service solution, because there are probably going to be some sensitive areas that only certain users should be able to access. For example, the Charge measure group relates to the Person dimension so that users can see which people were charged. The Person dimension includes some attributes such as Name and Date of Birth that are personal information, so these attributes would probably be disabled for most users by unchecking Allow Attribute on the Dimension Data tab for those attributes.

Dimension Data Security

Some scenarios require even more granular control over the data shown to the user, not just restricting the list of dimensions and measures. The Employee dimension contains information on all employees, including the chief of police and deputy chiefs, so this data would probably not be available to all users. On the Dimension Data tab of the role, you can select an attribute and define exactly what data a member of the role can see.

As shown in Figure 9-18, you can define the set of members that they can see in several different ways. You can explicitly list the members that they are allowed to see (allowed member set) or you can list those members that they should not see (denied member set). Both sets can contain either a list of members or an MDX statement that returns a set. In Figure 9-18, we have defined a denied set that removes all employee positions where the sequence is two or less (that is, deputy chief and chief of police).

Choosing an allowed set versus a denied set has a major impact on how new dimension members are handled. If you select a list of product groups and create a role with those groups in an allowed set, any new product groups that are added will not be available to the users in this role because they are not explicitly allowed. On the other hand, if you select a list of product groups that the users should not see and create a role with a denied set, any new product groups will be visible because they are not explicitly denied. This could be a serious problem in some contexts so using an allowed set is generally recommended.

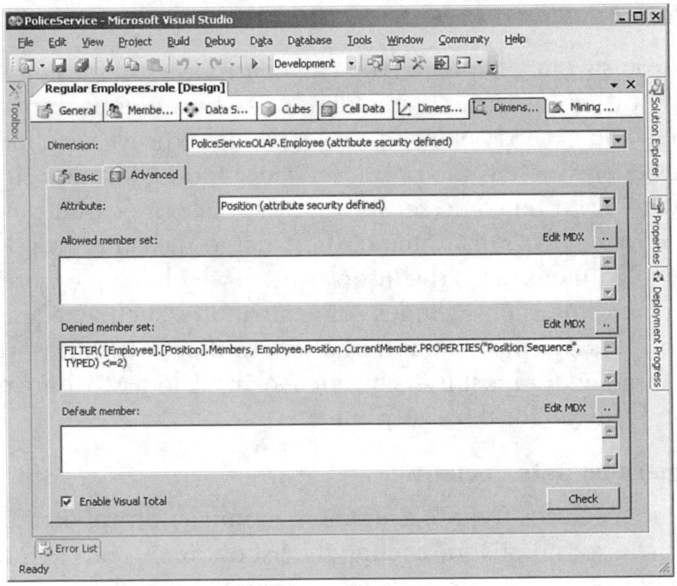

Figure 9-18   Defining dimension data security

The Enable Visual Totals check box on the Dimension Data tab controls what the totals above this attribute will display. If visual totals are disabled (which is the default and best-performing option), the total for all positions will still contain the actual total, including the value for all the members that have been hidden, such as chief of police. This means that users might be able to infer the hidden values by subtracting the visible rows from the total. If you would like to exclude the hidden numbers from the total for all positions, you can turn on visual totals, which will calculate the total based only on those members that are visible to the user.

Testing the Roles

After you have defined the roles, you can test the results by opening the cube browser and clicking the Change User button on the left of the toolbar. Doing so enables you to select a specific role or combination of roles and then browse as if you are a member of those roles rather than an administrator.

One thing to remember when defining multiple roles in a cube is that if a user belongs to more than one role, either by directly being added to the role or by membership in Windows groups, the user's permissions are the sum of all the permissions they have across all the roles they belong to. For example, if one role disables access to a dimension but another role allows it, the user will end up with access to the dimension.

Securing the Portal Web Site

The reports that display within the Reporting Services web parts will use the standard report security, but you will need to use the WSS security settings to control access to the Web site itself and to define what actions a user can perform on the site. You can modify the user permissions by clicking the Site Settings button on the toolbar of a page in the Web site and then selecting Manage Users.

You can add specific users or Windows groups to the list and select which site groups they belong to. A site group controls what actions they can take on the Web site, such as just being able to add documents to existing libraries, or being able to create whole new document libraries. The four site groups that WSS includes by default (Reader, Contributor, Web Designer, and Administrator) can also be extended so that you can control exactly which rights are provided to users.

Maintenance

The most common type of change to the portal will be adding web parts with new reports or rearranging the page. The tricky part is that the SharePoint Migration Tool is really a one-time-only deal: After users have started adding documents and other information to the site, you can't redeploy the site from development into production without deleting all their information. Any future maintenance changes to the site will either need to be manually made to the production site or you could write a script that copies the documents back from the production system into development so that you can use the migration tool.

As the police service's requirements evolve, we will end up making some changes and additions to the Analysis Services database. Any reports and OWC views that have been built on top of the database will need to be retested, because some changes such as renaming an attribute may cause reports to give an error message. OWC is typically quite forgiving about changes and often just ignores any missing columns that you may have deleted or renamed, but you need to check that the view still makes sense.

One other area to watch out for is that any new objects that you add to the cube such as new attributes or measures are not automatically added to any of the perspectives that you have defined. So, if you add a new attribute to a dimension that is part of a perspective, you must remember to go and turn on that attribute in the Perspectives tab.

Operations

All the information on the scorecard site, including items such as the definition of the pages, security settings, and even the documents that users add to the team site, are stored in the WSS SQL Server databases. So this adds another task to the list for your database administrators: In addition to backing up the data warehouse and Reporting Services relational databases and the Analysis Services database, they will also need to back up the STS_Config relational database, which contains the site configuration information, and the STS_<<server_name>>_1 database, which contains the content.

Next Steps

Now that the police service's employees can see their performance on the scorecard, they are likely to want the ability to drill down from the high-level information shown on the Web page down to the detail level information that relates to them. One of the ways in which the scorecard solution can be extended is to use drillthrough on the reports, as shown in Chapter 6, so that they can click on a KPI value or chart section and open a detail report.

Microsoft Office Tools for Scorecards

In addition to using Excel and Windows SharePoint Services, a few other tools in the Office family are useful for building scorecards.

Business Scorecard Manager

In this chapter, we have shown how you can build an effective scorecard using a combination of Analysis Services, Reporting Services, and WSS. The one drawback with the approach we took is that it requires the builder of scorecards to have expertise in each of the technology areas to deliver a full solution.

Microsoft has released a product called Microsoft Office Business Scorecard Manager that is intended to bridge the gap between the users and the scorecards. It is designed to allow people working within the business to create, manage, and use scorecards using Office and Share-Point technologies that they are already familiar with. Customers embarking on scorecard projects or who have a long-term vision for scorecards should take a look at this product.

FrontPage

Microsoft Office FrontPage 2003 (and the upcoming Office SharePoint Designer 2007) is now fully integrated with Windows SharePoint Services, so you can directly edit a WSS site from within the FrontPage graphical editor. This allows you to have much more control over the site compared with using the Modify Shared Page option within the Web site. For example, you can edit the page areas outside the web parts and define new zones for dropping web parts.

2007 Microsoft Office System

The next release of Office will have some new features that make it easier to create BI dashboards that include dynamic KPIs, information from Excel workbooks, and Reporting Services reports.

Supporting Multiple Languages with Analysis Services

If you have users with different languages, you can define **translations** in Analysis Services cubes that will be used when a client application connects to the database with a specific locale. Text such as captions or display folder names, as well as dimension and member names, can all have translations for various languages associated with them.

Summary

In this chapter, we extended a data warehouse and Analysis Services database to cover new areas to support the objectives. We decided to build reports that query the cube rather than the data warehouse so that we benefited from the performance increase from Analysis Services as well as more advanced and flexible reporting features such as key performance indicators. The scorecard reports were published on a Windows SharePoint Services intranet portal, allowing employees to see how the effects of new policies in their areas lead to improvements in the key performance indicators.

We built a single Analysis Services cube containing several different fact tables with different granularities. To help the users navigate the cube, we added several simplified perspectives focused on different subject areas. We identified any common dimensions across business areas and used conformed dimensions to allow cross-functional reporting.

We created a set of reports to display the KPI's using expressions to dynamically pick the relevant image based on the current value and used the Chart component to create graphical views of the information. We built the portal using Windows SharePoint Services to create a team site and used the Report Viewer web part to display reports in the portal. We used linked reports with specific parameter values to allow us to show parameterized reports in the web parts. We also added some dynamic PivotTable views to the site using the OWC controls.

To secure the information, we defined dimension data security in the Analysis Services database to hide some levels of the employee dimension from groups of user, and assigned permissions to specific groups to allow them to access the WSS team site and Reporting Services reports. We deployed the Web portal using Sharepoint Migration Tool (smigrate). Operations staff will now also back up the WSS SQL Server databases in addition to the reporting and data warehouse databases.

CHAPTER 10

Data Mining

As you have seen, Analysis Services enables you to build powerful Business Intelligence (BI) solutions that enable users to really understand the business. However, many business problems rely on the ability to spot patterns and trends across data sets that are far too large or complex for human analysts. Data mining can be used to explore your data and find these patterns, allowing you to begin to ask why things happen and to predict what will happen in the future.

In this chapter, we look at how to use some of the data mining features in Analysis Services 2005 to perform tasks such as customer segmentation and market basket analysis. The data mining results are presented in the form of new dimensions in cubes and are used in Web applications.

Business Problem

Our customer for this chapter is a large music retailer with stores across the country, and which also has an e-commerce site where customers can buy CDs. The retailer has also moved into the broader entertainment market and added product lines such as videos, computer games, and, more recently, DVDs. This latest product line has just been added to the Web site so that customers can buy DVDs online.

Problem Statement

The retailer faces strong competition in the online DVD market and is struggling to achieve profitability and gain market share. Its e-commerce system has built-in capabilities for conducting marketing campaigns and performing analysis; however, this is restricted to information learned from customers' online behavior and does not tie back into the retailer's extensive data warehouse, which is populated mostly with information from their stores.

This has led to the following challenges:

- There is currently no way to segment customers by combining the extensive customer profile information with the Internet-usage metrics. This segmentation is needed so that they can target direct mail and other marketing to segments that will potentially use the Internet channel.

- The profit margin on DVD sales is low because of extensive competition. The retailer needs to find ways to increase the value of items sold in a transaction, such as by promoting and cross-selling additional products at the time of the purchase.

Solution Overview

We will build an extraction, transformation, and loading (ETL) process to add the Web site's visit-tracking data to the corporate data warehouse. We will use the data mining features of Analysis Services to help discover patterns in this data and provide the information back to the business.

Business Requirements

The high-level requirements to support the business objectives are as follows:

- **Customer segmentation.** The data warehouse already has excellent profiling information on customers that is obtained through a popular store loyalty card program. This information includes demographic profiles and detailed purchasing histories, because the customer's unique card number can be used to identify store transactions. However, the business also needs a profile of customers' online activities.

  The main areas of interest are *frequency,* or how often the customer uses the Web site, and *recency,* or how much time has elapsed since they visited the site. There is already information in the data warehouse on the third area of interest, which is *intensity,* or how much money the customer is spending through the Internet channel.

When these Internet profiling attributes are available, customers can be segmented into groups with relatively similar behavior. Analysts can use the information for marketing purposes, such as producing lists of customers for direct mail campaigns, as well as performing further analysis using the attributes and groups that we identified.

- **Online recommendations.** They would like to add an online recommendations feature to the new DVD area of the Web site to drive additional profit per online transaction. When a customer adds a DVD to her shopping basket, she must be prompted with a short list of other titles that she may be interested in.

   The performance of this recommendation needs to be good because any delay in the responsiveness of the Web site has been shown to lead to more abandoned transactions. Also, the recommendation must include items sold through the physical stores as well as the Web site, because the stores currently make up the bulk of the sales.

High-Level Architecture

We will add the Internet visit information to the existing data warehouse and Analysis Services cubes. Because the e-commerce application already extracts data from the Web logs and inserts it into a relational database, we will use this as the source for the ETL process. The data in this source database already has discrete user sessions identified.

Many e-commerce applications (including those based on the Microsoft Commerce Server platform) provide this kind of extraction and log processing functionality, but for custom Web sites, the only available tracking information may be the raw Internet Information Server (IIS) logs. A full treatment of the steps to extract this kind of information from Web log files is beyond the scope of this chapter; see the sidebar "Extracting Information from IIS Logs" for a high-level explanation.

After this information is in the data warehouse, we will use the data mining features of Analysis Services to achieve the business goals for segmentation and recommendations, as shown in Figure 10-1. For each area, we will create a data mining structure that describes the underlying business problem and then run the appropriate data mining algorithm against the data to build a mathematical model. This model can then be used both for predictions such as recommending a list of products or for grouping information in cubes together in new ways to enable more complex analyses.

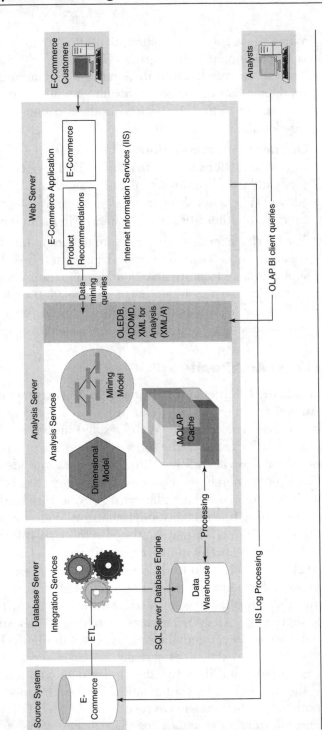

Figure 10-1 High-level architecture

Data mining in Analysis Services has several different types of algorithms to perform tasks such as classification, regression, and segmentation. We will use the **Microsoft Clustering** algorithm to create a customer segmentation mining model, and then the model will provide these categories of customers' online behavior as a new dimension for cube analysis. We will use the **Microsoft Association** algorithm to build a data mining model that can be used to make product recommendations, and then add code to the Web site to query this model to suggest appropriate DVDs for online shoppers.

Alternative Solution: Build a Feed from the Data Warehouse to the E-Commerce System

Because the e-commerce application already has some built-in BI capabilities, we could use these features for customer segmentation and product recommendations if we built a feed from the corporate data warehouse to supply extra information, such as detailed customer profile information or even sales totals for other channels.

However, this approach is not recommended in this case because it will be impractical to meet the business requirements. Product recommendations need to be based on sales through the physical store channel as well as online transactions, and copying all the sales transactions to the e-commerce data warehouse database is not viable. Also, customer segmentation is a core activity for the marketing department, and they need to have access to all the rich information in the data warehouse.

In summary, although many e-commerce applications have built-in analytical functionality, most large retailers that also have physical stores will already have an investment in a data warehouse, and the most appropriate approach will often be to find ways to extend this with information from the Internet channel.

Extracting Information from IIS Logs

Although in our example solution, we will be taking advantage of the log parsing facilities that are built in to the e-commerce application, many companies have built a custom Web site where the only available tracking information is the raw IIS logs.

The first step in extracting this information is to parse the log files and extract the information into a staging database. You could create an Integration

Services package to perform this extraction, possibly with an additional tool to make the data easier to work with. Microsoft has a free Log Parser utility (www.logparser.com), and third-party parsers are also available.

However, after you have extracted the raw information, the real fun begins, and is not for the faint of heart. Finding discrete "sessions" involves looking for an identifier in the logs such as username or cookie and then identifying a time period that could identify a "visit" fact.

If you also want to look at what pages the users visited, you need to parse URLs to deal with pages that are parameterized with identifiers such as product IDs (for example, product.aspx?ID=322442). On the whole, it is generally much easier to take advantage of an e-commerce application's existing parsing facilities if they exist, or otherwise find an existing tool that meets your needs.

Business Benefits

The solution will deliver the following benefits:

- Targeting direct mail and other marketing to identified groups of customers that will probably use the Internet channel will decrease the overall cost of marketing and increase the company's market share.

- Profitability will be improved by increasing the average number of items sold per transaction, such as selling more DVDs in one transaction and still incurring one shipping cost.

Data Model

Most of the data model for e-commerce is similar to the standard retail data model. The data that we need for product recommendations is simply a Sales fact that shows products that are sold over time. The interesting new areas in e-commerce are the facts that allow us to understand the behavior of visitors to the Web site.

Many BI solutions for Internet applications focus on how the site is used. Information such as the order that people visit pages, which page they start at, what Web site they came from—all of this can help companies to improve the effectiveness of their Web sites. Tracking information such as "click-through" rates, which measure how often users click an advertisement, can produce more optimized campaigns and a better experience for users.

However, for this solution, we focus on the other side of the Web equation: Who are the people visiting our site? To really be able to understand customers well enough to produce rich customer profiles, we need to keep track of the visits that users make to our site.

How Often Are Users Visiting the Web Site?

The new fact table in the data warehouse is Visit, which has one record for each completed customer visit to the site, as shown in Figure 10-2. So, if a customer signed on at 3:10 p.m. and then clicked through several pages with the last page hit logged at 3:25 p.m., the e-commerce application's log parser will see the last page hit and create a single record that spans the whole time period.

The measures that we will be tracking are the duration of the visit and the number of requests (or page hits) during the visit. Because we are interested in the date that the visit took place as well as the time, we will use the approach explained in earlier chapters and have separate Date and Time of Day dimensions. We can also include the Referrer Domain that the user came from which helps us to determine which Web sites are sending the most traffic to our site, and the type of browser platform that the customer was using, including browser version and operating system. This dimension is often called User Agent rather than Browser Platform because other software such as search spiders can also visit the site; however, we always use business-friendly names in the data warehouse rather than terms such as User Agent, which probably only makes sense to Web geeks.

If your log parser supports it, one useful dimension that we can add is Visit Result, which has values such as Browsed, Abandoned Transaction, and Completed Transaction. This is somewhat difficult for parsers to derive from the Web logs, however, because they would need to look for specific marker pages in the log, such as a confirmation page when the user completes a transaction.

The e-commerce application's database also includes another table with the actual page hits that took place, so in some ways it seems we are breaking one of the cardinal rules of dimensional modeling—always use the most detailed grain available. By using the summarized Visit table, we are losing the ability to analyze by a Page dimension, which shows which pages the user hit. Although powerful, the Page Hits fact table will inevitably be huge, and we would need a good business case to go to the trouble of managing this volume of data. Also, the kinds of analysis that Page Hits would enable are often already provided directly by e-commerce applications, and in this case don't need to be augmented with the extra information stored in the data warehouse.

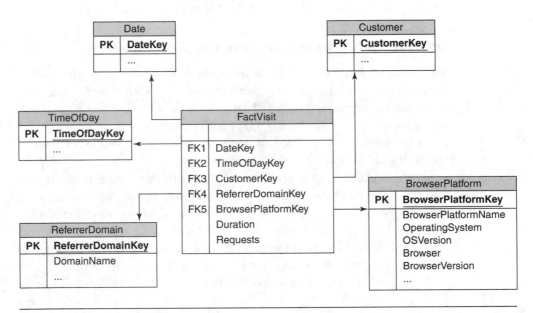

Figure 10-2 Visit fact

One question that arises is whether we can tie the Visit fact back to the Sales Transaction fact. If we could do that, maybe we could show information such as how profitable visits were. It turns out that for SQL Server 2005, it doesn't really matter if you have the information on the same fact record. Because a single cube can contain measure groups for both Sales and Visits, if a user has selected a date range and a customer or grouping of customers, measures such as total visits and total revenue display properly anyway.

In other words, the common dimensions between the two fact tables provide the means to tie the information together, and we don't actually need to link the two fact records. The site activity is tied to the sales transactions by way of the fact that they occurred in the same time interval to the same customer.

Who Is Using the Web Site?

The most important dimension is certainly Customer, but data warehouse architects face an interesting challenge when it comes to the Web—we often don't know who the customers are. Most e-commerce sites require users to create an online profile, and if the customer must sign in before placing any orders, we can usually associate the Web site activity after the user signs in with the customer's profile. However, online profiles usually contain little mandatory information (and as many online retailers will testify, the information they contain is often meaningless).

The goal for effective BI from the Web site visit information is to augment the minimal Internet profile information with rich, accurate demographic information. In our solution, the site profile includes an optional loyalty card number that is issued by the physical stores. Because customers build up credits to earn free CDs, this information is well populated and can be used to connect the online behavior from the Web site's customer profile with the data warehouse Customer dimension. (In case you have ever wondered why stores are so keen to hand out loyalty cards, now you know—they are trying to build a good Customer dimension!)

For customers who don't have a loyalty card number and an existing Customer record in the data warehouse, we have two choices: Either we can create new Customer records for each of the unmatched customer profiles with minimal information or we can use a single "Unknown Internet Customer" record that groups all these customer together. Because even the minimal online profile will allow us to track information such as how long they have been using our Web site, we will still be able to achieve some of our segmentation goals such as identifying frequent visitors, and so we will go ahead and create new Customer records for every distinct online profile that doesn't have a loyalty card.

Note that the CustomerKey will be blank for all visits where the user did not sign on but just browsed the site. If the user actually places an order, he must sign on and therefore there will be a customer key, but we will allocate all the other facts to an "Unknown Customer" record. It is important not to just discard these fact records, because even without the customer information, the Visit fact table is a valuable source of information about peak traffic levels on the site.

Alternatively, we could have solved the problem by modeling a separate "Internet Customer" dimension that is only used for this area and not related to other facts such as Sales, and thus avoid creating extra records in our Customer dimension. However, this would mean that we couldn't create a cube with a common Customer dimension that combines measure groups for Internet visit measures with sales and other facts for the business, which is really the central goal of this solution.

What Interesting Attributes Can We Track?

The first attribute we can add to the data warehouse Customer dimension is one of the easiest but most interesting: an InternetUser flag that indicates whether the customer has created a profile on the site, as shown in Figure 10-3. This is easy to populate and will enable analysts to start to understand the characteristics of people who use the Internet channel versus those who don't.

A related InternetPurchaser attribute can be derived by looking at the Sales transactions and flagging every customer who has made any purchases using the Internet channel. All InternetPurchasers will, of course, be InternetUsers, but the reverse is not true because some users will have created a profile but not yet made a purchase online. Although analysts could easily and flexibly get a list of customers who had purchased through the Internet by browsing the Sales cube and selecting the Internet channel and a time period, it is still a good idea to add the InternetPurchaser flag so that it is easy for both analysts and data mining models to distinguish those customers who have ever used the Internet channel from those who haven't.

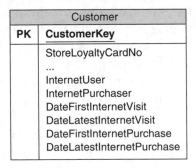

Customer	
PK	**CustomerKey**
	StoreLoyaltyCardNo
	...
	InternetUser
	InternetPurchaser
	DateFirstInternetVisit
	DateLatestInternetVisit
	DateFirstInternetPurchase
	DateLatestInternetPurchase

Figure 10-3   Customer dimension

Other interesting customer attributes are DateFirstInternetVisit, which tells us how long they have been using our site, and DateLatestInternetVisit, which tells us how recently they have visited. Both of these attributes are derived from the underlying Visit fact table, but will be added to the Customer table to make the dimension easy to query. Note that this means we will be updating our customer records much more often, so one way of simplifying the ETL process would be to create a view over Customer and the Visit fact table that returns the maximum date for each customer and is used as the source for the Analysis Services Customer dimension. We can also add equivalent date columns for the date of the first actual online purchase, and the most recent online purchase.

Technical Solution

We start this section by reviewing the changes that were made to add the Visit fact and customer information to the existing data warehouse, and then give a detailed description of the data mining sections of the solution.

Adding Visit Information to the Data Warehouse

To add the Visit fact table and associated dimensions to the database, we need to supplement the existing ETL procedures to load data from the e-commerce application's tables. As always, when adding a new data source to the warehouse, you need to perform data mapping to match any existing dimensions. We have already discussed that for the Customer dimension we will be using the store loyalty card number to map Internet profiles to customer records. Date and Time of Day keys are usually simple to map; however, because time stamps in Web server logs are either in the local time of the server or in UTC (coordinated universal time), we need to check this before implementing the ETL.

The Referrer Domain dimension will be sourced from the equivalent table in the e-commerce database, but if you are implementing ETL to extract this information from log files (see the sidebar "Extracting Information from IIS Logs"), you need to parse the URL of the referring page to extract the domain name. The Browser Platform attributes such as OperatingSystem and BrowserVersion also need to be extracted from the User Agent field in the log files.

Customer Dimension Changes

The new customer attributes can easily be added to the cube definition by refreshing the data source view (DSV) in BI Development Studio to pick up the new columns, and then adding these as attributes to the Customer dimension. However, they may not be in the best format for analysis purposes—having the specific date that a user first visited the site is not very illuminating for users of the cube. In fact, they would probably be better served by being able to select customers based on groups that show how long they have been Internet site users (for example, "3–6 months").

We can add this information into the DSV as a named calculation on Customer or add it to the underlying view in the database. You can implement the MonthsSinceFirstInternetVisit named calculation by using the `DateDiff` function to work out the number of months between the date of the first visit and the current system date:

```
DateDiff(m, DateFirstInternetVisit, GetDate())
```

Instead of showing the user a long list of numbers, it would be better to group the numbers together into ranges, such as 1–3 months, 3–6 months, and so on. Although we could do this manually using a lookup table of month ranges, we can take advantage of the Analysis Services **discretization** feature to do this for us. After adding the MonthsSinceFirstInternetVisit attribute to the Customer dimension, change the DiscretizationMethod property of the attribute to Automatic to allow Analysis Services to decide on the best method of grouping these time periods. If you want to specify the approximate number of groups (or "buckets") that are created, set the DiscretizationBucketCount property, too.

TIP:

Use the Data Load Date Rather Than System Dates

Although using the `GetDate` function to work out durations based on the current system date would work, bear in mind that because we will only be loading the data on a weekly basis, the `GetDate` function should probably be changed to return the latest date that the data was actually loaded. This date could be stored in a data warehouse table that is populated during the ETL process.

Visit Measure Group

Because we want to be able to look at both sales and visit information together, we can add the Visit fact table to the existing cube as a new measure group. Dimensions that are not used in the Visit measure group (such as Product and Promotion) will be grayed out in the Dimension Usage table of the cube editor.

One measure to be careful of is the Duration measure. Although this measure is additive across time (for example, we could determine the total duration that a group of customers spent on the site in the month of January), using the information by summing up the facts in this way does not make a lot of business sense. The Duration measure is there to provide an indication of how long people spent on the site; and so, we can change the AggregateFunction property of this measure to Average-OfChildren to display this information in the way that users will expect.

How We Will Be Using Data Mining

As discussed in the section "High-Level Architecture," we chose the Microsoft Clustering and Microsoft Association algorithms for our solution. Knowing which algorithm is appropriate for your business problem will take some experimentation and research in the documentation. In fact, in a lot of cases, there is no obvious candidate at the outset, and you will need to try different algorithms against the same underlying data to see which is most appropriate. The data mining designer also includes a Mining Accuracy Chart tab that you can use to compare algorithms.

The first decision we need to make is where the data will come from. Analysis Services can use either the relational tables in your data source view or the actual cube itself as the source of data for the models. Because data mining is even more sensitive to flawed data than most applications, it is important to ensure that you perform as much data cleansing as possible against the source data prior to processing your models; so, at the very least, you should probably be using the tables in your data warehouse rather than directly using source systems.

However, using the cube as the source for data mining has a number of benefits, so we will be using that approach for this solution. The cube data has already been supplemented with additional attributes and calculated measures that the data mining algorithms can take advantage of. Also, the load process for data mining models can take some time, so using the cube as the source means that the aggregates will be used if applicable, potentially speeding up the processing time.

Approaching the Customer-Segmentation Problem

Because users can slice and dice information by all the attributes in a dimension rather than just predefined drilldown hierarchies, analysts could use the new Internet-related attributes that we added to drill down through the data and start to understand how customers' online activities affect measures such as total sales or profitability. For example, they can learn that frequent visitors to the site often have high sales amounts, but that this isn't always the case—some frequent visitors are "just looking."

To really do a good job of targeting the DVD marketing campaign to customers likely to act on the information, analysts need to perform a segmentation exercise where all customers that have similar attributes are categorized into groups. Because the list of customers is huge and there is a large number of attributes, we can start this categorization process by using a data mining algorithm to search through the customers and group them into clusters.

The Microsoft Clustering algorithm is a great tool for segmentation and works by looking for relationships in the data and generating a list of clusters, as shown in Figure 10-4, and then gradually moving clusters around until they are a good representation of the data.

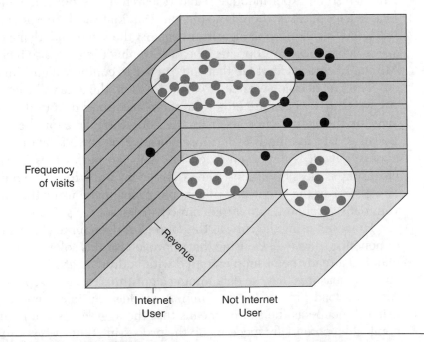

Figure 10-4   Clusters of data

Getting Started with Data Mining

We start the data mining process by creating a new mining model for the customer segmentation exercise, using an existing Analysis Services project that contains the cubes and dimensions with both the data warehouse information (such as in-store sales) and the new Internet information described earlier.

In Analysis Services data mining, we define a mining structure that describes the underlying data that will be used for data mining. Each mining structure can contain multiple mining models, such as a clustering model and an association model, that all use the same underlying data but in different ways.

QUICK START: Creating a Cluster Data Mining Model

We will be using the e-commerce sample project for this example because it already contains the necessary source cubes and dimensions:

1. Open the Business Intelligence Development Studio.

2. Select Open Project from the File menu and open the e-commerce sample project.

3. On the Project menu, select New Mining Structure.

4. After the first wizard page, select From Existing Cube for the definition method and click Next.

5. Select the Microsoft Clustering data mining technique and click Next.

6. Select the Customer dimension from the e-commerce cube and click Next.

7. For the case key, leave the default selection of the Customer attribute and click Next.

8. Select all the Internet activity-related attributes of the customer, such as Internet User and Internet Purchaser, as well as the Months Since attributes that we described in the first section. Also, select the Visits Count and the Sales Amount from the cube, and then click Next.

9. On the Mining Model Column Usage page, leave the default selections—all of our selected columns will be used as inputs. Click Next.

10. Leave the default settings for the column content and data types and click Next.

11. We will be using all the information in the cube for this mining model, so click Next on the Slice Source Cube page.

12. Specify Internet Models as the mining structure name, and Customer Internet Segmentation as the mining model name, and then click Finish (see Figure 10-5).

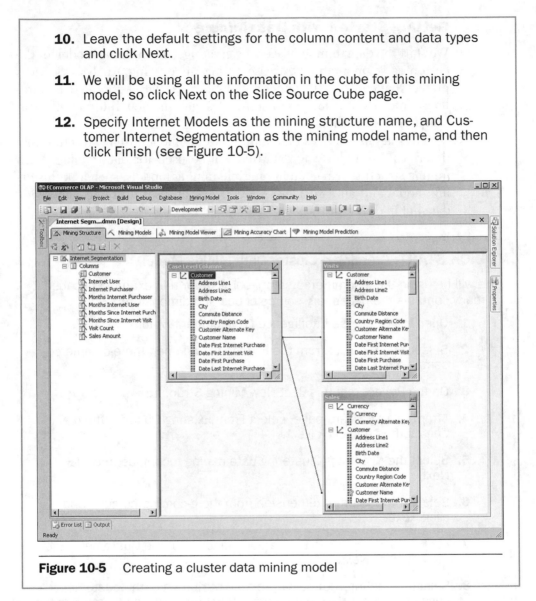

Figure 10-5   Creating a cluster data mining model

The wizard will create the mining structure and model and open the structure in the data mining designer. The underlying data that you selected is shown on the Mining Structure tab, and the Customer Internet Segmentation model is the only model in the list on the Mining Models tab.

Before working with the model, you need to deploy the solution and process the mining model. During processing, Analysis Services applies the algorithm you selected (Microsoft Clustering) to the data from the cube to allocate all the customers to their appropriate clusters—your next task in data mining is to understand the information that has been produced and relate it to the real world.

Looking at the Clusters Created

The Mining Model Viewer tab in the model designer enables you to view the model that has been processed. Each algorithm produces a different type of model, so there are specific viewers for each model. The initial view for clusters is the Cluster Diagram, which shows all the clusters in the model with lines connecting them. Each cluster is positioned closer to other similar clusters, and the darkness of the line connecting two clusters shows the level of similarity. The shading of each cluster by default is related to the population of the cluster (that is, how many customers it contains—the darker clusters have the most customers).

For our Customer Internet Segmentation model, we can see ten clusters named Cluster 1 through Cluster 10. Each cluster represents a group of customers with similar attributes, such as customers who are fairly new to our Internet site and have not made a lot of purchases yet. Our task at this stage is to understand the kinds of customers in each cluster and hopefully come up with some more meaningful names for the clusters.

We can start by using the Cluster Diagram's shading variable and state parameters to look at each attribute and see which clusters contain the most customers with the selected attribute. For example, if I select Sales Amount > 1275 in Figure 10-6, I can see that Cluster 5 and Cluster 8 contain the most customers who have total sales of more than $1,275, as shown in Figure 10-6.

You can use the cluster diagram to help you comprehend each cluster by looking at one variable at a time. To really understand and compare the composition of clusters (that is, what types of customers are in each group), you need to use the Cluster Profiles and Cluster Discrimination views. We can see in the diagram that Cluster 1 contains a fairly high percentage of customers with high sales and is arranged near to Cluster 2 and Cluster 6, but we need more complete information to be able to assign a meaningful name to these clusters.

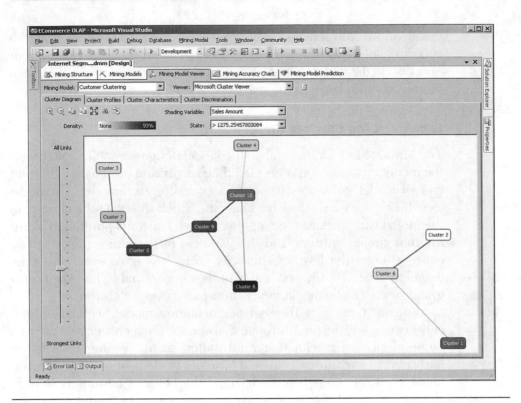

Figure 10-6   Cluster diagram

Understanding the Composition of Clusters

The Cluster Profiles view shows all the clusters that were identified as columns, and each attribute that you selected for your model as the rows, as shown in Figure 10-7. Looking first at Cluster 1, we can see that all the customers in the group have an Internet Purchaser attribute of False, as well as an Internet Visitor of False. So, the mining algorithm has grouped customers together who have never visited the site or purchased anything online—all their purchases have been at a physical store. Note that we can come to this rather useful conclusion only because we understand the underlying business, which is a key point about data mining.

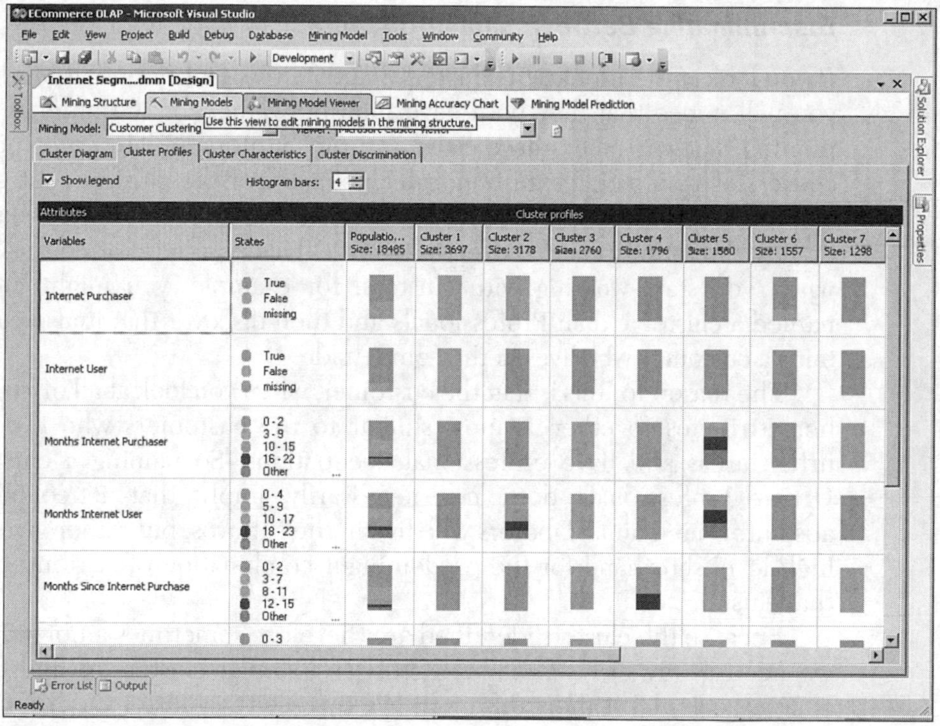

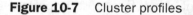

Figure 10-7 Cluster profiles

To give Cluster 1 the more sensible name of Store-Only Buyers, right-click the cluster name and select Rename Cluster. So, we now have a single cluster identified; what about the others? If you look at the next column, you can see that Cluster 2 differs from Store-Only Buyers in that all the customers in the cluster have actually visited the site, but they just haven't made any purchases online yet. We can call this cluster Browsers because they are customers who are (so far) using the site for information gathering only.

Cluster 6 contains visitors who have also made a purchase, but if we look closely at the Months Internet Purchaser and Months Internet User attributes, we learn that they are all relative newcomers to our site—all of them have been visitors and purchasers for between zero and three months (they are "Newbies"). We can continue the process of looking at each cluster, but the rest of the clusters are not quite so clear-cut, so we need a better tool for differentiating between them.

Discriminating Between Similar Clusters

If you look at the profiles of Clusters 8 and 9 in BI Development Studio, you will notice that they both have multiple values for the number of months that customers have been Internet visitors and Internet purchasers. This illustrates an important point about the clusters that the algorithm identifies: Every customer in the group does not have to have exactly the same value for every attribute. This is somewhat confusing when you start working with clusters; for example, you might have named a cluster Urban Professionals and then discover that it also contains a customer who lives in the countryside.

The reason for this is that the customer, when you look at all of his or her attributes together, is most similar to the customers who live in urban areas and have professional occupations. So naming a cluster Urban Professionals does not necessarily imply that it contains absolutely no manual laborers who live in the suburbs, but rather gives a high-level shorthand for the predominant combination of attributes in that cluster.

Because the clusters identified are therefore sometimes ambiguous, we need a way of discriminating between similar clusters to find out what exactly makes them different. We can use the Cluster Discrimination view, as shown in Figure 10-8, to select the two clusters we are interested in comparing and get an idea of what the most important differences are.

We can see in the discrimination view that although the cluster profiles of 8 and 9 look similar, in fact Cluster 9 contains mostly customers who have made a visit and purchase in the past few months, are fairly frequent visitors, and have spent a lot of money with us—we could call this group Frequent Visitors. Cluster 8, on the other hand, contains mostly customers who have not visited the site for many months, although in the past they have spent some money with us. This cluster is probably one that we want to pay careful attention to, because they may now be doing their shopping with a competitor. That is, they may be Defectors.

With the cluster profile and discrimination views, we can understand the clusters well enough to give them meaningful names, so we can now turn our attention to providing this information back to users to enable them to perform analyses on the data using the clusters.

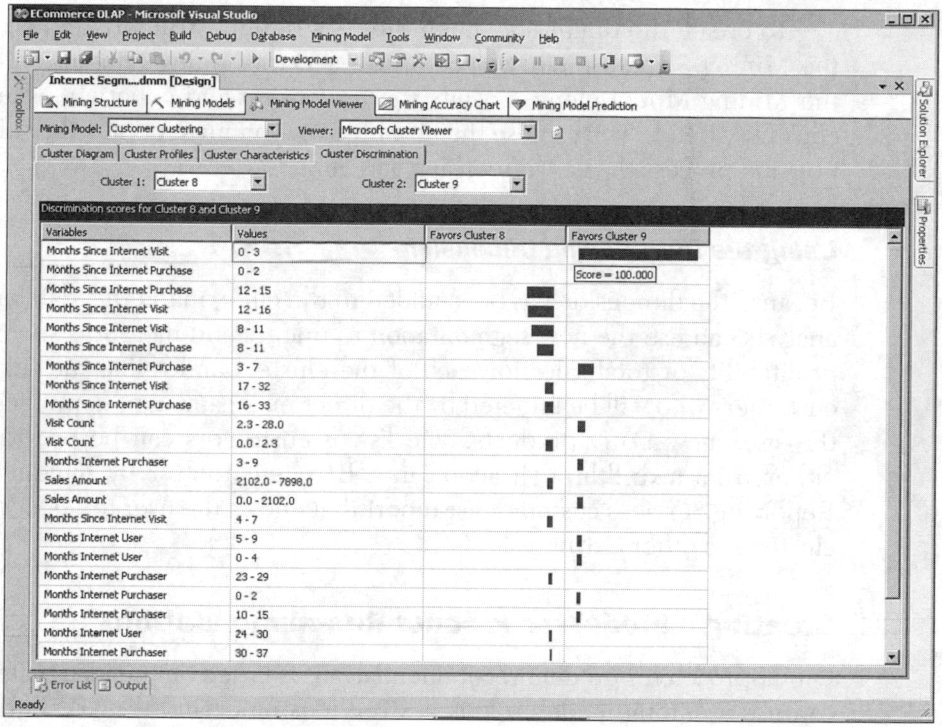

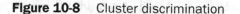

Figure 10-8 Cluster discrimination

Analyzing with Data Mining Information

Analysis Services allows you to create a special type of dimension called a **Data Mining dimension**, which is based on a data mining model and can be included in a cube just like an ordinary dimension. The Data Mining dimension includes all the clusters that were identified by the algorithm, including any specific names that you assigned to them.

Adding a Data Mining Dimension to a Cube

We will use the data mining model we created in the previous Quick Start exercise and create a new dimension called Customer Internet Segmentation, as well as a new cube that includes this dimension. The existing Visit and Sales measure groups from the e-commerce cube will be linked into the new cube to be analyzed by the new dimension.

To create the dimension, open the data mining structure and go to the Mining Structure tab. Select Create a Data Mining Dimension on the Mining Model menu. Specify the dimension and cube names and click OK. Before you can use the new objects, you must deploy the solution and process the new dimension and cube.

Using the Data Mining Dimension

Because the dimension has been added to the cube, marketing database analysts can use the new segmentation to understand measures such as profitability or total sales for each of the clusters and refine the set of customers who will be targeted by the direct mail campaign to publicize the site's new DVD products. The list of customers can be provided either from a drillthrough action in a BI client tool or by building a Reporting Services customer list report that allows the user to select the cluster and other attributes.

Creating a Model for Product Recommendations

Our approach for product recommendations is based on the idea that we can use a mining model to look at every customer and the DVDs that they have bought, and then look for patterns of DVDs that often occur together. The Association Rules mining model is often used for this kind of analysis (sometimes called market basket analysis) and produces a set of rules that say, for example, if the customer is buying a DVD of *The Godfather,* what are the other movies that other buyers of *The Godfather* have purchased?

Each of these rules has a probability associated with them. For example, many customers may also have bought similar films, such as *The Godfather Part II* or *Goodfellas,* so the rules that relate *The Godfather* to these DVDs would have a high probability. If only a single customer bought *It's a Wonderful Life* and *The Godfather,* this rule would have a low probability. In data mining terminology, the number of times that a set of items occurs together is called the **support**, so the example of *It's a Wonderful Life* and *The Godfather* appearing together would have a support of 1.

We can use these rules to make a prediction: For a specific DVD, give me a list of the most probable DVDs that a customer might also enjoy.

Asking the Right Question

The best way to successfully set up a sensible data mining model is to be precise about the question you ask. Because we are looking for DVDs that sell well together, is the question we are asking "Which other DVDs have been bought during the same shopping trip?" or rather "Which other DVDs did customers also buy at some point?." If you were doing product recommendations on groceries, the first question would probably be the most sensible. The reason is that if someone is buying beer and wine today, we can probably recommend ice and potato chips because those are often sold in the same transaction.

However, in our case, we are trying to determine the likes and dislikes of consumers, which have a longer duration than just a single transaction. We are really trying to understand what kind of movies customers enjoy, so the second question is more appropriate for this business solution. To set up the model, we need to look at each customer and determine the list of DVDs that they have purchased. The data we are looking for looks something like Table 10-1. In data mining terminology, the customer would be the **case**, and the list of products for each customer would be a **nested table**.

Table 10-1   Customer DVD Purchase History

Customer	DVD
Customer 3283	*The Godfather*
	The Godfather Part II
	Dark City
Customer 3981	*The Godfather Part II*
	Goodfellas
Customer 5488	*The Godfather*
	It's a Wonderful Life
...	...

QUICK START: Creating an Association Rules Data Mining Model

We can add the new product recommendations mining model to the same e-commerce solution as the segmentation model; but because we are using different underlying data, we need to create a new mining structure, too:

1. On the Project menu, select New Mining Structure.

2. After the first wizard page, select From Existing Cube for the definition method and click Next.

3. Select the Microsoft Association Rules data mining technique and click Next.

4. Select the Customer dimension from the e-commerce cube and click Next.

5. For the case key, leave the default selection of the Customer attribute and click Next.

6. Leave the other case level columns blank and click Next.

7. Click the Add Nested Tables button, select the Product dimension from the e-commerce cube, and click Next.

8. For the case key, leave the default selection of the Product attribute and click Next.

9. Leave the other case level columns blank and click Finish.

10. Check the Predict box next to the Product dimension. The wizard's column usage page should now look like Figure 10-9. Click Next.

11. Leave the default settings for the column data types and click Next.

12. On the Slice Source Cube page, select the Product Category hierarchy for the Product dimension and specify a filter expression of DVD.

13. Specify Cross Sell as the mining structure name and Product Recommendations as the mining model name and click Finish.

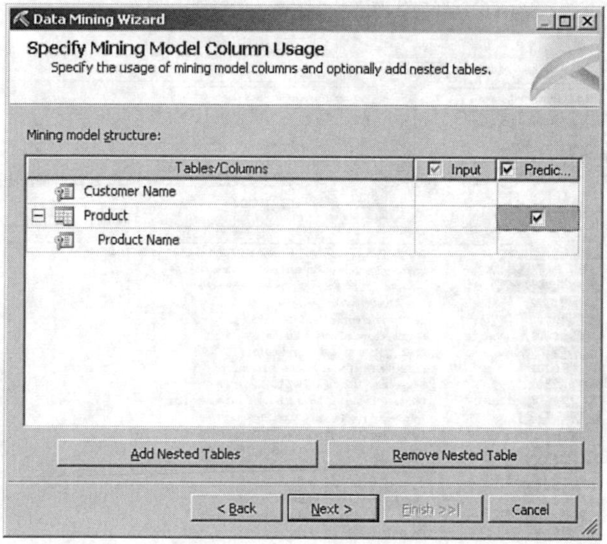

Figure 10-9 Product recommendations column usage

Understanding the Product Recommendation Rules

Once again, you need to deploy and process the model before you can view the results. The algorithm produces a list of products related to each other for a customer, and you can view these in the Itemsets tab of the mining model viewer. Each itemset also shows the support or number of times that the set occurred together. If you click the Rules tab, you can see the main feature of this mining model (see Figure 10-10): A set of rules that can be used to calculate the probability that a new DVD will be appropriate based on the existing DVDs in the customer's shopping basket.

For the Association Rules algorithm, the settings that you choose have a big impact on the set of rules created. You can change these settings by right-clicking the model in the Mining Models tab and selecting Set Algorithm Parameters. If you end up with long processing times and too many rules, you could increase the minimum probability parameter, which would discard rules with a low probability, or you could increase the minimum support, which would discard rules that do not occur very often in the data. If, on the other hand, you end up with too few rules, decrease the minimum probability and support.

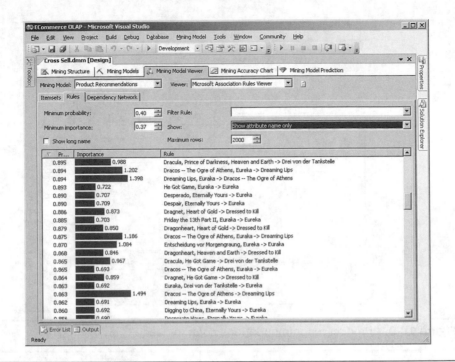

Figure 10-10 Product recommendation rules

When we have finished creating and training the mining model, we can move on to using the mining model to make predictions for our Web application.

Add Data Mining Intelligence into a Web Application

Web applications that include dynamic content typically access relational databases to provide information to users, usually by using a data access library such as ADO.NET to execute an SQL query against the database, then looping through the resulting rows to create a Web page. The process for adding data mining information to a Web application is similar. A programming library called ADOMD.NET provides classes for querying Analysis Services, and the Data Mining eXtensions (DMX) query language is used to request information from the mining model.

Querying the Mining Model Using DMX

The DMX language is similar to standard SQL, but there are enough differences that you will need to spend some time working with the language before it becomes natural. As with all new query languages, it is often better to start out using graphical designers, such as the prediction query builder in SQL Server Management Studio, before moving on to hand-coding queries. There is also a thriving user community for Analysis Services data mining, and there are lots of samples available to get you started at www.sqlserverdatamining.com.

QUICK START: Using the Prediction Query Builder

We need to build a DMX query that recommends a likely set of products based on a product that the customer purchases. The prediction query builder enables you to create a query based on either a list of values that you supply (called a singleton query) or to make batch predictions on a whole set of records contained in an input table:

1. In SQL Server Management Studio, open the Analysis Services database in the Object Explorer.

2. Browse to the Product Recommendations mining model, right-click it, and choose Build Prediction Query.

3. On the Mining Model menu, select Singleton Query.

4. On the Singleton Query Input box, click on the Product row in the Value column and click the ... button.

5. Add some products from the list to the input rows and click OK. We have now defined the input to the query. The next step is to define the output (that is, what we want to predict).

6. In the first row of the grid in the lower half of the designer, select Prediction Function in the source column, and select Predict in the Field column.

7. Now that we have selected the function we want to use, we need to supply the arguments to the function. In the Criteria/Argument column, specify `[Product], INCLUDE_STATISTICS`, as shown in Figure 10-11.

8. On the Mining Model menu, select Result to see the recommended product list.

9. To see the actual DMX that was produced by the designer, select Query from the Mining Model menu.

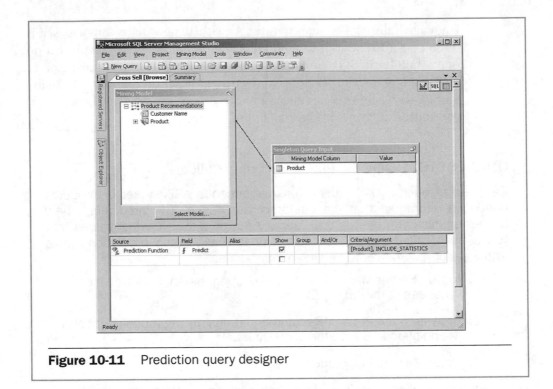

Figure 10-11 Prediction query designer

The prediction DMX query that we have built returns a long list of products, some of them with fairly low probabilities. What we actually need for the Web site is the top five or so best recommendations, so we can add a numeric parameter to the query to specify the maximum number of results to return. Our final DMX query looks like the following:

```
SELECT Predict ([Product], INCLUDE_STATISTICS, 5)
FROM [Product Recommendations]
NATURAL PREDICTION JOIN
  (SELECT
    (SELECT 'The Godfather' AS [Product Name]
      UNION SELECT 'Battlestar Galactica Season I' AS
➥[Product Name])
  AS [Product]) AS a
```

Executing DMX Queries from a Web Application

Our Web application is an ASP.NET application, so we can take advantage of the ADOMD.NET classes to execute the DMX query. The DMX query that we designed earlier returns the information in a hierarchical format, and we would need to navigate through it to extract the product names. We can simplify the code by using the SELECT FLATTENED syntax, which returns the information as a simple list of products that we can add to the Web page.

Managing the Solution

Data mining features are provided as part of the Analysis Services engine, so many of the usual management tasks are still applicable, but data mining also adds some new areas to be aware of.

Deployment

We are adding the visit information and customer-segmentation mining models to an existing BI solution, so the main deployment challenge that we face is for the product recommendations mining model. Because this model will be used on the live Internet site, we need to deploy an additional Analysis Server that can be accessed by the Web application servers.

Deploying the Mining Model to the Production Server

Because we built our mining model using an Analysis Services cube as the source, we need to find a way to get the processed cube and mining models onto the production server. The easiest way to do this is to back up the Analysis Services database and restore it in production.

If we had built our mining model using a relational database as the source rather than an Analysis Services cube, we could easily have deployed the mining model using DMX's EXPORT command, by running a DMX query in SQL Server Management Studio with the following syntax:

```
EXPORT MINING MODEL [Product Recommendations] TO
'C:\ProductRec.abf' WITH PASSWORD='MyPassword'
```

Remember that the path you specify is on the server, not on the client machine that you are running the DMX query from. The file will contain everything we need to make predictions, so we can copy it to the production server, create a new Analysis Services database, and import the model using a DMX query with the following syntax:

```
IMPORT FROM 'C:\ProductRec.abf' WITH PASSWORD='MyPassword'
```

Securing the Mining Model

Because we will be accessing the product recommendations mining model from a Web application, we need to set up the security correctly to allow the IIS user account to query the Analysis Server. We need to create a special role in the production Analysis Services database that has the IIS account (such as IUSR_machinename) as a member, and then enable Read and Read Definition permissions for the mining structure and model.

Maintenance

Any future changes that you make to the mining model definitions will need to be redeployed to the server and will also require processing the changed models. Mining structures can include more than one model on the same underlying data (for example, using different algorithms or even just different algorithm settings), so you might need to add new models to handle future business requirements.

Operations

Just like Analysis Services cubes, we need to reprocess mining models to train them with new input data. There is no "incremental process" option with mining models, however, so you need to reprocess using the full data set.

The product recommendations model probably needs to be reprocessed on a regular basis so that it is kept current with the latest products and sales trends. In our e-commerce solution, the model is reprocessed on a weekly basis and then copied from development into the Web production environment. The customer segmentation model will be used for marketing processes such as organizing marketing campaigns that take some time to complete, so the model will not be reprocessed often.

TIP:

Reprocessing Mining Models Drops Cluster Names
Another reason that the customer segmentation model is not reprocessed often is that the carefully selected cluster names such as Defector and Newbie are replaced with the default Cluster 1 and Cluster 2 names during processing. This is also important to know during development when you are designing your model, because you will be losing any cluster names every time you need to change anything in the model.

Next Steps

You can leverage data mining for various business requirements in many ways, and you have a whole set of new possibilities available if we add the Page Hits fact table to the data warehouse. This would involve handling a large fact table, which has ramifications for the relational database design, ETL processes, and even the cube structure. See Chapter 11, "Very Large Data Warehouses," for a full description of the issues associated with very large databases.

Sequence Clustering to Build Smarter Web Sites

Each visit has an associated path that the user took through the pages of the Web site. We could use this data with the Sequence Clustering algorithm, which finds clusters of cases that contain similar paths in a sequence. This mining model could then be used in the Web site to suggest the next page that the user might like to visit.

Other Data Mining Possibilities

This chapter has given a basic introduction to the rich and broad set of applications possible using the algorithms in Analysis Services data mining. One area that we have only scratched the surface of is prediction. For example, applications that require predictions of an attribute are possible using the classification algorithms including Decision Trees, Neural Network, and Naive Bayes; and continuous variables such as future profit levels can be predicted by the Time Series and Decision Trees algorithms.

Using Data Mining in Integration Services to Improve Data Quality

One of the major scenarios that we have not looked at in this chapter is the use of data mining in Integration Services. We could create a clustering model against a subset of data that is already in the data warehouse and is known to have clean, correct values, and then query this model in an Integration Services package that loads new data to determine the probability that each new record is valid. Records that are selected as likely "bad data" can be split out during the load process into a separate table for further validation or human checking and correction.

Integration Services also has other data mining features, such as loading data directly into data models within the data flow and specifying samples of data to be used for training models rather than just using all the data.

Summary

We added the Internet visit information to the data warehouse and Analysis Services database and built Integration Services packages to load the data from the e-commerce system's database. We created a mining model to add customer segmentation to the cube, and another model to supply product recommendations to the Web site. We decided not to use the e-commerce application's built-in BI features because the objectives required extensive data from the existing data warehouse, which was not available in the e-commerce database.

Marketing activities, such as Internet advertising and direct mail, can now be targeted more effectively at customers based on their use of the Web site and their customer profiles. The high-performance cross-sell feature on the Web site is recommending additional DVDs that the customer might like to purchase, hopefully leading to additional items sold per transaction.

Because many of the interesting measures in the Internet activity fact data are measures of the time elapsed between two dates, we added a set of time span calculations to the fact views that were used by the cube. To calculate the time up until the present day, the data load date was used rather than the current system date.

We used the Microsoft Clustering algorithm to create a customer segmentation mining model and data mining dimension so that analysts can use clusters of customers such as Newbies and Store-Only Buyers. We used the Microsoft Association Rules algorithm to create a product recommendations model, and added a DMX query to the e-commerce Web application to suggest a list of possible DVDs that a customer might also purchase.

The product recommendations mining model was deployed to a production server that can be accessed by the e-commerce Web application, and the security was configured so that the Web application can query the mining model. A new operations task is to periodically reprocess the product recommendations mining model so that it is kept current with the latest data.

CHAPTER 11

Very Large Data Warehouses

Very large databases (VLDBs) magnify inefficiencies that are unnoticeable in smaller databases into show-stopping issues. Common issues associated with very large amounts of data include problems such as speed of importing data, lengthy backup process, excessive unavailability due to long maintenance processes, lengthy processes to retire unneeded historical data, and poor query performance.

Another issue often associated with large databases is a high rate of growth. Large amounts of new data arriving need high-performance extraction, transformation, and loading (ETL) processing.

Even if your database is not multi-terabytes in size, you may be experiencing some of these problems as your database grows beyond expectations. The term *very large* is relative. You might have limited hardware, which can make some processes run more slowly even on a few hundred gigabytes of data. You might have a very small window of time to perform some maintenance operations. In these circumstances, you might be willing to give up some simplicity of your original design in return for more optimized operations.

In this chapter, we look at techniques available for handling very large volumes of data in the SQL Server 2005 relational engine and Analysis Services. We also cover how to work with Integration Services to handle very high rates of data flow into the data warehouse.

Business Problem

Our customer for this chapter is a telecommunications carrier, with millions of subscribers, and multiple interconnections to other networks and carriers to provide worldwide access for its subscribers. They handle millions of calls each day on their network. One of the challenges they constantly face is understanding their customer's calling patterns so that they can plan and optimize their network capacity. They analyze network usage based on time of day and the origin and termination locations of each call. The marketing group also reviews how the various calling plans they offer are being used.

Problem Statement

Many of the business problems our customer is experiencing would benefit from the kinds of BI capabilities that you have seen in previous chapters, but there is one huge technical problem that first needs to be overcome—the volume of data in a utility company's data warehouse can be staggering. The client has reduced the volume of data by loading filtered and summarized data into relational data mart databases for specific business applications. The business still finds itself constrained in many ways:

- The summarized level of information leads to limitations in the kinds of queries that can be answered meaningfully, because some of the dimension attributes are no longer available. For example, data summarized to the month level cannot be used to predict daily traffic levels.

- Data points from multiple systems are summarized and consolidated separately, leading to silos of information in the various data marts.

- The users cannot get timely information on events such as the effect of promotions on network traffic. As the database grows in size, increasing maintenance time is reducing availability of the system.

- Queries that span or summarize long time periods or many geographic areas are becoming too slow as the amount of data increases.

Solution Overview

Our customer faces the competing demands of faster query performance and providing more detail in the data. The increased level of detail will increase the data volume and thus reduce performance if nothing else changes. Based on the business requirements outlined below, we will design a solution that takes advantage of some new features in SQL Server 2005 to provide the desired improvements and still operate on the same hardware platform.

Business Requirements

The business has provided requirements about the increased level of detail they need in the data warehouse, about the longer hours of availability, and operational goals to reduce maintenance time and resource utilization.

Data Volume and Level of Detail

The business needs to analyze the data across all dimensions. The data is provided in a call detail record (CDR). The solution will eventually need to handle billions of rows in the fact table and be able to load and transform millions of facts per day. Recent data is queried far more often and at more detailed levels than historical data. However, queries summarizing current data and comparing it with parallel historical periods are also common, and need to perform well.

Data is kept for five years before being archived.

Availability

Data is generated nonstop, 24 hours per day. Analysts in three time zones expect access between 6 a.m. and midnight. At best, three hours are available during which the solution can be offline. However, taking the database offline would create a serious backlog of data waiting to be loaded, so this is not a viable option. Backups and other maintenance procedures still need to be performed, but with minimal impact on performance.

Operations

The operations staff who works with the data warehouse need the capability to easily remove and archive older data as it becomes less relevant, without requiring extensive reprocessing. Also, backups in general consume a lot of disk space before being transferred to offline storage. This space needs to be cut in half.

High-Level Architecture

Our customer's database is essentially overwhelmed by the data volume, forcing a reduction in detail just to be able to keep up. Much of the problem can be attributed to the time required to back up the data and reorganize the indexes. You might be asking yourself why we need to back up and perform index maintenance on all the data. After all, haven't we already done that for all but the most recent data? The historical data hasn't changed; we are just adding new data. If we could find a way to do the maintenance only on the new data, we could reduce the time for maintenance to almost zero. Figure 11-1 shows the components that are influential in supporting a VLDB.

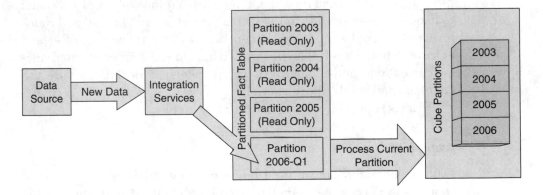

Figure 11-1   Major components of a VLDB solution

Partitioning the Problem

The core of the architecture supporting very large databases is partitioning of the relational tables and OLAP cubes. Each partition can be treated somewhat independently. This provides the opportunity to design shorter maintenance operations, faster backups, higher performance-loading OLAP cubes, and potentially more efficient querying.

In SQL Server, a **partitioned table** appears as a single table to a user, but the rows in the table are physically divided across a number of separate partitions. Partitioning the table can offer better performance through parallel operations. Partitions make it easier for you to manage the table because you can work with subsets of the data rather than the entire table.

Using multiple partitions associated with multiple filegroups in the data warehouse, we can dramatically improve backup times and maintenance times. A **filegroup** is simply a collection of files that you can use to distribute data across your available storage. Using filegroups, we also save a substantial amount of disk space that would be consumed by a full database backup. This comes from our capability to mark partitions read-only, which we will never have to back up or reorganize the indexes more than once. We only have to back up and maintain a relatively small "current" partition.

The cubes in the Analysis Services database will be partitioned in a manner similar to that of the relational database. This will allow us to import just the new data into a "current" partition, and process only the data in that partition. All the historical data will not need to be processed. The data in the cube will be online continuously, and only a small amount of resources will be consumed in the reprocessing.

ETL for Large Volumes

In our ETL processing, we will use the native high-speed pipeline architecture of Integration Services where it is advantageous, but trade some of the clarity and maintainability of using Integration Services transformations to take advantage of the performance of set operations performed by SQL queries.

One thing we need to do to guarantee good load performance is to make sure only the changes to the data are loaded, whether it is new facts or dimensions. At least, we should only have to reload a very small portion of existing data. We impose a business rule that no fact data is ever updated, because that would mean reprocessing all the data in the same partition. If a change is needed, a new fact containing the positive or negative adjustment required is used, as described at the end of Chapter 8, "Managing Changing Data." If dimensions change, consider whether they are Type 2 changing dimensions, where you create a new instance of the member rather than change an existing member's attributes.

Querying Large Volumes of Data

With the capability to manage larger volumes of data, we can now support the storage of more detailed data. However, this leads us into our next problem: longer query times.

As you have seen in previous chapters, Analysis Services is designed to precalculate aggregations of values to one or more levels, such as summing up the call duration to the month or quarter level. This means that a query no longer has to touch each row to determine the duration of all the calls per quarter. By using Analysis Services and taking advantage of the aggregations, we can meet the performance criteria for most queries. Analysts will be able to use Excel, Reporting Services, or other third-party tools to query the Analysis Services databases.

Dealing with Resource Constraints

Before you add or change resources to improve performance, it is important that you determine what constraints your application is experiencing. Usually, the bandwidth of the path to and from your mass storage, memory for caching data, and processor cycles is the resource constraint. The bottleneck tends to occur during the access to mass storage, because it is the slowest of all the resources. However, it is important that you monitor your system to determine which resources are hitting its limit. You can use Windows System Monitor to view the utilization of resources. In addition, you want to make sure that your application is using efficient queries and techniques. You can use SQL Profiler to look for long-running queries.

To improve immediate performance, increase the memory of the data cache. This is often the best choice. In a 32-bit system, your available memory is constrained by the architecture. This is not the case with 64-bit architecture. In the near future, 64-bit processors will be the norm, and you won't need to decide whether you need one, or you can get by with a 32-bit processor. Currently, price and some application restrictions mean you still need to evaluate this option. In our example, we were not constrained by memory. Yes, there is a large volume of data, but much of it is historical and not referenced often. Our dimensions are relatively small, and our partitioning scheme means we do not have to reprocess much data. We therefore can continue to use a 32-bit architecture.

Business Benefits

The solution will deliver the following benefits to the client:

- Increased efficiency and profitability through the capability to identify network route utilization trends and deploy equipment for optimal capacity
- Identify marketing opportunities where excess capacity could be promoted and premiums charged for prime routes and times

Data Model

We focus on the fact table in discussing the data model. The fact table is usually the largest table and therefore the most obvious candidate for partitioning. The dimension tables in our case are small and will not benefit from partitioning.

Our logical schema doesn't change significantly from what you might expect, but the physical implementation is very different. Partitioning requires a column that we can use to direct rows to a specific partition, so you do need to be sure you have an appropriate column. We are going to partition by date, and the CallDate column fulfills that requirement.

We have paid some attention to ensuring the data types are as small as possible to keep the row size down. This is not so much for saving disk space as it is for performance. The more rows you can fit on a page, the better the performance. Even if you have a relatively "small" VLDB with just a billion rows, each byte you save is a gigabyte you don't have to store or back up.

Our fact data sources are flat files, each containing call detail data from one of a number of on-line transaction processing (OLTP) servers, as shown in Figure 11-2.

In the fact table shown in Figure 11-3, we have converted the phone number into two parts: the area code, which we will use to determine the general location of the call; and the local number. This allows us to have a Geography dimension with a key that is independent of the phone number business key. Area codes are well defined and can be imported from standard industry sources. We have split date and time apart because we want independent date and time dimensions. We chose to use a data type of smalldatetime for the call date to shorten the row length. The range of dates is from 1900 to 2079, which suffices for our purposes. The Time dimension key can be computed as the number of minutes past midnight, saving a lookup.

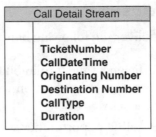

Figure 11-2   Data presented by OLTP system

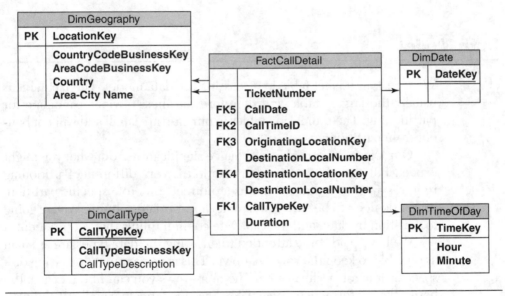

Figure 11-3   Call detail record in data warehouse

Our fact table has no declared primary key or unique key. This isn't unusual in a fact table, but in this case we can't have one. This is because of a restriction imposed by partitioning. Any columns in unique indexes must be part of the partitioning key. If we were to create a unique surrogate key to be used as a primary key, we would have to include it in the partitioning criteria. We don't want to partition by an arbitrary number, so even if you are in the habit of putting primary keys on your fact table, you will probably want to skip it this time. You can, and should, create a nonunique clustered index on the date column. If you must have a primary key, you can work around this restriction. Create a compound primary key using the date (or whatever column you are partitioning by) and any other unique column. If you don't have a unique column, create a surrogate key using a column with the Identity property set to true.

We've always recommended that you don't have a surrogate key for the Date dimension. This scenario is a good example of why, because we want to have a clear understanding what data is in our fact table partitions. The partition contents are defined by a key range, and Date is a human-readable value. A surrogate key wouldn't necessarily tell us directly what dates are in the partition. We also want the partitioning function to be easily read and maintained, and dates are more understandable than the IDs we would generate for a surrogate key.

Our Analysis Services database follows our data warehouse schema closely, as shown in Figure 11-4.

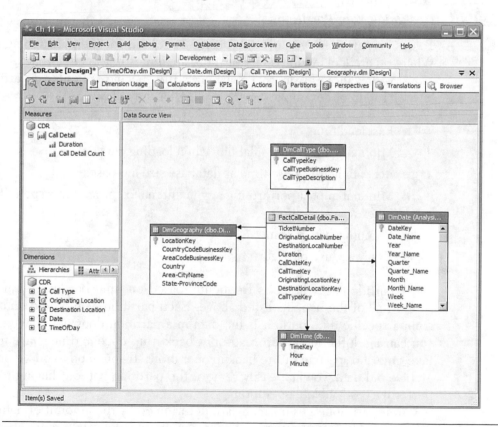

Figure 11-4 Fact and dimension tables

Technical Solution

Now we look in detail at our proposed solution. We start with how to design, create, and manage the partitioned tables in the data warehouse. Next, we look at the ETL processes we need to create to populate the tables in the data warehouse. Finally, we look at how to design, create, and manage the partitions that make up the cubes.

Partitioned Tables

You use partitioned tables for optimizing queries and management of a large relational table. Our partitions will be based on date because our usage of the data is primarily for a specific data range.

Designing Your Partitions

To design partitions, you need to decide on a basis for the partitioning. What you are looking for is one or more attributes in the table that will group your data in a way that maximizes the specific benefits you are looking for. In our example, we are looking for the following:

- Fast load time
- Minimal impact on availability when loading data
- Acceptable response time as database size increases
- Minimal impact performing any maintenance procedures such as index reorganization
- Minimize backup time
- Easily archive old data

A partitioning scheme is frequently based on time because it can support all of the benefits listed above. Each partition would hold data from a specific time period. If the data in a partition does not change, you can mark the file group read-only, back it up once and not have it take time and space in future backup operations. If you need to purge or archive old data, you can easily remove the partition without having to perform a costly delete operation.

Your partition sizes normally are determined by the amount of data estimated to be in a partition and a convenient time period. Larger partitions make management a bit easier, but may contain too much data to provide us with the efficiency we are seeking. Daily or weekly partitions are common. In this example, we will create uniform weekly partitions. It can take up to four weeks to receive all the data, so we will keep the prior four partitions writeable, and mark old partitions read only. This will mean we only need to back up four weeks of data.

Creating Partitioned Tables

No GUI exists for creating the partition function or the partition scheme, but even if there were, we still recommend that you use scripts to create partitioned tables so that you have a repeatable process. Here is an overview of the steps you take:

- Create a partition function.
- Create the filegroups.
- Add files to the new filegroups.
- Create the partition scheme.
- Create the partitioned table.

Creating the Partition Function

The partition function defines the boundary values that divide the table between partitions. You specify a data type that will be passed to the function, and then a number of values (up to 999), which are the boundary points. The name of the partition function is used later when you create the partition scheme. To illustrate the idea, the example below creates six partitions on a weekly basis, with the last partition holding everything beyond January 29.

```
CREATE PARTITION FUNCTION PartitionByWeek (smalldatetime)
AS RANGE RIGHT
FOR VALUES (
'2005-DEC-25',
'2006-JAN-01',
'2006-JAN-08',
'2006-JAN-15',
'2006-JAN-22',
'2006-JAN-29')
```

The partition function that you create determines which partition a row belongs in. Partitions don't have to be uniform in size. You can have partitions for the current four weeks, previous month, and another for everything else in a history partition if that suits your query profile. You can also specify more filegroups than you have partitions. The extra ones will be used as you add partitions.

Creating the Filegroups and Adding Files

A filegroup is simply a set of one or more files where data or indexes can be placed. A filegroup can support more than one partition, and a partition can be distributed over more than one filegroup. In our example, we use one filegroup for each partition. The partitions were defined by the partition function we just created previously. We will create one partition for each of the ranges defined in the function. We will add one file to each filegroup:

```
—Create "FG2005WK52" Group

ALTER DATABASE     CDR
ADD FILEGROUP FG2005WK52;
GO


—Add file "CD2005WK52" to FG2005WK52 group
ALTER DATABASE     CDR
ADD FILE
(
    NAME = Archive,
    FILENAME = 'D:\CDR\Data\CD2005WK52.ndf',
    SIZE = 3000MB,
    FILEGROWTH = 30MB
) TO FILEGROUP FG2005WK52
GO


ALTER DATABASE     CDR
ADD FILEGROUP FG2006WK01;
GO
ALTER DATABASE     CDR
ADD FILE
(
    NAME = CD2006WK01,
    FILENAME = 'D:\CDR\Data\CD2006WK01.ndf',
    SIZE = 3000MB,
```

```
     FILEGROWTH = 30MB
) TO FILEGROUP FG2006WK01
GO
.
.(repeat for the remaining partitions)
```

We expect that 3,000MBs is sufficient space for one week's data. If that's not enough, the file will grow by 30MB whenever it runs out. In SQL Server 2005, the new space is not formatted when it is allocated, so this operation is quick. Having multiple files in each filegroup would allow for some parallelism in query execution. If you have enough drives, you could spread the load across multiple drives. With high data volumes, such as we anticipate here, you will likely be using SAN storage with many drives and a large cache.

Creating the Partition Scheme

Now, you need to map the partitions to filegroups. You can map them all to one filegroup or one partition to one filegroup. We will assign each partition to its own filegroup because that will give us the performance and manageability we are seeking. The partitions and filegroups are associated one by one, in the order specified in the `filegroup` list and in the partition scheme. You can specify more filegroups than you have partitions to prepare for future partitions:

```
CREATE PARTITION SCHEME WeeklyPartitionScheme
AS PARTITION PartitionByWeek
TO (FG2005WK52, FG2006WK01, FG2006WK02, FG2006WK03,
FG2006WK04, FG2006WK05, FG2006WK06)
```

Creating the Partitioned Table

With the partition scheme now created, you can finally create a partitioned table. This is straightforward and no different from creating any other table, other than to direct SQL Server to create the table *on* a partition schema:

```
CREATE TABLE [Call Detail]
(TicketNumber     BigInt NOT NULL,
CallDate    SmallDateTime NOT NULL,
...
)
ON WeeklyPartitionScheme (CallDate)
```

In Figure 11-5, you can see how all the pieces fit together to store the data in a table. When a row arrives for insert, the database engine takes care of figuring out where it should go without any further work on your part. The partition column is used by the partition function to determine a partition number. The partition number is mapped by position to one of the partitions in the partition schema. The row is then placed in a file in one of the filegroups assigned to the selected partition. To reduce clutter in the diagram, we haven't shown all the files or filegroups.

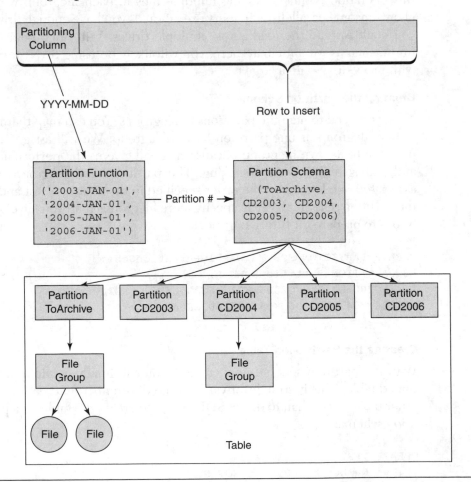

Figure 11-5   Assigning a row to a partition in a table

You can also partition indexes. By default, indexes are partitioned to be aligned with the data partitions you created. This is the most optimal configuration. If your data and index partitions are not aligned, you cannot take advantage of the efficiencies offered by filegroup backups.

Partitioning Restrictions

You need to be aware of some restrictions when designing the data model for your application. We have outlined the important ones here.

Consistent Table Schemas

Tables that are currently separate that you are planning to merge into a partitioned table should be essentially identical, with few exceptions. For example, if you have two tables, current and historical, and you plan to merge current data into a partition in the historical data table, you can't add additional columns to one table to support some functionality for current data and not carry the columns over into the historical data table.

Foreign Key Constraints

There can't be any foreign key constraints between tables you are planning to combine into the same partition. This restricts you from having self-referencing relationships in the model.

There can't be any foreign key constraints from other tables to a table that could be merged into another partition. An example of this would be a dimension table that is referenced in a constraint by a fact table. You are unlikely to have this situation in the portion of a data warehouse that is supporting a dimensional model. The fact table is usually the table you would be partitioning, and the foreign key relationships are usually from the fact table into a dimension table. Dimension tables generally are small enough that you do not need to partition them.

Indexed Views Not Supported

Indexed views are not allowed in either the source or the target, because schema binding is not allowed. If indexed views were implemented to improve the performance of an application, a cube built based on the data warehouse should be able to provide the same if not better performance gain.

Consistent Indexes

When you add a table to a partition, the indexes must be the same on both source and target.

Loading Large Volumes of Data

The pipeline architecture of an SSIS data flow is extremely efficient in loading and transforming data. After we have covered how the package is put together, we look at ways we can optimize it for high-volume data flows.

When talking about large volumes of data, bulk load or bcp utilities always come to mind. You can also use a Bulk Load task in your control flow. However, we want to transform the data, so these approaches won't help us.

Let's look at an SSIS package that can be used to import data from a text file and insert it into a data warehouse using the Fast Load option. This isn't strictly a VLDB solution, but it's an opportunity to show you another way of loading data. Flat files are a common way of recording or delivering larges volumes of data.

The first thing you need to do is to create a connection manager that points to your CDR input files. In the Connection Manager panel at the bottom of the window, right-click and then choose New Flat File Connection. Give the connection manager a name such as CDR Input. Browse to a file containing CDR data and select the file. Set the format to match your file. In our example, the columns have fixed width, and we just need to define the width of each column. If your data has a separator between columns, such as a tab or comma, choose delimited for the format. On the Columns tab, drag the red line to the right until you reach the end of the row. To define a column break, click the ruler.

Try to get the column breaks set correctly before assigning names to the columns. After that point, you need to use the Advanced tab to create new columns and set their widths, as shown in Figure 11-6.

When you are configuring the Advanced column properties, take care to select the right data type. The default is DT_WSTR, which is a Unicode or nvarchar data type. Clicking Suggest Types helps if you have many columns that are not character types. The name of the column is also set on the advanced properties. If you don't set the name, you will have a list of columns named Column 0 to Column n, which won't make it easy to maintain your package, so we strongly encourage you to supply names here.

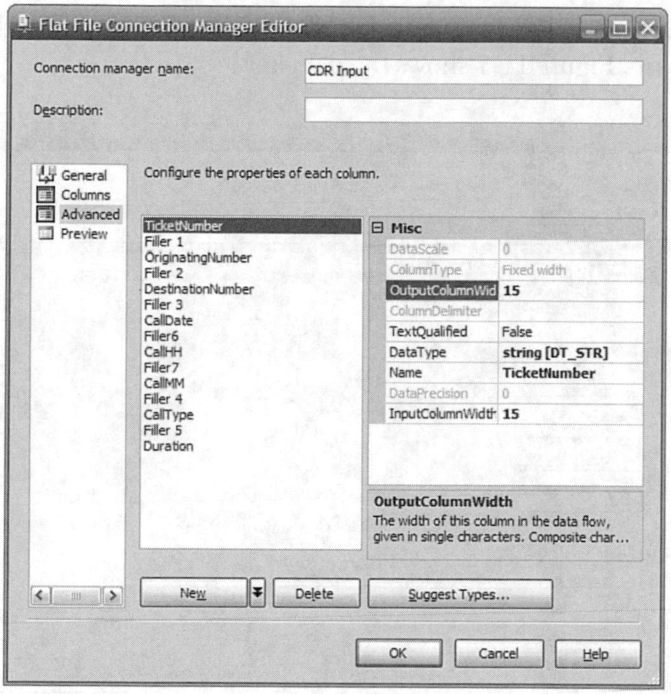

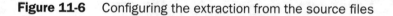

Figure 11-6   Configuring the extraction from the source files

Setting Up the Data Flow

Now you need to create the Data Flow task to extract the data from the CDR flat file, apply some transforms to create the keys in the fact table to link to the dimensions, and then insert the rows into the fact table in SQL Server.

We want to transform the originating and terminating country and area code into surrogate keys that reference our Geography dimension, and also transform the Call Type to a surrogate key that references our Time dimension, Date dimension, and Call Type dimension. We use a Lookup data flow transformation to do this.

We start the data flow by defining the flat file source to reference the "CDR Flat" connection we defined previously. We connect its data flow to the first lookup task. Each Lookup task does one transform. The updated rows are passed on to the next Lookup task, until all transforms have been completed. The last Lookup transform is connected to a SQL

Server destination connection, which writes the rows to the data warehouse. Figure 11-7 shows the data flow.

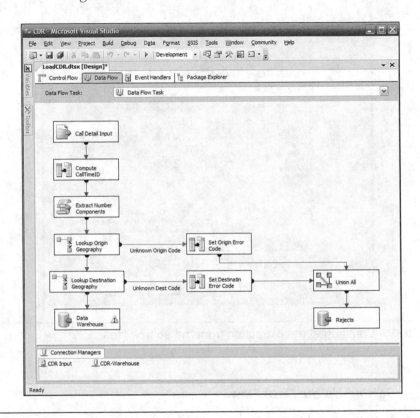

Figure 11-7 Call fact table processing data flow

On a Lookup task, SSIS tries to read as many rows as possible and perform in-memory operations. In the data flow shown above, each batch is processed by the first Lookup task and then passed on to the next Lookup task. The first Lookup task loads another batch, and the pipeline begins to fill as each Lookup task passes its results to the next task.

The Lookup data flow transform will try to use as much memory as is available, to enhance performance. You can restrict the amount of memory used for cache, but full caching (the default) is normally recommended if you have the memory.

If the reference table is very large, you may run out of memory and the lookup transform will fail. You can reduce the memory required by using a query instead of a table name for the reference table. In the query, select only the columns you are mapping to and the ones you want to look up. If that doesn't help, you can set the caching mode to Partial. Partial caching loads the rows from the reference table on demand (that is, when they are first referenced). In the Lookup transform that determines the PlanType, we have to reference the Customer table by the Origin Area Code and the Origin Local Number. Because the fact data is loaded so frequently, only a small number of customers show up in the CDR data, but those who do often make many calls. This is the kind of situation where partial caching may prove to be very useful. You set the caching mode either through the Advanced Editor or in the Properties window of the Lookup transform.

To optimize the data flow, don't select columns that you do not need, either in the data source or in lookups. In a union all transform, you can drop columns that you no longer need.

Joins Versus Lookups

As discussed in Chapter 4, "Building a Data Integration Process," SSIS Lookup transformations provide many advantages over loading the new fact data into a staging area and then joining to the dimension table using SQL to fetch the surrogate keys. Lookups are easier to understand and maintain, and they enable you to handle errors when the reference table does not have a matching row. Joins are generally faster than lookups, but for smaller data volumes, we were willing to sacrifice some performance for the clarity and error handling, because the total difference in time was relatively small. For extremely large reference tables, a join may be so much more efficient that the time difference is substantial, and you have no choice but to implement a translation using a join. You should do some testing before committing to either solution. In the case of a join, implement the join as an outer join so that you don't lose any facts.

You could implement a join either by creating a view in the source database or in the SSIS data source. Often, you don't have the permission to create a view in the source database, so you must create the appropriate SQL statement in the SSIS data source. You create your own SQL statement by selecting SQL Command, instead of Table or View, in the connection manager. You can type in the SQL directly, or you can use a graphical wizard to help you create the query. But there are some issues with doing joins in the query in the OLE DB data source. You usually join incoming facts to the dimension tables in the data warehouse. You have to explicitly name the source database in the query, and this makes it difficult to migrate to other environments without changing your package.

In our case, we can't use a join because our data source is a flat file. We have the option of using the Bulk Insert task to load the flat file into a temporary table and then performing the joins to the dimensions using that table. You don't need to spend time to index the temporary table because every row will be read, so the indexes won't be used.

Data Destination

If you are using an OLE DB destination, choose the Data Access Mode Table with Fast Load option. This option offers a significant performance enhancement over the standard Table or View option. If you are running the package on the same server as SQL Server, you can choose a SQL Server destination, which will provide further performance improvements.

Partitioning Analysis Services Cubes

Cube partitions enhance performance and manageability. They are invisible to users of the cube, so you have complete freedom to design and manipulate partitions according to your needs. Partitions offer the following advantages when working with cubes:

- Parallel loading of partitions.
- Only partitions that have been updated need to be processed.
- Easy to remove old data by simply deleting a partition.
- Different storage models can be applied to each partition. You could use a highly efficient multidimensional OLAP (MOLAP) for historical partitions, and relational OLAP (ROLAP) for real-time current partitions if necessary.
- Queries can be more efficient if only a few partitions are needed to satisfy them.

Designing Cube Partitions

In our example, we want to be able to efficiently add new data, while minimizing the impact on cube users. Smaller partitions perform better than larger ones, although it may mean a bit of extra management over-head. Ten to 20 million facts per cube partition is a good rule to follow. If you have queries that limit a search to one or a few partitions, it will be faster than if the query has to search one large or many small partitions. To improve performance, your objective is to create small partitions that cover the span of the most frequent queries. To improve maintainability, you want as few partitions as possible.

Weekly partitions are a good compromise between manageability and efficiency, so we'll implement uniform weekly partitions just as we did for the relational table.

Creating Cube Partitions

You can create cube partitions using the BI Development Studio or SQL Server Management Studio. You can also use the Integration Services Analysis Services Execute DDL task to execute commands to manage cube partitions. We'll use BI Development Studio while we're develop-ing our solution so that the partition design is captured as part of our source code. You will first have to modify the default partition's source so that it doesn't reference the entire call detail table. Next, you create additional partitions as necessary according to your design.

Because you have multiple partitions, you need to have an inde-pendent table or view for each partition, or a query that is bound to the partition. The data returned by the tables, views, or queries must not overlap; otherwise, the cube will double-count those rows.

For all our partition sources, we are going to use Query Binding rather than Table Binding. Query Binding enables us to use a single fact table as the data source, and then a where clause to restrict the call detail rows to a date-range matching the partition. You would use Table Bind-ing if each partition had its own separate relational table as a data source.

To make sure there is no data overlap in the queries for each parti-tion, we use a where clause like this:

```
CallDate >= '1-Jan-2006' and CallDate < '8-Jan-2006'
```

The use of >= to start ensures we capture every call that begins after midnight on January 1. The use of < for the end date ensures we capture all the calls right up to, but not including, January 8. If we had used <= '7-JAN-2006', we might miss calls made on January 7 if the time component in the fact table wasn't 00:00. We don't expect the time to be anything else, but this is defensive design in case future developers modify (or ignore) the design assumptions. We also won't use clauses like

```
CallDate BETWEEN '1-Jan-2006' and '8-Jan-2006'
CallDate BETWEEN '8-Jan-2005' and '15-Jan-2006'
```

because the ranges overlap at the endpoints and the facts on January 8 would be duplicated in adjacent partitions (in this example, 8-Jan-2006 would be included by both of these where clauses).

TIP:
Avoiding Gaps in Partition Ranges
A good practice to follow is to use the same value in the predicate for the boundary, but omit the equality comparison in one of the predicates. For the earlier partition, use less than (<), and for the later partition, use greater or equal (>=). An earlier partition includes facts up to but not including the boundary value. The later partition includes facts at the boundary value and greater. That way, there is absolutely no gap and absolutely no overlap. If there are gaps, you will have missing data, and if you have overlaps, you will have duplicate data.

QUICK START: Creating the Analysis Services Partitions

Start BI Development Studio and open your Analysis Services solution. Now, we'll go through the steps to create the partitions for your cube:

1. Choose the Partitions tab. Click the Source field of the initial partition, and then click the ellipses. Select Query Binding in the Binding type drop-down. Add the appropriate predicate to the where clause, as shown in Figure 11-8.

2. Add the additional partitions. Click New Partition to start the Partition Wizard. Choose the measure group that will reside in the partition. There is only one in our example. Next choose the Partition Source—the table that will supply the data for the partition. If you have many tables, you can specify a filter to reduce the length of the list you have to choose from. Check the table in Available Tables, and then click Next.

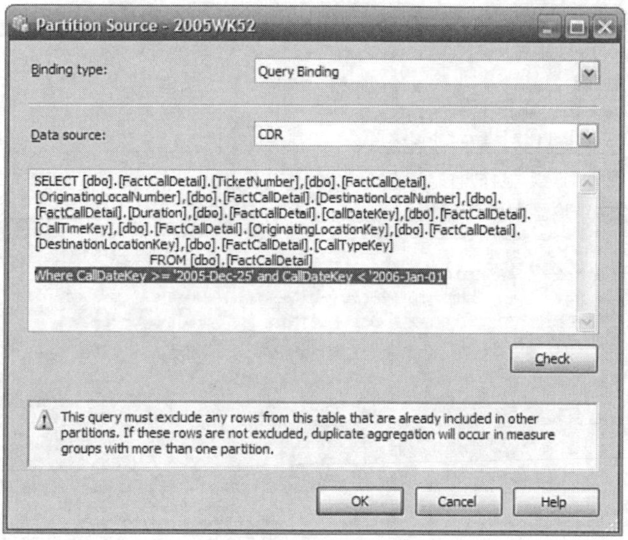

Figure 11-8 Setting the query for a cube partition

3. Be sure the check box is selected to specify a query to restrict rows. Supply the predicate for the where clause to limit the rows you will allow into this partition, as you did in Step 1. Click Next.

4. Accept the defaults for the processing and storage locations. Click Next.

5. Provide a meaningful name for the partition that will help you iden-tify its contents. Select "Copy the aggregation design from an exist-ing partition." If you are creating the first partition of its kind, choose Design aggregations now. Leave "Deploy and process now" unchecked. Click Finish.

6. Continue adding the partitions you need, repeating from Step 2.

You should end up with a set of partitions similar to Figure 11-9.

You must now deploy the solution for your changes to be visible to other applications.

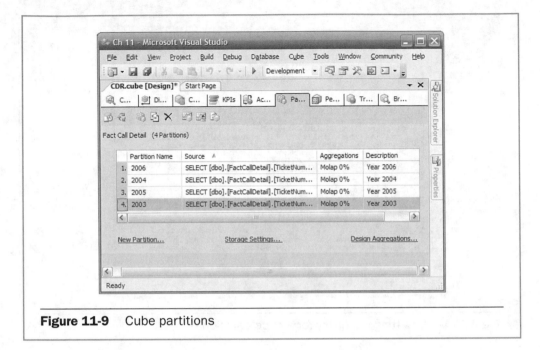

Figure 11-9 Cube partitions

TIP:
Create an Index on the Partitioning Column
To improve performance of cube partition processing, it is important to have an index on the partitioning column in the source table; otherwise, every row in the table will have to be read to process a cube partition.

Aggregation Design

Aggregations are used by Analysis Services to improve response time to queries that refer to a rollup of one or more measures. For example, Sales by month or quarter is logically rolled up by summing Sales by day. If Analysis Services precalculates the Sales by month, then to get Sales by quarter, only three values (for the three months in a quarter) need to be summed. If some aggregations are good, are more aggregations better for large cubes? Not necessarily!

The number of potential aggregations in your cube depends on the number of dimensions, attributes, and members in your dimensional model. It is not possible to precalculate all aggregations for most cubes because the number becomes astronomical quickly. The more aggregations that are stored, the better your performance, but it will also take longer to process new data, and partition size will increase.

Remember that you must specify the attribute relationships in your hierarchies for good aggregations to be created. This is particularly important in large databases. Refer back to Chapter 5, "Building an Analysis Services Database," to review how to set up the relationships.

Partitions can each have their own aggregation designs. This enables you to tailor the aggregations differently if you find, for example, that users pose different queries against historical data than for current data. However, a caveat applies here. When you merge partitions, they must have the same aggregation design. That is why we copied aggregation designs from other partitions when we created them.

In BI Development Studio, you can find the tool for designing aggregations on the Partitions tab of your cube. When you first design aggregations, Analysis Services creates a set of aggregations that it estimates will improve performance. You can specify how much space you are willing to provide for aggregations or how much performance improvement you want. You must limit the aggregations if the processing time becomes unacceptable. Consider starting with something like a 20 percent improvement.

Regardless of the initial aggregations you set up, when in production, you want to be sure the aggregations are appropriate for the queries that your users are sending. Analysis Services provides a means to do this, called Usage Based Optimization, or UBO. We describe how to use UBO in the section on "Managing the Solution" at the end of this chapter.

Large Dimension Support in SQL Server 2005

SQL Server 2005 Analysis Services has a much higher limit on the number of members that can belong to a node in a dimension compared with Analysis Services 2000. However, if you have a GUI interface that allows a user to drill into dimension levels, this might create a problem for the interface or the user, or both. You should consider very carefully whether you want to design such a large, flat dimension. If you can find a natural hierarchy for a dimension, it is usually better to implement it.

In our example, LocalNumber could be very large—seven digits means potentially ten million members. However, we don't need to use LocalNumber to solve our business problem, so we won't include it in a dimension. If it had been necessary, we could create a hierarchy that included the three-digit exchange number as one level and the four-digit subscriber number as a child of the exchange.

Managing the Solution

In a well-designed partitioned solution, it is easy to manage partitions. In a poorly designed solution, you can face huge performance issues moving large amounts of data between partitions. The most important consideration in designing your solution is to plan and test it end to end on a small amount of data.

Initial Loading of the Data Warehouse

You will see some performance benefit during the initial loading of large tables, if you create the table indexes after the initial loading is complete. When you create the indexes, be sure to create the clustered index first; otherwise, you will pay twice for the creation of the nonclustered index. You need to have about 150% more space for a work area when you create a clustered index on a populated table.

You need to create the table partitions for the weeks that are in the initial load.

Managing Table Partitions

On a regular basis and as quickly as possible, you will want to mark file-groups to read-only so that they won't require any more maintenance. You also need to create the partitions for the upcoming periods.

In the following section, we discuss some of the other activities necessary for keeping your system working well, such as the maintenance of the indexes of the active partitions, how to move old data out of the table, and an optimal backup strategy that avoids repetitively backing up unchanged historical data.

Index Maintenance

If data in a partition is changing frequently, the indexes can become fragmented and index pages will not be full, which reduces performance.

After you have populated a partition with all the data for its prescribed time period, consider performing an index reorganization to remove the empty space on index and data pages. One of the advantages of partitioning a table is that you can perform index maintenance on a single partition. If most of your partitions are historical, and so they haven't changed, they will not need to have any index maintenance performed on them. You only need to consider the current partition for maintenance.

You can tell how fragmented an index is using the system function sys.dm_db_index_physical_stats. For example, to see the fragmentation in the indexes in the Call Detail table, execute this statement:

```
SELECT IndexName, AvgFragmentation
FROM sys.dm_db_index_physical_stats (N'dbo.[Call Detail]',
DEFAULT, DEFAULT, N'Detailed');
```

You can view index fragmentation or rebuild or reorganize an index in SQL Management Studio by right-clicking the index in the Object Explorer and choosing Rebuild or Reorganize, as shown in Figure 11-10. As a rule of thumb, you would choose to reorganize an index if the fragmentation were less than 30 percent, and you would rebuild it if the fragmentation were greater than 30 percent. You can target all indexes by right-clicking the Index node rather than a single index.

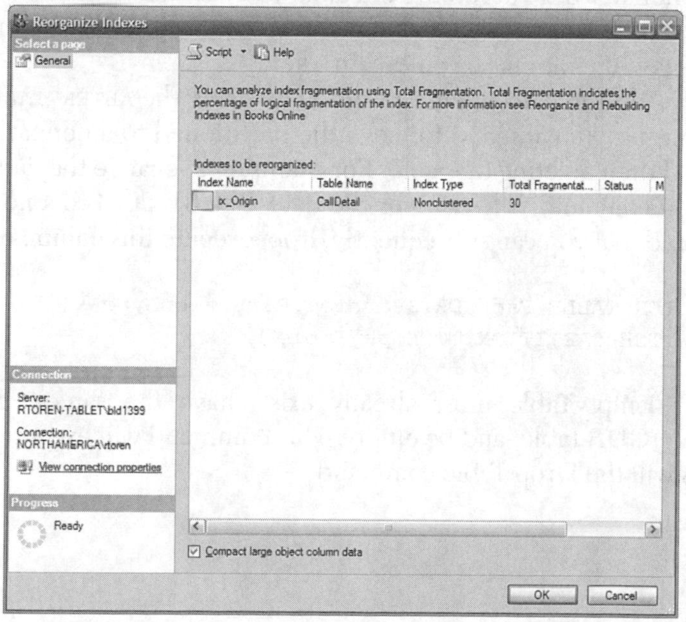

Figure 11-10 Managing fragmentation with Management Studio

TIP:
If you are used to using DBCC to optimize your indexes, you should switch to the new commands ALTER INDEX … REBUILD (or REORGANIZE). DBCC does not implement the online index operations and will not be available in future releases of SQL Server.

Marking a Filegroup Read-Only

When a partition contains all the data for its time period, you can mark the filegroup where it resides as read-only. After you've performed a final backup of the partition's filegroup, you will never have to back up this data again.

You set the read-only flag on a filegroup using the Management Studio. Right-click the database and choose Properties. Next, select the Filegroups page and check the Read-only box. Then choose OK.

Users cannot be connected to the database when setting the Read-only flag on a filegroup, so you will have to perform this operation during a scheduled maintenance period.

Deleting a Relational Partition

When it is time to remove old data, you can delete the data one partition at a time. This is a highly efficient way of removing data, but it is a non-logged operation, so you can't undo it.

You remove data in a partition by using the ALTER TABLE … SWITCH PARTITION command to move the partitioned to a nonpartitioned table and then deleting the table. For example, to change the data in the partition containing the data for the date Dec 31, 2004 to a non-partitioned table that you can subsequently drop, execute this command:

```
ALTER TABLE FactCDR $Partion.PartitionByWeek('31-Dec-2004')
SWITCH PARTITION TO EmptyTable
```

EmptyTable must already exist, have the same schema as the FactCDR table, and be empty. This command will execute very quickly, as will the Drop Table command.

Backing Up the Data Warehouse

Backup works with databases or filegroups, not partitions. Because we designed our partitions to each occupy their own filegroup, you can back up each filegroup independently. In addition, we have marked historical partitions to be read-only, so we don't have to back them up more than once. Our backup and restore times are now shorter.

In our example, source data arrives in frequent batches throughout the day. Because we have the source data available, we have the option of rebuilding the data from the last full backup and reloading the source data files. This would allow us to use the simple recovery model. In our example, we encourage using a bulk-logged recovery model, for manageability and faster recovery times. It is much easier to determine which log files need to be applied to restore the database than to determine which data files need to be reloaded. It is also faster to restore the database from log files than to reload the data.

If you do infrequent bulk loading of data into your data warehouse, you may be able to set the database recovery model to Simple. By infrequent, we mean a few times per day, but more than once or twice per day. This can reduce the amount of space consumed by the log file over a daily load. The more frequently you load data, the smaller the log file, but you will have to do more full backups, too. If you have not partitioned your warehouse so that the partition for "current" data is small, there may be little or no advantage in doing backups after loading data. To take advantage of the Simple recovery model, you must perform a backup of the modified partition immediately after you perform a load. If you do any loading by trickling in data, you should not use the Simple recover model; instead, choose Full, and then you will also need to perform log backups on a regular basis.

Table 11-1 presents our backup plan, which minimizes the amount of data you need to back up and provides for a faster recovery in the event you have to restore the data. Note that you do not have to back up the historical partitions.

Table 11-1 Sample Backup Schedule

Interval	What to Back Up
Hourly	Back up the transaction logs.
Daily	Back up the filegroup for the current month.
Monthly	Back up the filegroup for each of the three active months.
Annually	Back up the filegroup for the year just ended after the filegroup has been set to read-only, and place at least two copies of the backup in different secure locations.

Managing Cube Partitions

Partitions are continuously changing in an Analysis Services solution. You receive new data, want to archive old data, move current data to historical partitions, or perhaps your users have changed their query patterns and you need to reoptimize for those new queries. In this section, we discuss the ongoing management of partitions.

Remember that any changes to partitions that are made using SQL Server Management Studio are not reflected back into your Visual Studio projects. You will have to create an "Import Analysis Services 9.0 Database" project to create a project that matches the current design. If you deploy the original project, you will overwrite any changes you have made to the cube.

Populating a Cube Partition

When you process a partition, it reads the data specified by the source you defined when you created the partition. You can start processing a partition manually, under program control, or by a task in an SSIS package. You only need to populate partitions where the data has changed.

Processing New Facts

The ETL processes load data into one of the four recent weekly partitions. We fully process these partitions to bring in the new transactions. We can get away with this because it is only four week's transactions, not the entire five years. The prior periods in the relational table are read-only and therefore don't need processing.

Processing Updated Dimensions

A property you will want to set to improve processing times is the RelationshipType. This is a property of an attribute relationship in a dimension. For example, this is a property of the Quarter relationship to Month in the Date dimension. This property has two values: Flexible and Rigid. Rigid relationships offer better query performance, whereas Flexible relationships offer better processing performance in a changing dimension. If a member will not likely move in the hierarchy, as would be the case with dates, you can set the RelationshipType to Rigid. If a member does move in a rigid relationship, an error is raised. The default is Flexible.

You can initiate dimension processing manually by right-clicking the dimension in the Solution Explorer and choosing Process. You can also use an SSIS task or an XML/A command to process a dimension.

Merging Cube Partitions

You can merge smaller partitions into a larger historical partition to reduce your administrative overhead, although at some point you will see a degradation in performance.

To merge a partition into another partition, the partitions need to have similar aggregation designs. The way we created our partitions, aggregation design is inherited from the previous partition, so your designs should match up properly. If you want to change the aggregation design of a partition, wait until it is "full"—that is, you aren't going to add any more partitions. Then you can redesign the aggregations because it's not going to be merged with any other partition. If you want to copy the aggregation design from another partition, you can do that in Management Studio. Drill down into the cube, through the measure group, down to the partition you want to change. One of the right-click options is to copy the aggregations.

QUICK START: Merging Cube Partitions

You can merge partitions using the SQL Server Management Studio.

1. Expand the Measure Groups node in the Object Explorer until you see the partitions. You might need to refresh the measure group to see any partitions created since you started the Management Studio.

2. Right-click the Partitions node, and then choose Merge Partitions. In the Target Partitions section, set the Name to be the name of the receiving partition. You will see the other partitions show up in a list below.

3. Select the partitions you want to merge into the target partition, and then click OK.

4. Refresh the Partitions node, and you will see that the partitions you merged have been deleted. Their data has been merged into the Target partition.

Deleting Cube Partitions

The business requirements state that at least five years of data should be kept. At the end of each year, you can remove the oldest year partition, which now contains the fourth year of data.

You can delete a partition using Management Studio by right-clicking the partition and then choosing Delete.

Usage-Based Optimization

None of the aggregations built initially are based on anything but an educated guess by Analysis Services based on factors such as the number of members in the dimension. What you really want is an aggregation design based on actual usage. Fortunately, Analysis Services can track the queries being submitted by your users. You can use the Usage Based Optimization (UBO) Wizard to read the query log and design a better set of aggregations based on actual usage. UBO is done on a per-partition basis.

Before you can do UBO, you need to start collecting data in the query log. You enable this in the properties of the Analysis Services server. Look for the property Log \ Querylog \ CreateQueryLogTable and set it to true. Next, set the value of Log \ Querylog \ QueryLogConnectionString to point to a SQL Server table where you want to record the queries to be used for profiling. You want to collect data for a long enough period to provide a good cross-section of queries, but it's not recommended that you run with logging enabled all the time.

After you've collected data, you can have the UBO Wizard analyze the log and recommend some aggregations. You start the UBO Wizard from SQL Server Management Studio. You need to drill down from the cube, through the measure groups, to locate the partitions you want to optimize. Right-click a partition, or the Partitions node, and choose Usage Based Optimization. In the wizard, you can filter the data in the query log by date, user, or set of most frequent queries.

Next Steps

Here we provide some additional avenues for you to consider to improve your solution, after you have implemented the basic elements of this chapter.

Automating the Process

In this chapter, we described a scenario where the data is constantly arriving, or at least arriving very frequently in batches. Our purpose was to describe the ways you can efficiently process high volumes of newly arriving data and be able to query large databases efficiently. We want to leave you with some ideas on how to detect when new data has arrived. In Chapter 4, we discussed how you can browse a directory for files and pass a filename into a Data Flow task. Here are some other avenues you can explore:

- Two Control Flow tasks that you can look at for detecting file arrival are the Message Queue task and the WMI Event task.
- Chapter 12, "Real-Time Business Intelligence," on real-time OLAP describes methods for automatic background processing of cube partitions when new data arrives.
- A complete object model exists for working all aspects of partitions, ETL packages, and cubes. You can quickly build an application to automate the processing of data from the arrival of the flat files through to incrementally processing the cubes and creating new partitions in any language supporting the Common Language Runtime (CLR).

Partitioned Views

As noted in the introduction, you can also use partitioned views (PVs) to partition your data. This allows you to create a unified view of a table distributed over multiple databases. You can now manage each partition of the data independently. If the databases are on other servers, you have a distributed partitioned view (DPV). The advantage of DPVs is that the load can be distributed over several servers, and the partitions are searched in parallel. Each table has a constraint similar to one boundary point in the partition function. The individual tables are combined in a view that unions the tables together. This makes the use of the partitioned view transparent to a user. Select statements issue parallel queries to the relevant partitions. Data inserted through the view will be inserted into the table on the correct server.

The databases do not need to contain all tables, only the tables you want to divide into partitions. By using all but one database for historical data, you can find some operational benefits. If your partitioning is by time, you can reduce the backup time by marking the historical databases read-only; then, you only need to back up a much smaller current database.

You should consider PVs and DPVs only when you have extremely large databases, and queries that usually require data from only a few partitions. PVs, which by definition do not involve the network, are less resource intensive than DPVs. DPVs allow you to scale out over several servers, but the cost of initiating a query to another server across the network is relatively high compared to a PV or local query, so you should measure the performance of a DPV to ensure you are receiving a benefit from this design.

Scaling Out Using Analysis Services Database Synchronization

You can deploy the same database on several Analysis Services servers using Database Synchronization. This increases the number of users that you can handle. In this scenario, the Analysis Services servers have identical but separate databases. The partitions exist on locally managed storage (which could be a storage area network [SAN] drive). Each server has its own IP address and service name, but also has a virtual IP and virtual service name provided by the load-balancing service. The load-balancing service is either Windows NLB or a hardware device such as an F5 switch. Figure 11-11 shows a typical configuration.

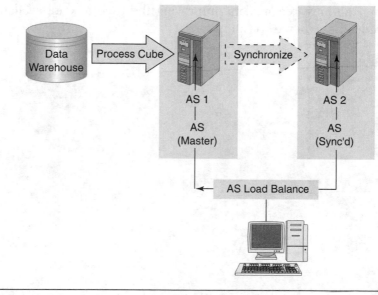

Figure 11-11 Analysis Services database synchronization

You can initiate synchronization from SQL Server Management Studio by right-clicking the Databases node of the *target* server (not the source server). You then specify a source Analysis Services server and database you want to synchronize with. Using the same wizard, you can create a script to enable you to schedule periodic synchronizations.

During synchronization, both the source and the target can continue to be queried by users. When synchronization finishes, Analysis Services switches users to the new data, and drops the old data from the destination database.

Summary

VLDBs present problems for both query performance and database maintenance. Partitioning can help in both areas. You can mark relational partitions as read-only and bypass subsequent lengthy backup cycles for those partitions. Also, index maintenance can now be performed online, increasing the availability of the database. For Analysis Services databases, you can restrict processing to the partition containing the most recent data, improving the time to data availability and reducing resource consumption.

CHAPTER 12

Real-Time Business Intelligence

There is a great need for current information in many business applications. In scenarios such as credit card fraud or outbreaks of serious contagious diseases, time is of the essence. However, many data warehouses on which BI solutions are based are loaded overnight, at best. The data you are analyzing is between 8 and 24 hours old. The reasons for this latency are often based on operational efficiencies or the lack of accessibility of the cubes during updates. New features in SQL Server 2005 address many of the issues relating to real-time analysis, and the process of building a real-time solution has been greatly simplified.

In this chapter, real-time design should be thought of as "real-enough" time, not necessarily instantaneous updating. In plenty of situations, latency from a few minutes to hours is more than acceptable, so don't feel your application won't benefit from some real-time features. Even if you just want to do better than the ubiquitous overnight update, this chapter offers you a solution.

Business Problem

Our customer for this chapter is a major hospital that wants to optimize its allocation of resources, by being more aware of the immediate needs driven by the current patient profiles such as specialized staffing or perishable supplies.

Problem Statement

A multidimensional database is used to manage hospital admissions and assist with patient diagnosis. Its purpose is to provide information to anticipate staffing requirements for the next shifts, determine medical-supply requirements, and provide early detection of elevated occurrences of contagious diseases or environmentally induced illnesses such as food poisoning. The data warehouse is populated overnight, but this does not give them sufficiently current information on which to base the day's operational decisions. At the same time, they cannot afford to take the system offline for more frequent updates. To ensure quality patient care, they have often overestimated the resources required for each shift.

Solution Overview

We will use Analysis Services proactive caching to enable real-enough time updates of our cubes. Proactive caching allows us to configure notifications of changes to the underlying relational table of a cube, and a maximum acceptable latency before the changes appear in the cube. We will isolate historical data and recent data from current data in separate partitions to reduce the amount of data that needs to be processed by the proactive cache. This will minimize the time between the arrival of new data and its availability to the user.

Business Requirements

The database consists of a large amount of historical data as well as very current data. New data needs to be available in an OLAP database within 30 minutes of its arrival at the hospital. The OLAP database must be accessible to users continuously, even during updating. The medical staff needs to be able to track the current symptoms and medical requirements of new and existing patients and be able to anticipate the resources required by those patients over the next 24 hours.

High-Level Architecture

A multidimensional database is required because of the large volume of data and multiple ways of analyzing the data. Our goal is to make new data visible as soon as possible after it arrives. One of the barriers to this is that with the MOLAP storage model, the data is only visible after the cube has been processed. We favor the MOLAP model because it is extremely an efficient way to store and retrieve cubes. It turns out we can trade some overhead for lower latency. The overhead arises from more frequent processing of the updated cube partitions, since processing is how data in the relational tables becomes available through the cube. By being smarter about what we reprocess, we hope to pay out as little as possible in overhead and in return receive a large reduction in latency.

For the Analysis Services database, we will use the **Proactive Caching** feature of Analysis Services to reduce the latency between the arrival of new data and the availability of the data to the user. For optimal access to the existing data, less-recent and historical data will be maintained as usual in MOLAP storage partitions. The new data will eventually make its way to one of these partitions or a newly created partition.

We will use the partitioning techniques discussed in the chapter on very large databases to limit the cube partitions that need to be processed. Ideally, only one very current partition needs to be processed.

As shown in Figure 12-1, SQL Server Integration Services (SSIS) will receive data from external sources by periodic polling of the sources, apply the necessary transforms to make the data conform to our data model, and store the data in data warehouse tables. SQL Server will notify Analysis Services of the arrival of new data in the data warehouse. Analysis Services will process the new data when a lull in the arrival of new data occurs or when the latency constraints dictate that the data must be processed. You have total control of the definition of a "lull" and the maximum latency.

Business Benefits

The hospital expects to reduce its operating costs by having the right number of staff with the right skills in attendance each shift. In addition, they expect to reduce waste of expensive supplies that have a short shelf life, kept on hand in quantities larger than usually necessary. They will now be able to analyze the current overall patient profile, bed utilization, and care-type requirements.

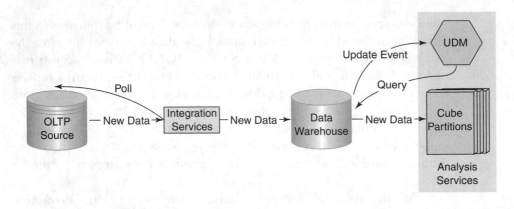

Figure 12-1 High-level architecture

A day is a long time in the context of epidemics. With near real-time analysis, local health authorities will have much faster notice of epidemics, which will reduce the number of victims, reduce hospital visits, and thereby free space for the critically ill and reduce overall health-care spending.

Data Model

Our facts in this example are patient diagnosis records generated throughout a patient's hospital stay. These records are created by the medical staff as a patient's condition changes. They are entered into the hospital's patient monitoring application. The dimensions we are concerned with are Patient, Diagnosis, Date, Time, and Ward. The Patient dimension changes quickly; the other dimensions are static. This yields a data model like that shown in Figure 12-2.

The main thing you need to do in your data model to accommodate real-time OLAP is to support partitioning and incremental loading. We are relying on a partitioning scheme to minimize the amount of reprocessing time, and we are relying on incremental loading to minimize the number of partitions affected during the loading of facts. We'll use the DiagnosisDate column for both purposes. Our Patient dimension is also changing in real time, so we'll need a column to track which patient records are new or updated. For that, we'll use the DateLastUpdated. We can compare these column values against those in the source tables and load only the newer records.

In real-time applications, sometimes the facts arrive before new dimension members do. This would normally be classified as missing members. For example, unidentifiable patients might arrive at the hospital, and their symptoms and resource needs would be recorded, but we would not have a member for them in our patient dimension yet. We need to support inferred members, which we discussed in Chapter 7, "Data Quality."

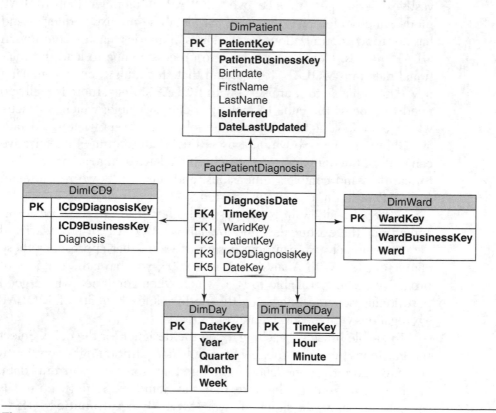

Figure 12-2   Data model

Technical Solution

We'll start by looking at what changes you need to make to your cube design for a real-time solution and work our way back to how we load data through Integration Services. Note that the basis of this solution, proactive caching, is only available in the Enterprise Edition of SQL Server 2005.

Cube Design for Real Time

In all the other chapters, we have implicitly or explicitly urged you to use MOLAP storage for your cubes and dimensions because of MOLAP's vastly superior performance over ROLAP. Remember that ROLAP mode simply references the relational database to answer queries and has no storage optimizations for the kinds of queries that are common in OLAP queries. However, you have to process a cube to load the relational data into MOLAP storage, and that step adds latency to making new data available to your users. With ROLAP storage, there is really no need to process the cube to make the data available, which is exactly what we are looking for in a real-time solution: present whatever data is available right now. So why not use ROLAP all the time? Because we can't afford the query performance hit if we have a large amount of historical data and complex dimensions, and this is why we recommend MOLAP. Wait, this is where we started....

What we really want is the best of both worlds. MOLAP performance for all the existing data and low-latency ROLAP for newly arrived data. Fortunately, we can now design a system that approaches these characteristics. With Analysis Services 2005, you have the services of proactive caching available to you, which when combined with a good partitioning scheme integrates the performance benefits of MOLAP aggregations with the low latency of ROLAP.

To enable proactive caching, open the designer for the cube. Select the Partitions tab. You probably have only one partition right now, but if you have more than one, choose the one that stores the "current" data. Click Storage Settings, be sure that the Standard Settings button is selected, and move the slider left, from MOLAP to **Automatic MOLAP** (see Figure 12-3). Save these settings. Congratulations, you're done! Go browse your cube and note the value of one of the measures, add a row to your fact table, wait 10 seconds, and then refresh the display. The new data really is there, and you didn't even have to process the cube.

Now that was too easy, you say, and there must be a catch. Well, there are some considerations, but no real catches. First, it's important to understand how proactive caching really works, and then you will have a better idea of the reasons for these considerations, and why there are not any big catches.

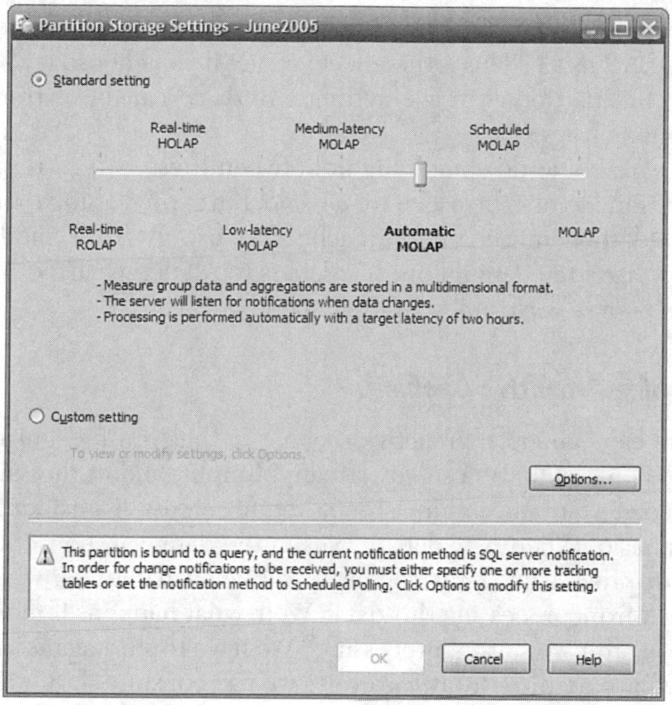

Figure 12-3   Enabling proactive caching

Overview of Proactive Caching

Let's take a closer look at what we just did with proactive caching. Proactive caching sits between the user and the data they are after. In a static situation where MOLAP storage is used, a request for data is satisfied by the cache, which obtains all the data from the MOLAP store. Simple enough. When new data arrives in the relational store, the MOLAP cache is out of sync with the relational store. What are our options for dealing with the next request for data?

We could simply continue to serve up data from the cache and in the background begin rebuilding the MOLAP store. The data would be out of date until the reprocessing was finished, but we would still be responding to requests quickly because we are using the cache. How stale the data becomes is a function of how long it takes to reprocess the data.

If we need to have the most up-to-date view of the data, we could have the cache immediately invalidated when new data is received. Now our only source of data is the relational database, which means we are in ROLAP mode. This is the effect you get if you choose real-time HOLAP for the partition storage settings. ROLAP can be extremely slow for some queries.

We could do something in between these two extremes. We could continue to use the cache for a while, but if processing took too long, we could then invalidate the cache and use ROLAP mode. If we can reprocess the data before the data is too stale, we avoid having to go to the poorer-performing ROLAP mode.

Tuning Proactive Caching

You can configure proactive caching so that you recognize and wait for the completion of a steady stream of input, and at the same time don't exceed your maximum latency requirements. Consider the following scenario. When new data arrives in the data warehouse, the sooner we start processing it, the sooner it will be available. So, what's holding us back from processing this data? Well, what happens if more data arrives soon after we started processing? We have to start again, and that means we have to throw away the cycles we just consumed. Remember that we are not processing just the new data, but all the data in the partition. This could be your entire set! If we wait just a little while to see whether any more data is going to arrive, we could process it all at the same time. But how long should you wait?

Avoiding Too Much Reprocessing

Suppose that a batch upload to the data warehouse is occurring. There will be little time between the arrival of each row, and we certainly wouldn't want to be restarting the processing after each row. So why don't we wait, say, ten seconds after a row arrives, and if nothing else arrives, then we can start processing. If another row does arrive, we start waiting for ten seconds again. The time we wait to see whether the activity has quieted down is called the **silence interval**. If no data arrives for the duration set by the silence interval, and there is new data, processing begins.

You can set the value of the silence interval to any value from zero upward. Ten seconds is common. (That's why you had to wait 10 seconds before refreshing your browser when we first started looking at proactive caching.) If you set the silence interval to zero, processing starts immediately when data is received but might be interrupted by the arrival of more data. If you set it to a very large value, processing does not start at all until that time is up, and you might get excessively stale data. However, we do have a solution to the problem of false starts of the reprocessing task, and you can tune this to your situation. But what happens if data continues to trickle in?

Dealing with a Continuous Backlog of New Data

If you have set the silence interval to ten seconds, on a bad day the data will arrive one row every nine seconds, and nothing will ever get processed because the silence interval criteria is never met. After a while, we need to be able to just say "enough!" and start processing. This is where the **silence interval override** value comes in. The silence interval override timer starts as soon as the first new data arrives after processing. Even if data trickles in just under the silence interval value, when the override period is exceeded, processing starts regardless of whether the silence interval requirement has been satisfied.

You set the silence interval override to a value that makes sense for your requirements (of course you would!). By that we mean if you have batch updates occurring every hour, and they take about 10 minutes, you might set the silence override interval to 20 minutes. This means that there will be sufficient time to complete a batch update before processing starts, and as soon as the batch is finished, the silence interval will likely kick in and start processing ten seconds after the batch completes. If you have an exceptionally long batch, or the trickle updates are still defeating the silence interval, processing starts anyway.

Okay, we are doing well. We have solved the problem of being so swamped with new data that it never gets processed. But what if processing takes too long? Our data will be too stale to meet our business requirements. In a worst-case scenario, we have data that is 20 minutes old (the silence override interval) plus the time it is going to take to process the partition.

Guaranteeing Data Currency

So far, we have learned about optimizing when we reprocess an updated partition. We didn't want to waste resources if we were just going to have to restart with the arrival of new data. However, the user is still being given data from the MOLAP cache, and the cache is getting staler the longer we wait for processing to finish. If you have a requirement to present users with data that meets an "age" requirement, your only choice is to abandon the cache at that age. When the cache is not being used for data, queries are satisfied directly from the relational database (that is, by using ROLAP mode). Performance might not be good, but at least the data will be fresh.

You control when the cache is dropped by setting a time for the **drop outdated cache** property. The timer for this starts as soon as the first new data arrives, just as it does for the silence interval override. If you cannot afford to have data more than one hour old, set this value to 60 minutes. This setting guarantees that regardless of the arrival of any volume of new data, or how long it takes to process it, the data delivered to a user will meet this "freshness" criteria. You can set this value anywhere from zero up. If you set it to zero, the cache is invalidated immediately, and new data is available immediately. This might put quite a load on the server because most queries will now be resolved using ROLAP mode. Unless there is a long quiet period, data trickling in may keep the cache invalid most of the time, and you have traded performance for very low latency.

Minimizing the Cost of Reprocessing

In all the tuning parameters we have discussed, we were always confronted with the time required to reprocess a partition. If you have a lot of data, it's going to take a while to process it. However, we've already processed most of it; why bother to process it again? It's because the unit of processing is a partition, and so far we've only set up one partition containing all our data. Performance will deteriorate over time, depending on how much data is added over time.

What we want to do is to put as much of the "old" data as possible in a partition by itself and leave it alone. We don't enable proactive caching for this partition, so it will not be reprocessed unless we manually initiate it. In another partition, we can put the most recent, or "current" data. We would enable proactive caching only on the "current" partition, which we expect to be substantially smaller and so require much less time to process.

We would merge the current partition into the historical partition when there's enough data in it that performance is affected, and then we'd create a new "current" partition. Let's take a look at how that would work in practice. For this example, we'll assume that our historical and current partitions are split at June 1, 2005.

QUICK START: Setting Up Partitions for Proactive Caching

In this Quick Start, we configure proactive caching so that it meets our requirements for real-enough time updates of our cube. Start by creating another partition so that you have one for historical data and one for current data. You learned how to create partitions in Chapter 11, "Very Large Data Warehouses," so we won't repeat those steps here. The current partition shouldn't be so large that the reprocessing time exceeds your requirements for making new data available to your users.

Open your Analysis Services project in BI Development Studio, and we'll begin configuring the proactive cache settings.

1. On the Partitions tab of the cube designer, select your current partition.

2. Click Storage Settings, and set the slider to Automatic MOLAP.

3. Click Options. Based on our measurements, our partition takes less than a minute to reprocess. We want a latency of less than five minutes, so we'll set the Silence override interval to four minutes, as shown in Figure 12-4. This means the partition is guaranteed to start to be reprocessed within four minutes and will complete in less than five minutes, because we know from testing that the partition processing will complete in less than one additional minute.

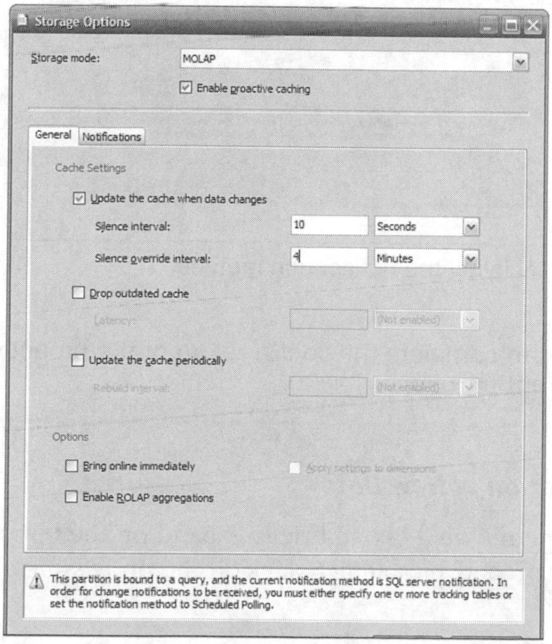

Figure 12-4   Configuring proactive caching

4. On the Notifications tab, Select SQL Server, and then check Specify tracking tables. We need to tell Analysis Services which table to monitor for changes because we specified a query instead of a table to define the data that will populate the partition. Click the ellipses (...) and select the fact table specified in your query where you defined the partition. Click OK to save the tables to be monitored, as shown in Figure 12-5, and then click OK and to save the Notification settings.

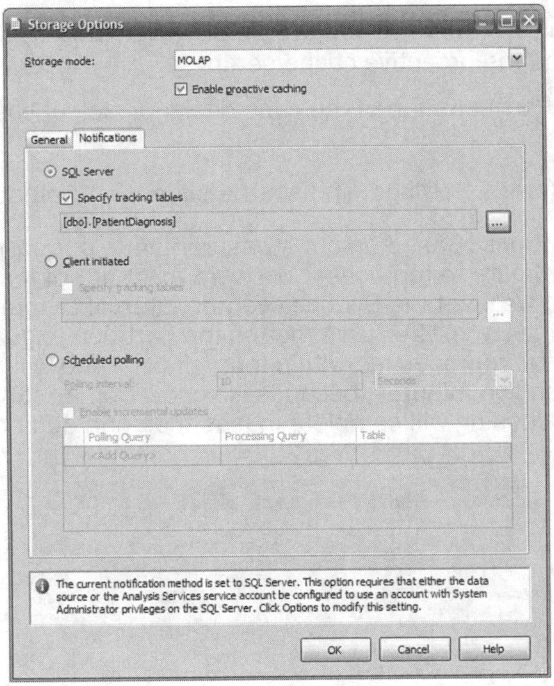

Figure 12-5   Specifying the notification method

5. Click OK to complete the configuration of the proactive cache for the current partition.

Notification of New Data

At this point, we'd like to briefly expand on the options for notifications used by proactive caching to kick off the processing of a partition.

Specifying Change Notification Method

Proactive caching requires a notification to make it aware of new data. There are three basic methods available to you: **notification** "pushed" by SQL Server when a table changes, sending **client-initiated XMLA message** from a service or programmatically to Analysis Services, or **polling** at intervals to check for new data. You specify which method you want to use on the Notifications tab on the Storage Options dialog, as shown in Figure 12-5. As you saw earlier, you access the Storage Options dialog by clicking the Options button on the Partitions Storage Settings panel. But how do you choose which method is appropriate for your business requirements?

SQL Server Notification

SQL Server notification uses SQL Profiler to capture events that indicate a relevant table has been updated. This approach means that a notification is pushed to Analysis Services, which is much faster than Analysis Services polling for changes. Profiler does not guarantee that absolutely all update events will be detected, so it is possible that Analysis Services will not be notified, and your cube will not be as current as you expect. However, missed events usually result from heavy activity on the database, so it is likely that another event will trigger notification within a short time, and your cube will still be very current.

SQL Server notification only works with SQL Server 2005 databases, because it uses the SQL Server Profiler to detect table changes. If your data source is something other than SQL Server 2005, you cannot use this method to notify Analysis Services of a change.

Events are tracked through SQL Profiler using table names. Analysis Services can determine which table you are using in the partition and automatically monitor it. If you are using a view to populate the cube, you should specify the underlying tables that are actually being updated.

In the preceding example, we used SQL Server Notification.

Client-Initiated Notification

You can use the XMLA command `NotifyTableChanged` to alert Analysis Services of a table change. You use this notification method when your data source is not SQL Server and you need faster response time than you might get by polling. In the sample code shown next, an XMLA command is sent to the server MyAnalysisServer. Analysis Services will be notified that the PatientDiagnosis table has changed. This table is used by the OLAP database DiagnosisProfile, as specified by the

DatabaseID. The table resides in a database referenced by the data source Health Tracking DW, specified by the DataSourceID.

```
Dim command As String =
"<NotifyTableChange
xmlns=""http://schemas.microsoft.com/analysisservices/2003/
➡engine"">" + _
        "<Object>" + _
        "   <DatabaseID>DiagnosisProfile</DatabaseID>" + _
        "   <DataSourceID>Health Tracking
➡DW</DataSourceID>" + _
        "</Object>" + _
        "<TableNotifications>" + _
        "   <TableNotification>" + _
        "      <DbSchemaName>dbo</DbSchemaName>" + _
        "<DbTableName>PatientDiagnosis</DbTableName>"
+ _
        "   </TableNotification>" + _
        "</TableNotifications>" + _
        "</NotifyTableChange>"

        Dim client As New Microsoft.AnalysisServices.
➡Xmla.XmlaClient
        client.Connect("MyAnalysisServer")
        client.Send(command, Nothing)
        client.Disconnect()
```

Polling by Analysis Services

Polling is a method where a query is periodically sent to a data source by Analysis Services. It is useful when the data source is not SQL Server, and there is no application that can send an XMLA command to Analysis Services. Polling is usually less efficient and often means greater latency than other notification methods.

On the Notifications tab, you specify a query that is to be used to check for new data, and how often it is to be sent. This query must return a single value that can be compared against the last value returned. If the two differ, a change is assumed to have occurred, initiating the proactive cache timing sequence.

Ensuring Consistency During Processing

Just when you thought we had sorted out all the potential problems that could occur, some new fact records arrive in the data warehouse right in the middle of the cube processing—how do we avoid having an inconsistent picture? SQL Server 2005 has a useful new transaction isolation level called **snapshot isolation**, which uses row versioning to make sure that a transaction always reads the data that existed at the beginning of the transaction even if some updates have been committed since then.

To get Analysis Services processing to use snapshot isolation, you can change the Isolation setting on the Analysis Services data source from the default ReadCommitted to Snapshot. If you try this out, you will get a warning message that snapshot isolation won't be used unless "MARS Connection" is enabled. You can turn on the MARS Connection property by editing the connection string in the Data Source Designer and then clicking the All button on the left to see all the advanced properties.

Real-Time ETL—Working with the Data Source

We've got Analysis Services reading from the data warehouse automatically. How do we get data from the source into the data warehouse in real time? Periodic polling of the source system is the easiest to implement. You can use SQL Agent to schedule an SSIS package to run periodically to import new data into the data warehouse. This works well when you can accept latency on the order of several minutes or more, which is acceptable in many applications. Avoid using polling when the latency requirement is measured in seconds, because of the cost of initiating the package every few seconds (even if there's no new data).

In our example, we used polling because we can accept a latency of a few minutes. We created a job in SQL Server Agent with an SSIS package step that invoked our import package that loads the data warehouse. We set a schedule for this job that specifies a recurring execution every two minutes. When setting this time for your schedule, consider how long it takes to reprocess the current partition and either reduce the frequency of execution if the processing takes a good part of the two minutes or reduce the time window on the current partition so the processing time will go down.

You can initiate the importing of the data in other ways without polling if you have some control over the application that creates the data.

Using a Message Queue

A message queue is a guaranteed delivery mechanism for sending data and messages between applications. The applications do not need to be on the same machine but, of course, do need some connectivity and authentication. MSMQ (Microsoft Message Queue) is a service that provides these features and is part of Windows Server.

You can use an MSMQ task in an SSIS control flow to listen for messages indicating that new data is ready, and then launch the data flow task to begin the data import.

Using Event Notifications

Windows Management Instrumentation (WMI) monitors the entire system for certain events, such as file creation. You can use a WMI task in SSIS to wait for an event and then proceed to the data flow task when the event occurs. For example, your data source application might push a flat file to a directory that you monitor with WMI. When the file is dropped in the directory, your package detects this and begins the process of loading the data.

Managing the Solution

As we have described, the changes you need to make to enable real-time BI mostly relate to Analysis Services partition settings and Integration Services packages. The management of a real-time solution does not differ much from that of standard BI solutions, except that you need to pay careful attention to the complete process of handling new data. (Because there is no overnight processing window to give you time to smooth out any mistakes, users will be aware of any problems right away.)

Operations

Operation of a real-time OLAP database does not differ much from a regular OLAP database. You have the additional task of creating new partitions and merging old partitions.

Backup

In a real-time application, data usually trickles into the relational database on a continuous basis. There is no batch loaded at regular intervals. This means you must use the Full recovery model and back up the transaction log files to protect your database. You only need to back up the partitions that are read-write, which should just be the most recent partition.

Unlike a relational database with partitions, for Analysis Services you need to back up the entire cube each time. You may have expected to get away with only backing up the current partition, but you can't because you cannot select which partitions to back up.

Although you can technically delete the relational tables underlying the partitions after the data has been loaded into Analysis Services, you should not do this. Partitions set to use proactive caching may revert to ROLAP mode depending on the settings and require the relational tables. More important, if you ever need to reprocess or rebuild the partitions, you must have the relational data. So, be sure that the data sources are formally backed up and are accessible to you.

Rolling Partitions

Remember why we created partitions in the first place: so we wouldn't have to reprocess more data than we had to. Therefore, we created a partition for history and another for the current month. We only reprocess the partition for the current month. In a perfect world, June data arrives in June, and July data arrives in July. However, this is not our experience. Data is delayed, or post-dated. It arrives out of sequence. Because of the reality of our business, we cannot simply close off the previous month and open the current month's partition to updates.

Depending on your business rules, you might need to keep monthly partitions open for two or three months, and the current month's partition must be open to all future dates. To maintain your partitions, you create enough "current" partitions to accommodate the latest data that could arrive out of sequence. If that's 90 days, for example, you want three monthly partitions. Each partition will have a definite start and end date specified in the query to restrict the rows. The exception is the last partition, which does not restrict the end date of the fact rows.

When you create a new partition, you will likely retire an earlier partition by merging it with the historical partition.

After merging a number of current partitions into the historical partition, you need to reprocess the historical partition to improve the aggregations and efficiency of their organization. You should do this during a maintenance period due to the resource consumption of the operation. You need to monitor the performance of the server to determine how frequently this needs to be done.

Next Steps

With real-time data, you have the opportunity to do some interesting just-in-time analysis. Credit card companies look for spending that doesn't conform to your usual patterns. In our health-care example, we could use data mining to understand the normal patterns of initial diagnosis at an emergency ward and look for deviations that might provide an early indication of the start of an epidemic or an outbreak of local food poisoning.

Maintaining a Consistent View of the Source Data

In a real-time application, the source data constantly changes. If you need to have a time-consistent view of the data loaded into the data warehouse, you can use snapshot isolation to ensure all the data you read through a package is exactly the same set of data as it was when you initiated the package. You set the isolation level property in the package Transaction properties. Select Snapshot from the drop-down list.

Loading Data Directly into Analysis Services Using Integration Services

Integration Services enables you to push new data directly into a cube or dimension. In the same way that you can define a SQL Server table as the destination in a data flow, you can use a Partition Processing destination and add new data right into the cube, or use the Dimension Processing destination to update the dimensions. This allows you to be quite creative with exactly how "real time" you want your solution to be, without always necessarily having to rely on the proactive caching settings in Analysis Services.

Notification Services

Imagine if the hospital supervisor could get a notification to her cell phone when the number of new admissions to the hospital in the last hour exceeded a critical value. You can implement this scenario in SQL Server 2005 by taking advantage of Notification Services' provider for Analysis Services. Notifications can be triggered based on an MDX query, so with a near-real time BI solution, you could define some KPIs and then send notifications to subscribed users.

Summary

Real-time solutions aren't just for applications that need up-to-the-minute information; you can also use them to reduce latency to whatever level your business requires. Proactive caching is the foundation for real-time data availability from Analysis Services. Proactive caching works best when the new data is destined for a cube partition that contains only a small amount of recent data. Analysis Services can receive "push" notifications from SQL Server databases that new data has arrived. Other data sources can be polled to determine the availability of new data. You can tune the proactive cache settings to meet any latency requirements, and minimize unnecessary restarts of the partition reprocessing when data arrives in bursts. When proactive caching is reprocessing a partition, the current data is still accessible by users. The partition structure of the cubes will change over time.

Index